D0832766

WIMBLEDON SCHOOL OF ART LIBRARY
WIMBLEDON SCH
MERTON HALL ROAD, SW
Tel: 540 0231

THE COTTESLOE AT THE NATIONAL

'INFINITE RICHES IN A LITTLE ROOM'

Contributors

Jason Barnes
Simon Russell Beale
Michael Billington
Bill Bryden
John Bury
John Caird
John Caulfield
Roger Chapman
Alison Chitty
William Dudley
Richard Eyre
Sebastian Graham-Jones
Peter Hall
Jenny Harris
Sue Higginson
Iain Mackintosh
Genista McIntosh
Ian McKellen
Ronnie Mulryne
Trevor Nunn
Nick Ormerod
Margaret Shewring
Ian Williams

MULRYNE AND SHEWRING

in association with

THE COTTESLOE AT THE NATIONAL

'INFINITE RICHES IN A LITTLE ROOM'

Edited by
Ronnie Mulryne
Margaret Shewring

Technical Editor
Jason Barnes

First Published 1999
By Mulryne & Shewring Ltd
3 Benson Road
Stratford-upon-Avon
Warwickshire CV37 6UU

ISBN 1 900065 02 9 Casebound
1 900065 01 0 Paperback

Produced, Designed and Typeset by:
A.H. Jolly (Editorial) Ltd
Yelvertoft Manor
Northamptonshire NN6 6LF

Printed by:
Clifford Press Ltd, Coventry

Cover Illustration:
Detail of a photograph by Michael Mayhew of *The Passion*, part of *The Mysteries*, as staged at the Cottesloe in 1978.

CONTENTS

And thus methinks should men of judgement frame
Their means of traffic from the vulgar trade,
And as their wealth increaseth, so enclose
Infinite riches in a little room.

Christopher Marlowe
The Jew of Malta, I.i. 34–37

The phrase 'Infinite Riches in a Little Room' was first used in connection with the Cottesloe by Iain Mackintosh. *See* FIG 11, p. 20

PREFACE

THIS BOOK has two sources, our pleasure in the work of the Cottesloe, and the enthusiasm of our co-authors, Jason Barnes and Iain Mackintosh. Without Iain the theatre might not have been built (John Bury pays tribute in this book to his 'persistence'), and without Jason it would not have survived its twenty-one years with such great success. Iain, working with John Bury and Richard Pilbrow, brought the theatre into being. Jason, Production Manager from the first show until now, has nourished its work in every practical way. We are privileged to have been able to collaborate with them.

It was a good day when the four of us agreed that the twenty-first anniversary of the Cottesloe should be greeted by a book celebrating the theatre's achievements, and honouring those who have worked there. That good day has been followed by a succession of good days, as we have experienced the generosity and the genial good humour of Royal National Theatre staff, directors, designers, actors, technicians and people working in the Production Office, the Press Office, the Touring Office, the Archives, the Bookshop and elsewhere. It has been a pleasure to get to know them better.

We owe a special debt to Trevor Nunn, the present Director of the National, who encouraged us to write the book as soon as the idea was put to him, and to Sir Richard Eyre, Sir Peter Hall and Genista McIntosh, all of whom were generous with time and advice. Nicola Scadding, Archivist of the National, went out of her way time and again to help us find our path among the lofty stacks of her beautifully-ordered domain. Lyn Haill, the National's Head of Publications, kept us to the strait and narrow and saved us from many an error. Roger Chapman, Head of Touring, shared his immense knowledge of that important area of the National's work with readiness and great good humour. Sue Higginson, Head of the Studio, gave us generously of her time, and shared her huge enthusiasm for the work she presides over so successfully. Jenny Harris, Head of Education, made us far more aware than we were of the range and significance of her Department's work. Diane Willmott and Jo Maund, of the Production Office, made us welcome and allowed us to see some of the busy work they undertake. Ian Williams, Chief Lighting Technician, received us in the Cottesloe to enthuse about lanterns and follow spots. John Caulfield, Stage Manager for longer than almost anyone can remember, showed no sign of waning interest or failing vigour. Toby Radford, Bookshop Manager, gave us shrewd advice and the occasional warning. Angus MacKechnie arranged a platform in the Cottesloe with exemplary promptness. Fiona Walsh, Head of the Press Office, and all her staff, were ready to help on any occasion, however fraught their own immediate business. Alice Dunne, also of the Press Office, prompted us when deadlines approached. Sarah Collins and Moragh Darby of the Directors' Office were invaluable in making contacts and shepherding us and their employers; so was Corinne Beaver, Sir Peter Hall's assistant.

We received great kindness from many others including Richard Mangan, Miles King, Gita Cohen and Elizabeth Bury. Michael Billington shamed us all by writing his excellent contribution precisely to time and exactly to length. Bill Bryden and Sebastian Graham-Jones, once very much of the National, welcomed us at Birmingham Rep and treated us to their undimmed enthusiasm for the Cottesloe and all its works. Alison Chitty allowed us to visit her studio, gave us permission to use her drawings, and was wonderfully informative about her work. William Dudley was, as ever, full of verve and vision. John Caird pondered and enquired, and gave us the benefit of his time and thoughts. Nick Ormerod saw us and discussed his work while mounting a major production at Stratford; we are grateful to him and to Declan Donnellan for their forbearance. Ian McKellen, courteous as always, telephoned us in the interval of the opening night of his engagement at the West Yorkshire Playhouse. Simon Russell Beale wrote for us with his customary helpfulness and insight. Matthew Frost and Lauren McAllister of Manchester University Press have been greatly encouraging and supportive.

The way has been hard and the time short. We could not have made the journey without the industry, expertise and ready commitment of Alec Jolly of A.H.Jolly (Editorial) and of Jane Martin his assistant. This is our fourth book with Alec, after *This Golden Round: the Royal Shakespeare Company at the Swan, Making Space for Theatre* and *Shakespeare's Globe Rebuilt.* His unstinting interest in our work, and the untold hours he is prepared to spend on it, go far beyond the call of duty. We are enormously grateful to him – and to his wife, Anne.

We have once again trespassed on the goodwill of our families. We say thank you to John, James, Richard and Evelyn, and to Eithne, Grania, Peter, Lucy, Sam, Sarah, Kevin, William and Edward. We hope you will be pleased with the results of our labours.

Ronnie Mulryne and Margaret Shewring.

Ronnie Mulryne and Margaret Shewring have collaborated on the writing and editing of nine books, including four for their own Company, Mulryne and Shewring Ltd., and others for Cambridge University Press, Manchester University Press and Macmillan. Ronnie is Professor of English, former Pro-Vice-Chancellor and Director of the Centre for the Study of the Renaissance, University of Warwick, and was Chairman of the Drama Projects Committee of the Arts Council of Great Britain and Chairman of the Drama and Dance Committee of the British Council.
Margaret is Senior Lecturer in Theatre Studies at the University of Warwick, and was national secretary of the Standing Committee of University Drama Departments. She is the author of a study of Shakespeare's Richard II *in the Shakespeare in Performance series (Manchester University Press).*

and vivid words of our contributors, and of the reviewers we have cited, the living tissue of theatre performance can be only partially recovered. We have nevertheless thought it entirely worthwhile to make the attempt, and have committed many highly enjoyable if taxing weeks, days and hours to searching that other source of National Theatre riches, the theatre archives, under the benign and expert guidance of the archivist, Nicola Scadding. The riches shelved on those towering stacks include not only all kinds of visual material, together with theatre programmes, reviews, interviews, the prompt-book 'bibles' (drawn up by the stage management team), and production and rehearsal photographs, but also the invaluable file of each production in the Cottesloe, compiled by Jason Barnes and replete with every kind of technical drawing and specification, negotiating letters to suppliers and local authorities, budgets and (often revealing) communications between artistic and technical staff. Our keenest regret is that we have not been able to include even a tiny fraction of this material. In some future technological age, or indeed even now, it may be possible to share some at least of these riches with a wider audience, but not at an affordable cost, and not within the covers of a book. We have done what we can, particularly in the sections entitled 'Working the Cottesloe', and 'Living Spaces', to reveal, through illustration and through the words of contributors, as much as is feasible of the entire *process* of creating and running a Cottesloe show, and not merely of its staged outcome.

We have kept faith with our initiating emphasis on the theatre space itself. Iain Mackintosh, to whom the task fell of designing as a theatre auditorium the cavernous hole so wisely left within the shell of the National building by its architect, Sir Denys Lasdun, has written of the circumstances in which he undertook the task, and the solutions he adopted. He has given perspective to his account by reprinting alongside his current thoughts an article he wrote under the immediate stimulus of the 1977 brief. He has also published for the first time original notes and sketches from which more permanent plans were later derived. His position as the far-sighted author of opportunity becomes quite clear. Jason Barnes (who as Production Manager of the Cottesloe for all twenty-one years of its existence is in an unrivalled position to do so) has written technical summaries of the production of each of the plays we feature, specifying in some detail the ways in which the Cottesloe space has been dressed and adapted for each show. These summaries are complemented by floor and vertical plans of the theatre, including plans specially commissioned for this book from Miles King (who has worked in the Cottesloe as stage and production manager). These plans illustrate the use of the space, including the disposition of the stage area, and the audience seating (or for promenade productions the shared performance and audience area). Jason has also, through interview, and through an edited version of his published article on *The Mysteries* (in the Cottesloe, in Edinburgh and at the Lyceum) offered vivid insights into the extraordinarily skilled, multifarious and demanding role of production manager. The acclaimed adaptability of the Cottesloe would be impossible to implement without the practical know-how of the production office (including, now, Diane Willmott as well as Jason Barnes) so that, without them, the visionary reconfigurations of space by directors and designers would run to waste.

The Cottesloe, like every other theatre, exists within an administrative and financial context that determines, or at the least very heavily influences, the work it does. We therefore invited the three successive Directors of the National Theatre, Sir Peter Hall, Sir Richard Eyre and Trevor Nunn, together with the Executive Director, Genista McIntosh, to set out their thoughts about the place of the Cottesloe within the economy of the National Theatre generally, and the contribution its work has made to theatre in Britain. The three Directors were also invited to talk about working in the Cottesloe, and Trevor Nunn about what he sees as the future for this smallest of the National's auditoria. The most notable common element in all four discussions proved to be the warmth of regard in which the Cottesloe is held, both in terms of its artistic product and the skills of its technical staff. All four emphasised the Cottesloe's role as a centre of innovation, a proving ground for new approaches to established plays, and the arena for finding an appropriate language of theatre for new writing – not an experimental space (the role of the Studio) but a public forum in which directors who are passionately engaged with a particular play may bring it to performance, working with a skilled cast and skilled technical support. Such an opportunity is costly in the case of a theatre that seats, in different configurations, at most four hundred or so, but sometimes as few as 250 (exact figures are given in the chronology in this book). The National's belief in the value of the Cottesloe translates into a cross-subsidy between the three auditoria, with the box-office of the Olivier and the Lyttelton supporting the Cottesloe's inevitable deficits.

This is a point underscored by Bill Bryden, the first and indeed the only Artistic Director of the Cottesloe, with whom we also talked. Bill's sense of obligation to Peter Hall, who authorised and sustained the concealed subsidy (though he was forced to close the Cottesloe for four months in 1985 as a high-profile gesture to government) is emphatic. It is, we found, a sentiment shared by his colleague and co-director Sebastian Graham-Jones, and by others who worked under Hall's directorship in the early years of the Cottesloe. The wisdom of the National's artistic policy under successive Directors has been to encourage the work of this innovative theatre by offering it financial security – though by no means lavish budgets – while, equally important, not constricting its play selection within a narrowly specified policy. Conviction on the part of a stage director and designer about the worth of a particular playscript, and the need to do it now and in the Cottesloe, seems to have counted for more than definitions of the theatre's role and therefore its repertory. The Cottesloe's place in the National is currently evolving, with notice (by Jonathan Miller, for example) of what appears to be an emerging policy for productions to gather plaudits in the Cottesloe before transferring to the Olivier or the Lyttelton, and with Trevor Nunn's plans for a shared ensemble in the Olivier and the Cottesloe. Under such plans, touring (as Roger Chapman remarks in this book) may be curtailed. A new Cottesloe is in the making within the framework of the National's development generally, and in response to new economic and cultural conditions. We can hope that the artistic freedom of which the Cottesloe has made such distinguished use will continue to be available to it. There are few signs to the contrary.

The Cottesloe not only generates its own productions but plays host to visiting shows, most notably perhaps those from the Market Theatre, Johannesburg and Théâtre Repère, but also from British companies such as Leicester Haymarket, the Liverpool Playhouse, Théâtre de Complicité, Shared Experience and English Touring Theatre. It also takes in shows drawn from the work of the National's Education Department and the National Studio. We have tried to represent this important part of the Cottesloe's annual repertoire by setting out the aims and listing some of the performances of the Education department, and by interviewing its head, Jenny Harris. We have also interviewed the Head of the Studio, Sue Higginson, about the Studio's distinctive work and its role in discovering, developing and nurturing experiments in writing, directing, designing and performance, some of them leading to production in the Cottesloe. Again, the wisdom of National policy has been to create a strong working Department and to trust it to get on with its allotted role. The gain to both of these Departments in terms of morale, loyalty and enthusiasm, and therefore to the work of the National and in the Cottesloe, appears to be great. As with other areas of this book, we are aware we have been unable to represent these aspects of the Cottesloe adequately, and regret that this is so.

Our most intractable problem has been how to select from among the very numerous Cottesloe productions a small number for more detailed treatment. It was obvious to us from the start that to consider (say) twenty or thirty plays as representative of the Cottesloe's work would produce only skimming, superficiality and dullness. Discussion with Iain Mackintosh and Jason Barnes produced criteria for selection that might not have seemed obvious, but which on reflection led to a list of productions which is, we believe, both interestingly varied and defensible. Our prime aim in writing about the Cottesloe, along with the wish to celebrate its success, has been, as we have emphasised, to explore the ways in which this most adaptable of theatres has lent itself to artistic vision and technical expertise. It began to seem logical to make the principle of selection not (or not only) the high profile and artistic achievement of a show (though that would remain a criterion) but the variety of ways in which the theatre space has been configured to host performances. Thus we have tried to include shows that have used the Cottesloe as a promenade space, in traverse (or long traverse), as an end stage, as a proscenium arch theatre (almost), and in the round (a full list of configurations, and an explanation of their meaning is given in the Chronology). It is usual to speak of the Cottesloe as a courtyard theatre, and the description is useful, for it draws attention to the embracing balconies which contribute so much to that sense of shared presence which is among the Cottesloe's greatest attributes. But so often Cottesloe shows are not courtyard shows, when, for example, steeply-raked stalls nullify the separation of stalls and balconies characteristic of a courtyard, or when no end-stage is in use at all. A prime example is David Edgar's *Entertaining Strangers*, where the use of a moving bridge repeatedly modified the audience-stage relationship. We have tried in discussing the selected shows to avoid, or at any rate to de-emphasise, any categorising of the theatre space, in favour of giving prominence to the distinctive qualities of the chosen format for a particular show. In other words, we have tried to see the configuration of the space as an integral aspect of design, and as, therefore, an influential element in what the show has to 'say'. No doubt some use of category has crept in, as it has above, to help us decide which shows to include. But our aim has been to identify experiment and distinctiveness in the use of the Cottesloe's resources, especially its resource of space. As a result, we have excluded from consideration shows which on other grounds it would be fruitful and fascinating to discuss. And, it has to be admitted, we were constrained by the number of pages available to us. For this we have tried to compensate by inviting Michael Billington, with his extraordinary powers of recollection, and his encyclopaedic knowledge of Cottesloe productions, to survey the Cottesloe's work over its twenty-one years. As we anticipated, this has turned out to be far more than compensation, and readers will find in Michael's chapter vivid evocations of shows not otherwise discussed in the book.

Our method of discussing shows has been to set out initially as much information as we thought useful to readers about the production in question, including author (or adapter), director, designer and so on, together with cast (sometimes, in the more complex shows, curtailed) and a note of opening and closing dates and where appropriate transfers and tours. We have expanded this information, again where we thought useful, into more extended treatment of the author's life and work, and/

FIG 3 The National Theatre and Théâtre de Complicité co-production of *The Street of Crocodiles*, devised by the Company and based on short stories by Bruno Schulz. Director Simon McBurney, designer Rae Smith. This visiting co-production opened at the Cottesloe on 13 August 1992.
César Sarachu (Joseph), Matthew Scurfield (the Father), Lilo Baur (Adela), Annabel Arden (the Mother), Joyce Henderson (Agatha). Background: Eric Mallet (Theodore) and Stefan Metz (Leon).
PHOTO: *Nobby Clark*

FIG 4 *Titus Andronicus* (William Shakespeare) presented by the Market Theatre, Johannesburg, in association with the Royal National Theatre Studio, July 1995. Director Gregory Doran, settings by Nadya Cohen. The work of the Studio in forging links with overseas and British companies has greatly enhanced the repertoire of the Cottesloe.
Jennifer Woodburne (Lavinia) and Antony Sher (Titus).
PHOTO: *Ruphyn Coudyzer*

or the subject-matter of the play (Ma Rainey's singing or Stanley Spencer's art, for example), and/or the work of a leading actor, director or designer, sometimes using grey-tint 'boxes' to set this information off from more descriptive material. In every case, Jason Barnes has supplied a technical summary of the play's staging, juxtaposed with floor and vertical plans of the Cottesloe set out for the show in question. We next attempt to evoke as vividly as possible the experience of being present at the show, by choosing issues and perspectives that are distinctive of it, and by using as fully as we can the comments of reviewers (and sometimes others) a source which offers immediacy and freshness of response, if not unanimity. In all of this we have tried to lay emphasis on design – an area of commentary too often neglected – and on the directors' and actors' management of audience response. One early and very influential show, or set of shows, *The Mysteries*, we have treated at greater length, to take in not only the kinds of commentary just mentioned, but to include Jason Barnes's lively discussion of the challenges thrown up by transferring the shows to other venues, in Edinburgh, and at the Lyceum. In most cases, eight or ten pages are devoted to a single show, always illustrated as fully as possible by photographs and drawings depicting as much as we can of settings as well as costume (photographers tend to be much influenced by the media's preference for close-up shots of individual actors). In every case, the endeavour is to give readers insight into the process of staging a Cottesloe show, from the point of view of technical and artistic personnel, as well as audiences.

A similar motive governs the selection of material we have included under the heading 'Working the Cottesloe'. We have used interviews to gain insight into the work of a range of theatre people, from directors and designers to actors, stage and production management, a senior lighting technician and the head of touring. These are supplemented by a full account of the process of mounting a Cottesloe show, with a week-by-week timetable of preparing and rehearsing it. Photographic and hand-sketched illustrations are included to give some sense of the detail of mounting the technical aspects of a production, including props, scenery, flying-arrangements and costume, together with the kinds of practical challenges that different productions throw up (a collapsing wall, a practising painter at work). As with other parts of the book, the need for economy has restricted what we can offer, but we hope to have afforded readers at least a glimpse of the extraordinarily skilled and demanding task of mounting a typical Cottesloe show.

There is sometimes a disposition among those who have not been closely involved in a Cottesloe production to think that mounting a show in the smallest auditorium poses few technical challenges. Trevor

Nunn detects a hint of condescension even among National personnel working in the other theatres. Our own experience in researching and preparing this book has been to emerge with a profound respect for the sheer inventive capability of technical staff and the vision of artists taking part in the work. As contributors to this book make clear, the Cottesloe is by no means a small space, and 'studio' is a misnomer (not only because the term is used for the experimental department of the National). In every respect, Cottesloe shows require a degree of skill comparable to that demanded by larger auditoria, and perhaps more often are given it.

The Board and the Beginning

When the Board of the National Theatre (then at the Old Vic) first considered the provision and use of the theatre ultimately known as the Cottesloe, British theatre at large was in something of a ferment resulting from the rise and expansion of the phenomenon known as 'fringe' or 'alternative' theatre. Theatre in this category was making all the running, first at venues such as the Traverse Theatre in Edinburgh (where Jim Haynes arguably began the movement in 1963), and then in the work of (usually young) companies such as 7:84, Shared Experience, Hull Truck and Joint Stock. Work reaching this country from abroad influenced the movement, as the La Mama company from New York or Jerzy Grotowski's and Tadeusz Kantor's work from Poland became known.

The subject-matter (and indeed the style) of such practitioners offered uncomfortable models and precedents for the National Theatre Board, even if some of its members, notably Peter Brook, had themselves been engaged in furthering it. As David Edgar puts it in a highly diverting article in *Making Space for Theatre* (ed. Ronnie Mulryne and Margaret Shewring, 1995): 'The two defining characteristics of the fringe theatre of the late 60s and early 70s were its distrust of the establishment in all its forms and its hostility to theatre buildings'. He adds, 'the generic fringe theatre location was either a room above a pub or a cellar below, roughly converted for home-produced theatrical presentation ... almost all of my early non-touring work was presented in small low-ceilinged rooms, their architectural, electrical and plumbing peculiarities obscured (but, happily, never entirely hidden) by ubiquitous black emulsion, including the now sadly defunct Pool Theatre, Edinburgh, the still thriving Bush Theatre and the much-relocated Soho Poly (for which, when in Ridinghouse Street, agents prepared special lists of short actors; I am six foot four, and had to attend rehearsals on all fours)'.

The problem for the National Theatre Board in planning their third auditorium was how to tap into the vitality of the fringe movement without sacrificing either principle or architectural style. Even the more conventional building-based companies were in these years setting up spaces for experimental work, often attached to the major Repertory theatres across the country. The Royal Shakespeare Company was to open The Other Place in 1974. The Royal Court had established its Theatre Upstairs in 1969 (Lord Goodman at the Arts Council, Peter Hall remarks in this book, thought that experimental work was appropriate for the Royal Court but not for the National Theatre). How was the National to provide a space for experimental work, an aim that must have seemed an obligation – to some Board members certainly – and one that was fully shared by Peter Hall? Notes prepared on an informal meeting of the National Theatre Building Committee on 26 January, 1968, show Peter Brook asserting that 'The experimental theatre "must be a laboratory". It should have the possibility of making the walls "alive". Actors must be able to make unexpected entrances through apertures in the walls'. Plainly, in Brook's mind, the more bizarre characteristics of contemporary small-scale theatre must be possible, and were desirable, in the National's third auditorium.

Help of a practical kind was at hand. John Bury, Head of Design at the National, 'explained with the aid of a model a scheme which would make the Cottesloe completely flexible as between various forms of stage/audience relationships' – though this was not until July 1974 (Minutes of the 102nd meeting of the National Theatre Board). Money was however unavailable, and it was 1977 before Iain Mackintosh's scheme, as explained by Mackintosh in this book, was realised. The more perplexing matter was the role the third auditorium was to play. Minutes as early as March, 1968, show the Board regretting the finance-driven sacrifice of the experimental theatre, while insisting that it 'was a vital part of the National Theatre complex and concept'. A partial compensation for the loss was attempted by the establishment in 1969 of an experimental season at the Jeanetta Cochrane Theatre, a remedy it was thought for flagging impetus in the National company at large, and one where 'the actors were excited and re-energised by the new opportunities presented to them' (Board Minutes, 10 February, 1969). Peter Hall's influential 'Policy Thoughts for the new South Bank Theatre' presented to the Board in March 1973 shows him wavering between concepts for the third auditorium, stimulated in part by Peter Brook's Parisian experiments, and in part by the responsibilities of the National to theatre in Britain. Under the heading 'The Studio. Third auditorium of the National Theatre' he writes:

> Its use is not as a Workshop or a place for people to learn their jobs. It is rather a Laboratory for advanced work, and this work should be done by the leaders of the profession. An example is Peter Brook's current work in Paris. A major firm always has a research laboratory; the National Theatre must have a laboratory to extend and examine all its work.
>
> Roughly half the year in the Studio should be used for research, with no absolute *necessity* to perform. Only with this freedom can we research. ...

> The Studio should also be a facility for all the young creative groups up and down the country. We should invite them to use our facilities. It is important that new talent can use the National Theatre and attract their audiences to our building.

There must be some question about the practicality of these thoughts, and competing strands are evident within them. Yet the seminal nature of what Hall had to say is evident. The Cottesloe has not taken on all the tasks he assigns. The Studio carries out the research function, and to a considerable degree Education maintains the country-wide liaison with young people to which he points. Yet both of course make use of the Cottesloe for important parts of their work. A later paper for the Board, dated November 1973, and simply headed 'The Cottesloe Theatre', modifies one of the roles the Cottesloe would be called on to play: 'Strictly studio or "laboratory" work which is not yet ready for or appropriate to a paying audience can also continue in the theatre's principal rehearsal rooms, moving subsequently to the Cottesloe and an audience when ready and if relevant'. Even if the location has changed, this division of functions between the Studio and the Cottesloe has become a matter of fact. Another insight that has proved fruitful and prophetic comes later in the same paper. Noting that the repertoire in the Olivier and the Lyttelton has to be fixed well in advance, the authors ('the directorate') suggest that 'The Cottesloe's role will be to counter-balance this unavoidable predictability with its own important ephemeracy, volatility and continuous changing interest'. In architectural terms, 'seating capacity and fixed installations are secondary to the requirements of flexibility, mobility and adaptability of the entire area'. These are desiderata which the Cottesloe as built and in operation has been able to meet. The path to the theatre's birth may have been strewn with sizeable rocks and may have had several wrong turnings and blind alleys, but its goal of a third auditorium which combines the energy of the experimental with the requirements of a paying audience has been, one might say triumphantly, realised.

The present book chronicles the ways in which this realisation has come about, and its characteristics. It should be read in conjunction with Simon Callow's fine book on the National, which quite properly pays major attention to the two principal auditoria, and makes little more than passing reference to the Cottesloe (Nick Hern Books in association with the Royal National Theatre, 1997). Callow's book provides the broader context for the development of the National, within which the work of the Cottesloe can be understood. Our book should also be read as a tribute to Lord Cottesloe, Chairman of the South Bank Theatre Board at the time the third auditorium was opened, and after whom, following some diversions, the theatre was eventually named (the early favourite as a name was simply 'The Studio'). A letter of 23 October 1972 from Richard Lynex, Secretary of the South Bank Board, to Sir Max Rayne, the then Chairman of the National Theatre Board, explained that 'I have experienced at first hand both his [Lord Cottesloe's] regret when, for reasons of drastic economy, the studio theatre was abandoned in March 1968 and also his determined efforts thereafter to get it reinstated. ... I am sure that no one man can have been more effective than he in getting the theatre built'. The letter was received less than effusively by Rayne, but despite some coolness on the part of the Board, the proposal to attach the name Cottesloe to the theatre was finally adopted in a tabled paper for a Board meeting on 12 November, 1973.

Our book is, however, offered above all as a tribute to those who have worked in the Cottesloe over the twenty-one years of its existence, and as an acknowledgement of the outstanding technical and artistic riches to which the theatre has given birth. A not very little room, it is true, but almost infinite riches.

THE NATIONAL'S STUDIO AND THE COTTESLOE

Sue Higginson

Based on an interview with Ronnie Mulryne and Margaret Shewring

Sue Higginson is Head of the Royal National Theatre Studio. She has worked with Cameron Mackintosh, Sir Peter Hall, London Weekend Television and the English National Opera.

FROM the earliest discussions, members of the National Theatre's Board wanted an experimental space in addition to the two large auditoria planned for the South Bank. This experimental space was described variously as a studio and a laboratory, a space in which writers and performers could develop their skills and take risks, without putting personal reputations or the box office in jeopardy.

At first, the Cottesloe (when it was eventually incorporated in the South Bank building) seemed to meet this need. But given the Cottesloe's four hundred seats, its comparatively large space and its role within the repertoire of the National overall, a play produced there has to be robust to survive. Some new writing, for example, can be very exposed in the Cottesloe. In 1984, therefore, the Studio was set up to provide an appropriately challenging, but also appropriately sheltered, environment for artists to work in.

The great joy of the Studio from its inception has been that it has not had to rely on box-office for its income. As conceived by Lord Rayne, Peter Hall and Peter Gill, the Studio has always been protected in commercial terms, and dedicated to research and development, not public performance.

The Studio has been fortunate in its physical location. It is housed in the Annexe of the Old Vic, previously leased rent-free to the National by Ed Mirvish, and now, since early 1998, owned by the National itself. Once the production workshops for the Old Vic, the Annexe became in 1963 the purpose-designed production workshops for the National (at that time at the Old Vic), then the home for a time of the Prospect Theatre Company, before a one-off capital grant in 1984 allowed a modest refurbishment of the run-down building and its opening as the Studio.

FIG 5 The National Theatre's production of *The Murderers* by Daniel Mornin, one of the Festival of New Plays originating in the National's Studio, which re-opened the Cottesloe on 23 September 1985 after Peter Hall's forced closure of the space in response to insufficient Arts Council funding. Director Peter Gill, designer Alison Chitty. Ewan Stewart as Tommy.
PHOTO: *Michael Mayhew.*

The Studio is at once physically separate from, and yet part of, the National Theatre, which allows it the freedom to develop its own ethos in a context run by and for artists. It is neither a Conservatoire nor a studio theatre, but a space set aside for experiment. A new writer, for example, can work in the Studio alongside professional actors, often in larger casts than could ever be financially acceptable in a commercial context. Actors currently working in the National make themselves available without fee, and others can when necessary be 'bought in' as appropriate. New writing is explored in this way, and the writers encouraged to develop their craft. When a piece strong enough for public performance comes along, it may be offered production in the Cottesloe, or go on elsewhere.

When the Studio first opened, this chance for public performance took the form of Studio Nights at the Cottesloe, with one night within each of the National's booking periods set aside for readings or semi-staged performances. However, because there was little opportunity for set-up in the Cottesloe, and staging was usually minimal, these Nights were found to be intimidating for new writers and directors, and sometimes hampered rather than promoted creative development, and so were allowed to lapse. A major Studio foray into the Cottesloe came, however, in 1985, when the Greater London Council gave sufficient money to reopen the auditorium after Peter Hall had been forced to close it for lack of funds. The re-opening was celebrated with a nine-week Festival of New Plays from the Studio. Peter Gill's season included ten pieces, five of them in a single bill, by authors such as Mick Mahoney, Debbie Horsfield and Gill himself.

More recently, work initially developed at the Studio has led to major collaborations between the National and a visiting company. For example, Théâtre de Complicité worked on *Street of Crocodiles* at the Studio before its presentation at the Cottesloe. Again, one of the great achievements of the Studio has been its development of links with companies from abroad, such as the Market Theatre of Johannesburg (whose *A Place with the Pigs, A Lesson from Aloes, Master Harold and the Boys* – all by Athol Fugard – and *Titus Andronicus* have been presented at the Cottesloe) and the enormously successful residencies developed with theatres in Vilnius in Lithuania, taking people like Antony Sher and Juliet Stevenson to work with Lithuanian theatre practitioners. Three successful residencies have also been held at the Edinburgh Festival and one in Belfast.

Work on new writing is complemented by work on design, directing, lighting, voice and text. Directors and designers are put in touch with each other, for example by a 'dating day' during which new designers can introduce their portfolios of work to senior directors. Links have been developed with the Motley theatre-design course, and with Central St Martin's. Out of such collaborations, fruitful developments in design have come about, for example in the case of Tim Hatley, who began his career working at the Studio with Tony Harrison on *Trackers of Oxyrhynchus* and who has now, among much else, designed *Stanley* for the Cottesloe. One major function of the Studio is indeed to put creative teams in touch with each other, and in this the social ecology of the place – for example in the presentation of unrehearsed play readings with good sight-reading actors – is important. Recently, two bursaries have allowed individual directors to be based at the Studio, each for one year, with one of the bursaries being in association with the English Touring Company.

The Studio can commission work. It can also promote work already in hand. For example, in the last two years, Martin McDonagh worked on *The Cripple of Inishmaan* while the writer was on attachment at the Studio, and Patrick Marber's *Closer* was given workshops and a rough draft developed. Both plays went on to the Cottesloe (as well as the West End and further afield). The Studio therefore complements the Cottesloe, and feeds it. But it remains separate, and unique. There is nothing like it abroad, nor at home, especially in terms of its creative autonomy and its freedom from the pressures of the box office.

FIG 6 The National Theatre's production of *As I Lay Dying* by William Faulkner, adapted by Peter Gill. One of the Festival of New Plays, opening at the Cottesloe on 15 October 1985. Director Peter Gill, designer Alison Chitty. Robert Hamilton (Anse Bundren), Joanne Whalley (Dewey Dell), Ewan Stewart (Vardaman), Phillip Joseph (Cash), Paul Moriarty (Vernon Tull), Gillian Barge (Cora Tull), Daniel Webb (Darl).
PHOTO: *Michael Mayhew.*

FIG 7 *Alice's Adventures Under Ground* by Christopher Hampton in collaboration with Martha Clarke opened at the Cottesloe on 8 November 1984. Director Martha Clarke, designer Robert Israel. The play was developed over two years through a series of workshops at the National's Studio. Sasha Hanau (Alice) and John Carlisle (Mock Turtle).
PHOTO: *Michael Mayhew.*

THE COTTESLOE AND THE ROYAL NATIONAL THEATRE'S EDUCATION DEPARTMENT

SINCE 1982, the National (subsequently the Royal National) Theatre, has put an increasing emphasis on its role in making theatre accessible to all, and in particular to young people, not only in London but throughout Great Britain. One important component in carrying out this aim has been the work of the Education Department.

The Cottesloe has played its part in this Education and outreach work by providing a venue in which touring productions could begin, or in which tours could conclude.

Until 1988, Education outreach took the form, largely, of NT Workshop presentations, touring in a single van to numerous small-scale venues throughout the country. From 1990 this developed into the NT Mobile Productions. In both cases, the Cottesloe was used as the venue to present this work in London. A list of the productions concerned is given alongside.

In 1993, a new Head, Jenny Harris, was appointed to the Education Department, and a new tour co-ordinator, Venu Dhupa (now Executive Director of Nottingham Playhouse). The role of the Education Department has continued to develop over these years, and the Cottesloe continues to be used for performances.

1994 saw the first Showcase for new plays by youth groups to be presented in the Cottesloe, sponsored by British Telecom. This event, under the title BT National Connections, has seen two further major projects in 1995 and 1997.

BT National Connections involves a portfolio of twelve new plays being made available to 200 youth theatre groups meeting in ten venues across Great Britain. Each venue sends one production to take part in a Showcase at the National, either in the Olivier or the Cottesloe.

Jenny Harris, Head of the NT Education Department, summarises the place of the Cottesloe in the work of the Department:

The significance of the Cottesloe is that we aim in the Education Department at creating the next generation of theatre-goers, and young theatre-goers respond to challenging work in small spaces. In the Cottesloe, the audience participates in a shared experience. The energy generated by the performers is not dissipated by the size of the auditorium. So there is a relationship between the performers and the audience which is immediate and direct. They are all engaged within the same space.

The Cottesloe is wonderfully flexible, and so can offer a wide range of different and exciting experiences. The staff of the Education Department, together with the Cottesloe Production Office, have grown very skilled at developing work within that space, and at changing the space in accordance with the needs of the show. It is therefore exciting for an audience to come into it. They never know what they are going to find. Its unpredictability makes theatre an exciting possibility worth experiencing.

National Theatre Education Department Workshop and Mobile Productions which have played in the Cottesloe

1982	Bertolt Brecht, *The Caucasian Chalk Circle*, directed by Michael Bogdanov and Justin Greene.
1983	William Shakespeare, *Macbeth*, directed by Michael Bogdanov
1986	William Shakespeare, *Hamlet*, directed by Cicely Berry
1986	Bertolt Brecht, *The Mother*, directed by Di Trevis
1988	James Hayes, *Russell of the Times*, directed by James Hayes
1988	David Hare, *Fanshen*, directed by Les Waters
1987	Arnold Wesker, *Roots*, directed by Simon Curtis
1990	Molière, *Tartuffe*, directed by Jatinder Verma
1991	Dario Fo, *Accidental Death of an Anarchist*, directed by Tim Supple
1991	Chris Barton, *More Tales from the Magic Carpet*, directed by Chris Barton
1992	Keith Waterhouse and Willis Hall, *Billy Liar*, directed by Tim Supple
1993	Bertolt Brecht, *Mother Courage and her Children*, directed by Anthony Clark
1994	Garry Lyons, *Wicked, Yaar!*, directed by John Turner
1995	Winsome Pinnock, *Leave Taking*, directed by Paulette Randall
1996	Aristophanes, *The Frogs*, directed by Fiona Laird
1997	Caryl Churchill, *Light Shining in Buckinghamshire*, directed by Mark Wing-Davey
1998	William Shakespeare, *Twelfth Night*, directed by Brigid Larmour

There were, in addition, BT National Connections presentations of Play Festivals for young People in the Cottesloe in 1994, 1995 and 1997.

Fig 8 The National Theatre Workshop presentation of *Hamlet*, directed by Cicely Berry, designed by Chris Dyer and with music by Terry Davies. Kate Buffery as Gertrude and Tim McInnerny as Hamlet. The production was specially devised with a minimal use of sets and props for presentation at colleges, schools and small scale arts centres. It was cast from the Richard Eyre/David Hare group of actors and opened at the Cottesloe on 10 January, 1986.
Photo: *Graham Mitchell.*

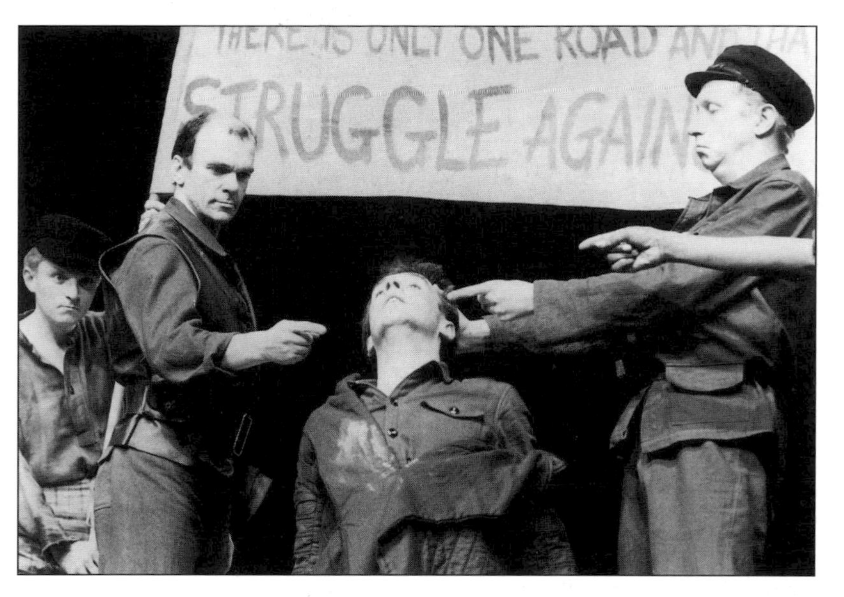

Fig 9 *Fanshen* by David Hare was one of a series of Education tours, devised for touring to schools, colleges and arts centres. It played at about 25 places before coming into the Cottesloe for 6 performances in April 1988. The play offers 'an accurate historical record of what once happened in one village four hundred miles south-west of Peking' (Programme), and was written initially for the experimental Joint Stock Company, who gave it its London premiere in 1975. The Education Department production was directed by Les Waters and designed by Bunny Christie, and was sponsored by British Petroleum. The photograph, by Michael Mayhew, shows (*left to right*) Kilian McKenna, Des McAleer, John Keegan and Mark Williams.

Fig 10 Caryl Churchill's *Light Shining in Buckinghamshire* was one of a series of Royal National Theatre Mobile Productions, instituted to bring top quality theatre to small and middle-scale theatres, arts centres, colleges and found spaces throughout the UK, before joining the repertoire at the Cottesloe. This production, directed by Mark Wing-Davey and designed by Madeline Herbert, opened at the Cottesloe on 10 January 1997. The photograph, by Geraint Lewis, shows Tim Crouch, Fergus Webster and Tim Welton, three of the company of six making the tour, which played at 27 venues before the Cottesloe, where it was staged for 19 performances. The simple 'fit-up' design can be clearly seen.

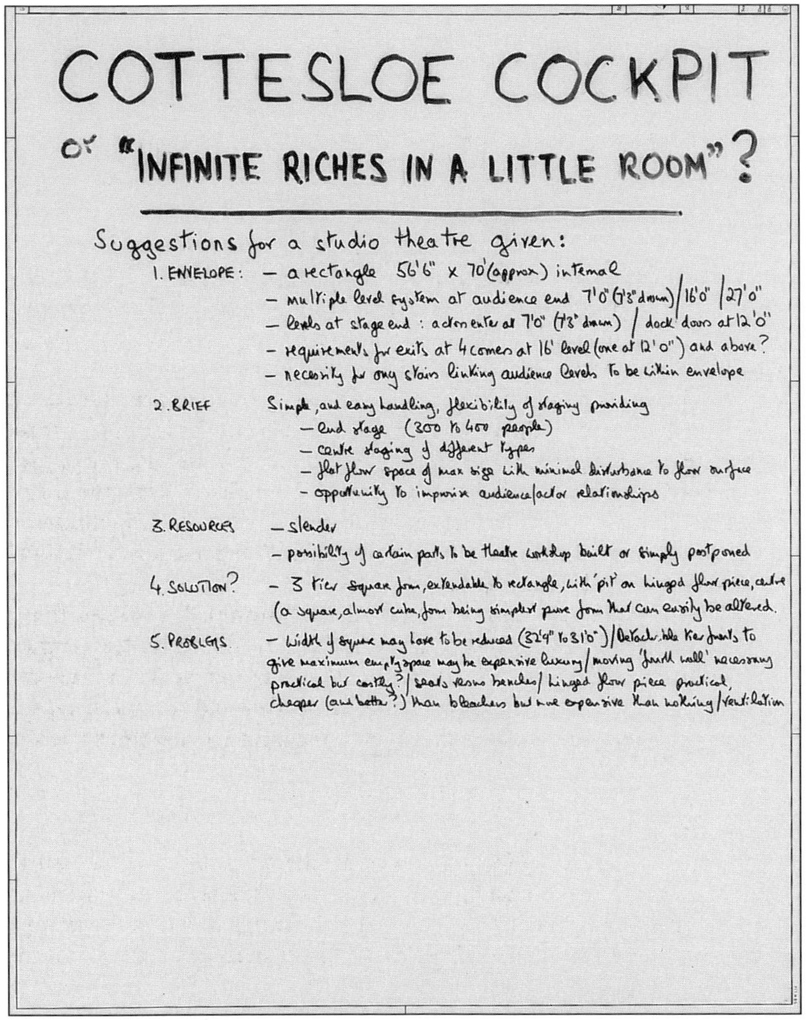

COTTESLOE COCKPIT or 'INFINITE RICHES IN A LITTLE ROOM'?

Suggestions for a studio theatre given:

1. ENVELOPE:
   - a rectangle 56' 6" x 70' (approx) internal
   - multiple level system at audience end 7' 0" (7' 3" drawn)/16' 0"/ 27' 0"
   - levels at stage end: actors enter at 7' 0" (7' 3" drawn)/dock doors at 12' 0"
   - requirements for exits at 4 corners at 16' level (one at 12' 0") and above
   - necessity for any stairs linking audience levels to be within envelope

2. BRIEF:
   - simple and easy handling, flexibility of stage providing
   - end stage (300 to 400 people)
   - centre staging of difference types
   - flat floor space of max size with minimal disturbance to floor surface
   - opportunity to improvise audience/actor relationships

3. RESOURCES
   - slender
   - possibility of certain parts to be theatre workshop built or simply postponed

4. SOLUTION?
   - 3 tier square form, extendible to rectangle, with 'pit' on hinged floor piece, centre (a square, almost cube, form being simplest pure form that can easily be altered)

5. PROBLEMS
   - width of square may have to be reduced (32' 9" to 31' 0")
   - Detachable tier fronts to give maximum empty space may be expensive luxury
   - moving 'fourth wall' when necessary, practical but costly?
   - seats versus benches/hinged floor piece practical, cheaper (and better?) than bleachers but more expensive than nothing/ ventilation

FIG 11 Iain Mackintosh's first 'back of envelope' thoughts on the design of the Cottesloe. Many of these have proved to be remarkably prescient.

THE IDEAS BEHIND THE COTTESLOE

Iain Mackintosh

Iain Mackintosh examines the concepts and problems behind studio theatres in general and the Cottesloe in particular.

Reprinted with small editorial alterations from THE STAGE, March 1977.
(*The three notes were written in 1998 with the advantage of hindsight*)

DESIGNERS of studio theatres soon discover that the phrase studio theatre means different things to different people. It is not a description of form like open stage, thrust stage, opera house or picture frame stage.

It is not, quite, a description of theatrical character such as West End, Broadway, Boulevard or Fringe. Studio Theatre certainly suggests risk or experiment to most people but when questions of shape, character and size are posited one gets very different answers.

Let us see whether the extent of these differences can be shown by comparing opposite points of view to three questions:

1. **Simplicity or Sophistication?**
First answer: a studio theatre is an utterly simple space in which a performance can be put on with the minimum of technical preparation. Switch on the lights, put up the set (if any), cut costs on inessentials, sell the seats and get on with the real business of theatre. Both audience and professionals will learn more, risk more, experiment more if they can all get down to fundamentals with a minimum of fuss.

Second answer: a studio theatre is a flexible space in which far-reaching experiments, possibly about the very nature of theatre, and certainly about actor/audience relationships can be made. Changes in form must be total as well as rapid and labour-saving if such a sophisticated laboratory theatre is to be used intensively by different groups of people.

2. **Liberate/Abolish the Scenic Designer?**
First answer, a studio theatre liberates the designer and director from the confines of the picture frame proscenium, with its baroque traditions. In the studio, the designer can design not merely the actors' world but the entire space. If it is a season of Athol Fugard, you may sit on an oil drum within the shanty town: if the evening is presented by some eastern European group of artist-actors, you might have wished you had put on older clothes with all that glue and feathers around.

French designer Chaix wrote in 1976: 'During the '50s it became evident that there was a need for an alternative to the traditional *commedia dell' arte* theatre layout, for staging spectacles. The spectacle should no longer be confined to the stage, but should invade the entire space.'[1]

For this first group, a studio theatre is a canvas or living sculpture to be repainted and recreated for each show. The second answer comes from those refugees from the picture stage who have left not because the picture frame confines the scenery but because behind the picture frame the use of scenery is at once necessary and unwelcome. For these a studio theatre is essentially a non-scenic theatre, where actor/audience relationship is literally just that and nothing else.

Edmund Jones, an American scenic artist, has written: '... the best thing that could happen to our theatre at this moment would be for playwrights and actors and directors to be handed a bare stage, on which no scenery could be placed, and then told that they must write and act and direct for this stage. In no time at all we should have the most exciting theatre in the world.'

3. **Renewal or Rejection?**
First answer: the motive for building studio theatre is to renew the theatre we already have. New actors, new writers, new directors are needed, and in the studio theatre opportunities will be given for this new talent to emerge which, once proven, will graduate to the larger theatres of the establishment.

Second answer: studio theatres, especially those actually within the citadels of the establishment, should be spaces able to accept easily and naturally an iconoclastic, experimental or fringe theatre pledged to overturn

1 At the Cottesloe, it did invade the entire space as early as 1977, when Bill Bryden and William Dudley created the first Cottesloe promenade, *The Passion*, which culminated in *The Mysteries*, the full trilogy presented at the Cottesloe and Lyceum in 1985.

> establishment forms of theatre. Here again are two groups of people whose spatial needs are very different: the first wanting a studio theatre able to serve as a smaller-scale approximation of existing theatres, the second wanting a studio space totally removed from all past or present theatrical conventions, which are to them bourgeois and boring.

This quick resume shows that studio theatre design is a game in which the player can only please some of the people some of the time. The central issue is probably the opposing demands of simplicity and freedom-from-scenery on the one hand, and the demand for total flexibility in which everything is possible on the other.

There are two other aspects of the design problem that must be mentioned. The first of these is the difficulty of purpose-building for experiment.

It is a fact that most experimental theatre in Britain today takes place in converted premises: church halls, rehearsal rooms, basements, warehouses, tin sheds or tenements. Throughout the last 15 years, fringe theatre has generally treated architects and designers with suspicion. The few architects who have opened dialogues with the fringe have often concluded that the improvised and inadequate nature of their existing premises are far from a hindrance, but rather a necessary condition for their sort of theatre. There are those who simply prefer converted premises to a purpose built theatre.

The second remaining problem is one of size. Here it is best to illustrate the problem by comparison. The Theatre Upstairs at the Court, the Traverse at Edinburgh, the Other Place at Stratford and the old Open Space in Tottenham Court Road all hold under 150. Most are empty spaces in which it would seem that almost all is possible. But all are small. If a designer were to try the same empty-space approach on a space four times as large, he would get all the theatricality of an aircraft hanger. This is fine for Ronconi's *Orlando Furioso* or Mnouchkine's *1789* but a bit demanding for a two hander played to a small audience. From this it is apparent that the design of larger studio theatres is a rather different affair from the design of small ones.

Back to the Cottesloe, which was to be at once large and small. In 1973, Peter Hall called for his third theatre. ... The brief asked for the following: a top capacity, on occasions, of 400; provision for a scenic end stage so that the theatre might serve as London showcase for the National Theatre mobile productions; a flat floor, as much for television and film work as for free-space theatre, plus, of course, all the usual features of a studio that would serve both as the experimental wing of the National Theatre Company and as the venue for best fringe productions.

All things to all men? Well, why not? A National Theatre ought to be available to very different groups of people. The design had to achieve as much of the impossible as possible: a reconciling of some of the very different views expressed above.

The response to this brief was to turn this large empty space into a form of courtyard. Galleries were introduced on three sides of a central, much smaller, empty space. Two objectives were thus achieved: the increase in capacity, by papering the walls with people on three levels (one row seated, one row standing) and the reduction in free space to a much smaller, more manageable volume that does not need the resources of a Broadway musical – as would have been needed to achieve a fully scenic effect in the empty 57ft by 66 ft room. ...

The middle level of the galleries is at foyer level. And since the linking stairs between the three levels are within the theatre, everyone aiming to sit at the lower levels must pass through the upper levels, thus removing any feeling of it being a hierarchical layout. When the audience enters for the opening show, the courtyard is set out in end stage form, but it must be remembered that nothing at the lowest level is fixed or permanent. Since stage level is the same as 'first' tier level, all that need be done to achieve a flat floor throughout is to lift and remove the encircling rostra, level up the central space to stage level, and take away the seats to a subterranean store. ...[2]

A series of sketches would show the formal options: end-stage, arena, thrust, traverse, etc. However, such a series might be misleading on two counts. First, because the point about a courtyard is not that the stage area can be altered through a set of fixed options, but that the place and character of the stage within the courtyard can be varied infinitely — largely because every level is available to either actor or audience.

The second reason why a set of sketches might be misleading, is that the Cottesloe is, as it now stands, incomplete.

Missing Bits

The missing bits are missing through a lack of money, not a lack of thought. Without them, the theatre may seem a bit inflexible. It is therefore worth listing the additions yet to come.

First, the moving fourth wall, which will be available to either audience or performer depending on the layout of the theatre. This spans the end of the rectangle at middle and top gallery level. It has three positions. Firstly, the parking position at the back of any conventional scenic end stage. Secondly, at the ends of the rectangular galleries, where it either offers a multi-level architectural alternative to built scenery (again in the end stage layout) or becomes the fourth side of a rectangular theatre-in-the-round. Thirdly, drawn right in to form a perfect square 9.9m x 9.9m, in which even an audience of 150 need not feel lost. The moving fourth wall is a device which can both reduce the need for scenery and/or reduce the volume of the space.

The second missing element is the adjustable floor system within the rectangle of galleries. At present, screwed-down bench seats and a permanent-looking edge to the end stage suggest inflexibility. At present, labour must be brought in to move seats and re-position the rostra on which the seats are set, in order to form theatre-in-the-round.

The final layout will include some lifts with which to adjust the levels of the central area with far less fuss. The usefulness of the lift system can be judged when one compares how much extra timber and labour is needed now to achieve layouts which ultimately will be done mechanically, for example,

2 The flat floor feature was familiar in most Georgian playhouses where it was used regularly for balls and occasionally for pony racing. The closer link was to *Orlando Furioso* at the Murrayfield Ice Rink, Haymarket, Edinburgh in 1970.

the steepening of the rake of the central block of seats so that it reaches to the middle rather than the lowest encircling tier.[3] This arrangement would achieve the seating capacity and the actor/audience relationship of the Hampstead Theatre club, i.e. 150 or 160 in a single tier. In such a layout the galleries would be superfluous.

Although lacking some bits and pieces, the Cottesloe is in a sense, a clean slate. It is now up to actors and artists to do just what they like with it. Push it around, even repaint if they don't like black. This would be relatively easy because almost every inch can be reached with a pair of domestic step ladders.

The only limitation on what can be done is the theatricality inherent in the courtyard form, a form at once ancient and universal, a form which may suggest some fresh ways of achieving a theatrical relationship. … Even when this studio theatre is complete with fourth wall and lift system, it should still feel incomplete. Only by leaving a lot to the experience of use can the designers of brand new theatre encourage the improvisation and the vital response to problems of theatrical relationship more often found only in converted premises.

So much for design philosophy. Now it is up to the first groups of actors and artists who have to break in the Cottesloe while it is still new if not shiny. March 4 [1977] was the first night, but there are many more first nights to come, because there will be as many first nights as there are changes to be rung. In a few years, however, it may be possible to assess whether the NT's third theatre is their sort, your sort, our sort of studio.

The author submitted a design study to the NT in 1973, an exercise in filling the existing space. This study was then developed by the architects in discussion with the NT.

3 It was done mechanically in 1986 with the introduction of the retractable seating unit which is still there. However while this speeded the changeover from flat floor to end stage it has meant that the shallower rake to the lowest level, with its increase in capacity and with a large part of the audience below the actor's eye line, has not been used since.

JOHN BURY

John Bury was Head of Design at the National Theatre when plans for the Cottesloe were first considered by the Theatre Board. His model for the Cottesloe, conceived in consultation with Richard Pilbrow, and built (he recollects) by Theatre Projects Consultants, was shown to the Board in July 1974. Before and since that time John Bury has been Britain's leading stage designer, working in particular with Peter Hall on such memorable productions as The Wars of the Roses, Richard II, Richard III *and* Twelfth Night. *In the Cottesloe he designed, among other productions, Harold Pinter's* Family Voices, Victoria Station *and* A Kind of Alaska.

Based on a conversation with Ronnie Mulryne

WHEN the Cottesloe was first being considered we were all terribly busy. The other theatres weren't right, and our days were taken up with adjustments to the Lyttelton and especially the Olivier. All of us in the theatre liked the idea of the Cottesloe, but it was Iain Mackintosh's persistence that got things done.

We had all sorts of problems. The space wasn't always available to work in. It was used for various purposes, including at one time a scenery store. Then there was the problem of the galleries. Iain wanted three galleries all round, but it wasn't financially possible or practical at the time. And Peter Hall threw us by wanting a rake different from the original plan. Some suggestions would have led to a tiny number of seats, and would have been wholly uneconomical. We sometimes felt we were being pushed from pillar to post. We did the best we could.

The theatre has, despite these initial problems, turned out to be very useful, and it works well. My own design work in the Cottesloe has not been such as to use the space in its more adventurous forms. I'm not a theatre-in-the-round man, and I find the traverse very difficult to design for, and difficult for the audience – you have to have the right show. I've used the space conventionally. End stage or thrust stage offer good opportunities in the Cottesloe. The theatre is about the right size and you can get to the bars easily. What more can you ask?

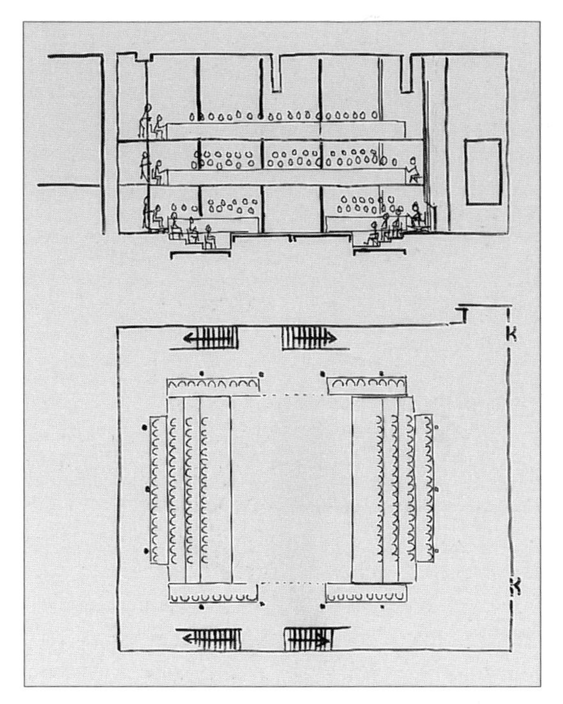

FIG 12 Traverse layout

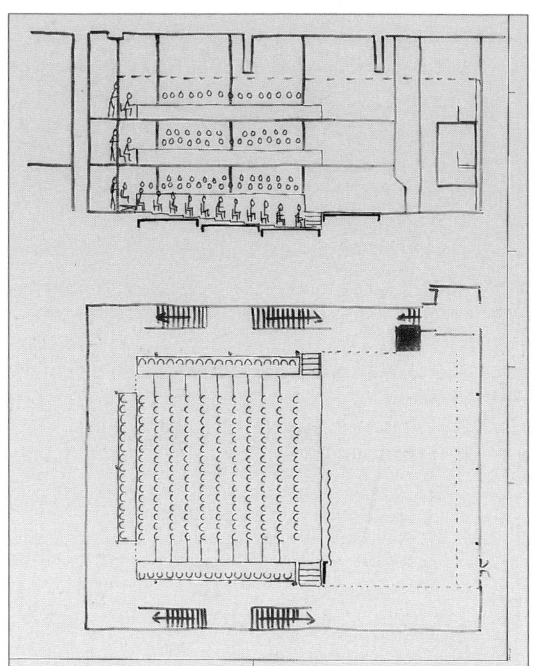

FIG 13 End stage layout

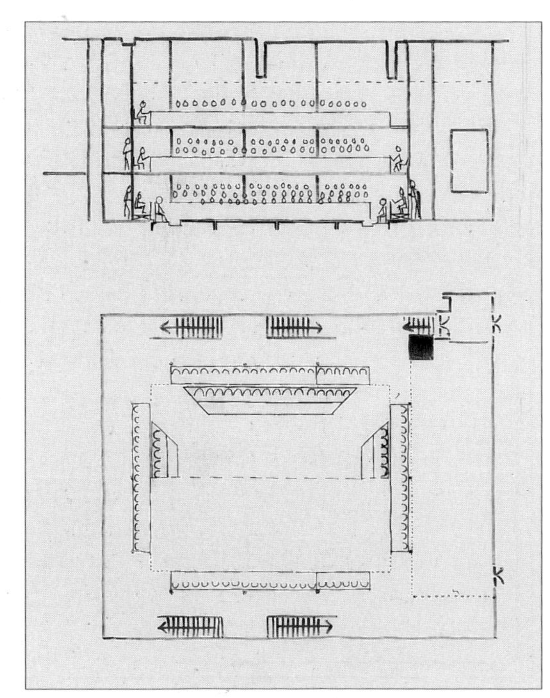

FIG 14 Centre stage layout

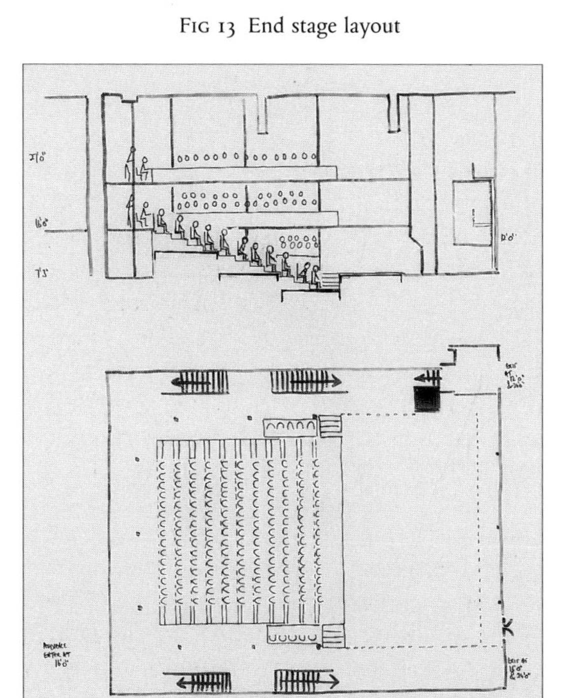

FIG 15 'Cottesloe cockpit'

FOUND SPACE IN A NEW BUILDING

THE CREATION OF THE COTTESLOE

Iain Mackintosh

Iain Mackintosh is Design Director of Theatre Projects Consultants Ltd. After graduating from Worcester College, Oxford, he co-founded the Prospect Theatre Company in 1961 and in 1973 joined Richard Pilbrow as a director of Theatre Projects. In addition to the Cottesloe, Iain has participated in the design of the Tricycle Theatre, London, the Wilde Theatre, Bracknell and the Lawrence Batley Theatre, Huddersfield, among others, and in the re-ordering and re-modelling of many more, including the Edinburgh Festival Theatre. He is currently working on the Royal Court. Iain produced the Cottesloe Mysteries *for Theatre Projects at the Lyceum in 1985, and has been responsible for several major exhibitions, including the 1975 Hayward exhibition,* The Georgian Playhouse 1730–1830, *the 1982 Royal Academy* Royal Opera House Retrospective 1732–1982 *and the British Council* Making Space for Theatre: British Architecture and Theatre since 1958 *(1995). He is the author of* Architecture, Actor and Audience *(Routledge, 1993).*

THE COTTESLOE as built was conceived in the winter of 1973/74. Exactly how this happened is a strange story.

Twenty architects had been chosen in the summer of 1963 from the 120 who had applied to design the new National. Each had been sent a brief which called for a main theatre, seating about 1000, adaptable to provide (a) an amphitheatre with an apron or peninsular stage (not a theatre-in-the-round) and (b) a proscenium arch stage. They had also been asked to include a small theatre seating about 400, mainly for experimental purposes. The interviews took place in November and Denys Lasdun (now Sir Denys) was appointed on 22 November 1963.

The first meeting of the South Bank Building Committee after the appointment of Lasdun took place soon after, on 9 January 1964. The committee had first met a year earlier on 3 January 1963. Its membership included, in addition to Laurence Olivier, Norman Marshall as joint chairman, George Devine, Peter Hall, Stephen Arlen, Michael Benthall, Peter Brook, John Dexter, Frank Dunlop, Michael Elliott, William Gaskill, Michel St Denis, Sean Kenny, Jocelyn Herbert, Tanya Moiseiwitsch and Robert Stephens. Richard Pilbrow became a member in April 1966, on the death of George Devine, having been on the Technical Sub-Committee since early 1964. Pilbrow resigned in 1968 when his firm, Theatre Projects Consultants, was appointed as technical theatre consultant to Denys Lasdun's architectural firm.

The conclusions of the South Bank Building Committee had to be presented to the National Theatre Board, who then had to seek sanction from the Government for any change from the original architectural brief. In May 1964 there was such a change. Prior to that the brief was for two spaces, a 1,000 seat adaptable theatre and a 400 seat studio. After that, the brief was for three spaces, with capacities still being discussed: an open stage, a proscenium theatre and a studio. Some committee members, with advice from Kenneth Tynan, had formed the view that a proscenium theatre was a *sine qua non* if the classic repertoire was to be served, while Lasdun and others shared the instinct that the inherent technical complexity of an adaptable theatre on a 1,000-seat scale was simply not practical.

The civil servants' view that a single large 2000, or even 3000, seat theatre would need less subsidy had already been rejected. In May 1964, the government endorsed the Board's view that, although the precise site was still uncertain, there should be two main theatres, an open stage and a proscenium. While discussion intensified on what was to be the Olivier, the debate on the proscenium dwindled. (It was once dubbed the 'any other business theatre' by a recalcitrant member of the Building Committee.) Most of the discussion took place around Lasdun's original idea of an open-stage theatre with the stage 'in the corner of a room', which had been conceived as early as March of that year. In November 1964 Olivier finally accepted that a proscenium theatre should be included. Little reference of any kind was made to the studio theatre, although Brook pressed its importance.

The committee did not meet from January 1965 to March 1966. But after March matters moved fast. The design of what was to be named the Lyttelton, with its 'non hierarchical single gallery', was approved at the end of 1966. It was not spotted that no one in the stalls of this theatre, as designed, could see the audience in the gallery and vice versa. This, plus the absence of any audience on the side walls, led inevitably to the 'two house' feel of the Lyttelton. During 1967, the final design of the open stage theatre (the Olivier), complete with drum revolve and fly tower both introduced by Pilbrow, emerged to the satisfaction of the

Building committee and Board. Between February and September 1967 the GLC (the Greater London Council), the South Bank Theatre Board and the National Theatre discussed with Lasdun and others the moving of the already-sketched design to the present site east of Waterloo Bridge from the earlier site to the west of Hungerford Bridge. John Elsom and Nicholas Tomalin in their 'official' *History of the National Theatre,* published by Jonathan Cape in 1978, record that vast changes in the design were not required, other than the exclusion of the proposed opera house and the angling of the National's entrance upstream rather than downstream. Planning permission for the change was sought in September 1967, so that detailed design could commence.

At this point, there was still little discussion on the nature of the studio theatre. What discussion there was must wait until publication of the confidential minutes of the Building Committee. Elsom and Tomalin state that 'in December 1966, the South Bank Theatre and Opera House Board agreed to the addition of a studio theatre, which would basically be plain rooms with moveable seating for 150–200.' However soon after it was 'indefinitely deferred'.

Here we must stop the story to praise Denys Lasdun for what seems to have been a Nelsonian touch in not reading his architectural client's signal. He had anticipated just such an eventuality as the proposed indefinite deferral, and had located the studio theatre under the upstage right corner of the main open-stage theatre, irrespective of where the whole building was to be constructed. Hence it could not be abandoned, 'only perhaps shut off and left as a useless hole, a solution which no politician would surely contemplate', as John Elsom puts it. And so the detailed design of the whole building on its new site commenced with, in one corner, an empty space for the cancelled studio.

At earlier building committee meetings, Peter Hall had always preferred a single main open-space theatre and had been against any proscenium theatre, on the grounds that the latter was 'an historical hiccup from 1700 to the present day'. But Hall, like Brook, had been adamant that a studio was a necessity. In the summer of 1972, he was appointed director designate of the National to succeed Olivier, in complex circumstances which do not concern us here. In February 1973, he revised his first notes on his task of making the new building work. The paper was entitled *Policy thoughts for the new South Bank* and in it Hall set out his idea of a 'Theatre Centre for the Nation not a Cultural Fortress for the National Theatre Company alone'.

According to this paper, the Olivier was to be the centre of the company's work – a company of actors engaged for three years. The Lyttelton, as it was now designed, would be 'a first class theatre with facilities better than any other proscenium theatre in Britain', which would welcome visiting companies as well as productions staged by the National itself. Those National productions first staged in the Lyttelton if successful would then transfer to the Olivier.

He then turned to the Studio, which had not yet been christened the Cottesloe, although the other two had by then received their names. The Studio was to be 'a laboratory for advanced work and this work should be done by the leaders of the profession'. The main happening of the National's year would be the 'National Theatre Festival', eight weeks from mid-July to mid-September each year. Hall listed what would happen in each space and against the Studio he wrote: 'New Groups, Experimental Groups from all over the world in the Studio. We would also show any important new research work done by the National Theatre Company itself.'

However, in February 1973 when he wrote this, there was no Studio, simply the huge empty bricked-up hole under the rear stage at the Oliver with, at one end, a free-standing column supporting a corner of the fly tower above.

During the summer of 1973 John Bury, head of design for the National, who was to become the benevolent and clear-minded midwife for the birth of the Cottesloe, started the search for ideas. One of the persons he talked to was Richard Pilbrow, with whom he had collaborated on the Barbican Theatre, designed a couple of years before the Olivier concept was finalised. Pilbrow in turn was delighted that Hall had the authority to reinstate the studio, in the preliminary design of which he had been involved six years earlier. In November 1973 his first action was to have a card model built of the hole.

While I was writing the present article Pilbrow showed me for the first time a paper he wrote in collaboration with Richard Brett and David Collison dated 25 October 1967, referring to the design of the proposed National Theatre and entitled *Preliminary Report on Proposed Stage Equipment Lighting and Sound Installations.* The section on the studio was more than that, being in effect a design guide for an interior which bears a strong similarity to the interior Pilbrow designed the following year for the Sheffield Crucible's studio. The latter opened in 1971 but was subsequently remodelled in the late 80s.

Pilbrow envisaged four levels for the National's studio: a stage level with basement below; an audience entrance level at +7ft; a technical gallery at +15ft and a grid at +29ft. The gallery 7ft above the stage level (there was to be no stage riser) was to run on three sides of a 60ft square space. Audience members would not sit on this gallery which was, presumably, to be no more than an aisle width, except at the audience entrance end, where there would be 'a small block of raised permanent seating'. The remainder of the seating was to be on eight retractable units, each holding about 30 people. 'Six of them [the units] should be able to be stored under the audience gallery at the entrance end'. Capacity would seem to be 300 in the round, assuming 60 on the fixed block of raised seating, and 240 for thrust. As in all such square concepts, an end-stage arrangement would have had the smallest capacity, 120, end stage being thought of as the least likely arrangement in a studio. (In fact, more than half the performances in the Cottesloe have been end stage.)

The Pilbrow paper of October 1967 coincided roughly with the decision to move the site, followed soon after by the decision to defer the studio. There had thus been little opportunity for detailed design collaboration between architect Lasdun and theatre consultant Pilbrow. Why what was eventually built differed so much from these initial plans is uncertain. Possibly site considerations determined that stage level, at the level of the National's internal scenic street (linking the Lyttelton stage to the workshops, rehearsal rooms and the foot of the Olivier drum), was not 7ft below foyer-entrance level but only 4ft lower. And the two levels of the Cottesloe foyer as built were 11ft apart rather than the 9ft Pilbrow's plans assumed. Hence, what had been envisaged in 1967 could not be developed in 1973, because the levels had worked out differently. A new approach was required.

This is where I enter the story. As I recall, in early November a meeting was to be held at short notice with John Bury at the Theatre Projects office, in response to Peter Hall's success in persuading the Board that the studio theatre should be finished 'to rehearsal room standards'. (Hall later told Peter Lewis 'If there's one thing I want on my tombstone, it is that I saved the Cottesloe' – *The National: A Dream Made Concrete* published by Methuen in 1990.)

Pilbrow was busy designing the lighting for *Gomes*, a grand guignol with sets by Michael Knight, which opened on 20 November at the Queen's Theatre in Shaftesbury Avenue. I was the new boy at Theatre Projects, having thrown in my job as administrative director of the Prospect Theatre Company, of which I had been co-founder. I had felt that the increased support from the Arts Council's embryo touring department, run by Jack Phipps, made the most challenging part of my job at Prospect superfluous, since now 'they' were to decide what the company presented where. Having deeply enjoyed my short experience in 1972 and 1973 as theatre design consultant to architect Graham Law and consultant John Wyckham at the Eden Court Theatre in Inverness (not to open until 1976), I decided to try my hand as a theatre consultant. Pilbrow liked the Inverness concept when Law, Wyckham and I presented the plans to the ABTT (Association of British Theatre Technicians) Theatre Planning Committee earlier that year. He issued an invitation. I accepted.

I had been a full-time theatre consultant for all of six weeks when I saw Pilbrow's model of the empty hole and, without either being shown the 1967 paper or having any opportunity to visit the space, I asked Pilbrow if I could put together some ideas. Pilbrow said he had intended asking me, later pointing out that it was for just such an opportunity that he had offered me a job. The ideas were put together over one weekend in the form of sketches made with a thick black pen, and these were then carried over to the stalls at the Queen's Theatre, where Pilbrow was working, probably during the second weekend in November. It is these rough drawings which are printed before this article.

The Cottesloe foyer, with its concrete stair (which was removed in 1997) and those two levels 3.4m (11ft 1 inch) apart, was already there when I began my design work. Space had been left each side of a large opening for cloakrooms and lavatories. There was then a brick wall behind which was the empty space. To reach the space behind the brick wall one had to travel a circuitous route through the bowels of the building. Inside the space, standing with one's back to the bare brick wall, one looked at a huge aircraft hanger 40ft high, 56ft 6 inches wide and 66ft long. At the far end, behind the free-standing column supporting the Olivier fly tower, was the scene door leading directly to the internal scenic street. As has already been mentioned the height of the scenic door matched neither of the foyer levels. At the same end, on the corner opposite the scenic entrance, was a pair of exits, in the wall one above the other. These were at yet different levels, connected at the lower level to the scenic entrance via a fire-protected passage behind the back wall. This was the only point at which emergency exits were possible.

Such was the empty space which was to contain a flexible studio, on which so much seemed to depend. Nobody who then formed part of the National had seen or were to see any of the architect's designs for what was to go into the space. Thus it was, in so far as what happened next, 'found space', rather than a pre-determined coherent design. And then there was Peter Hall's instruction that, rather than 250, which was the capacity Lasdun had been told to provide for just before the Studio was cancelled, the new Studio on the same site was, if possible, to revert to the original idea of holding 400.

Six weeks later, in January 1974, in a paper accompanying an early model, I described this empty space:

1. If the space for the National Theatre's third auditorium is an 'empty room' then it is a very, very big room. In plan the main area, apart that is from audience access and foyers, is 66 ft long by 56 ft 6 inches wide – bigger than the audience and acting area of Garrick's Drury Lane, wider than the Duchess Theatre and almost as deep. The 'room' is 41 ft high, which is reduced to 25 ft if one excludes a 9 ft deep basement under three quarters of the area and a 6 ft space above any ventilation and lighting grid hung between the roof trusses. It is certainly bigger than any studio theatre in Britain.

2. The usual contemporary solution to equipping a studio theatre is to lay a flat floor and to provide on this floor large seating units that can telescope and that can trundle around to form 'in the round', 'end stage' and 'thrust' situations. Except in the smallest studios such units tend to be unwieldy and do not use the space efficiently, there being only one level of people for each part of the floor area. While the front row is close to the actor, the seats stretch away at a constant 30° and the whole space which the actor is to fill remains constant. The walls are empty.

3. The design study that is offered for further development is rather different. The approach has been pragmatic – the problem posed includes the fact that the audience enters at a level 8 to 9 feet above the natural level of the main floor at one end of the building, and must be provided with exits at similar levels at the other end, where actors and any scenery must also arrive.

4. The width of the rectangle has allowed the introduction, inside the envelope, of stairs which link three audience levels that fit neatly within a 25 ft height. This width is greater than, say, the tennis courts which Davenant and Killigrew were able to transform into theatres – and, if a metaphor be allowed, to play within this contemporary Cottesloe 'cockpit' should be like playing squash in a court with faces lining three walls, or, if one chooses, all four.

Toward the end of the same paper I described what such a space could do for the National:

> Courtyard, Cockpit (a bit big for cock fighting, better for a boxing ring) or whatever – [the new theatre] should be particularly useful for experiment in non-scenic theatre: the movement of the outdoor Fortune or indoor Blackfriars, according to either Hotson or to Hodges, [or for] the more formal expression of Grotowski or anyone else who has explored the notion of a ritual gathering of onlookers. The form and scale is also Restoration/early Georgian, when spectacle was as yet subservient to the spoken word. The finish should be simple and workmanlike – it is designed to be unfinished in the sense that actor, director and designer must 'fill' the whole space, and the audience complete the furnishings as wallpaper does a room.

The idea born in November 1973 was very simple. Rather than put the stage at the level of the scenic road and design around this level (1.36m higher than where the stage is now), I decided to work off the foyer level, and make that the middle level of a three-level courtyard.

The lower level of the theatre, which would also be stage level, would be 8 to 9 ft. lower than the foyer entrance, and the upper level would be 8 to 8ft 6in higher. The former coincided roughly with the stage-to-entrance level envisaged by Pilbrow in 1967. The upper level did not chime with the already-built higher level of the foyer, hence the little flight of stairs in the completed building which brings you down a metre from upper-foyer level to the top level of the Cottesloe auditorium.

My idea for a courtyard packed with people on three levels was the product of five influences:

- a love of 18th century playhouses: I had led Prospect to reopen the 1788 Georgian Theatre in Richmond, Yorkshire, in July 1963. This was a rectilinear theatre on three levels – pit, boxes, gallery – which held 230, and was as intimate as any theatre-in-the-round but yet demanded 'big' acting. (On taking our fourth show there in 1965, I met my wife, actress Jan Carey, on its stage. She had been cast in Etherege's *A Man of Mode* by Prospect director Toby Robertson.)

- another love had been the Assembly Hall, Edinburgh, where for the 1969 Edinburgh Festival Prospect had launched the double bill of Marlowe's *Edward II* and Shakespeare's *Richard II*, and also the career of Ian McKellen, who played both kings. This was the Assembly Hall which Tyrone Guthrie had transformed into his first thrust-stage theatre for *Ane Satyre of the Thrie Estaites* in 1948, and which was also the inspiration of Bill Howell's Young Vic, created in 1970 in collaboration with Frank Dunlop, who was then administrative director of the National and had been founder-director of Pop Theatre (of Festival fame) at the Assembly Hall prior to Prospect.

- a promenade production of *Orlando Furioso*, a version of Ariosto's Renaissance epic thrillingly brought to the Murrayfield Ice Rink from the Piazza in front of the Duomo at Milan by its director Luca Ronconi in September 1970. (It was therefore no surprise when in 1977 someone called me to say, 'you'll never guess what they've done to your theatre [the Cottesloe], they have removed all the seats'. This was for the Cottesloe's first promenade, *The Passion*.)

- an uncertainty in my own mind whether the two large theatres at the National, the concrete steppings of which I had already seen, were going to be beyond human scale: a roofed-in Epidaurus, and a super cinema with perfect sightlines. Both were so very different from everything I had learnt about the British theatre from touring the older theatres of Britain with Prospect over the preceding dozen years. (I had never quite understood why Gordon Craig was held in such esteem, with those huge screens and the actors reduced to pigmies.) This was not an opinion to be voiced in 1973, and it would have been ungracious to do so, because Pilbrow, with his own commitments to the National design, offered me 100% support for the courtyard concept, especially under questioning from Lasdun. But now I can confess that my own uncertainty over the half-built Olivier and Lyttelton theatres was a spur to do something rather different at the Cottesloe.

- The fifth influence was a stirring talk by Michael Elliott on the Third Programme of the BBC entitled *On not building for Posterity*. (This was reprinted first in *TABS* Vol 32 No 2 of June 1973, and subsequently in *Making Space for Theatre*, edited by Ronnie Mulryne and Margaret Shewring and published for the British Council exhibition which opened at the National in June 1995.) As Elliott put it, 'as one leans on the parapet of Waterloo Bridge pondering the huge mushrooming concrete of the new National Theatre, all one's doubts centre round one question – was this the right theatre to build *now*?' Elliott confessed his membership of the Building Committee of the National Theatre, which 'reminds one organisationally more of a battleship than a theatre'. Reviewing the theatres of Britain he contrasted 'the large, expensive, grand square and boring on the one hand, and the intimate, cheap, informal, exciting left wing on the other'. Without coming to any conclusion, other than explaining his own personal passion for what was to become the Royal Exchange, Manchester, in 1976, he suggested that rather than monuments for posterity Britain needed 'to imagine to what kind of place we would all most be drawn for an evening – what kind of building and atmosphere has the most life, warmth and immediacy.' Elliott cited the fringe, the Young Vic and the Roundhouse, as it then was, and suggested we needed 'more buildings that are "almost" theatres' rather than theatres that are 'huge, inflexible, hard to demolish'. My personal reaction to this call-to-arms was to wonder whether we could plant just such a subversive space inside the grand monolith of the National, which of course had to have big spaces but might also contain a small one for 'human beings (to) communicate with each other', with an emphasis different from 'the unparalleled technical sophistication and vastly improved amenities' which Elliott, as a member of the Building Committee, knew were going to be provided upstairs.

Once John Bury was convinced that the simple courtyard I had conceived was the right direction to be going, a meeting was set up between Peter Hall and myself. Nervously, I did the chat and showed the model, stressing the Georgian antecedents. After half an hour, Hall said 'Fine, let us go ahead', and returned to rehearsal. Later, John told me that Hall had said he liked the design very much, and blessed the project, provided he, John, did not let that fellow Mackintosh into his office again to lecture him about the eighteenth century. And so it was that John pushed the project through. We never met with Hall again on the design of the Cottesloe. *Carte blanche* for a black box.

Over the next eighteen months, the design evolved in a series of special meetings involving Peter Softley for the architects, John Bury and Simon Relph (Technical Director) for the National, and myself and colleagues from Theatre Projects Consultants as required for their special skills.

At one such meeting, with the drawings already issued to the contractor, I blithely announced I had just visited the studio theatre at Sheffield Crucible, and as a result reckoned 9ft too great as the difference between stage level and entrance level, and 8ft 6ins too much for the difference between mid entrance-level and the higher level. (The 6ins difference between the two was compensated by the six-inch-thick rostra on which the removable side-seats sat, on the lower encircling tier at stage level.) I would, I said, like everything six inches tighter, and could it be changed please?

Peter Softley, to his eternal credit, smiled and said he would let the contractor know next week. Richard Pilbrow did not fire me, as I might today a junior who had 'a good idea' like this a year too late when the job was already under construction. The claims would be just too horrendous to contemplate.

Before such niceties, we had had to prepare two schemes: one with the galleries as built and one without, but with 'future provision' for galleries. The sums involved were piddling – the galleries cost £180,000 I believe – but there was no money, and every penny had been committed for the expensive two theatres upstairs and next door. By September, 1974, there were still not to be any walkways in the roof, only a tubular steel grid. The light and sound controls were to be on wandering leads, able to go anywhere on the top level; only later did the technical department, responsible for lighting and sound, bag the prime Louis XIV position, dead centre on the middle level.

At an early point, Denys Lasdun asked to see the model. In a moment, I discovered I was alone, others having remembered pressing appointments. It was a large 1:25 model. Lasdun peered. Silence. 'What are these?', he asked, pointing at the columns which, in the model, continued (as they do not now) through the ceiling of the mid level into the top level, to meet the existing ceiling. 'Well, er, they are part of the, er, web which enfolds audience and actor in the same space which is um er a statement ...'. 'I don't understand metaphysics. Columns hold up roofs. I have already built the roof. Take them out'. There were no other comments. The interview was at an end.

Three years later, I thought of the answer: 'Oh the columns? They are a part of the access system to the lighting walkways'. (These had already been designed, if not agreed, and in the absence of such a 'system' are now reached by hook-on ladders.) I feel that Lasdun, who always tempered his design sense with doses of functionalism, would have accepted that. A pity, because the top level, built without these columns, is windy.

As I write this, I realise that Lasdun did not pounce on what he might have regarded as another functionless conceit. Upstage right, there already was the free-standing column to the Olivier. This in my design became a protuberance from the audience-left escape passage through a new sound lock for the scenic entrance. I added more concrete, and a slot to provide a useful lighting position and improve the proportions. Upstage left, I sketched an exact duplication of the Olivier supporting column and added slot. This was duly cast in concrete. It 'does' nothing, except make the room look symmetrical. And later still, the National inserted some fibreglass brickwork in the back wall to make that look symmetrical too. Such are the lengths we theatre folk will go to, to prevent architectural asymmetry intruding upon the province of the director and designer.

Through 1974/75 the galleries were confirmed, and the egg-box design of walkways, snug against the ceiling, using a small square hole existing in the concrete truss for front-to-back access. John Bury got his raking stage, or rather the front portion of the end stage, which still rakes if required. (This is not often the case, due to the later modification to the principal end-stage arrangement.) I did not get my travelling fourth wall, described in *The Stage* article of 1977, re-printed here. But this did come about later in scenic guise, first in *The Beggar's Opera* in 1982. None of us got the elevator system we wanted in the centre of the floor: a mosaic of elevators each 65 inches square which would make permutations in form easier in repertoire.

One might ask why 65 inches was chosen as the design unit. At Pilbrow's insistence, it had been decided that the working areas of this theatre, like the Olivier and Lyttelton, were to be designed in metres, although measured in feet. 65 inches equals 1.65 metres. Multiply by 6 and you get 9.9m, the width between the galleries of the Cottesloe. Moreover, 9.9m equals 32 ft 6 ins, which is the standard proscenium width of a West End or No 1 touring date (e.g. Leeds, Glasgow) up to the 1920s, when the bigger Empires were built. And 9.9m divides easily. The distance between the columns at the side and end of the Cottesloe is 3.3m (10 ft 10 ins), which feels right. Most important, a 1.65m (65 ins) square is just right for 3 seats measured in width at 550mm centres, or two rows measured in depth at 825mm (32½ ins) back to back. Reduce or increase the 1.65m and it does not work. Hence a module based on 1.65m would prove flexible in design and construction.

All this was complex to calculate, but eminently sensible. It was complicated by the British construction industry's bad idea of practising 'going metric' by inventing 'the metric foot'. The 24ft 6ins level on the National plans was known as 24.50. There were ten units to the metric foot. This arcane practice adds another dark glass through which to look back on the past.

Usually, the design of a theatre is driven by capacity as much as anything else. The end-stage arrangement of the Cottesloe, as built, held 311 seated, 171 in the stalls and three levels of a single front row at each level, holding respectively 42, 46 and 52. 311 seated, plus 75 standing, and places for two wheelchairs, gives a total of 388, near to the 400 target for which Peter Hall had asked.

From the outset it was envisaged that either by the use of lifts (never installed), or by using scaffolding, the stalls/pit seating, instead of rising in increments of 100mm from a front row 1.1m below stage level, to stage level at the back of the stalls, could alternatively rise in increments of 315mm to the mid (main entrance) level.

In 1986, a mechanical device to achieve just such a steeper rake was installed. This arrangement reduced the end-stage seating capacity to 284 (plus 41 standing). In the late '80s, some of the resulting loss was recovered by adding a second row to the centre tier at the top level, which took the seating capacity for end stage up to 302 with 34 standing and two wheelchair positions. This gave 338, 50 less than the original design. It is possible to ask why the National went for a reduced capacity as the norm.

There were two reasons. The National at that stage in its development was artistically driven, rather than managerially driven. Directors preferred the Cottesloe in this seating configuration, so it happened. The loss of capacity was no problem. And of course it is the steepness of the rake of these central seats which makes John Bury's option of a raking end-stage superfluous, since a stage rake would only be required if the stalls rake is shallow.

The second reason was that after the success of Bill Bryden's promenade productions (the *Mysteries* from 1978 to 1985 and *Lark Rise* in 1979), licensed for 400 at first, 450 later, the priority seemed to be to get from end stage to flat floor as rapidly as possible when in repertoire. In this context, the investment in a retractable seating unit above stage level, and a system of covering up four stepped rows at the front, seemed worthwhile.

Since then priorities have shifted. The long traverse is now in the ascendant, having been first introduced by directors Bill Bryden and Sebastian Graham-Jones and designer William Dudley for *The World Turned Upside Down* in 1978, and again most thrillingly in the Declan Donnellan/Nick Ormerod *Fuente Ovejuna* in 1989. The refinement of raising the traverse stage above datum level (normal stage level) came in *Racing Demon* in 1990, and this was again used in 1997 for *King Lear*.

The raising of the stage level above the front few rows in any format restores the dominance of the actor, which in a small room can be electrifying. It is no coincidence that comedians prefer to have half their audience below eye level, because then the performer controls the audience. Put most of the audience above, and they are in charge. The actor is pinned out on the table like a butterfly under chloroform. Many directors, who direct at the dress rehearsal overlooking the actor from the back of steeply raked stalls, like to be just that, in control.

At the Cottesloe, there have been times when the front four rows have been covered over in the end-stage format, leaving the front row of audience at the same level as the actor on stage, under the belief that this places the actor in closer communion with the audience (as it does in small fringe theatres). This does work at the Cottesloe, but only for the front three rows. When Ian McKellen moved downstage in Sheila Hancock's production of *The Cherry Orchard* (1985) to sit in a window seat placed at the knees of the front row, the middle and back of the steeply-raked central tier could not see him, and felt left out. Communion with the front two or three rows had been bought with alienation of the larger middle and rear section. This is the same phenomenon as happens in the middle of a rake of seats in a theatre without a stage riser, and led Per Edstrom, the Swedish architect/designer, to write of such theatres: 'the whole stage is too low in relationship to the audience. The majority of the audience is forced to look down from above and if a naked ballet came on the stage most of the audience would only be able to see that the dancers had hair on their heads' (*Why not Theatres made for People?* Varndo, 1990).

The retractable seating unit is there to make repertoire changes easier. But whether or not the Cottesloe is worked in intense repertoire is determined by many factors other than the physical ease or difficulty in making changes from one format to another format two, three or four times a week. There was a time when each of the National's three theatres had their own company working in repertoire, and another when three companies worked in repertoire across the three theatres. There have been 'runs' and occasions when actors have been contracted for single plays. At the time of writing, repertoire requires markedly less frequent change-overs than previously, although the change-overs are individually heavier as directors and designers compete to create ever more ambitious environmental effects.

These considerations make the point that designers of theatre space should never shape their ideas entirely to the client's brief. The brief, meaning the way that the building is to be used, can change, often during construction. The designer must play his hunch, having first won the confidence of the client. And, if at all possible, he should not spend the available money on technical solutions to the problems as they are presently posed.

This is not just because the people posing the problem change. It is because if the technical machinery is programmed to provide too specific a series of layouts (end stage, in the round, thrust, traverse) then that is exactly what you get. The engineer asks what you want in shape or form and produces machines to achieve it. You get variations A, B, C and D. But the very existence of the machinery makes it impossible to achieve variation E & F, and, more importantly, variations X & Y, which nobody had thought of before the space had been created. Hence at the Cottesloe the most flexible sort of centre for a fixed courtyard: an empty hole without any machinery. Even my simple unobtrusive modules of 65-inch square sections, which were intended to rise and fall mechanically, could be considered too prescriptive. Think of Peter Stein's Schaubühne in Berlin, a high-tech conversion of a 1927 cinema into a theatre holding no more than 600, with no workshops, no rehearsal rooms and little or no foyer space. This single space cost DM 82 million in 1981, more than the entire National had cost in 1976, with its three theatres, rehearsal rooms, workshops and much larger foyers than in Berlin. The Schaubühne had gizmos galore including seventy-eight 7m x 3m hydraulic lifts. Stein was quickly bored, resigned in 1990, and although he is back there working again he often builds the theatre spaces he needs with scaffolding, inside the theatre as built. Perhaps it is a good thing we couldn't afford our little 5ft square elevators at the Cottesloe.

What is there has withstood the test of time. It is still black. Those of us who remember what it was like in 1976, when the steel columns and tier fronts were in their red undercoat against black walls are fewer in number as the years go by. (It was more like Bill Howell's scarlet-stained theatre at Christ's Hospital, which opened in 1975 and was the inspiration for The Swan in 1986.) There has been neither a need to change the fabric of the space, nor any call for change, as there has been for the Olivier and Lyttelton. It remains what it was intended to be: a simple and unpretentious framework for freedom.

Fig 16 Charles Wood's *Has Washington Legs?* opened in the Cottesloe on 29 November 1978. The production was directed by Geoffrey Reeves, with settings by William Dudley and costumes by Pamela Howard.
Photo: *Michael Mayhew*

THE COTTESLOE YEARS

Michael Billington

TRY to imagine the National Theatre without the Cottesloe. What would it be like? Grand, populous and, probably, successful. But it would lack a vital third dimension. The Olivier and the Lyttelton between them would cover a lot of ground: classics, musicals, large-scale new plays. Without the Cottesloe, however, something crucial would be missing: a flexible space that could accommodate everything from *The Mysteries* to Beckett, Shakespeare to Ken Campbell, Lepage spectacles to the intricacy of Pinter. If the Olivier – as directors constantly tell us – is the National's prime showcase and the measure of its popular success (three flops in a row and the journalistic doom-mongers, as well as the accountants, start to gather), then the Cottesloe is its creative engine-room: what Shakespeare calls 'the quick forge and working-house of thought.' Indeed, after 21 years, it is impossible to imagine the National without it: when Peter Hall was forced to close the Cottesloe in 1985 for five months, because of a funding crisis, it was as if a vital limb had been lopped.

But why does the Cottesloe work so well? And what has it contributed both to the National and the theatre at large? I suspect there are several interlocking answers.

For a start one has to go back to a decision taken on 1 November 1973: the first day of Peter Hall's official tenure as the National's director. In his *Diaries* he records a crucial meeting with his associates: 'There was a good deal of talk about the tendency of the theatre today to move away from from the cathedrals of art to small rooms. The concept of the Studio in the new building actually functioning as a studio was totally demolished. It is now to be thought of as our third theatre – the Cottesloe theatre: a small space.' Which is one of the best decisions Hall and his team ever took. Experiment is vital for any artistic institution. But it is something that, of necessity, requires a degree of privacy: exactly what the National Theatre Studio (housed in the Old Vic annexe) is for. The Cottesloe meanwhile is a public space with a seating capacity of 400: exactly the same as the Royal Court. The decision to treat it as the National's third auditorium was right at the time and has been vindicated by history: you can certainly take risks in the Cottesloe impossible on larger stages but it would have been a wasteful disaster if it had been used purely as a private laboratory.

The second shrewd decision was an architectural one: to combine classical principles with contemporary intimacy. The Cottesloe clearly has echoes of the Elizabethan courtyard and the rectangular Georgian auditorium of the Richmond Theatre, Yorkshire. But it is wholly modern in its emphasis on the spectators' closeness to the action. To me, this is more important than its famous flexibility: its ability to be promenade space, traverse stage or even theatre-in-the-round. In fact, the bulk of directors and designers over the past 21 years have used it as a straight-edged stage. But the supreme virtue of the Cottesloe is that it locks you into the action in a way the Victorian-age Royal Court doesn't: you can see Ian Holm's lower lip trembling in panic as King Lear, or the mixture of envy and lust in the features of Simon Russell Beale's Iago as he gazes at David Harewood's Othello. The Cottesloe accommodates the revolution in theatre going taste that has occurred in the television age: we want to be able to see not just actors' eyes but every twitch of their facial muscles. We don't go any more to watch a play: we want to be intimate eavesdroppers. And part of the luck of the Cottesloe is that it opened in the late 1970s: it was therefore able to benefit from the radical shift in taste that occurred with the publication of Peter Brook's *The Empty Space* in 1968 and with the explosion of small spaces that, in London, included the Soho Poly, the King's Head, the Theatre Upstairs, the Orange Tree and the Bush. The Cottesloe was not like any of them in shape. But it was part of the same ethos: the move away from theatre as cathedral towards dissenting chapel.

But the Cottesloe also had another huge stroke of luck in that it found, from its inception, a director keen to explore its peculiar dynamic and to make it the base for a quasi-permanent company: Bill Bryden. It might so easily not have happened. Peter Hall records in his *Autobiography* how, after the failure of *Il Campiello* in the Olivier in 1976 (a not very dainty dish set before a visibly displeased Queen) he was under pressure from the Board to fire Bryden. Thank God he didn't. Because it was Bryden who went on to show – with the help of his associate Sebastian Graham-Jones – that the Cottesloe was not an experimental cornershop tacked on to a theatrical supermarket but a unique space with enormous popular potential. And he did it through *The Mysteries,* which started its existence with Tony Harrison's version of *The Passion* staged on the NT terraces at Easter 1977 and which ended, nearly a decade later, restoring Irving's Lyceum to theatrical life.

FIG 17 Arthur Kopit's *Wings*, first performed on American National Public Radio, opened at the Cottesloe on 15 August 1979, after a production at the Yale Repertory Theatre in February 1978, and subsequently in 1979 at the Wilbur Theatre, Boston, the Kennedy Center in Washington, D.C., and the Lyceum Theatre in New York. All three stage productions, and the radio production, were directed by John Madden. The photograph, taken for the Washington opening, shows Constance Cummings as Emily Stilson, the part she played in the stage productions, which were all designed by Andrew Jackness, with costumes by Jeanne Button.
PHOTO: *Jeffrey Richards*

The Mysteries helped to define what the Cottesloe could do: not least that it could be an open promenade space in which we, as members of the audience, chose our own angle of vision. It also led to the creation of a strong company of actors, admittedly very male-dominated, that fed into other work: Brian Glover (who sadly died in 1997), Jack Shepherd, Gawn Grainger, Tony Haygarth, Trevor Ray, Derek Newark and James Grant were pillars of the Bryden team with Brenda Blethyn, Morag Hood and the late Susan Fleetwood as co-opted members. But the strangest aspect of *The Mysteries* was the least discussed: that, in an agnostic age audiences were moved to tears by a dramatisation of the Bible story that took us from the Creation – with Brian Glover as a West Riding God on a fork-lift truck – to Doomsday and the Harrowing of Hell. Did we willingly suspend our disbelief and become Christians on an away-day ticket? Or did *The Mysteries* tap into some residual faith that many of us had grown up with and had casually let slide? My instinct is that it was the latter. What happened in the Cottesloe transcended aesthetics: it became, with the help of the Albion Band, an act of celebration and atonement.

There were, of course, many other famous productions in the Bryden period: *Lark Rise* (a piece of genuine English pastoral), several pieces about the film business including Charles Wood's *Has Washington Legs?* and Bryden's own play *Old Movies,* plus numerous excursions into American life and drama including Miller's *The Crucible,* O'Neill's *The Long Voyage Home* (a truly great production) and *The Iceman Cometh,* Mamet's *American Buffalo,* Arthur Kopit's *Wings* and an adaptation of Michel Herr's study of the Vietnam war, *Dispatches,* which long before *Miss Saigon* showed how you could bring a helicopter on stage. I once asked Bryden about his dual fascination with Americana and cinema and he attributed it to growing up in working-class Greenock in the 1950s when America seemed a distant Utopia and cinema was the ultimate escape route.

But it's a measure of his success in creating a genuine house-style in the early years of the Cottesloe that I stumbled, amongst my cuttings, on a lumbering parody I wrote in 1979 at the time of *Lark Rise.* I suggested that Bryden and Keith Dewhurst were at work on a celebration of communal life in and around Waterloo Station to be dubbed *From Waterloo to Hounslow.* 'To foot-twitching music from the Albion Band,' I surmised, 'it will contain time-honoured dances like The Lurch of the Meths Drinkers and such festive commuter rites as Rushing the Barrier, Misdirecting the Foreigner and Cheating the Inspector. A semi-religious interlude will also reveal the wrath that occurs when trains are suddenly cancelled by strike action. That will be called Station of the Cross.' Not very funny, I admit. But it proved that the Cottesloe – unlike the Olivier or Lyttelton – had a style one could lampoon. More significantly, perhaps, I went on to suggest that, having created its own company, the

Cottesloe should now explore some of the byways of the classic repertory including plays by Jonson, Otway and Massinger.

In fact, the Cottesloe's policy did change in the 1980s in line with Peter Hall's modification of his plans for the National. Instead of having single directors for each theatre, he moved towards the idea of creating companies who would switch between the Olivier, the Lyttelton and the Cottesloe. Inevitably this broadened the Cottesloe's base and led to greater diversity. In the period from 1980-87 one finds standard classics (*A Midsummer Night's Dream* vigorously directed by Bryden with Scofield and Fleetwood, *Antigone, The Beggar's Opera*), rare revivals (*The Mayor of Zalamea, The Prince of Homburg, The Fawn*) and a wide variety of new plays (Pinter's *Other Places,* Peter Gill's *Kick for Touch* and *Small Change,* Fugard's *Master Harold and the Boys,* Hare's *The Bay at Nice* and *Wrecked Eggs).* The Cottesloe may have forfeited a distinctive housestyle. Increasingly, however, it seemed to become, by virtue of its rapid turnover and its emphasis on discovery, the motor that was driving the National Theatre: the quick forge where the really innovative and exciting work was being done.

1985 was, in every sense, the watershed year. As the National hit financial crisis, the Cottesloe went dark. It re-opened in September with a special grant of £375,000 from the GLC: one of the local authority's last acts of munificence before being vindictively abolished by Mrs Thatcher. Characteristically, the theatre kicked off with a season of new plays which included one genuine discovery: Debbie Horsfield with a pair of plays (*True Dare Kiss* and *Command or Promise*) about four female Manchester United supporters and their divergent lives. At the time I dubbed Ms Horsfield 'the funniest woman dramatist to have emerged since Shelagh Delaney': an all-too-accurate parallel since she hardly ever wrote for the theatre again but went on to a thriving career in television. But if the Cottesloe emerged from the crisis of closure as the National's chief source of new writing, it also became a place where familiar classics were subjected to fresh scrutiny: a case in point was Mike Alfreds' production of *The Cherry Orchard* for the McKellen-Petherbridge Company which is still one of the best British versions I've seen. Alfreds used the intimacy of the Cottesloe to highlight the characters' tactile quality: they constantly laughed, cried, kissed, hugged and embraced each other in a vain attempt to break out of their implacable solitude. Alfreds' production also serves as a reminder that the Cottesloe both was, and is, a place of overwhelming individual performances: one thinks of Judi Dench in *Other Places,* Juliet Stevenson in *Yerma,* Michael Gambon in A *View From The Bridge,* Antony Sher in *Stanley.* In the case of *The Cherry Orchard,* it was Ian McKellen's Lopakhin. He partook of the family warmth yet remained an inviolate outsider: I still recall him, after the purchase of the estate, whirling the house-keys above his head as if going to put someone's eye out yet rushing over to clutch and comfort Sheila Hancock's weeping Ranyevskaya. Amidst a group of tribal egoists, McKellen's Lopakhin was the loneliest character of the lot: brimming over with peasant gregariousness yet unable to make genuine emotional contact.

FIG 18 David Edgar's *Entertaining Strangers,* first performed as a community play in 1985, opened at the Cottesloe in a promenade production on 15 October 1987. The production was directed by Peter Hall and designed by William Dudley, with music by Dominic Muldowney and the Mellstock Band under David Townsend. Tim Pigott-Smith as Henry Moule. PHOTO: *John Haynes*

FIG 19 Henrik Ibsen's *Rosmersholm* opened at the Cottesloe in a new version by Frank McGuinness on 6 May 1987, directed by Sarah Pia Anderson, designed by Roger Glossop and with music by Mike Figgis. Suzanne Bertish as Rebekka West, David Ryall as Kroll and Roger Lloyd Pack as John Rosmer.
PHOTO: *John Haynes*

Individual performances and ensemble achievements are part of the Cottesloe aesthetic. Or, to put it another way, the space is very good at conveying both claustrophobia and communality. Chekhov works beautifully in a small theatre. So too does Ibsen. A fact noticed by the RSC as well as the National. Alongside Adrian Noble's *A Doll's House* and Katie Mitchell's *Ghosts* in The Other Place and The Pit, I would place Sarah Pia Anderson's 1987 production of *Rosmersholm* at the Cottesloe. It is always a difficult play: so much of the action is retrospective and one is never sure how much Rebekka West, in inspiring Rosmer's radical conversion and his wife's suicide, is – as Freud suggested – repeating the pattern of her incestuous relationship with her mother's lover. On a big proscenium stage Ibsen's play can seem a suffocating bore. In the Cottesloe it made perfect sense largely because Roger Glossop's design, a raked platform framed by 28 ancestral portraits, took us inside the penitential gloom of John Rosmer's Norwegian house. Gazing at this ferociously bewhiskered assembly of ancient generals, priests and public servants one felt at any moment as if they might step down from the canvases like the ghosts in *Ruddigore.* The power of the past over the present was made tangible. So too was the influence of Suzanne Bertish's Rebekka over Roger Lloyd Pack's Rosmer. At one point she silently mouthed to him the need to offer hospitality to his old teacher, Ulrik Brendel: at another she stood behind his chair as if seeking to dominate him through sheer willpower. In the intimacy of the Cottesloe we were locked into Ibsen's world.

Oddly enough the spirit of Ibsen also hovered over David Edgar's *Entertaining Strangers:* a work that started as a community play in St Mary's Church, Dorchester with a local cast of 180 and that was turned into a Peter Hall promenade production at the Cottesloe with a much smaller professional cast. It was Ibsenite in the sense that Tim Pigott-Smith's Reverend Henry Moule descended on the parish of Fordington in Dorset with a Brand-like severity and harshness: there was even something of Ibsen in his clash with Judi Dench's Sarah Eldridge, a pub-keeper and founder of a famous Dorchester brewery. But Hall's production also showed that the Cottesloe could be used for a very different kind of promenade show to the earlier Bryden achievements. In the Bryden shows you chose your own angle of vision. While using the same designer, William Dudley, Hall focused the action more precisely. Moule and Sarah, for instance, occupied different ends of the Cottesloe. And Dudley used two mobile iron bridges which advanced upon the audience bearing at one moment the fairground sideshows of Dorchester races and at another a giant Stephenson steam engine. The Bryden shows were festal celebrations: Hall's production, determined by the different nature of the material, was an evocation of a Hardyesque world of rural squalor and lowering fate.

Like Bryden, however, Hall used the Cottesloe to explore the Englishness of England, and one little-noticed aspect of this theatre has been its ethnic flexibility. At times, it has seemed like a downtown New York venue taking us through the different varieties of American experience. At other times, it has seemed peculiarly Spanish, evoking the atmosphere of Golden Age rectangular *corrales.* At yet other times, it has seemed quintessentially South African: not only the base for visiting productions from the Market Theatre of Johannesburg but also for a stunning show from The Earth Players of that same city, Percy Mtwa's

Bopha!, dealing with the tragic dilemma of a poor, jobless black who joins the South African police force to make a living and in so doing becomes a traitor to his own people. A cynic might argue that the National salves its conscience by siphoning off minority shows into the Cottesloe. But it has never seemed that way to me. Largely because of the bold decision taken by Hall and his associates in 1973 the Cottesloe has never appeared to be the junior partner amongst the National's triple auditoria: if anything, as the most architecturally satisfying and human in scale of the three theatres, it is the one that every actor, director and designer most wants to work in. The point cannot be made too strongly: there is nothing third-class or threepence-off about the Cottesloe. Taking part recently in a Radio Three discussion about the marginalisation of women playwrights, I was informed by Charlotte Keatley that no living woman playwright had ever had her work done in the Olivier or the Lyttelton: only in the Cottesloe. In fact, Micheline Wandor was quickly on the phone to point out that her joint adaptation of *The Wandering Jew* had been presented in the Lyttelton. But I was struck by the irrelevance of the complaint: as I said at the time, to have one's work done in the Cottesloe is a mark of respect rather than an implied slur. Indeed one of the particular hallmarks of Richard Eyre's years at the National (from 1988 to 1997) has been the recognition that the Cottesloe is as much a natural space for new writing as the Royal Court: it relieves the dramatist of the pressure of filling the vast cubic capacity of the two bigger theatres while possessing a style and character of its own. I would have thought it was a writer's dream in so far as the space serves the text.

Eyre, in fact, gave the Cottesloe a high definition profile by encouraging three particular strands of work: visiting productions from directors of the calibre of Robert Lepage, Simon McBurney and Peter Brook; new writing from a wide variety of sources, and the National Theatre's own mobile, educational work. Lepage, in particular, was encouraged to treat the Cottesloe as his permanent London address: *Tectonic Plates*, and *Needles and Opium* played there and showed that anything is technically possible inside that rectangular black box. Eyre, I know, has a profound admiration for the Quebec spellbinder: I, personally, feel more ambivalent about his work. No-one working in theatre today makes more imaginative use of light, space and perspective: I sometimes hunger for more emotional and intellectual substance.

What is beyond dispute is that Lepage has worked miracles in the Cottesloe. Take *Needles and Opium* seen there in 1992. Set in a Left Bank Paris hotel in 1989, the show evoked the place's historical associations with Sartre, Cocteau, Juliette Greco and the world of the late 1940s existentialists. But one's chief memory is of the relationship between Lepage's own body and a backlit canvas screen. At one point, evoking Cocteau's intellectual acrobatics, the harnessed Lepage seemed to plunge

FIG 20 *Needles and Opium*, a solo piece written, designed and performed by Robert Lepage, was first seen in October 1991 at the Palais Montcalm in Quebec city, then in Ottawa and on tour in France and Germany before opening at the Cottesloe on 30 April 1992.
Production photographed by *Barbara Staubach* and *Silvia Frey*

FIG 21 *Closer*, written and directed by Patrick Marber, and with designs by Vicki Mortimer, opened at the Cottesloe on 29 May 1997.
Ciaran Hinds as Larry and Sally Dexter as Anna.
PHOTO: *Hugo Glendinning*

downwards as stencilled skyscraper blocks unrolled behind him at dizzying speed. Later he seemed to be sucked into a whirling vortex on the screen behind him, calling up memories of the Dali-esque dream sequence in Hitchcock's *Spellbound.* For the purposes of that show the Cottesloe was transformed into a dazzling technological dreamscape.

I was more impressed, however, in that same year by another visiting show: Theatre de Complicite's *The Street of Crocodiles* drawn from the 1930s short stories of a Polish Proust, Bruno Schulz. Recreating life in a city in south-east Poland, Simon McBurney's production was both a conscious remembrance of things past and a chilling reminder of the city's occupation by the Nazis in 1941 and of the fact that Schulz himself was shot in the street by a Gestapo officer. Where Lepage relies heavily on technology – always subject to gremlins – McBurney and his designer, Rae Smith, give symbolic life to mundane objects. Raised chairs very simply represented a spring dusk: adults, in a deliberate echo of Kantor's *The Dead Class,* sat behind tilting schoolroom desks for a crazy woodwork session. The surreal grew out of the real. Form also merged with content since the show largely dealt with Schulz's father: a textile merchant who retreated into a world of dreams and inventions and who, at one point, was seen perching on a ledge like a bird. Once again, it seemed that anything was possible in the Cottesloe.

But if any one production defined Eyre's belief that the Cottesloe was the National's creative engine-room it was surely Declan Donnellan's astonishing version of Tony Kushner's two-part *Angels in America.* This ranks, alongside the David Hare trilogy about the state of Britain, as the high-water mark of Eyre's tenure at the National. I suppose it would have been possible to stage Kushner's plays in the Olivier or the Lyttelton. But there was a positive aesthetic gain from mounting them in the Cottesloe. Their roller-coaster energy, their constant switch from private to public worlds, their buttonholing directness gained from the intimacy of the Cottesloe and the fluidity of Donnellan's direction and Nick Ormerod's design. In the Cottesloe, to take a tiny instance, you could see close-up the images of Hollywood icons – Mae West, Greta Garbo, Bette Davis – decorating the gay lovers' bedhead. And the performances, not least Henry Goodman's Roy Cohn with his buzz-saw voice and stabbing forefinger, were even more powerful at close quarters. I remember walking into the Broadway theatre where *Angels in America* played while they were putting up the set. I am sure the end result was very impressive but it looked like a big show: at the Cottesloe, it became an intimate life-changing experience.

New plays have, I would suggest, done more than anything to define the character of the Cottesloe over the last decade. Just occasionally, one has felt that they needed more room to breathe. Jim Cartwright's *The Rise and Fall Of Little Voice* gained from transfer to a West End house.

FIG 22 Théâtre de Complicité's *The Street of Crocodiles,* directed by Simon McBurney, designed by Rae Smith, opened at the Cottesloe on 13 August 1992. The echo of Tadeusz Kantor's *The Dead Class* is evident in the staging of this scene.
Left to right: Lilo Baur (Adela), Stefan Metz (Leon), Eric Mallet (Theodore), Clive Mendus (Uncle Charles), Matthew Scurfield (The Father) and Hayley Carmichael (Maria).
PHOTO: *Nobby Clark*

Tom Stoppard's *The Invention of Love,* which later moved to the Lyttelton, also felt like a big-stage play struggling to expand beyond the Cottesloe. But, more often than not, new plays sit naturally and easily in this space: you can appreciate both the detail and texture of writing and performance. In David Hare's *Skylight* the cluttered confinement of Kyra's flat, which is a significant part of the play's meaning, looked dead right in the Cottesloe. Martin McDonagh's *The Cripple of Inishmaan,* with its stylised sets and comic-poetic dialogue, also invited our conspiratorial participation. And Patrick Marber's *Closer,* analysing the truth and lies that are part of sexual intimacy, drew us into the action. That too transferred to the Lyttelton, and, while I can see the pragmatic reasons for the move (more people could get to see it), I slightly regret the increasing use of an internal transfer-system. The Cottesloe makes its own aesthetic statement: in my experience, shifting a play to another space usually results in loss rather than gain.

The NT's own mobile productions also, of course, touch down periodically in the Cottesloe: *Mother Courage, Billy Liar, Twelfth Night,* Winsome Pinnock's *Leave Taking,* Caryl Churchill's *Light Shining in Buckinghamshire* in recent years. Ken Campbell, that extraordinary mix of Ancient Mariner, Ken Dodd and garden gnome, has turned the space into his own back garden in recent years. And Shakespeare's plays, most notably Richard Eyre's *King Lear* and Sam Mendes' *Othello,* have palpably gained in domestic resonance through being staged in such a bruisingly intimate theatre. All that is a measure of the space's infinite adaptability. But what is most striking about the Cottesloe, as one surveys its rich history since the late 1970s, is how it seems to accord with the needs of artists and playgoers alike. Over that period the formal barriers between actor and audience have gradually been eroded. Performers are less and less rarefied beings encased behind footlights and proscenium-arch. And we, as lookers-on, no longer wish to be isolated spectators: we crave a shared experience, a sense of imaginative involvement, a feeling that we are part of the event. In big spaces – whether it be the Olivier or the Royal Shakespeare Theatre – it often requires a conscious effort to achieve that sense of instant rapport. In the Cottesloe it is built into the dimensions of the space. In the long day's journey from *Illuminatus* in 1977 to *The Invention of Love* in 1997 the key fact about that magical theatre is ease of communication. Whether the stage-configuration be straight-edged, circular or traverse, we are all in the same room. To use the terminology deployed by Peter Hall in his *Diaries* in 1973, we have left the cathedral behind. In the Cottesloe we are all worshippers in the same chapel; and there is a much greater chance that we shall get a tiny glimpse of heaven.

FIG 23 A scene from *Perestroika,* Part Two of Tony Kushner's *Angels in America.* Directed by Declan Donnellan and designed by Nick Ormerod, the production opened at the Cottesloe on 19 November 1993. Nancy Crane as the Angel and Stephen Dillane as Prior Walter.
PHOTO: *John Haynes*

FIG 24 *Entertaining Strangers* by David Edgar with Tim Pigott-Smith and Judi Dench opened in the Cottesloe in October 1987, directed by Peter Hall and designed by William Dudley. The photograph shows the moving bridge which reconfigured the space during the performance.
PHOTO: *John Haynes*

THE COTTESLOE AND THE NATIONAL

A CHANGING ROLE

SIR PETER HALL

Sir Peter Hall was born in 1930 in Bury St Edmunds and educated at the Perse School, Cambridge, and St Catharine's College, Cambridge. At the Arts Theatre in London he directed the world premiere of the English-language version of Waiting for Godot *(1955). He created the Royal Shakespeare Company (in 1960) after directing productions at Stratford in 1956–59 with, among others, Peggy Ashcroft, Laurence Olivier and Charles Laughton. He directed eighteen plays during the ten years he ran the RSC, including such notable productions as* The Wars of the Roses, *the David Warner* Hamlet *and premieres of plays by Harold Pinter, Edward Albee and John Whiting. Peter Hall was Director of the National Theatre for fifteen years (appointed in 1973), moving it into its new building on the South Bank. With his own Company, the Peter Hall Company, he has since directed some twenty-four major stage productions in London, New York, Sydney and many European countries. He has directed films and television films, including* Akenfield, The Homecoming, The Camomile Lawn *and* The Final Passage. *He has also directed more than forty operas all over the world, and was Artistic Director of Glyndebourne from 1984–90.*

PHOTO: *Clare Clifford*

Based on an interview with Ronnie Mulryne and Margaret Shewring.

I CAN claim that without me there would never have been a Cottesloe theatre. From the earliest discussions in the South Bank Building Committee, only two auditoria were planned. Peter Brook, George Devine and Michel St. Denis wanted a main house and a studio space, while Laurence Olivier and Kenneth Tynan very much wanted the second house to be a proscenium theatre. In the event, the Olivier and the Lyttelton were the outcome. Any smaller, studio space was cut for economic reasons, coupled with Lord Goodman's belief that the National Theatre did not require an experimental space. Goodman, as Chairman of the Arts Council, believed that experiment was the province of such theatres as the Royal Court.

Talking with Denys Lasdun I discovered that the third auditorium could not be cut entirely, since the space was there for it in the building plans, even though it was left empty. It was, in fact, *under* the whole building, like a foundation stone. I decided to hold fire. When the opportunity came to convert the space that Lasdun had left I thought that what the National needed was a flexible theatre in which we could experiment with performer-audience relationships, and where we could take risks without too much financial consequence. John Bury was the chief creator-designer of the space that eventually emerged.

Lord Cottesloe was Chairman of the South Bank Theatre Board. It was his Polonius-like wiliness that got a National Theatre built at all. He embarked on the project with statesmanlike determination, to the point where it couldn't be stopped. When others thought he had stepped out of line his attitude was, 'What are they going to do to me now? Put my head on a silver platter?' He certainly deserved to have one of the spaces named after him.

What I didn't predict was that before long everyone would want to work in the Cottesloe rather than in the other two auditoria. I found myself, as captain of the ship, needing to lead by taking on the largest space, the Olivier. The work of the other two theatres allowed the Cottesloe to exist as a heavily subsidised space – although I was careful to disguise that fact.

What happened was that the artistic seed-bed of the National moved from the larger spaces to the Cottesloe. Any attempt to cut the work in the Cottesloe would be to amputate one of the main arms of the whole enterprise, artistically even if not financially. When I *had* to close the Cottesloe for a brief period (in 1985), in the face of Arts Council under-funding, I chose to do so because I knew that the closure would make a big point not only politically but also artistically. Now, the cross-subsidy of the Cottesloe by the other two auditoria means that a successful musical, like *Guys and Dolls*, in the Olivier can make it possible to explore *King Lear* in the Cottesloe.

Working in the Cottesloe offers a special experience. In that space it is possible to use the full vocal range, from a shout to a whisper. This gives it great virtue as a Shakespearean house. The analogies with the Blackfriars, the indoor space used by Shakespeare's company, seem to me quite marked. That is why I chose to do the Shakespeare Late Plays in the Cottesloe. The eventual transfer to the Olivier was not planned from the beginning. I wanted to stage these plays from Shakespeare's Blackfriars years in a space with the same possibilities as the Blackfriars. In the event, in one performance, the lighting failed and, without electricity, we were forced to play the second half of *The Winter's Tale* by candlelight, as Shakespeare's company would have done. It did get us into some trouble with the Fire authorities, but it also allowed for a magical intimacy and concentration on the performers in the space.

Again, I chose the Cottesloe as the appropriate space for David Edgar's *Entertaining Strangers*. The set was extraordinary, filling the space with a mobile gantry that could sweep down the auditorium taking the performers right into the heart of the audience. The piece had been written as a community play, performed in Devon, and the Cottesloe allowed a parallel sense of community engagement.

Developing the Cottesloe as a shared or community space was a major part of the work of the first and only Artistic Director of the Cottesloe, Bill Bryden. Bryden's work offered a fine and challenging use of the Cottesloe space. In those early days, the Cottesloe had its own group of performers, and Bill was able to develop their work together, particularly in Promenade performances. Later work, after Bill had left the National, has often required cross-casting between auditoria, which tends to dissipate the energy derived from group work.

Above all, it is the proportions of the space, as envisaged by John Bury and realised by Iain Mackintosh, that make it so special. Not many so-called flexible spaces really *are* flexible, but the Cottesloe manifestly is. It has affinities with courtyard theatres – I think Iain Mackintosh is completely right about the virtues of the courtyard and of Regency theatres. But the Cottesloe transcends the courtyard. It shares something of the ideal proportions of the courtyard, yet its unassuming 'black box' architecture is extraordinarily flexible. Most courtyard-style theatres really only work in end-stage configurations. The Cottesloe is not restricted in this way. Nor has it settled down to a regular format. It isn't predictable, but offers, with each show, a genuine challenge.

Challenge and risk-taking are very important features of the Cottesloe. Right from its earliest shows I wanted the Cottesloe to be different. *Illuminatus* offered the ideal opening show. I knew Ken Campbell's work at this time (1977). *Illuminatus* had been playing in Liverpool, and when it turned out that the Cottesloe dates could fit the schedule, it seemed a fitting choice. *Illuminatus* was wonderful as a kind of 'stream of consciousness' applied to the theatre. It had its own emotional logic, rather than any linear narrative, so that it was possible during each long performance to go out and have coffee or a snack and come back in. The play shook up people's ideas of what theatre was, and what it can do, thus providing just the kind of risk-taking I wanted for the Cottesloe.

Selecting shows for the National should, in my view, be a process of risk-taking and moving theatre on. When a board member would look at a planned production and say, 'Oh dear! Not at the National Theatre', my instinctive response would be that things that are not obvious choices are absolutely things that ought to be done at the National. Theatre needs to be at the cutting edge in its public performances, and not only in private experiment.

The National Theatre has, and should have, several functions: to perform in public (as in the three auditoria), to develop in private (as in the Studio), and to look forward to the next generation of theatre-goers (as in the Education work). Sometimes, these areas overlap.

The Studio's role is strictly non-public. Under Peter Gill, its first director, it developed in a focused, particular way, sometimes using the Cottesloe as a public element within the laboratory context. Sue Higginson's great achievement with the Studio has been to open it up to the whole profession. I have great admiration for what she has done.

Equally the Education department has drawn itself more and more into the life of the National as a whole – into the life of the building and into the life of the Cottesloe. I just wish the resources were available to allow the National to enter on the primary tasks of education. I don't think the government has understood what music and drama have to offer. They are not optional extras but an integral part of our culture and our environment. To limit resources in this area is to demonstrate a woeful lack of vision. I remember hearing Gerry Robinson (the present Arts Council Chairman) give a lecture praising the outreach programme in Los Angeles. It transpired on further enquiry that the Los Angeles programme had been inspired by the London outreach programme in schools. The major difference was that, with all it has to offer artistically, London was working on a shoestring.

When I invited Bill Bryden to become Artistic Director of the Cottesloe I wanted him to have the freedom to take risks. He took on the challenge very readily, and both in Bill's time and since the Cottesloe has proved its value to the National precisely as an arena for taking risks. The space is one that encourages and rewards risk-taking, and I am glad that my two successors as Directors of the National have followed me in providing the circumstances in which cutting-edge work has proved possible. The rewards are obvious from the artistic achievements the Cottesloe has generated and nurtured.

SIR RICHARD EYRE

Sir Richard Eyre was Director of the Royal National Theatre from 1988 to 1997. Born in Barnstaple in 1943, he directed his first production, The Knack, *at the Phoenix Theatre, Leicester, in 1965. He was Associate Director and Director of Productions at the Royal Lyceum Theatre, Edinburgh (1967–72) and Artistic Director of Nottingham Playhouse (1973–78), before becoming Associate Director of the National Theatre in 1981. He joined the* BBC *as producer of* Play for Today *in 1978, and has directed films including* The Ploughman's Lunch *(1983) and* Laughterhouse *(1984; Venice Film Festival Award for Best Film) as well as opera* (La Traviata *at the Royal Opera House, 1994) and television (including a version of his Cottesloe* King Lear *in 1998). Eyre's memorable productions at the National include* Guys and Dolls *(1982),* Futurists *(1986),* Richard III *(1990) and the David Hare trilogy,* Racing Demon, Murmuring Judges *and* The Absence of War *(1993). Sir Richard is now pursuing a freelance career, and has recently been prominent as the author of the Report on the Royal Opera House.*

PHOTO: *John Haynes*

Based on an interview with Ronnie Mulryne and Margaret Shewring.

My first experience of working in the Cottesloe came in 1982. I was at the National for the first time, directing *Guys and Dolls* in the Olivier when Peter Hall asked me to do *Beggar's Opera* in the Cottesloe 'for zero cost'. All the elements of set and costumes came out of stock, a feature which led us to set the piece in a thieves' kitchen – since a diversity of superannuated items could be convincingly employed in that context. All the creative team came from people already at the National. Peter asked me, for example, to use Dominic Muldowney for the music. This was the first time I had worked with him, though he has since become a good friend and trusted collaborator.

This first opportunity of working in the Cottesloe revealed the strengths and drawbacks of the space, in both aesthetic and commercial terms. *Beggar's Opera* came alive in very gratifying fashion in the relatively large 'studio' space. At the same time, its success was dependent on the fortunes of *Guys and Dolls*. The two productions had to be cross-cast from the same group of actors, a fact that inevitably placed restrictions on the artistic choices available for the successful but far less lucrative *Beggar's Opera*.

Even the most successful productions in the Cottesloe show a deficit in real terms, when budgets are broken down into surplus and loss. This

FIG 25 *Harley Granville Barker's* The Voysey Inheritance, *directed by Richard Eyre and designed by William Dudley, opened at the Cottesloe on 27 June 1989. The photo (by Gerald Murray) shows David Burke as Mr Voysey in front of one of the realistically-conceived windows. Granville Barker was an early advocate of a National Theatre, taking part in 1900 in a lobbying committee along with influential friends including Gilbert Murray and William Archer.*
The Voysey Inheritance *(1906) was Barker's initial play for the Court Theatre (now The Royal Court) in Sloane Square. William Dudley's design for the Cottesloe revival was the first to use the theatre in the round format, and while employing only small sections of a realistic set, was able to create the impression of a four-walled interior, enhanced by the daylight quality of the neon lighting within the windows and door. 'Like all the best products of the Edwardian imagination,' wrote Peter Kemp,* 'The Voysey Inheritance *exhibits the woodworm in the mahogany … Under the impeccable surface, as Richard Eyre's production penetratingly displays, lies a warren of twisted voracity and hollow rottenness.'*
(Independent, *29.06.1989*)

FIG 26 *Skylight* by David Hare opened in the Cottesloe on 4 May 1995.
Lia Williams as Kyra Hollis and Daniel Betts as Edward Sergeant.
The production was directed by Richard Eyre and designed by John Gunter.
PHOTO: *John Haynes*

FIG 27 *White Chameleon* by Christopher Hampton, opened in the Cottesloe on 14 February, 1991. David Birkin (Chris) and Suzanne Burden (Chris's mother).
Directed by Richard Eyre and designed by Bob Crowley.
PHOTO: *John Haynes*

is both inevitable and acceptable within the context of the National's budget overall. It's a situation which gives the Cottesloe a great advantage over other studio or fringe venues, which need to balance their books without the cushion of box office revenue from two much larger spaces. Another financially-relevant consideration is that overall budgetting at the National is dependent on good returns from the Lyttelton and the Olivier, so that it is tempting to be cautious over scheduling even an apparently commercial piece in one of these theatres, until it has proved itself. Hence, for example, our decision (in late 1989) to mount *Racing Demon* in the Cottesloe, which in such cases doubles as a genuine and a try-out venue. This can have artistic as well as financial consequences. It may be that I would not have staged the play as I did, had I not been devising it first for the Cottesloe. At the same time, the Olivier production retained some of the strengths we discovered in the Cottesloe staging.

I'm aware of Tom Stoppard's jesting remark that the National has recently tended to open shows – and win excellent reviews and accolades – in the Cottesloe, and then to reap the royalties by transferring them to a bigger venue. There's some truth to Tom's observation, at least in financial terms. But it is also the case that the Cottesloe is so hospitable to different styles of production, and so versatile in its use of space, that it often makes good aesthetic and artistic sense to use it, even for plays that might well fill a much larger auditorium. So, for example, the Cottesloe offered the ideal venue for *The Invention of Love* (in 1997), even though, as a new play by Stoppard, and with John Wood in its principal rôle, one could predict a big box-office success. In this instance, certainly, the Cottesloe offered the right space. For example, the first act consists of a thirty-five minute duologue between characters sitting on a bench, and for this the Cottesloe offered the appropriate conversational context. Staging *The Invention of Love* in the Cottesloe may have seemed over-cautious in commercial terms, but the choice struck us as right artistically.

Another instance will illustrate the Cottesloe's adaptability and the aesthetic possibilities it opens up. The Cottesloe seemed to me absolutely right for my staging of *The Voysey Inheritance* (in 1989). I wanted to make a case for the play as a piece of English Chekhov, so I had to take it out of the immediately post-Victorian production style for which it was written (in 1903–5), with its conventional proscenium-arch frame, and open it up in the round. This had the effect of freeing the piece from critical preconceptions, and so offered me the aesthetic freedom to explore the play afresh.

Some plays just feel right in the Cottesloe, sometimes against all the logical arguments. My approach to *King Lear* (1998), for example, meant that it could only be done in that space. (See pp. 162–170 in this book.) I am reminded of Brecht's remark, on hearing Elizabeth Hauptmann's report on Playfair's splendid production of *The Beggar's Opera*: 'that smells like theatre'. One could say the same of Declan Donnellan's staging of *Fuente Ovejuna* at the Cottesloe (1992), even though its cast of twenty five would suggest that, in both financial and artistic terms, a Cottesloe performance was scarcely appropriate. The space fitted with the way in which the work of Donnellan and Nick Ormerod was developing. They would almost certainly not have done the show in one of the National's larger spaces. (See p. 67 in this book.) Thus the Cottesloe made it possible for the National to stage – magnificently – a show we would otherwise have failed to secure.

More and more directors want to use the Cottesloe, often preferring it to the Lyttelton or the Olivier. Its popularity says as much about theatre architecture as it does about the current preference for staging even 'large' plays in relatively small spaces. Or rather, it has much to say about the *absence* of intrusive architectural presence. The Cottesloe has no one dominant configuration or spatial form. It is extraordinarily self-effacing. It allows the configuration chosen for a particular production to develop its own aesthetic in a liberating environment, rather than requiring it to work, as in some other spaces (including the Lyttelton and the Olivier), against an ever-present, intrusive and often opposing aesthetic.

It is the liberty afforded both by the physical space, and by the relative financial security of the Cottesloe (within the resources of the National generally), that has ensured the National can carry out its responsibility towards the development of British drama as a whole. Time after time, the National has staged the most innovative work anywhere in British theatre – and this work has happened in the Cottesloe. Indeed, it is the opportunity and the challenge offered by its third auditorium that has kept the National in the game in this respect.

FIG 28 *Futurists* by Dusty Hughes opened in the Cottesloe on 17 March 1986. Directed by Richard Eyre and designed by William Dudley. PHOTO: *John Haynes*

Challenge is an important issue. The Cottesloe may be small in relation to the other auditoria at the National, and it may enjoy a privileged place in relation to the Company's budget, but it nevertheless needs to fulfil the high expectations, in terms of artistic achievement, which are appropriate to the work of a major 'flagship' company. A failure in the Cottesloe is very exposed. The Cottesloe does not offer a safe, small, inconspicuous space, where risks are cheap. It can therefore be very daunting to new writers. The National Studio, by way of contrast, can offer a much more protected laboratory environment in which new work can evolve. (See the interview with Sue Higginson, pp. 16–17 in this book.)

Work at the Cottesloe needs to be understood in terms of overall Company policy and planning. Only in the context of the Company's total ecology can individual repertoire choices, for the Cottesloe as well as the other auditoria, be understood. In this context, the Cottesloe can be seen as taking a crucial place, not only in the work of the National, but in emancipating what I believe has been some of the most interesting theatre work in this country.

GENISTA McINTOSH

Genista (Jenny) McIntosh was educated at Hemel Hempstead Grammar School and the University of York. She joined the Royal Shakespeare Company in 1972 as Casting Director, a post she held until 1977, when she became Planning Controller. After a two-year absence she returned to the RSC as Senior Administrator and then Associate Producer. She joined the Royal National Theatre as Executive Director in 1990, and was Chief Executive of the Royal Opera House for a five-month period in 1997 before re-joining the National in October to work alongside Trevor Nunn. Jenny McIntosh is a Fellow of the Royal Society of Arts and was awarded an Honorary Doctorate by the University of York in July 1998.
PHOTO: *Gautier Deblonde*

Based on an interview with Ronnie Mulryne and Margaret Shewring

THE COTTESLOE plays a role in relation to the National similar to that of The Other Place in relation to the Royal Shakespeare Company. The Cottesloe picked up on Peter Hall's perception that working at different scales is beneficial both to actors and to audiences. Small-scale spaces in the national theatres were a development of the fringe movement, and offered the actors an opportunity to experience variety. Within the National building, the Cottesloe is the only truly flexible space: it is able to offer a paintbox for creative artists of all kinds, with wide scope to develop their craft.

Perhaps because of this creative freedom, a significant proportion of work forged in the Cottesloe has gone on to very different kinds of life – in the other National spaces, in the West End, on television and on tour. *Othello* and Patrick Marber's *Closer* are good recent examples. But even if such an after-life is not envisaged, the flexibility and scale of the Cottesloe are still important factors in encouraging artists to extend their range. They can experiment in the Cottesloe with a freedom that cannot often be offered in one of the larger spaces, without risking serious financial consequences. Indeed, this sense of commercial obligation can inhibit an artist from taking risks in a large space.

Its role at the risk-taking edge of our work on the South Bank gives the Cottesloe a particular cultural currency, as a result of the more dynamic interchange it encourages between performers and audiences. Traditional theatre, traditionally performed, can get stuck within its own cultural boundaries. Audiences have fewer preconceptions about what they will see in the Cottesloe. For most people, new ideas are communicated in and shaped by the media: television, advertisements, journalism. The Cottesloe makes it easier for artistic and ideological exchange at the cutting edge of our culture to take place in the theatre. In this respect, the Cottesloe allows the National to fulfil a very important aspect of its remit.

The Cottesloe is a seed-bed of ideas and a hot-bed of artistic achievement, continually pushing out the boundaries of theatrical possibility.

TREVOR NUNN
THE COTTESLOE AND THE FUTURE

Trevor Nunn has been the Director of the Royal National Theatre since October 1997. He joined the Royal Shakespeare Company in 1964 after a period as Resident Director at the Belgrade Theatre, Coventry, was made an Associate Director of the RSC in 1965 and became the RSC's youngest ever Artistic Director in 1968. He continued to run the RSC until 1986. His work at Stratford was associated not only with the main house, but also with The Other Place (where he directed the final production at the first Other Place and the opening two productions at the new Other Place) and with The Swan, a theatre which he conceived and in which he directed one of the earliest productions. In London, he opened the RSC's new home at the Barbican (1982). His long list of directing credits includes such world-famous productions as Nicholas Nickleby *(with John Caird; the production won five Tony Awards),* Les Miserables *(eight Tony Awards; the most performed musical in the world) and* Cats, *as well as many outstanding productions of the plays of Shakespeare and other dramatists. He has also directed three films and a number of plays for television.*

PHOTO: *Gautier Deblonde*

Based on an interview with Ronnie Mulryne and Margaret Shewring

LOOKING at the place of the Cottesloe in the overall context of my, as yet limited, experience of programming for the National, it is clear there has been much more planning discussion relating to the small theatre, because of its more rapid turnover of productions and the much greater demand for the small space, than about the other two auditoria. Indeed, my problem is often to persuade directors, designers and performers to take on the two big spaces. This attraction to the Cottesloe is not just evident from the extraordinary range of plays that have been done there. It is bound up with what, by its very existence, the Cottesloe has initiated, the stylistic approaches which have been introduced there, and the extent to which these have changed the work of the rest of the organisation.

There is something of a parallel here to the situation in Stratford when I opened The Other Place as a second or alternative auditorium. In its first season, actors and directors did not want to work in this uncomfortable little building which had for years been used as a storage space. By the second season, company members wanted to work *only* in The Other Place, and had to be heavily persuaded to contribute work in the Main House. That response from actors is still there at Stratford – but focused now on the Swan rather than the rebuilt Other Place.

Unquestionably, directors at the National would much prefer to do great, intractable classics in the Cottesloe rather than the other spaces (witness, for example, Peter Hall's enquiry into Shakespeare's *Late Plays* and Richard Eyre's *King Lear*). Most new writing is also aimed at the Cottesloe, with its flexible and spare ability to accommodate many scenes unfolding in almost cinematic style, and certainly, in a style totally at variance with what is possible in the larger auditoria. In this regard, therefore, the Cottesloe has in its turn shaped new writing policy and output, the characteristics of which have flowed from the Cottesloe's inherent black box flexibility.

I have noticed a tendency within the National for the accepted perception of the opportunities offered by each of the three spaces to be locked into an unchanging pattern. Those who are experienced in making the larger spaces work can develop a degree of condescension in relation to the Cottesloe. And yet the Cottesloe offers a particular intimacy which leads to both a sense of immediacy and danger, and a tangible expectation, to be discovered in performer and audience alike. No pause dies. Laughter is infectious and sustained, whereas in larger auditoria laughter often dwindles away like water into sand. So conditions in the Cottesloe are admirable and enviable for everything that benefits from intimacy or interactivity.

The Cottesloe, because it was something of an afterthought, has a certain separateness architecturally from the National complex. It has a separate entrance and is separated spatially from the main foyers of the building. Perhaps that is why audiences, too, behave as though they regard the Cottesloe as a separate space. And this separateness may offer a clue to one of the ways I see the Cottesloe developing in the future. I would love the National to present more at weekends, and during the week in the mornings and afternoons; as more and more people want leisure activities to be available on Sundays, it would be good to use periods of Sunday too. It can be prohibitively expensive to open the whole of the National complex for additional performances, but, since the Cottesloe is self-contained physically, it would be viable to open the small theatre independently.

Then too, perhaps, more of the end-stage work at the Cottesloe could tour to University town theatres, where there is a need for middle-scale touring. Where necessary, productions might be adapted. To take a recent example, *Othello* (which opened at the Cottesloe on 16 September 1997) didn't start off as end-stage, but became more so on its tour, where it played proscenium theatres, even (though this was not always a good thing) very large proscenium theatres.

FIG 29 Set for *Mutabilitie* by Frank McGuinness which opened in the Cottesloe on 20 November 1997. Directed by Trevor Nunn and designed by Monica Frawley. PHOTO: *Philip Carter*

FIG 30 Trevor Nunn's production of *Mutabilitie* with Patrick Malahilde (Edmund), Diana Hardcastle (Elizabeth), Lauren Bird (Edmund's child) and Anton Lesser (William). PHOTO: *Stephen Vaughan*

The Cottesloe's individual identity is clear, not just in its separate space and its unique artistic history. The team working in the Cottesloe has also established its own identity. There is a strong sense of continuity and even proprietorialness among the technical team, which offers the kind of togetherness of spirit that one otherwise finds only with actors in the rehearsal room. The sense of unity that is present among the people working in the Cottesloe makes it a very enjoyable experience to come in and work with them.

There is, in addition, an identifiably different audience expectation in the Cottesloe. For example, with Patrick Marber's *Closer* (opened 29 May, 1997), the audience going in clearly had an expectation that, because this was a new play, it would be pushing the limits of vocabulary and content, and they were happily complicit. When *Closer* transferred to the Lyttelton, some of the audience shared that Cottesloe expectation, but an equally large number did not, were not expecting to be challenged as in a Cottesloe performance and were palpably discomfited.

It has to be said that we are living in much more financially-constrained times now than when the Cottesloe first opened. The Cottesloe, it is true, survived its period of token closure (in 1985) but, on the whole, it has been used throughout its twenty-one years as a totally flexible space, and that involves the National in a great deal of hidden expenditure. A crew often needs to be in all night to change the configuration of the space from one show to another, which is an expensive option. We may have to rediscover a greater basis in the simplicity of the actor-text relationship, and do without such bold scenic solutions. At present, we have had to make the rule that only two configurations for Cottesloe seating can co-exist at any one time in the same repertory run. This causes some distress, as it is seen to limit an artistic freedom that has become part of the expectation of work in the Cottesloe. I know myself how challenging this rule can be, as I have had to consider both *Mutabilitie* and *Not About Nightingales* (my first two shows in the Cottesloe) as very different plays needing to share the same basic configuration.

Mutabilitie is a very good example of risk-taking in the Cottesloe. Being a minimalist, I enjoy the challenge of working in small spaces, as I did with *Macbeth* at The Other Place, but I have had relatively little experience of the Cottesloe. So, I decided to use the Cottesloe space in its most environmental configuration, using a full-length traverse stage. Frank McGuiness (the play's author) had conceived the play for a larger space, but I felt his text was so dense and so rich, difficult, allusive, contradictory and elliptical that it was ideal for the conditions of a small space, especially because it was without a strong narrative thrust to carry the action in a large auditorium. The play also needed live singing, much music, sounds of all kinds, to be provided in a real way and not amplified. Frank agreed to the Cottesloe, and the traverse. The castle occupied by the colonial English and the forest occupied by the fugitive Irish could be seen physically to oppose each other at each end of the space – almost like the use of symbolic areas in liturgical drama. My choice of traverse was based on my belief that everyone in the audience would be

Fig 31 *Not About Nightingales.* The world première of a play by Tennessee Williams (c.1938), opened in the Cottesloe on 5 March 1998. Directed by Trevor Nunn and designed by Richard Hoover. The photograph shows Nunn's use of the traverse configuration of the Cottesloe.
Photo: *Philip Carter*

Fig 32 Trevor Nunn's production of *Not About Nightingales* with Finbar Lynch (Canary Jim) and Corin Redgrave (Boss Whalen).
Photo: *Nobby Clark*

in steeply banked seating, and would therefore be looking down on the stage floor surface in the middle of the space. This was important because the play made great use of the contoured earth, bisected by a stream and emblematically standing for Ireland. It was not until the production was set up in the theatre that I realised the angle of vision was not as I had imagined it, and that not all the audience could see the floor.

The subject-matter of the play is important, its insistence that the history of the English in Ireland is largely unknown or unheeded, so that the present turmoil derives from an ignorance that is both repeated and ingrained. The play's people are more or less figures in an allegorical landscape confronting the cultural misunderstanding and wilful ignorance we have all inherited and which we share equally. We conveyed these things in a theatre space that embraced and expressed them, in the manner of a debating chamber or a parliament. It was disappointing to me that some of the English press responded to this ambitious and difficult play with the same ignorance and misunderstanding that had characterised English reactions to Ireland during the preceding four hundred years. But in the Cottesloe, critical disappointments are not ruinous.

I very much hope the Cottesloe will continue in its ability to initiate new approaches, to fertilise the rest of the organisation and to make risk-taking viable.

FIG 33 The company and crew for *Dispatches*, 1979

WORKING THE COTTESLOE

Jason Barnes, Margaret Shewring, Ronnie Mulryne

PART ONE
THE TECHNICAL TEAM

Jason Barnes has been Production Manager for the Cottesloe throughout its twenty-one year history.

Based on an interview with Ronnie Mulryne and Margaret Shewring

THE COTTESLOE is the smallest auditorium at the National. It may appear to operate as an uncomplicated, black-box, 'empty space'. But any illusion that this space places few demands on its personnel is wholly mistaken. The process of realising scenography and performance in this flexible, hospitable space is complex, requiring skill and imagination on the part of the creative team and on the part of the team responsible, under the Production Manager, for the physical aspects of each show. The success of the Cottesloe over the past twenty-one years owes almost everything to the fruitful interaction of these two teams.

This section of the book aims to give a glimpse, no more, of the range of work which lies behind every production. The National's archive houses separate production files for each show, and we have drawn extensively on these, with Nicola Scadding's guidance, to summarise the theatre's pre-production and performance process. The master-file for a Cottesloe production, compiled by Jason Barnes, is divided into the principal aspects of the physical preparation for a show, and offers a rich source of information ranging from facts and figures to letters, sketches, photographs and anecdotes. We have supplemented this vivid material by interviewing several of those who have been involved in both the technical and the creative work of the Cottesloe, from directors, designers and actors to production-office and stage-management staff and a lighting technician.

Production Management

THE Production Manager's office is central to a successful collaboration between the creative and technical teams for any show. With my colleagues, currently Diane Willmott and Jo Maund, I concentrate on all the physical aspects of a Cottesloe production: settings (including construction, carpentry and metalwork, painting and drapes), properties (from large stage furniture to hand-held items), electrics (especially lighting), sound, wardrobe, wigs, armoury and special effects. Each of these is the province of a department with its own head and staff. The Production Manager's job is to co-ordinate all these activities, analysing the overall needs of each production, and matching them with the available resources (including the production budget and in-house and bought-in contractors' skills) and the time available. Each production mounted from scratch in the Cottesloe follows a similar schedule, adapted as need arises, from the initial conception of the show to the press-night (a count-down is given overleaf). Among the Production Manager's responsibilities is monitoring and participating in this process.

Scenery

Any proposal from a director or designer for movable elements of a stage-setting has to be considered against the limited technical resources we have available. The Cottesloe has no fly-tower, although we do have a suspension system which has recently been renewed and is now safer and partially mechanised. This serves as a substitute for a full flying system. The location of the lights also affects scenic preparations (see the interview with Ian Williams in this chapter). For example, for much of its twenty-one years the area used for an end-stage configuration has had to rely on access towers to reach the lighting rigs. A motorised access system is about to be installed over the whole performance space to meet this shortcoming.

Decisions relating to scenic elements have to take into account not only creative wishes and judgements but also the budget available and questions relating to changeover in the repertoire system as well as storage feasibility. All scenery used in repertoire has to be capable of being dismantled and re-assembled rapidly – even given that it is usual to restrict the spatial configurations employed to two in each repertoire. Scenic judgements also need to be tempered by the extent to which a desired audience configuration may reduce seat availability, or affect seat pricing (due to restricted sightlines, for example).

Seating

A detailed seating plan is produced once the configuration of the space is precisely known. The exact location of each seat is marked, on each seating level. The plan makes clear which seats (if any) will have a restricted view, the number of wheelchairs which can be accommodated, and how many standing tickets can be sold. Sometimes these decisions have to come at a late stage, as a memo from Genista McIntosh (Executive Director) referring to the production of *Stanley* makes plain:

> Holding 8 seats off-sale is annoying, but probably sensible at least until we have a better sense how the show will work ... as to pricing, we must assume impeded view and discomfort, price accordingly and above all *warn* people. If it turns out better than we feared it's tough but greatly preferable to ill-feeling and argument. (20 November 1995)

Properties

Decisions on large properties may be taken at the Planning Meeting (see 'Countdown to Performance'), in order to ensure that they are ready for the start of the rehearsal period. Throughout the preparation period, props research is undertaken by the designer and his or her assistant, by the props department, and by the appropriate construction departments. All of this work is co-ordinated by the production manager's offce. The process of supplying and altering props goes on throughout the rehearsal period, with the stage-management team liaising with the production office. Costumes and wigs follow a similar pattern.

The Production Office and Countdown To Performance

22 Weeks before Opening. The Pre-Production Meeting

By this date a play has been chosen, and a creative team, led by a director, has been appointed. Most of this team work on a freelance basis, and their availability has consequences throughout the preparatory weeks and into rehearsals and the previews. Following the pre-production meeting, the Production Manager draws up a skeleton plan of major requirements, in terms of people needed and issues to be addressed.

---

18 Weeks before Opening. The Planning Meeting.

The Planning Meeting determines basic design requirements, and is attended by the director and the designer(s). Any special requirements are taken into account – for example the need to accommodate musicians on or adjacent to the performance space. A stage manager has been appointed and a budget set.

---

14 Weeks before Opening. Working Drawings.

By this date, working drawings have been prepared, including designers' drawings and construction/technical drawings. Technical drawings are prepared in house or by an outside contractor as appropriate (outside contractors are normally appointed following the receipt of three tenders). Construction estimates have been received, and the Production Manager co-ordinates these with an eye to the production budget. A model and detailed design drawings are usually available.

---

9 Weeks before Opening. The Construction Process.

The construction process starts. About half of the Cottesloe scenery is built in the National's own workshops, with the rest going to outside contractors.

---

8 Weeks before Opening. The Production Meeting.

All those involved in the physical aspects of a show are called to a Production Meeting. This meeting draws together the conclusions of the individual construction meetings, and offers an opportunity to check the final logistics of the work. Both the Press Office and the marketing team attend this meeting. A green light is given for rehearsals to start. Ground plans are prepared for the stage-management team, enabling them to work out requirements for the rehearsal space, and any rehearsal furniture required.

---

7 Weeks before Opening. Rehearsals.

Rehearsals begin. During the rehearsal process, the stage management team remains in touch with the production office, to ensure that all the detailed requirements that emerge from rehearsals can be accommodated in time for the technical rehearsals and dress rehearsal.

3½ Days before Opening. Changeover and Get In.

Only 3½ days are usually available between striking a set on a Saturday night and opening a new production in the vacant slot in the repertoire. During this change-over period the Cottesloe is dark. (Occasionally, an extra day may be available to meet complex demands, but each day the auditorium is dark costs money in terms of box-office receipts.) During the get-in period, music and sound calls are held to deal with such matters as microphones and amplification levels. There are special rigging sessions. The new set is constructed *in situ*, the lights focused, colour adjusted and the 'plug-up' undertaken. Useful combinations of lights which can be pre-set on the computerised board are determined. Properties and stage furniture are pre-set (on stage or at an appropriate off-stage location for use during the show). Costumes required for quick changes are put in place, while technicians ensure that moving elements of the set operate as designed. The full technical rehearsal takes place (often known as the 'stopping' dress rehearsal).

About twenty hours are available for the technical rehearsal and the dress rehearsal. The pace varies. The opening moments of a show may require as much as three or four hours of rehearsal time to achieve the exact technical requirements for running the show. The creative team may decide on last-minute cuts or transpositions. These, in turn, have a knock-on effect in all technical areas, as well as in props and costumes. Major changes at this late stage are rare. Rehearsals continue on preview days leading up to Press Night.

Props for Ma Rainey

Props for any show can be very numerous, from large stage units to hand-held items. The design and supply of props is shared between the creative and technical teams, with the ultimate responsibility resting with the Props department to oversee the research, design and making, or the hiring, borrowing or buying of the relevant pieces.

The props list for *Ma Rainey* (September, 1989) runs to some 56 'personal' props (items carried by individual characters), 29 small on-stage props and 27 large pieces of furniture, plus musical instruments ranging from two pianos to 'a silver cornet in a case'. Stage management notes relating to the props indicate the level of detail. For example, 'The wall 'phone should have dimes set in it, so that when the actor plays with the return button, he can collect the money out of it.' Or, 'Three of the chairs really get thrown about during the fight, so they need to be fairly solid. One gets thrown down the stairs.' Or, on the musical side, 'Both Hugh and George use Valve Oil for their instruments, so please may we have period containers for them?' The personal tastes of the performers have to be taken into account. So, for example, 'George Harris does not smoke, and as he has to roll reefers during the play, there is a problem of what to put in the tobacco pouch. Herbal tobacco has been declined. We will have to experiment.'

FIG 34 The props workshop at the National Theatre, with trees for the Cottesloe production of John Marston's *The Fawn* (1983) under construction.

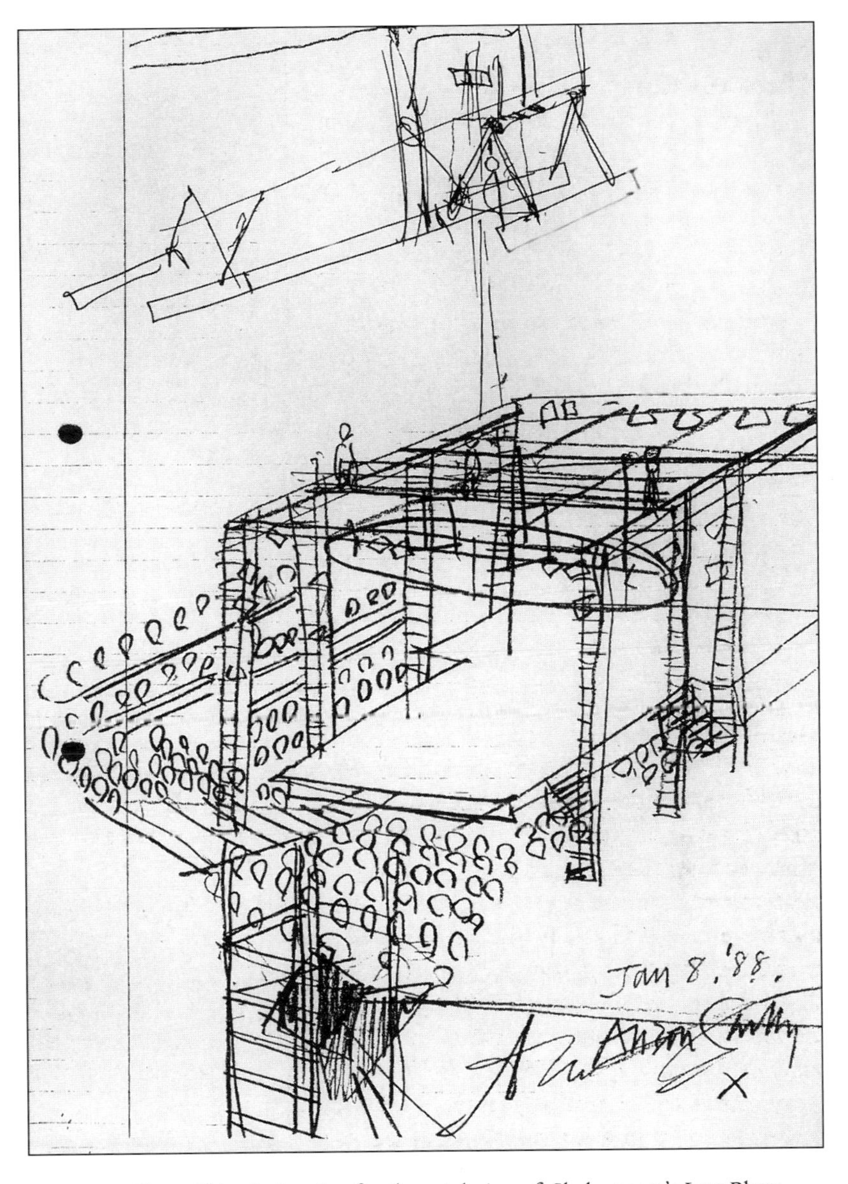

FIG 35 Alison Chitty's drawing for the set design of Shakespeare's Late Plays.

Costs

The set design for Shakespeare's Late Plays, with its suspended ceiling (see Alison Chitty's drawing of January 8, Fig 35), removable panels and trap under the stage, was so complex that the Production Office went out to engineering firms to tender for the installation, rather than building it in house. A late re-design of the back wall led to additional contractors' costs. (For a discussion of the production see pp. 112–121 in this book).

FIG 36 John Tams as Robin Starveling (left) in the National Theatre production of *A Midsummer Night's Dream*, opening at the Cottesloe in November 1982 and transferring to the Lyttelton in April, 1983. Directed by Bill Bryden, settings Bob Crowley, costumes Deirdre Clancy. The other actors, left to right, are Stephen Petcher (Francis Flute), Derek Newark (Nick Bottom), Tony Haygarth (Tom Snout) and James Grant (Snug). John Tams provided the music, or acted as Music Director, for a number of Cottesloe shows, beginning with *The Long Voyage Home* and *Dispatches* in 1979, and including *The Mysteries* (with Ashley Hutchings).

Lighting

Throughout the rehearsal period, the stage management team record lighting needs. Plays running in any one repertoire need to share a basic lighting rig (*see right* the interview with Ian Williams for this and related points). Most plays have some specially rigged lights.

Sound

During the period of rehearsal, the stage management team record sound cues, and relay special requirements back to the Production Office. Most music is performed live, as a result of agreements with the Musicians Union.

Costume

One member of the stage management team is usually assigned principally to costume requirements during the rehearsal period. This is particularly important in the case of a costume plot involving quick changes.

IAN WILLIAMS: LIGHTING THE SPACE

Ian Williams is Chief Lighting Technician at the Royal National Theatre. He has worked as part of the Cottesloe team of technicians (now two Chief Technicians, one Senior Technician and one Technician) throughout the twenty-one year history of the theatre.

I BECAME part of the technical crew about twenty-five years ago, when the National Theatre was still based at the Old Vic. I moved with the Company into the new building on the South Bank, and formed part of the team who first opened the Cottesloe with *Illuminatus*. At that time, the Cottesloe had only twenty-five to thirty lighting units/lanterns, and a temporary wooden structure at the back of the first gallery, where the control boxes for light and sound are now more permanently situated. For the first two years in the Cottesloe we went on with this very basic system until, just prior to the opening of *Don Juan*, the auditorium closed to permit the re-laying of the floor and some refurbishment. At that time, the lighting was enhanced, up to 180 units. These needed to be distributed carefully because various designers used the space in different configurations, and each needed to be lit from the same basic format.

By the late 1980s much of our original equipment was worn and obsolete. This led to a period of modernisation, introducing a rig of 250–300 units above the space. This increase in equipment sounds lavish, until the demands of the repertoire are fully understood. With only two hours to do a change-over between shows, the lighting formats for each show have to be in place simultaneously, double and triple rigged. Even with an increase in units to 400, we had no more than 180 dimmers available to share out between the shows. Now, in the late 1990s, the 400 units are matched by 400 dimmers, but we still need to double and triple rig to meet the demands of the repertoire. And, though the equipment has become more sophisticated, allowing us to pre-set various combinations of lights from the computerised board, we still need manual operation throughout the show night by night.

The Cottesloe really is a totally flexible space. The focus is on the performer and on the performer's relationship with the audience. The technical aspects of a show have to take second or third place. Sometimes, the control boxes have to operate virtually blind – behind a wall in *King Lear*, or peering through what amounted to no more than a letterbox in *Entertaining Strangers*.

On the Cottesloe's creative team there are a number of lighting designers, who often work with a particular director with whom they establish an artistic relationship. These designers have to work within the constraints of the repertoire system, which can mean that artistic wishes have to be tempered by practicalities. One show has to respect the needs of another programmed in the same time-period. In that respect, a visiting show may have more freedom than an in-house piece, since it tends to be programmed in a continuous run, rather than as part of the repertoire system.

Working in the Cottesloe makes many demands, some of them hard to meet, but it offers nevertheless a very satisfying environment for both skill and artistry.

JOHN CAULFIELD

STAGE MANAGEMENT IN THE COTTESLOE

I HAVE worked in the Cottesloe from the time of the earliest show there, Ken Campbell's *Illuminatus*, in 1977. I worked with Bill Bryden and I am still working on Cottesloe productions as well as shows in the Olivier and the Lyttelton.

When the Cottesloe first opened people didn't quite know what to do with it. The early months saw a mixture of shows, with no clear direction. Gradually, it was understood that flexibility was the Cottesloe's real strength, its ability to accommodate any kind of show. In a gap in an early production schedule, Bill Bryden came up with the idea of *The Passion,* staged in promenade. This obviously extended our sense of what the Cottesloe could handle. Quickly, the stage management team learned to cope with a wide range of configurations, hospitable to a seemingly infinite variety of productions.

For each production it is the stage manager and his or her team who co-ordinate all the departments involved in the production, and then look after the day-to-day business of rehearsal through to first performance and on into the repertoire. Liaising with the production office, stage management mark out the rehearsal room floor, ensure the necessary elements are present in the rehearsal room, and sit in on all rehearsals with the director, recording all cues and any other needs. Actor calls, voice calls, fight calls, music calls, costume and wig fittings all need to be co-ordinated by the stage manager to ensure they do not interrupt the smooth running of the rehearsal process.

Once the production is running one of the stage management team co-ordinates each performance from a base within the body of the auditorium, close to the lighting and sound boards. Productions have become increasingly reliant on technology to the extent that the assistant stage manager can no longer co-ordinate the show successfully from a prompt corner back stage. Nowadays, while the assistant stage manager works out front, the stage manager co-ordinates the team back stage, preparing for and responding to moment by moment requirements.

Once an ideal pattern has been established for each production it is recorded in what becomes the 'bible' of the production. The 'bible' is a file in which pages from the script are inserted on right-hand sheets while on the left all the relevant light, sound, actor and prop cues are recorded, linked directly to the exact moment they are required in the script. The 'bible' is the complete record of the show, or, to put it another way, the blueprint. It is used when a show tours as the plan for the complete reconstruction of the Cottesloe production. Only when the show is no longer required is the 'bible' lodged in the National's archive in order to provide a lasting account of the full process of each production. Even then, I suppose, it might inspire later directors with ideas for their own productions. (For illustration of a 'bible' see p. 60.)

FIG 37 Members of the cast rehearsing *Fuente Ovejuna* (staged December 1988 to August 1989), directed by Declan Donnellan, designed by Nick Ormerod. Note the back cloth, table and other scenic elements provided by stage management to assist the cast in preparing for the Cottesloe space.
PHOTO: *Robert Workman*

FIG 38 Diane Willmott (right) and Jo Maund in the Cottesloe Production Office. Diane worked for eleven years as a freelance stage manager before joining the Cottesloe, where she has managed a number of notable productions, including *War and Peace, Cardiff East, Fair Ladies at a Game of Poem Cards, Closer, The Invention of Love* and a world tour of *Othello*. Jo has worked in the Cottesloe Production Office since December 1997 as an Assistant Production Manager.

ROGER CHAPMAN

THE COTTESLOE ON TOUR

Roger Chapman is Head of Touring at the Royal National Theatre, a post he has held since 1988. He was a founder member of the Theatre in Education Company at the Belgrade Theatre, Coventry, and has been Director of Theatre in Education Companies at the Octagon Theatre, Bolton and at Leeds Playhouse. He has directed productions in England, Ireland, Hong Kong and Australia, where he has been, among other appointments, the Director of the first Australian International Puppet Festival and Executive Director of the Ninth World ASSITEJ Congress. He has negotiated tours across the world for the National Theatre, has been a member of the Drama Panel of the Arts Council of Great Britain, is a member of the Board of the University of Warwick Arts Centre, and has published Snap Out of It *for Eyre Methuen.*

IN TERMS of touring, the Cottesloe shows offer both special opportunities and huge problems. These arise partly from the nature of the Cottesloe itself. Directors working for the National really want to work in the Cottesloe. It is a special space, larger than one at first thinks, yet still deceptively intimate. The intensity of the experience of any play is enhanced, for both actor and audience, by this intimacy. There is a greater chance of making an impact – and of kicking up a storm – with work in the Cottesloe. It's not just a matter of its seating capacity of 250–400, it is that the auditorium, which can be configured in a rich variety of ways, has the focus of a cockpit. The gallery running round the space means that the audience can either be close to the performers on stage level or be hanging over the space looking down from the gallery, but again almost in touching distance of the performers.

The nature of the space, then, entices major directors to work on 'big' plays, and with great success. This in itself creates a problem. The house is almost always more than 80% full, and often all the seats are taken. But if the show then transfers to one of the larger auditoria, or tours, its nature is changed by the new space or spaces it occupies.

The experience of the Cottesloe is unique. There are just no other spaces like it. For touring, this poses a problem. Sometimes we are forced to use proscenium-arch theatres. The best of these in Britain are the Matcham houses, with their intimacy and their galleries forming a horseshoe wrapping around the audience. But sometimes we have to replicate the Cottesloe in touring venues by using quite heroic measures. With the extraordinary skills of Jason Barnes and his team, we have literally rebuilt the interior of the Cottesloe in a variety of spaces. Sometimes we do this by building a stage out over the stalls, and making this, as in the Cottesloe, a shared floor between performer and auditorium. This plus the galleries can suggest a Cottesloe format.

In England, the theatre of Christ's Hospital School, Horsham, offers a good approximation to the Cottesloe's courtyard space – in fact they were both conceived by the same team, Theatre Projects Consultants. Abroad, the challenge is often much greater. At Bobigny in France, it's true, the theatre offers a similar but much larger 'box' shape, so we can tour there without much difficulty. But we have had to virtually re-build the Cottesloe in a sixth-century church in Istanbul and in a dockyard warehouse in Thessaloniki. And we built out over the stalls of a theatre in Seville, to construct a space for *Fuente Ovejuna*. Yet even these copies are not totally satisfactory, because it is hard to replicate the intimate acoustics of the Cottesloe itself. In the Cottesloe the performers can whisper and still be heard. Also, external noises do not obtrude into the space. In a sixth-century church, or a dockyard location, not only the natural acoustics of the space but their environments can cause noise problems – like the ship's hooter in Thessaloniki.

Touring, then, seldom does the director any favours. A success in the Cottesloe can be dissipated at a tour venue, and then everyone feels let down – both the Company and the audience who have come because they have heard about the play's success in its home venue.

Touring will become more difficult in the foreseeable future, for the Cottesloe in particular, for organisational as well as practical and spatial reasons. Trevor Nunn is currently developing a large shared company of actors who will work in both the Olivier and the Cottesloe. This means that shows in these auditoria will be cross cast, so that if either show were to tour it could only be at the expense of the other. Only the Lyttelton will have a free-standing casting arrangement which, in turn, will make it the logical auditorium from which to tour out.

The Cottesloe can, of course, accept some shows in, or mounted in collaboration with other companies (such as the Théâtre de Complicité and the Market Theatre, Johannesburg). It will also remain an option for some work originating in the Studio, and from the mobile productions of the National's Education Department. I don't for a moment think that the glory days of touring out from the Cotesloe have come to an end. However, these are days of considerable change, which may mean less of an external profile for its product.

Health and Safety

An important element in the preparation of any public occasion is the need to comply with health and safety regulations. For the Cottesloe team, this means informing the local authorities about the specific details of each production, including the construction and materials used in the scenery, and the overall layout of stage and auditorium. Any potentially hazardous elements, for example flame effects, require special attention. All uses of real flame and dry ice have to be approved by the London Fire and Civil Defence authorities, previously under the Greater London Council, and more recently under the Borough of Lambeth.

The Production Manager writes to the local Council two weeks prior to the show's opening. The Council's safety inspector visits the auditorium and inspects the performance and seating arrangements two days prior to the opening preview performance. Only after this visit can a production be licensed for performance. If anything causes concern, the inspector can require the production team to make what alterations he deems necessary. The license can be withheld until the changes are made to the inspector's satisfaction.

Touring

When the National Theatre mounts a co-production at the Cottesloe with a British company – the Liverpool Everyman, for example, or the Leicester Haymarket – there is usually a big input on the physical side from National Theatre staff. Much discussion is needed about how to fit the show into the Cottesloe, about flammability questions and about safety generally. The problems can be reduced through staff contacts, especially production manager to production manager. Sometimes, existing contacts make things easier, as in the case of *Guiding Star*, which opened at the Liverpool Everyman, where the safety officer had previously worked at the National.

In the case of overseas tours into the Cottesloe, we sometimes have to make a bigger contribution. With *Titus Andronicus*, mounted by the Market Theatre of Johannesburg (1995), we had to rebuild the set to fit the Cottesloe and to tour. We even sourced the jeep locally. Only the props and costumes came from South Africa.

For an outgoing tour, a lot of work has to be done. We have to consider feasibility, by answering for example questions about how long a tour will be appropriate, and how many performances we should do in each venue. We have to organise our repertoire here in such a way that the outgoing show has enough time off for the planned tour. We have to visit the overseas venues to ensure the Cottesloe show will fit. When it comes to the tour itself, we have to plan the itinerary very carefully. There are often long distances to be covered by road in Europe, and this can lead to delays at land borders, in shipping and so on. When we use air freight, there can be delays in this too. The airlines are not always helpful in scheduling our containers, especially if they are doing it free (as they are sometimes willing to do). There are complex inventories to be made of everything we are taking with us, and valuations have to be undertaken for countries outside the European Union. We have to estimate the number of containers or lorries we need – which can be considerable, especially if the host venue is different in scale or facilities from the Cottesloe, or is a non-theatre venue and we have to build everything from scratch. And then sometimes the overseas theatre is not equipped to the standard of the National, and we have to supply whatever items are not to hand. The production manager is required to travel with the tour about fifty per cent of the time, when there are physical difficulties with the freight or with the venues we are working in. Touring takes time – in a dozen ways – but we accept it as a valuable part of our work.

TECHNICAL MIRACLES

The sky's the limit: Lark Rise *and* Candleford

Jason Barnes wrote to an American acquaintance, explaining, as an example, how the sky cloth for *Lark Rise* presented a challenge even to a very experienced Production Department:

> *Lark Rise* with its horizontal sky cloth posed enormous problems. The material was to be white, seamless (27'3" wide across the theatre) and 78' long from the bottom of the horizon behind the corn field, up along the length of the theatre, and finishing up above the heads of the audience at the rear of the second level gallery. [See the illustration *right*] It had also to be translucent when lit from above, but precisely diffusive to avoid the image of the lamp elements when looked at from below. The underside needed to be reflective, in the sense of a bounce cloth (cyclorama material). No such material is available as inherently non-flammable nor durably treated (a process of baking in chemicals at very high temperatures for a very short time). The process renders the fabric resistant to washing. The relevant British Standard laid down for such materials, and incidentally for children's nightwear, demands that the material must resist twelve machine washings of thirty minutes' duration each, without affecting the finish or nature of the cloth. Against the background of bureaucracy sensibly in operation to preserve the life of both spectator and actor, you may imagine my frustration in trying to achieve Bill Dudley's celestial expanse, which so dramatically dominated the model of his design.

Despite all the difficulties, the Production Office once again found a solution, and the very important design element was manufactured.

A Cause for Concern: Lear's *Walls*

A memo from Deborah Jaffer to Maggie Whitlum (General Manager) and David Roberts (Head of Technical Department) headed 'Incident involving member of public' (31.3.97) reported that:

> During the storm scene in Monday's performance of *King Lear*, the rush of air caused by the flats falling onto the stage caused a foreign particle to enter the left eye of Mr Besch, a member of the audience. During the interval he was attended to in the Cottesloe foyer by the duty nurse who irrigated his eye and removed the offending particle. Mr Besch had declined to go to the medical room because he was at that time enjoying a drink in the foyer and was concerned that he would miss the beginning of the second part of the play.
>
> There has been concern from both the Safety Dept and Front of House Management that incidents such as this would happen as a result of the flats falling, but this seems to be an isolated incident so far and the problem does not appear to be as bad as first anticipated. However we shall continue to monitor the situation and if further incidents are reported we may recommend more thorough cleaning of the stage area, and that failing, a re-direction of the air-flow by modifying the barriers in front of the stage area.

FIG 39 The Winter Scene from *Candleford* (1979), directed by Bill Bryden and Sebastian Graham-Jones, designed by William Dudley.
Note the great skycloth also used for *Lark Rise* (which gave Jason Barnes and the Production Office so much trouble) over-arching the playing area.
PHOTO: *Michael Mayhew*

Jason Barnes had already anticipated this problem (memo of 27 January, 1997, to Gurinder Johal, Health and Safety Officer), suggesting remedies for keeping the stage clear of dust particles. He also, in the same memo, proposed devices for ensuring members of the audience were not struck by the falling panels (including the provision of a steel handrail, and a safety gap) and suggested that the company 'engineer the panels to combine as light a structure as possible, using aerolam and aluminium, with a stable surface for the acting area formed by the panels in part two'.

The Walls that do not Fall

Diane Willmott (of the Production Office) explained in a memo (25.4.97) to Richard Eyre (the National's Director and stage director of *King Lear*) why the wall in *Lear* failed on occasion to fall:

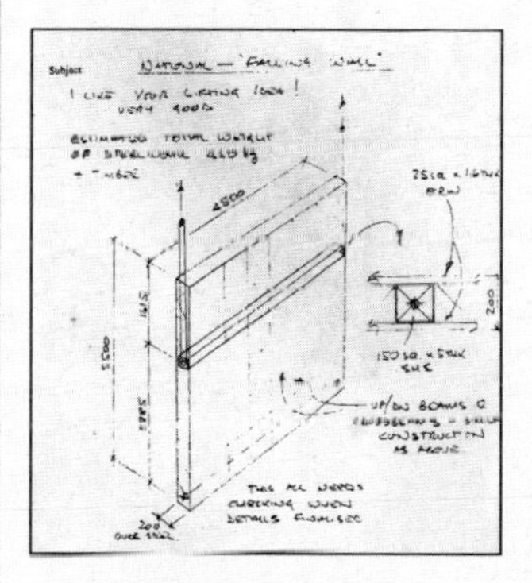

FIG 40 Technical sketch for the wall in Skakespeare's *Lear*

> Following a meeting with Michael Passmore from Level Services at 2.00pm this afternoon, I am now in a position to tell you the U/S [up stage] *King Lear* wall did not fall last night because the arm holding the electromagnet/hook system on S/R [stage right] was not correctly aligned with the eye on the door – it was positioned too high, the consequences being that when the hook dropped it did not release the eye and the wall was not able to fall. This incorrect alignment was due to lack of time in the changeover and exacerbated by the amount of 'play' in the arms in the horizontal and vertical planes.

She recommended that various remedial steps should be taken, but concluded:

> I discussed with Stuart Smith & Michael the possibility of replacing the current electrically operated system with a manual one and we concluded that any system we introduce will involve a considerable level of sophistication as we need to ensure the walls sit absolutely on the vertical because of the doors. Therefore we are quite likely to find ourselves in a situation where we are struggling with an entirely new set of problems arising from the replacement system, having made very little net gain in reliability.

Preparing for the Deluge

Jason Barnes's pre-performance letter of 10 March, 1997, to Mike Timlin of the Directorate of Environmental Services at the London borough of Lambeth (see 'Countdown to Performance') explains the materials used for *King Lear*, including those used for the area which receives the heavy rainfall:

> Upstage of the playing space is an area of mud, comprising side areas of textured foam, together with peat free compost. The compost has been the subject of time tests to confirm no organic development in the material. It is anticipated that this material will in any case be replaced on repertoire change-overs.
>
> Upstage of the mud area is a water impervious backcloth. Above the mud area is a bridge which extends, for performers only, the second level gallery around the back of the stage. Under the cross stage run of the bridge is a rain effect, which will discharge during the storm sequence into a lined reservoir containing the mud. Waste water will pass by means of a sump into storage tanks in the stage basement. Fresh water will be pumped from separate storage tanks also held in the basement.

Engineering drawings were provided for the panels, and a ground plan and seating layout, together with a section showing the proximity of the front row of the audience.

Oil Painting and Stanley

A memo from Jason Barnes (17.1.96) explained to David Munday (Head of Security at the National) how the requirements of naturalism posed risks in the performance of *Stanley*, and how these should be minimised:

> Mr Sher is using oils, not water based paints, for, as an established painter himself, having naturalistically to reproduce parts of several of Stanley Spencer's paintings before the public, and as part of the action, he needs to use the same materials as Spencer himself. …
>
> Mr Sher has four painting 'stations' … As part of these stations, he requires quantities of white spirit to wash brushes during the action. … I have asked Mr Sher a) to rehearse with these vessels fixed in position, and b) to limit the quantity of white spirit to one inch in each.
>
> The play calls for smoking. We have limited this to two occasions, and separated the action as far as possible from the paint stations. …
>
> The play calls for one candle. The action for this is also detailed on the enclosed sheet.

Jason accompanied the memo with a drawing. David Munday in turn faxed Mr Terry Collins of the Entertainment Licensing branch of the London Borough of Lambeth, to explain how the authentic smell of the painter's studio was to be made compatible with safety:

> I understand we are using 50% diluted fluid. We propose to drop in three places (nowhere near the public) very small droplets, so there is a 'turps' fragrance to help the audience believe they are within a painter's studio. Gurinder Johal, our Safety Officer, is satisfied with the use of this medium, and I sincerely hope you will have no reason to reject it.

In the end, the requirements of both authenticity and safety were satisfactorily met.

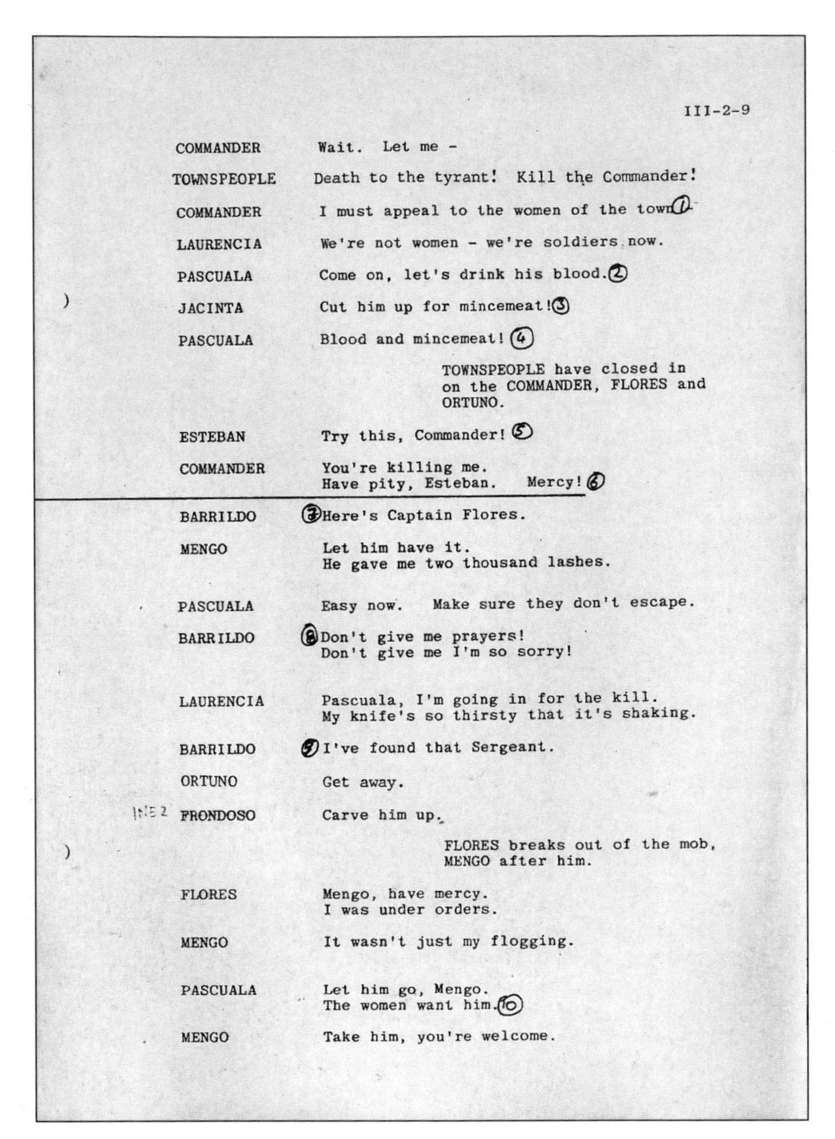

III-2-9

COMMANDER Wait. Let me -

TOWNSPEOPLE Death to the tyrant! Kill the Commander!

COMMANDER I must appeal to the women of the town ①

LAURENCIA We're not women - we're soldiers now.

PASCUALA Come on, let's drink his blood. ②

JACINTA Cut him up for mincemeat! ③

PASCUALA Blood and mincemeat! ④

TOWNSPEOPLE have closed in on the COMMANDER, FLORES and ORTUNO.

ESTEBAN Try this, Commander! ⑤

COMMANDER You're killing me.
Have pity, Esteban. Mercy! ⑥

BARRILDO ⑦ Here's Captain Flores.

MENGO Let him have it.
He gave me two thousand lashes.

PASCUALA Easy now. Make sure they don't escape.

BARRILDO ⑧ Don't give me prayers!
Don't give me I'm so sorry!

LAURENCIA Pascuala, I'm going in for the kill.
My knife's so thirsty that it's shaking.

BARRILDO ⑨ I've found that Sergeant.

ORTUNO Get away.

FRONDOSO Carve him up.

FLORES breaks out of the mob, MENGO after him.

FLORES Mengo, have mercy.
I was under orders.

MENGO It wasn't just my flogging.

PASCUALA Let him go, Mengo.
The women want him. ⑩

MENGO Take him, you're welcome.

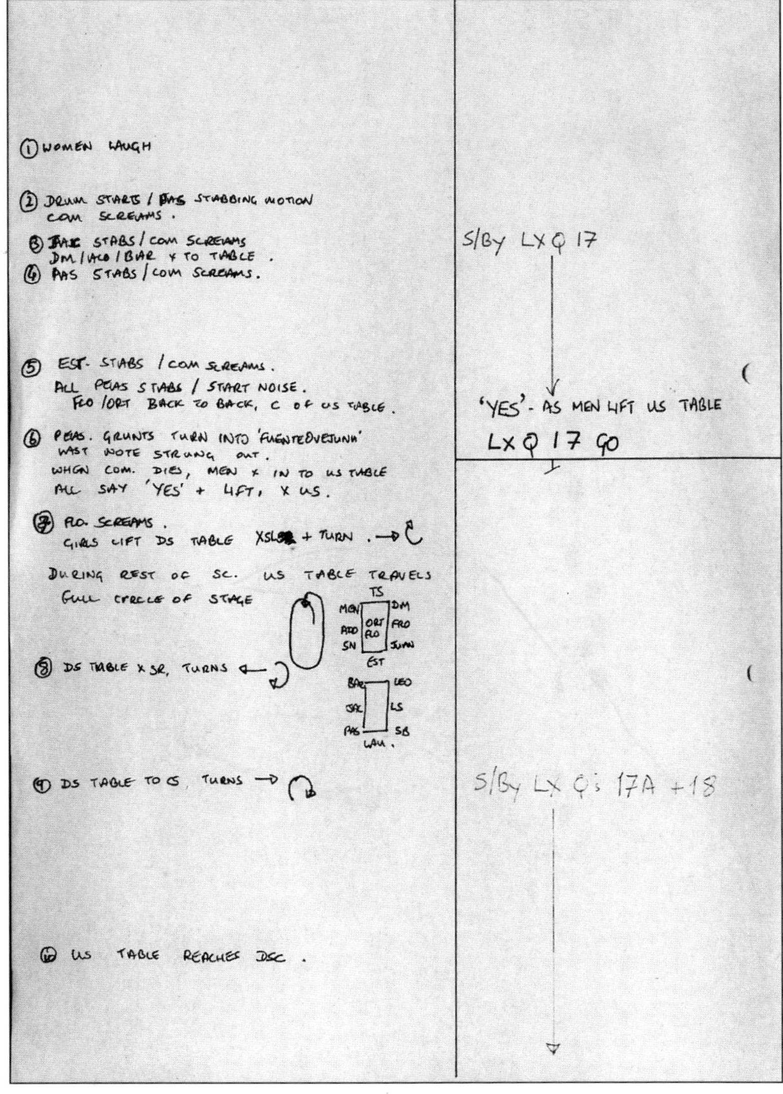

① WOMEN LAUGH

② DRUM STARTS / PAS STABBING MOTION
COM SCREAMS.

③ BAR STABS / COM SCREAMS
DM / JACO / BAR X TO TABLE.

④ PAS STABS / COM SCREAMS.

⑤ EST. STABS / COM SCREAMS.
ALL PEAS STABS / START NOISE.
FLO / ORT BACK TO BACK, C OF US TABLE.

⑥ PEAS. GRUNTS TURN INTO 'FUENTEOVEJUNA'
LAST NOTE STRUNG OUT.
WHEN COM. DIES, MEN X IN TO US TABLE
ALL SAY 'YES' + LIFT, X US.

⑦ FLO. SCREAMS.
GIRLS LIFT DS TABLE XSL + TURN.

DURING REST OF SC. US TABLE TRAVELS
FULL CIRCLE OF STAGE

⑧ DS TABLE X SR, TURNS

⑨ DS TABLE TO CS, TURNS

⑩ US TABLE REACHES DSC.

S/By LX Q 17

'YES' - AS MEN LIFT US TABLE
LX Q 17 GO

S/By LX Q; 17A + 18

FIGS 41 and 42 The prompt-book 'bible' in which stage management record the running of a show as exactly as possible. The 'bible' may be subsequently be used as the basis of a revival or a touring production. In the opening shown here (from the *Fuente Ovejuna* 'bible') sound, movement and lighting cues are all specified and the general stage action sketched.

FIG 43 The Cottesloe Family photographed in March 1998

Tim Bray, Stuart Smith, Micky Day, Harry Burden, Stephen Wentworth, Christopher Shutt, Jane Suffling, Tony Collins, Henryk Borowski, John Langley, Diane Willmott, Jo Maund, Billy Penston, Rosemary Beattie, Peter Gregory, Fraser Burchill, Richard Reddrop, Simon Baker, Cathy Joyce, John Phillips, Ian Williams, Laurie Clayton, Stuart Calder, Paul Neilson, Arthur Jeffrey, John Noakes, David Price, Rob Barnard, David Roberts, Sarah Sanderson, Kevin Leeman, Adèle Brandman, David Milling, Miles King, David Edelstein, Jason Barnes, Peter Kidd, Richard Pocock, Liz Ainley, Bruce Dunning, Marie Dunn, Tracey Wilson, Brewyeen Rowland, Patrick MacMullan, John Pickersgill, John Rothenberg, Chris Watts, Mike Atkinson, Sylvia Carter, Gabby Haynes, Richard Mangan, Alison Rankin, Mark Jonathan, Bella Rodrigues, Jon Driscoll, Trish Montemuro, Brenda Edelstein, Fiona Bardsley, Mary Kidd, Jane Slattery, Anna Stamper, Chris Jones, Joanna Quilley, Jean Green, Hilary Vernon-Smith, Leslie Woolnough, Eugenie Nielson, Terri Anderson, Jude Wheway, Ronnie Merralls, Mark Seaman, Kirsten Shiell, Valerie Fox, Wendy Hall

PHOTO: *Michael Mayhew*

FIG 44 Drawing by Alison Chitty for the production of the Shakespeare Late Plays, directed by Sir Peter Hall (1988). The drawing sketches the setting for the pastoral feast in *The Winter's Tale*.

PART TWO
THE CREATIVE TEAM

ALISON CHITTY

DESIGNING FOR THE COTTESLOE

Based on an interview with Ronnie Mulryne and Margaret Shewring

Alison Chitty has designed over forty plays for the Victoria Theatre, Stoke-on-Trent, and in London has designed for Stratford East, Hampstead, the Riverside Studios and the West End as well as for the RSC and the Royal National Theatre. Her work at the National Studio led to her designing a number of pieces for the Studio's Festival of New Plays in the Cottesloe (1985), including Peter Gill's In the Blue *and Mick Mahoney's* Up for None. *Her major design challenge in the Cottesloe came with working on Peter Hall's productions of the Shakespeare* Late Plays *(1988).*

MY EARLY connections with the Cottesloe came with the work I did for the National Studio, for the Festival of New Plays we mounted in the Cottesloe in 1985. I vividly remember the challenge of working to a small or sometimes (it seemed) non-existent budget, which in turn led to simple design statements, and to ingenious and by necessity economical solutions. The Cottesloe is so wonderfully flexible, one doesn't need to 'cover up' or to 'decorate' the space. It allows the designer and the director to concentrate on the text. For Peter Gill's *In the Blue*, for example, as part of the Festival of New Plays, the design was minimal: a raked, painted floor, five electric blue taut bungies (for tension and atmosphere), two actors and a pile of books. In the Cottesloe it looked wonderful.

As a designer I always work from the text outwards. That is to say, I start from the play-text, respecting the writer, and try to find the essence of the play for the space. I spend time exploring the text with the director, finding out where the performers need to be at any particular moment, and trying to find a space that can help them tell the story in the strongest possible way. I see the job of a set as 'holding' and 'supporting' the actors, and so in turn 'holding' and 'supporting' the narrative. The Cottesloe makes a designer's work a pleasure. Its nature and scale already 'hold' performers in a positive way. All the possible permutations of the actor-audience relationship are already focused there, whereas in the Olivier, for example, it is necessary to add a scenic element between the proscenium and the performer, to help actor and audience alike.

The Cottesloe is a strong space. There are tensions across the space, which derive from its architecture. It holds its performers in *three* dimensions, offering a sculptural space to the designer. In my case, the Cottesloe allowed me to draw on my eight years of experience of theatre-in-the-round with Peter Cheeseman at Stoke-on-Trent. Peter has a passion for the text. He taught me to give emphasis first to the performer, then to the floor, then to any volumes placed within the space, and only then to add other visual elements as appropriate.

One of my largest challenges in the Cottesloe was designing the Shakespeare *Late Plays* for Sir Peter Hall. We used the space almost in end-stage format, trying to see how far it was possible to use the Cottesloe's courtyard design to recreate the shape and atmosphere of a Jacobean private theatre, like the Blackfriars, which Shakespeare must have had in mind when writing these final plays. We wanted to learn from the architectural design of the Blackfriars, and experience these plays in this sort of theatre space.

Peter also wanted some scenic elements that would be appropriate to both then and now. The fact that the three plays, *Cymbeline, The Winter's Tale,* and *The Tempest,* were to be played as a season meant that the basic set-structure had to work for each of them. A major consideration was the need for the gods to descend, as they traditionally did, from 'above', from the 'heavens' (or their equivalent in the Jacobean private theatre). The Cottesloe has no flying system and little space above the stage. We designed a single large scenic element, which could be raised and tilted as needed. (See the drawing on p. 53.) In practical terms, it 'held' the action and 'held' the actors, and it could when necessary disgorge the gods from above. In iconographic terms, it evoked man's perception of his world, a post-Copernican world. It expressed the level of knowledge and understanding at the time the play was written. The iconography drew on the astrological culture of the Jacobeans, which has survived sufficiently to offer a bond between the world of the play and the audience. All the other scenic elements we designed provided a practical equivalent for Shakespeare's inner stage, upper stage and fore stage. They allowed, too, for side entrances, and entrances through the audience to the stage.

I always design costumes as well as sets, which allows me to control an audience's visual experience of a play. Often, the clothes can have more visual power than the sets. For example, a stage full of actors dressed in the black garments and white collars of Puritans creates a monochrome world which can be shattered with just one splash of brilliant colour, a scarf, a handkerchief, a flag. It's like working on an oil painting, gradually controlling the colour and its power. In technical rehearsals you can adjust the colour and orchestrate it by working with the lighting designer. Of course, some plays control the colour palette for you. This is true of the plays of Shakespeare. In all plays costume and colour underpin the narrative, and the designer needs to be sensitive to this.

Colour and shape can have a subconscious effect on the way an audience perceives a play. For example, in *The Winter's Tale* I worked on one palette in the scenes in Sicily, then shifted to a new palette for the Bohemian scenes, and shifted again for the return to Sicily. An overall impression of colour is also enough to suggest period. Of course, it isn't necessary to go in for detailed, historical reconstructions of period clothes – which can be costly and actors often find it difficult to work in them. Most importantly, though, these obsessive reconstructions of originals leave no space for the imagination. They leave no space for the audience to take part and the experience is distanced for them. The events of the play are perceived as something far removed from their lives, the opposite of the main purpose of theatre. Peter Hall wanted in the Shakespeare Late Plays to complement the sense of intimacy offered by an indoor private theatre with a sense of a time of change, and changing ideas and perceptions of the world as expressed by our scenic firmament. So we decided on the Carolinean period, a period of clothes which has a purer line than the Jacobean. This period also had the advantage that the actors had longer breeches, covering their knees!

Peter Gill's work for the Studio Nights and for the Festival of New Plays (1985; see the interview with Sue Higginson, pp. 16–17 in this book) helped to prove the power of the Cottesloe space. It also helped to suggest that simple design solutions can have the greatest potency. Thus, for example, Ewan Hooper did a platform production set on a sea-shore, for which when the tide was out I went down to the riverbed of the Thames and collected all kinds of driftwood and debris, which we then used to make a high water mark in a sweep along the floor of the performance space. This, with a simple deck-chair, was enough and right.

When I returned to the Cottesloe at the end of 1996 I had the opportunity to design a classic Peter Gill production, *Cardiff East* – a very poetic play, a collage, offering glimpses into people's lives, sometimes shocking, sometimes romantic. At first, I felt the play needed a sense of landscape, otherwise it would be too tight and domestic. I built a rough model to look at, trying out the idea of putting the playing area down the long side of the Cottesloe (a Riverside Studio look – where Peter Gill and I did a lot of work together), using the full length of the space. This arrangement would have offered both a vast landscape and a contained space, but we decided it would have been very difficult for the audience, switching their attention from end to end like a crowd at Wimbledon. *Cardiff East* needed to evoke the Cardiff of people's lives and their memories. We finally used the end-stage format, with a large stage of paving stones, stretching from side to side under the overhanging balconies, and from the back wall to under the feet of the front row of the audience. We hung a long pebbledashed back wall with a wonderfully photographic painting of a row of council houses floating in and out of focus in front of the Cardiff East marshes. With fifteen different wooden chairs from different periods over the last fifty years we told the lives of the characters of this community. It's an episodic play with naturalistic requirements, prams, cups of tea and kitchen knives, but the play is poetic and not wedded to naturalism. The design created a visionary, not a literal world.

The Cottesloe repertoire provides an enormous range of design challenges, with perhaps greater potential than elsewhere of possible spatial and visual solutions to those challenges – always an exciting experience for directors, designers, actors and especially for audiences.

FIG 45 Sketch by Alison Chitty for figures in the masque from *The Tempest*.

JOHN CAIRD

DIRECTING IN THE COTTESLOE

Based on an interview with Ronnie Mulryne and Margaret Shewring

John Caird became Associate Director of the Royal Shakespeare Company in 1977 and directed over twenty productions for the Company, including the internationally acclaimed Les Misérables *and* Nicholas Nickleby *(both with Trevor Nunn). At the Swan Theatre in Stratford, he directed two Jonson plays,* Every Man in his Humour *and* The New Inn. *For the National he has directed* Trelawny of the 'Wells', The Seagull *and* Peter Pan. *Caird now has a varied freelance directing and writing career in the theatre, musicals, opera and film, in England and throughout the world. At the Cottesloe, he has directed Pam Gems's play* Stanley *(opened 1.2.96), for a discussion of which* *see pp. 154–161 in this book.*

THE MOST important fact about the Cottesloe is its versatility. It is, though, by no means anonymous, which is rare for a 'black box' space. This is, I think, because of its courtyard design, which, for modern studio theatres, was a bit ahead of its time. Although it uses black and steel and concrete, it is more of a cousin, among RSC theatres, of the timber-built Swan at Stratford than of the underground Pit at the Barbican. There is a real sense of community at the Cottesloe when the audience is in. There are always people above looking down, sitting over the top of the space, witnessing what is going on. It's a practical solution that reminds one of the experiments Grotowski was carrying out in the sixties and seventies.

Pam Gems asked me to look at her play, *Stanley*, with a view to directing it. It had been mooted as a possible West End production, but Pam wasn't happy with that. I agreed to do it. I saw that she had created something very remarkable by using the painter Stanley Spencer to explore what it is to live the life of an artist. There is a strong autobiographical element to it. I showed it to Tony Sher, who is himself an artist in several kinds of work (theatre, writing, painting) and he agreed to play Stanley. The problem was to find the right space. Pam had already written extra narrative scenes to 'explain' the play to a West End audience, but I wasn't convinced that in its original and most challenging form it needed a proscenium arch. I couldn't imagine *Stanley* as an Other Place (Stratford) production – for one thing, it would transfer to the Pit (at the Barbican in London) and it needs far more height and air than the Pit offers. The Cottesloe seemed the ideal space. I showed the play to Richard Eyre and he snapped it up.

Directorially, the answer to *Stanley* was to find a physical correlative for Spencer's whole life. The solution came to me quite suddenly, in the Cottesloe, the first time the designer Tim Hatley and I went into the space together. The play is episodic. Pam plays brilliantly with time, so that five years can pass in the middle of a scene, or two babies can appear within one page of the script. It wouldn't work to break up each section of the piece into 'filmable' units, where time has only one value. It would fragment the play dramaturgically, and you'd never get a sense of flow. The idea of representing Stanley's life and Stanley's work, and of accommodating the play, by placing them in a church-like setting came to me sitting in the theatre itself. The space is like a church nave, a rectangular shape like a non-conformist chapel of the mid-nineteenth century. Pam emphasised in her play Stanley's phrase, 'the church of me'. He wanted a Hilda chapel, a Patricia chapel, a 'me' chapel, following Wilde's dictum that your life and your art are one. Stanley genuinely saw his artistic life in terms of a quasi-theological whole, Father, Son and Holy Ghost, Virgin, Mother, Whore. His life was, by his own lights, a lived Gospel. It followed that one could use the theatre as if one were performing in a church, one could draw on the fact that much of Stanley's work was in churches or about churches, and one could even have him *living* in a church while he was painting, with his bed and chair and stove there too. The audience's perception of Stanley needed to be partly theatrical and partly liturgical, with the kind of intimate relationship you get during the Mass between the people and the celebrants.

Stanley talked of sex in religious terms, as ritual or sacrament. How do you do a play with so much physical and emotional nakedness? In a theatre like the Haymarket or Wyndhams (in London's West End), you would have to disguise the play's nakedness. When nudity is used in a proscenium-arch theatre it often leads to a sense almost of aggression on the actors' part – it takes nerve to perform in those circumstances, and actors use various devices to accommodate themselves, the most common of which is to assume a kind of physical and moral superiority over the onlookers. But with the audience so close in the Cottesloe it made the onlookers almost uncomfortable about being in the same room as the performers. I wanted that frisson of discomfort, making it impossible for the actors or the audience to hide. In the Cottesloe, the intimate emotional scenes and physical nakedness are so close that an 'attitude' is not needed, and scarcely possible. Fascination, shyness, nervousness are all allowed. Sexuality and nakedness become entirely unprurient, as they do in a Spencer painting.

The other main challenge to a director was to get the play flowing. Pam has scenes merging into one another without any indication of a change of place and without any break in the action. In the same way, people and events flow into and out of some of Spencer's famous canvasses. People in fact sometimes appear more than once in the same painting. The production tried to echo that quality, where the normal bounds between reality and perceived reality are not applicable. Tim Hatley used all the paintings we were allowed to use for his design (though Spencer's daughters refused permission for all of the paintings in which they hold the copyright). In that way we tried to incorporate the essential qualities of Spencer's work and of his experience of life.

I love the Cottesloe space. It's a pleasure to work in it. In fact, I have loved it ever since seeing *Illuminatus*, the very first production, on stage there.

FIG 46 The Townspeople in front of the pastoral backcloth in *Fuente Ovejuna,* directed by Declan Donnellan and designed by Nick Ormerod (1992).
PHOTO: *John Haynes*

NICK ORMEROD

DESIGN AND THE SPACE

Nick Ormerod has been stage designer for, and co-director of, Cheek by Jowl since he founded the company with Declan Donnellan. He was trained at Wimbledon School of Art, and has designed many shows for the National Theatre in both the Olivier and the Cottesloe, including Fuente Ovejuna, Angels in America, Peer Gynt, Millennium Approaches (*Time Out Award for Best Design*), and Sweeney Todd. *He has recently designed* School for Scandal *for the RSC. He has designed* Macbeth *and* Philoctetes *for the Finnish National Theatre and* The Rise and Fall of the City of Mahagonny *for the English National Opera. In 1988 he received an Olivier Award Nomination for Designer of the Year.*

THE SPECIAL thing about the Cottesloe is its magical combination of the epic and the intimate, a combination Declan Donnellan and I tried to achieve in the production of *Fuente Ovejuna.* Our first impulse on entering the space was to use a traverse stage, as we eventually did, so providing long, sweeping runs down the length of the space for the actors, together with an opportunity to focus on a few performers using the centre of the space. The Cottesloe had not really been used in traverse before, so that much of our budget went on buying seating for the audience on either side of the performance space. The traverse configuration also allowed us to develop the idea of the play as a performance before the King and Queen of Spain, who sat at one end of the traverse, balanced by the rural life of the village, with its drop curtain depicting the rural landscape, at the other. (*see left*)

When a traverse is used, each member of the audience sees the action from a different perspective. This in turn puts a great deal of emphasis on the actors' presence in the space. The Cottesloe is thought of as the National Theatre's small auditorium, but in fact the space is relatively large, so that the visual emphasis on the actors is crucial. The actors need to engage with each member of the audience, including those on the sides and those in the gallery. It is important to use the height of the space, as well as the length of the traverse, if the energy and engagement of the piece are to be sustained.

As a designer, I find I work best when I can work with a three-dimensional grouping of actors. The more I try to concentrate on two-dimensional pictures, the less successful the work is. The Cottesloe is perfect for this three-dimensional approach, since it is so wonderfully flexible and hospitable to groupings of actors, giving them the opportunity to make up the most striking images. The architects have not intruded or imposed a pattern on the space, allowing the actors to energise it by their performance.

I have also designed for the Cottesloe as an end stage, for both *Sweeney Todd* and *Angels in America* (see p.39). It is undoubtedly one of the great spaces among contemporary theatres, offering a variety of both two-dimensional and three-dimensional perspectives. Declan and I chose the Cottesloe for *Sweeney* and *Angels*, and there can be no doubt that the space had a magical effect on the energy of the performance. When we transferred *Sweeney* to the Lyttelton, the engagement of actor and audience very noticeably altered and declined.

The restriction of technical resources and the absence of large budgets at the Cottesloe turn out to be an advantage. You have to make shows work without relying on elements other than the actors. This also leads to inventive use of what resources there are. For example, in *Sweeney* we used a mobile bridge which moved from the back of the end-stage space right up to the audience, and mobile, sliding walls around it. Jason Barnes's technical skills made this possible – indeed the show looked to the audience very technically advanced, even though the devices used to achieve the effects were actually very simple.

Music is central to our kind of theatre, but usually we allow it to emerge as an organic part of the creative process rather than imposing it as a separate effect. Again, this maintains the focus on the performer. For *Sweeney* we placed a band on the first gallery, where they remained throughout the show, an arrangement that proved very satisfactory. For *Fuente Ovejuna*, we both instinctively knew that the long traverse was right in allowing the maximum space for movement and choreography, and for the musical elements to emerge and be received as part of the whole experience.

Some designers leave the directors to talk to the lighting designers, who then get on with the business of lighting the show. On the whole, Declan asks me to work with the lighting team. I don't 'design' the lighting, but I usually work with a lighting team I know well, and whose work I trust. The result is, we hope, a show designed in a consistent and cohesive way.

Putting such a strong emphasis on the performers means that my engagement with design extends throughout the rehearsal period. Some solutions are only found quite late in the process. This has its risks, but I have learned over the years which design problems need to be solved in advance, and which can be left till late in rehearsal. It's for audiences to decide how successful our practices are.

FIG 47 Cast members of *Sweeney Todd*, directed by Declan Donnellan and designed by Nick Ormerod (1993), showing the main stage and upper level. Left to right: Stephen Hanley, Martin Nelson, Ernestina Quarcoo, Di Botcher, Megan Kelly, Philip Curtis, Antoni Garfield Henry, Nick Holder.
PHOTO: *John Haynes*

SIMON RUSSELL BEALE

PLAYING THE COTTESLOE

Simon Russell Beale began his acting career at the Traverse Theatre in Edinburgh before going to the Royal Lyceum, Edinburgh, to play Osric in Hamlet. *His London career began with William Gaskill's production of* Women Beware Women *at the Royal Court, after which he spent many years with the RSC at Stratford and the Barbican playing such roles as Ariel, Richard III, Edward II, Edgar, Thersites and Konstantin* (The Seagull). *At the Royal National Theatre he has played Guildenstern in* Rosencrantz and Guildenstern are Dead, *Mosca in Matthew Warchus's production of* Volpone *(1996 Olivier Award for Best Supporting Actor) and, in the Cottesloe, Iago in Sam Mendes's production of* Othello *(nominated for the 1997 Olivier Award for Best Actor). Simon has also worked widely in the West End, television, radio and film.*

I REMEMBER my first visit to the Cottesloe, as a member of an audience, very clearly. Not so much for the performance, excellent though it was, as for the sense of excitement I felt as I entered the theatre. The National Theatre was presenting a performance of Bill Bryden's now-famous production of *The Mystery Plays*, designed by William Dudley. There were no seats at ground-floor level for this promenade performance, and the audience was allowed to go almost where it pleased. I wandered around the theatre under a panoply of kitchen utensils and workmen's tools that were hung from the ceiling and glittered under the lighting like tinsel. It was like being inside a Christmas decoration.

I had just decided to train as an actor, and though hugely inexperienced as a theatre-goer, and filled with the usual unspecific ambitions of a new student, I knew that this was the sort of theatre I wanted to be involved in, that this was where I wanted to work.

Years later, I played Iago in a production of *Othello* at the Cottesloe. And the thrill was still there. This rather grand studio space has always been proud to present experimental and exploratory work, but, partly as a result of a history of audience expectation, each night is something of an event. Will Patrick Marber's second play be as good as his first? What will Ian Holm do with King Lear? What will Tom Stoppard do next? How will the designer

FIG 48 Simon Russell Beale as Iago and David Harewood as Othello in Sam Mendes's production of *Othello* (1997), designed by Anthony Ward.
PHOTO: *Mark Douet*

use the space? Promenade, three sides, traverse, in the round? Excited anticipation should be a part of the atmosphere in any theatre foyer, of course, but the tradition of work in the Cottesloe seems to breed a confidence in both audience and practitioners that, despite a few failures, what they will see or present will be of quality.

Of course, this confidence is a result primarily of a *relatively* well-subsidised National Theatre. Good work anywhere needs care, attention, and, above all, time. But the Cottesloe is also a place that actors like to work in. It is, like the RSC's The Other Place, intimate – especially from the audience's perspective – and that always feels good. It is very adaptable – which means that it is actor-friendly. It is also a large and high room that surprisingly needs a great deal of the performance energy required in theatres that are more obviously majestic. For a great classical play like *Othello* it is an almost perfect space.

I cannot, obviously, predict the Cottesloe's future. But a theatre this hospitable should and must thrive.

IAN McKELLEN

FIG 49 Sir Ian McKellen as Ivan Petrovich Voynitsky (Uncle Vanya) in the 1992 production of Anton Chekhov's *Uncle Vanya*, in a new version by Pam Gems, directed by Sean Mathias, designed by Stephen Brimson Lewis. Sir Ian writes (privately): '*Uncle Vanya* felt wondrous to be in. It was devised in the National Theatre's Studio and fitted the Cottesloe's intimacy so snugly.'
PHOTO: *Mark Douet*

Fig 50 Brian Glover as God on the fork-lift-truck 'maypole' with radiating streamers depicting the elements of Creation.

THE MYSTERIES

THE MYSTERIES (*The Nativity, The Passion, Doomsday*)
A version of the English Medieval Mystery Plays by Tony Harrison and the company.

Directors	*Bill Bryden* and *Sebastian Graham-Jones*
Design	*William Dudley*
Lighting	*William Dudley* and *Laurence Clayton*
Music Director	*John Tams*
Dance	*David Busby*
Sound	*Chris Montgomery*
Production Manager	*Jason Barnes*
Photography	*Nobby Clark* and *Michael Mayhew*

The Company (*in alphabetical order*)

	The Nativity	**The Passion**	**Doomsday**
Brenda Blethyn or Dinah Stabb	Mary	Mary Magdalene	Mary Magdalene
David Busby	Morris Dancer	Disciple	Angel
Jim Carter	Mak	Fourth Soldier	Fourth Soldier
Edna Doré	Mrs Noah	Mary Mother	Mary Mother
Christopher Gilbert	Wise Man	Simon of Cyrene	Disciple
Brian Glover	God	Cayphas	God
Howard Goorney	Noah	John Baptist	Paul
James Grant	Wise Man	Peter	Peter
Dave Hill	Joseph	Third Soldier	Third Soldier
Karl Johnson	Abel	Jesus	Jesus
Phil Langham	Disciple	Angel	
Eve Matheson	Eve	Mary Salome	Eve
Derek Newark	Abraham/Wise Man	First Soldier	First Soldier
Robert Oates	Cain	Barrabas	Disciple
Stephen Petcher	Adam/Isaac/Shepherd	Blind Man	John
Trevor Ray	Shepherd	Second Soldier	Second Soldier
Jack Shepherd	Lucifer	Judas	Satan
Robert Stephens	Herod	Pontius Pilate	Pontius Pilate
John Tams	Shepherd	Thomas	Thomas
Anthony Trent	Herod's Son	Annas	Annas
Don Warrington	Angel Gabriel	Angel Gabriel	Angel Gabriel

Music by The Home Service: Bill Caddick (guitar, vocals), Jonathan Davie (bass, vocals), Howard Evans (trumpets), Michael Gregory (percussion), Stephen King (keyboards), Graeme Taylor (guitar), Roger Williams (trombone, tuba), with Andrew Findon (flute, saxophones), Phil Langham (accordion, vocals), Philip Pickett (woodwind), and Linda Thompson (vocals).

This production of *The Mysteries* opened at the Cottesloe on 19 January 1985 (previews from 12.12.84) and ran in repertoire until 20.4.85. It transferred to the Lyceum (refurbished for this show) opening on 18.5.85 and running until 3.8.85. The first of the series of three plays, *The Passion*, opened at the Cottesloe on 19.4.77, running until 28.4.77; excerpts were also played on the terraces of the National Theatre, the first at Easter 1977. It was revived at the Cottesloe on 26.9.77 and again on 8.8.78, running until 2.9.78. A revised version, in two parts (*Creation to Nativity* and *Nativity to Judgement*), was staged at the Edinburgh International Festival (Assembly Hall and street locations, 18–30 August, 1980). The first part of the revised version opened at the Cottesloe on 23.9.80 (previews from 19.9.80) and ran until 17.10.80. *The Passion Part Two* (with the title *Baptism to Judgement*) opened at the Cottesloe on 24.9.80 (previews from 20.9.80) and ran until 18.10.80. A third play, *The Nativity*, employing material from the existing plays, opened at the Cottesloe on 16.12.80 and ran until 28.1.81. A European tour of *The Nativity* and *The Passion* took place in mid-1981, including performances in Rome and at the Kirche Gross St Martin, Cologne. The production was also staged at the Vivian Beaumont Theatre, Lincoln Center, New York.

The 1985 revival, under the general title *The Mysteries*, comprised three parts, *The Nativity, The Passion, Doomsday*. All three parts were filmed for Channel 4 television.

'THE MYSTERIES'
STAGING AND SCENOGRAPHY AT THE COTTESLOE AND ELSEWHERE

Jason Barnes

In April 1977, for the first of five major works to be staged in promenade form, the Cottesloe was transformed rather to brewhouse than to the 'kitchen' to which Peter Hall had referred at a company meeting earlier in the year. The occasion resulted from the suggestion of the English poet Tony Harrison, who proposed an exciting, and certainly challenging, twentieth-century adaptation of a selection from the medieval English Mystery Plays, drawn largely from the York and Chester Cycles of the late fourteenth and fifteenth centuries.

In presenting *The Mysteries*, Bill Bryden wanted to reflect the traditional staging method of using carts that had originally toured the streets of York or Chester, pausing to perform individual parts of the Bible stories at selected locations, some, it seems likely, with specially-constructed platforms. We needed a sense of popular jostling town life, together with a feeling of progression necessary to recreate in a modern idiom the development of the Christian story from Creation to Last Judgement.

Bill Dudley and I examined the shallow-rise end-stage seating layout which had been used for the first two productions in the Cottesloe. By removing all the seats from the lower pit section of the theatre to a chair store in the basement, and turning over the rear rostra blocks into the front, deeper, portion of the void, we provided a 9.9m (32'6") square playing area 2 feet below stage level. This kind of sunken garden, enclosed by the loose-railed seating units (which in turn could be used as required as raised playing areas – the Mystery Cart equivalents), offered a sufficient vantage over the audience promenading at the lower level. Overhead, the two upper galleries, thronging with both seated and standing spectators, recreated the upper windows of what would originally have been surrounding buildings and balconies, filled with sporting faces, eager to catch the festive attraction. In modern terms, these upper levels are not unlike the upper floors of a shopping centre, or London's restored central market hall in Covent Garden, now itself a lively mix of puppet performances, spontaneous dance and street theatre, combined with the bustle of a public market place.

Beginnings

The first selection from *The Mysteries* to be staged, entitled 'The Passion', covered stories from the New Testament, from Christ's Baptism to the Crucifixion, and embodied music by the Albion Band (led by Ashley Hutchings and John Tams), with participation in the action by the musicians. Having created a playing space in the lower central pit, we needed to accommodate the band in a focal way, and to provide an upper performance space. To effect this, Bill Dudley chose to build the bottom half of a 'fourth wall', as proposed by Iain Mackintosh as part of his 1973 design study, and subsequently used in *The Beggar's Opera*, *A View from the Bridge*, and *Ma Rainey's Black Bottom* (*see* p. 22 above). Mackintosh had suggested this 'fourth wall' as a device for reducing the need for scenery – and increasing the focus – in a space where there should be an opportunity to experiment with the power of performance alone. Such a bridge, Mackintosh proposed, would be available to actors or spectators, and, had it been able to travel up and down stage, would alter the volume of the performance space.

The bridge for *The Passion* linked the ends of the existing galleries, and could be reached via them, or by stairs from the stage below. The band was sited upstage, beneath this fourth central gallery, which also provided a very strong upper focus, particularly for the Herod Scenes, and for the Crucifixion play. In this episode, the Roman Soldiers, having nailed Christ to the full-sized and very heavy cross, could just manage to haul it vertical, and fix it securely, for the twenty minutes the actor playing Christ must remain aloft. The soldiers' dialogue in the original text refers to mortise and wedges, and these indeed proved mechanically necessary in stabilizing the cross in this re-enactment five centuries later.

The Cottesloe itself provided an exciting physical environment for this project. Parallels were drawn in preparing the show between the modern staging and the original fluid backdrop of the spectators, the raised levels of the carts themselves, and the focusing element of the onlookers overhead. Decoration of the space, and the creation of atmosphere through lighting, were the final touches necessary to creating the performance circumstances we needed.

The plays had been written originally for the contemporary trade guilds. Bill Bryden saw the new version as a twentieth-century celebration by ordinary working people of the greatest story ever told. High above the upper gallery, Dudley placed nineteenth-century Trade Union banners, in faithful full-sized reproductions, prepared in the National Theatre's workshops, with the help of John Gorman. Gorman's definitive

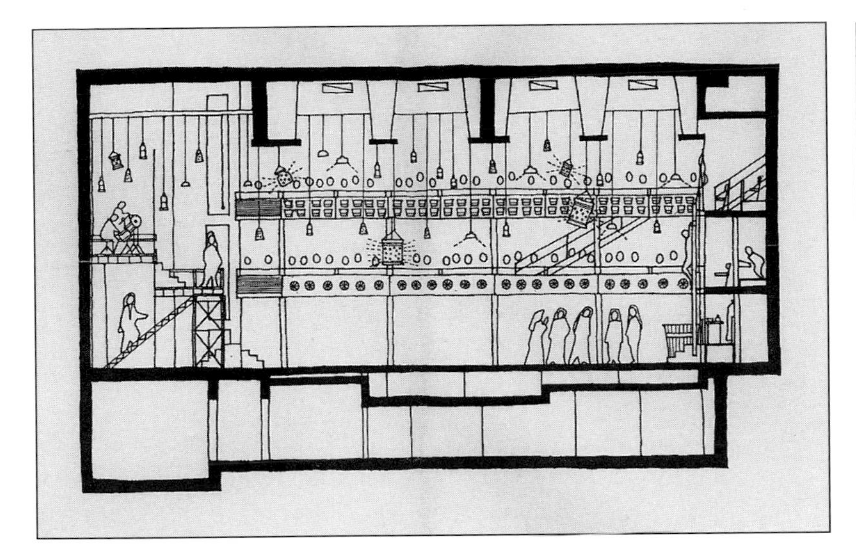

FIG 51 Vertical plan of the Cottesloe for *The Mysteries*.

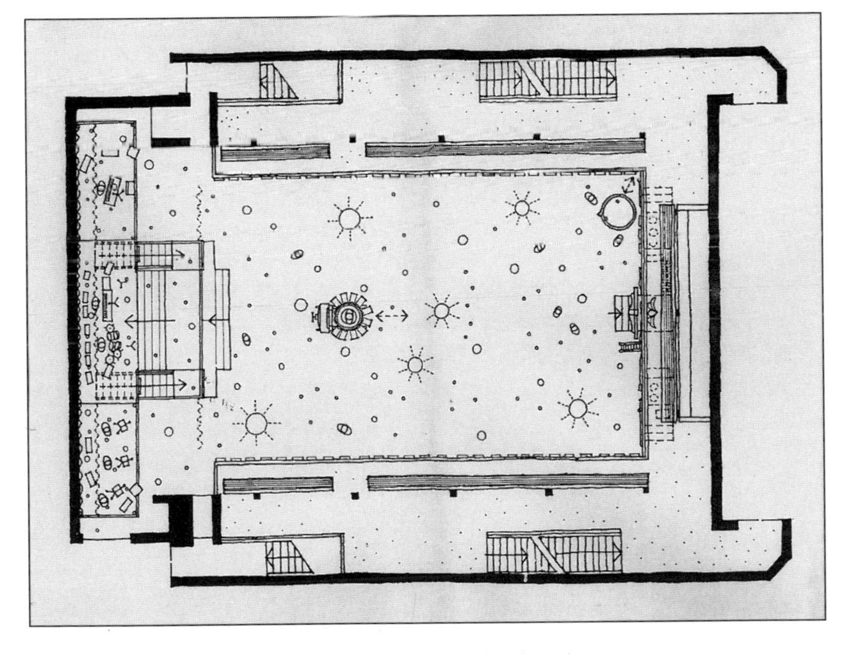

FIG 52 Floor plan of the Cottesloe for *The Mysteries*.

book, *Banner Bright*, contains many beautiful colour plates from which Bill chose appropriate banners for the plasterers, bakers and nail-makers who had traditionally and appropriately presented the Creation play, the Last Supper, and the Crucifixion.

Programme Notes
Ronnie Mulryne

The Scripts

THE VERSIONS of the Mystery Plays performed at the Cottesloe were adapted from edited texts of the medieval English plays collected as the York, Wakefield, Chester, and 'N-Town' (previously 'Coventry') cycles. From 1977 to 1985 (see detailed chronology on p. 71), the Cottesloe company under Bill Bryden developed a series of one-, two- and three-play performances, beginning with a brief Crucifixion play presented on the open-air terraces of the National at Easter 1977, and culminating in a three-play 'cycle' given in repertoire in the Cottesloe at Christmas and New Year, 1984–85.

The English Mystery Plays take their material from Biblical and extra-Biblical narratives, in complete form telling the story of mankind from Creation to Last Judgement. The playscripts were originally compiled and performed by members of the trade guilds of leading towns (the term 'mystery' means 'craft'), working with writers and with actors specialising in the more important roles. In working out the final shaping of the performance with the Cottesloe company, Bill Bryden was paralleling the role of the medieval trade guilds, though, like their forebears, the modern company created the performance in association with professional writers, principally Tony Harrison. Sharing of responsibilities in this way seemed to Bryden to justify Godfrey Matthews' description of the plays as 'the most democratic thing in English literature ... of the people, by the people, for the people'. (*The Chester Mystery Plays*, 1925)

The plays, performed from the fourteenth to the sixteenth centuries, were presented normally at the feast of Corpus Christi (the first Thursday after Trinity Sunday, in late May or early June), as part of the Procession of the Host (or 'body of Christ'). Typically, two-tier pageant carts were used as stages, either hauled manually from station to station on the processional route, with the play performed several times, or with the carts drawn up around an open space (such as the cathedral square). In either case, performance would take place both on the cart, which carried a stage setting or scenic elements, and on the immediately surrounding area (or '*platea*').

The textual re-ordering and limited modernisation by Tony Harrison can be seen as carrying on a process already evident in the medieval playscripts themselves, many of which show signs of re-writing and revision as audiences and doctrines changed. Nor was the original *mise-en-scene* crude. Documents show that sets, props and special effects (such as the Red Sea or the destruction of the world) were as fully developed as current technology allowed. The skills of the various crafts, for example the carpenters and nail makers at the crucifixion, or the bakers at the Last Supper, ensured that action and running props were as convincing, practically or symbolically, as craftsmanship could make them. The ambitious technology of the Cottesloe's Ferris Wheel (for the Last Judgment) was therefore just as appropriate to the original texts as the medley of household utensils employed for the lighting.

Haze from a smoke machine, running gently throughout the performance in order to replenish smoke drawn off by the air conditioning, was punctured by a firmament of twinkling orange lights, housed in early twentieth-century kitchen and household articles – cheesegraters, paraffin stoves, sieves, colanders and dustbins, each containing a flickering neon candle lamp. This unusual lighting rig gave the overall impression of a candle-lit barn, with a distinct feeling of a Byzantine Church. In the first version of *The Passion* in 1977, no production lighting units were used at all, with the exception of one beam light, which reflected from a circular prop mirror held by the Angel Gabriel, and sent a shaft of contrasting white light from above the heads of the audience down to the figure of Christ at prayer in the Garden of Gethsemane.

Edinburgh

This first production of *The Passion* remained in the repertoire, including two revivals, for 63 performances from April 1977 to October 1978. In August 1980, we added a second programme consisting of adaptations of many of the Old Testament stories, beginning with the Creation and running up to and including the Nativity. This opened initially at the Assembly Hall in Edinburgh for the International Festival. Iain Mackintosh points out that the nineteenth-century Assembly Hall of the Church of Scotland had been converted into what was in effect the first major open-stage theatre in the English speaking world when it was employed by Tyrone Guthrie in 1948 for his production of *The Three Estaites*, following a city-wide search. His thrust stage had proved a resounding success, and became the progenitor of 'a whole new generation of theatres, all linked to Guthrie ... the Stratford Festival Theatre, Ontario; the Tyrone Guthrie Theatre, Minneapolis; the Young Vic, London, and the Crucible, Sheffield.' (Iain Mackintosh, *Architects Journal*, 1972)

In common with all stagings at the Assembly Hall, the 50 foot by 50 foot Promenade 'Arena' for *The Mysteries* had to be raised considerably to skim over the sacred Church of Scotland's Moderator's dais and surrounding balustrade. (This remained the case until the visit of the Cottesloe production of *Fuente Ovejuna* in 1992, when for the first time the Church was persuaded to allow a dismantling of the balustrade – a comparatively easy job as it turned out!). However, as in many eighteenth- and nineteenth-century 'Italian' theatres, where the stage is level with the floor of the rear stalls, the enforced arena height for *The Mysteries* was almost level with the rear surrounding walkways, which normally led to the pew seating for the General Assembly of the Church. By boarding over the normal aisles with gently sloping runways, the promenading audience of 400, and the cast, could reach the central space. A further 600 viewed from the existing gallery on three sides, although many who had paid a higher price regretted not being with the promenaders below. Raising the arena undoubtedly improved the gallery sightlines, and helped minimize the black-hole effect of the rear pew areas, unused except for property storage during the performance.

FIG 53 Noah's Ark in the Cottesloe with Edna Doré as Mrs Noah and Howard Goorney as Noah.

London again

For *The Nativity* in Edinburgh, Bill Dudley had designed elements which could be introduced among the promenaders from storage positions on each side of the arena. These could be handled by cast or crew, but needed a level playing area, which required filling in the Cottesloe's lower pit level when *The Nativity* and *The Passion* returned to London to play in the repertoire. This posed a problem for larger items, though items needing less head room would pass under the mid-level seating galleries, which offered a clearance of 2.2m. Presenting Brian Glover's God above the crowd set some design challenges. A twentieth-century solution was clearly appropriate: a scarlet fork-lift truck bearing a crow's nest radiating white shafts of light, like a salutary lighthouse. The whole basket arrangement strapped to the forks of the truck provided an off-the-peg, mobile *deus ex machina*. The truck was manoeuvred among the crowd by theatre technicians wearing boiler suits suitably emblazoned with the name of ROLATRUC, the company who had kindly lent the truck – industrial sponsorship after all had been a feature of the Passion Plays for over 500 years!

Some further adjustments were required. The larger promenading space resulting from these post-Edinburgh changes needed a little more con-

FIG 54 The Crucifixion scene with Karl Johnson as Jesus, Eve Matheson as Mary Salome, Edna Doré as Mary Mother, Lynn Farleigh as Mary Magdalene and Stephen Petcher as John.

trol over the lighting of the actors' faces, and 100 small 'minuet' spotlights were added discreetly among the flickering junk overhead.

Dance has always formed a significant part of traditional drama. For the Creation play, Bill Dudley with dance director Dave Busby con-

(*Programme Notes continued from page 73*)

It is not only in the work of identifiable writers such as the Wakefield master or the York realist that the dramatic power and theatrical sophistication of the cycle plays emerge. Reviewing the 1985 three-play promenade season, John Peter wrote: 'There is nothing quite like these plays in any other literature: they combine theological sophistication, theatrical craftsmanship, a robust realism and a sense of freewheeling imagination which is both deeply original and deeply English ... They are that rare thing, a genuine popular theatre, both serious and entertaining, and speaking with the language of the people who created them and played in them'. (*Sunday Times*, 27.1.85)

Tony Harrison: writer

Born in Leeds in 1937, the son of a baker, Tony Harrison became progressively alienated from his roots as a result of his education at grammar school and at Leeds university, where he read classics. 'The poet,' he says, 'should have a similar mission to the historian of "rescuing from silence the class into which he was born, and to articulate for them certain moments of the past."' (Interview with Peter Lennon, *Times*, 21.12.84) Invited by Bill Bryden to adapt the Mysteries he agreed 'so long as he could give God and Jesus Yorkshire accents – the accents they would have had in those medieval pageants'. 'These are local northern classics,' he said, 'that have been taken away from northerners and betrayed, made genteel.' (Interview with Hugh Hebert, *Guardian*, 18.1.85)

Harrison took the job of adapting the Mysteries seriously but by no means solemnly. 'When we talk about faith in the Middle Ages being simple and its drama crude,' he said, 'that's wrong. The drama is more brilliantly written than it's given credit for ... From broad farce to sermon – they could encompass the whole range. ... This drama had the task of pleasing and instructing at the same time. We've lost that. Our plays of instruction – political plays – can end up being very solemn.' (*Guardian*, 18.1.85)

Harrison's translations of the *Oresteia* (1981), of Molière's *Le Misanthrope* (1973) and Racine's *Phèdre* (1975) were all considerable successes at the National. He sees his tasks of translation and adaptation in a self-effacing light, insisting that 'I use a kind of translator's judo. It's not pugilistics. You don't batter the original into submission, you use the weight of its political assumptions'. (*Times*, 21.12.84) In each case, he considers the pulse of the theatrical language to be of prime importance. His adaptation of *The Mysteries* accordingly preserves the alliterative emphasis of the original, right from the opening speeches of God and Lucifer. 'Later the rhythms and the alliteration get subtler, but they are always there, crashing out in fierce hard-edged consonants from the villains, lilting softer sounds for the women.' (*Guardian*, 18.1.85)

Harrison says he is the man who comes to read the metre. But this is no small task. 'If I could separate my intelligence from my heart,' he says of his work at large, 'my intelligence receives very grim pictures of the world and has an enormous tendency to pessimism. It seems to me that the strong rhythms I employ are a way of preserving a momentum into optimism, even though my mind is registering nightmares.' (*Times*, 21.12.84) *The Mysteries*, likewise, as they survey the destiny of man from cradle to grave,

FIG 55 The Tree of Knowledge of Good and Evil with Stephen Petcher (Adam) and Eve Matheson (Eve).

FIG 56 The *Doomsday* 'ferris wheel' with the damned writhing in torment.

ceived an elaborate maypole dance. Brian Glover's God slowly ascended five metres in the fork-lift crow's nest, providing the 'maypole', while silk streamers unrolled bearing images of birds, fishes and other creatures. On the theatre floor, the company interwove in an accelerating traditional dance until the radiating beams of light from the ascending framework flashed across the faces of the spectators on the surrounding galleries. A tremendous enclosure of excited faces had become a living environment, in which we could share the very beginning of the world.

There were other scenes for which Bill Dudley needed greater height in the new programme. The tree of life for the Creation play followed the twentieth-century style: a low stacker truck, also donated by Rolatruc, carried a bright-blue fibreglass garden pond filled with earth-coloured cork chippings, from which at God's bidding emerged, like Venus from her shell, the clay-clad naked forms of Adam and Eve. (One ground-floor shower room had to be reserved for their clean-up, a tell-tale track of terracotta footprints betraying its location.) Over the pair, from a shuttered concrete column sprouted re-enforcing rods, which bowed over into the branches of the tree of life. These were formed from aluminium conductors of high-tension electric cables, with the insulation stripped back to reveal their primary colours. Hung on the bouncing twigs were spinning apples with piercing barbs, the fruit of the tree of the knowledge of good and evil. To accommodate the height of this and other scenic devices, the upstage fourth-wall bridge gave way to a higher scaffolding walkway, and the band moved up from stage level, where they had been in the first season, releasing valuable storage space. A raised platform in front of the bridge giving better sight lines for some static scenes, and a framework for securing the cross, moved downstage to double with the Last Supper platforms.

Certain conclusions can be derived from this experience of promenade work. The inclusion of a rectangular or circular dance form by performers, with perhaps spectators as well, needed a central area of about 30 feet diameter. On a flat floor, the public were able to 'back off' under the galleries, to re-converge for the development of the next scene. Most plays need space away from the action for entrances and exits. In the absence of approaches from outside the auditorium, it was possible to create these entrances between or below upper seated areas. 'God's bin', however, as the fork lift became known, required 50mm chopped off the house-light shades under the Cottesloe's galleries. Due to its length, Noah's ark, a kit-form keel and curved ribs, carved out of demolition timber, and secured with turned wooden pins into a skeletal boat-shape by the cast, provided another sort of problem, one of storage. All the properties, furniture and featured items had to store in remote corners of what would normally be audience circulation. Directors Bill Bryden and Sebastian Graham-Jones, and their stage manager John Caulfield, had to anticipate in the rehearsal room what space would be available in performance, by marking the outline of the theatre, the fire-safety routes, and a reinforced path for the fork lift truck, which weighed over half a ton.

Doomsday and after

In January 1985, a third and final part of the story, 'Doomsday', took us from the Crucifixion to the end of the world. Bill Dudley again remodelled the upstage bridge and band platform, this time into a two-level extension of the theatre's galleries. He also introduced another spectacular design item. In this final production, imperceptible within the framework in parts one and two, and covered over until the last section of *Doomsday*, was a 'ferris wheel' 6m in diameter and 1.2m deep, dressed with a gilded-aluminium global grid. Within it, suspended on body harnesses, nine actors writhed in torment, as the whole globe turned, their contortions backed by showers of welding sparks and a cataclysmic score from the band. Doomsday approached.

In this revival we embarked for the first time on what were christened 'Epic Days' by our devoted company executive, Michael Hallifax. In these, all three parts were given in one day, an epic undertaking indeed! The complete cycle opened to the press in January 1985, and played what was to become at the time the closing season of the Cottesloe, since at the end of the run, on 20 April, 1985, we ceased operations for six months, due to lack of Arts Council funds.

When the theatre closed for live performance, plans were already well advanced for the company and staff to record the whole cycle for Channel

(*Programme Notes continued from page 75*)

from creation to doomsday, employ the rhythmic energy of their language to transform tragedy into festival.

Brian Glover: performer

The down-to-earth and demotically humorous qualities Bryden was looking for in *The Mysteries* were memorably incorporated by the casting of Brian Glover as God. The son of a professional wrestler, and for twenty years a professional wrestler himself, Glover was a Yorkshireman who spoke with a strong Yorkshire accent, and represented in his appearance and manner a thoroughly unconventional notion of God. 'The first strange pleasure', wrote Michael Ratcliffe of a Cottesloe performance, 'was to watch the polished pink scalp of an egg-bald God ... moving through the cosmos of shining tin without cutting itself on the stars as he created the world in a thick Yorkshire accent from the top of a fork-lift truck. "Ego sum alpha et omega," he declared to the milling spectators below and then, with a hint of exasperation lest we had missed the point, "Nowt is but I".' (*Observer*, 27.1.85)

Glover's stage work before *The Mysteries* included a spell at the Royal Court under Lindsay Anderson, playing especially in pieces by David Storey, followed by fourteen months with the Royal Shakespeare Company at Stratford, where his first main part was as Charles the wrestler in *As You Like It*. He also played frequently on television, and wrote scripts for stage and film. Sadly, Brian Glover died before this book could be published.

Looking at the Mysteries

William Dudley's design for *The Mysteries* was comprehensive, inventive and busy. Michael Ratcliffe referred to 'actors who leap, jump and sway under a smoky orange firmament flickering with lamps built from punctured utensils of everyday life – dustbins, braziers, colanders, graters, paraffin stoves, compost burners and hurricane lamps. Above these, the decorative banners of unions and guilds billow down like great sails from the universe beyond.' (*Observer*, 27.1.85) Michael Coveney too noticed with appreciation the exuberance of the overhead design elements: 'William Dudley has hung a glittering firmament of twinkling orange braziers, dustbins, lights and lamps from the roof, while colourful union banners decorate the top tier and the two balconies are fitted out with heraldic badges of the guilds and industrial implements.' (*Financial Times*, 21.1.85).

The overhanging firmament was not just decorative. Francis King (*Sunday Telegraph*, 27.1.85) drew out some of the visual conflicts and paradoxes: 'What could be more simple and homely than that, at one's first entrance, the auditorium, transformed into a murky guildhall, should be illuminated by flickering candlelight from an amazing assortment of colanders, graters and perforated dustbins, that Jesus and Mary should ascend to Heaven on forklift trucks, and that Noah's passengers should cower under modern umbrellas? But what could be more sophisticated than the vast ferris-wheel, representing a hollow world, inside which, as it inexorably revolves, the damned are seen writhing and jerking in torment?' The high- and low-tech inventions of the third play, *Doomsday*, attracted particular attention. Michael Billington (*Guardian*, 21.1.85) relished the serious absurdities of the visuals: 'Adam and Eve emerge from 4,600 years in

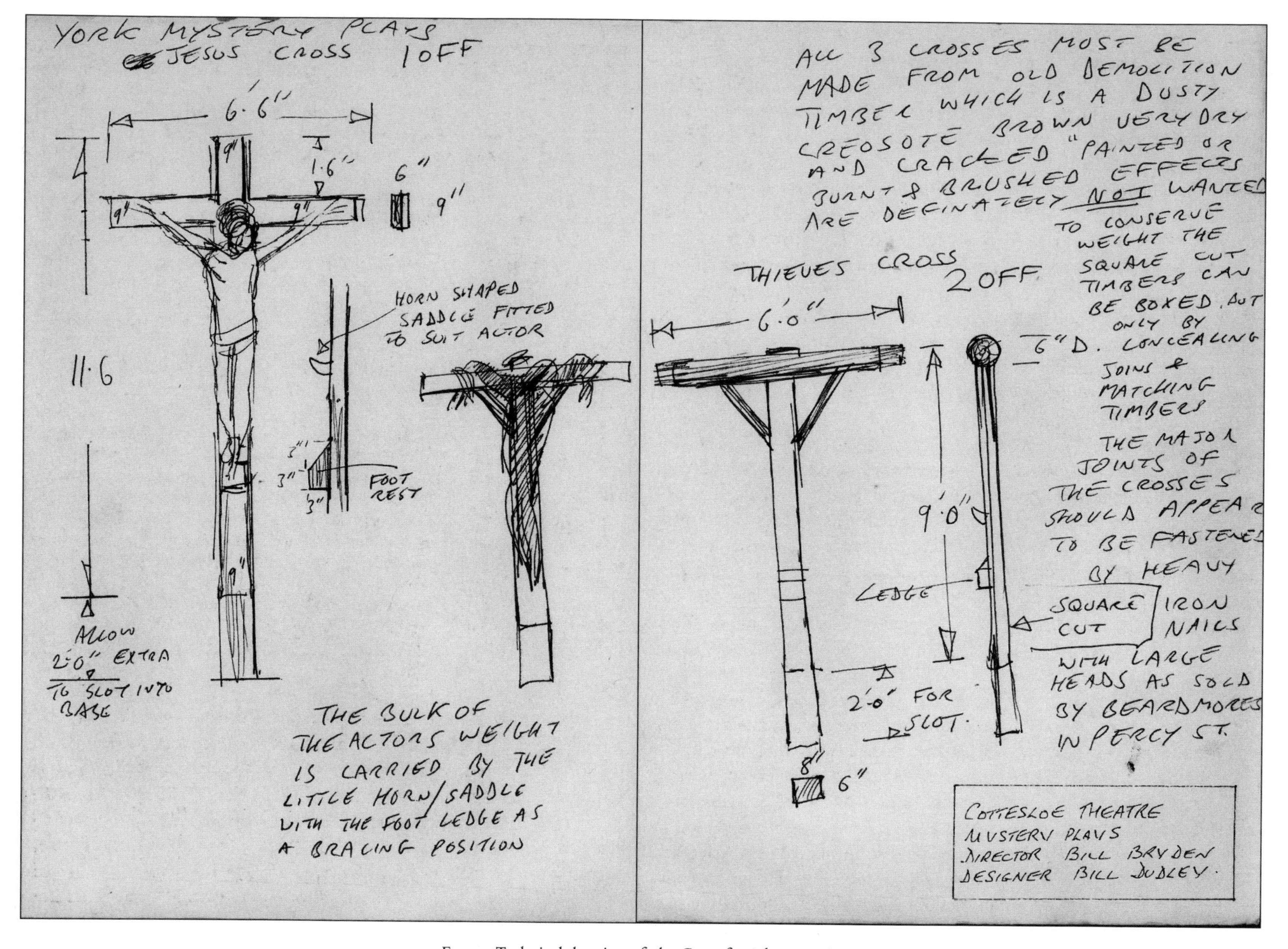

FIG 57 Technical drawing of the Cross for *The Mysteries.*

4 Television, and for the second time, the Cottesloe became a TV studio. The recordings were made with the theatre thronged with invited audiences, who had been unable to see the plays during the sell-out season. They were broadcast on British television screens the following Christmas, and subsequently over most of the world at Christmas 1987.

The Mysteries at the Lyceum

When the closure of the Cottesloe was imminent, and we were faced with an unflagging demand at the box office, we began a search for a flat-floored space within London's commercial sector that would accommodate *The Mysteries* and twice the Cottesloe's 400 admissions. Iain Mackintosh of Theatre Projects Consultants, a firm which had a long connection with the National Theatre, as consultants for the South Bank building as a whole, and more particularly as proposers of the original design study for the Cottesloe Theatre, came up with an idea which had also occurred to Bill Dudley. Mackintosh and his partner Richard Pilbrow set about persuading Mecca Leisure, leaseholders of the Lyceum since 1945, to squeeze in a three-month season between its closure as a dance hall and proposed major restoration work on the sadly dilapidated building. A seedy fifties dance hall within an eighty-year-old theatre with overwrought plasterwork would provide the perfect setting for Bryden's and Dudley's three-part show. *The Mysteries* have happily occupied a variety of venues over the years, the only facilities needed being a flat floor, the possibility of accommodating spectators above and to the side of the playing arena, the ability to suspend items overhead and some architectural contribution from the host space. In the Lyceum, this last was provided by the original circles, boxes and proscenium arch set around the level dance floor.

The principal brief for the Lyceum transfer was that it should accommodate over 1000 patrons and provide access from below through traps for some sequences in *Doomsday*. A lighting grid would be required, covering the whole promenade area beneath, to carry 150 or so lighting units, plus the several hundred twinkling objects, loudspeakers and associated cables. Our own bandstand would move across with the productions, and the whole layout would have to provide safe access and emergency exit routes for public and company. One 'deal breaker' had to be negotiated: the use of smoke throughout the performance space, permission for which had reluctantly been given for the revivals at the Cottesloe after flammability, toxicity and oxygen levels had been checked by the GLC scientific branch, and found to be well within their rigorous safety margins. GLC licensing regulations normally prohibit theatre smoke entering the auditorium, but the rules are somewhat unclear when stage and auditorium are one, as in the case of *The Mysteries*, presented as a promenade production on an open stage.

I started on feasibility studies with Theatre Projects in February, and sketched scaffold tiers across the circle end and sides of the Lyceum's existing and world-renowned dance floor – actually two floors, one atop the other. They were installed at the end of the war, and constructed entirely of Morrison air-raid shelters, supported on a maze of brick piers standing directly on the original stalls rake, which dates, as does the whole Bertie Crewe interior, from December 1904. Sir Henry Irving's original auditorium had been demolished early in 1904, because it did not meet the new LCC licensing provisions of the time, although the famous portico remained. Our scaffold tiers were to extend from the first circle front, down the length of the auditorium and on through the main proscenium to meet the 1945 band-stage and second proscenium half way up the stage area.

It was just possible in designing the layout to provide sufficient headroom for promenaders who wished to leave the floor to occupy the standing terraces provided beneath the seated rows above, while linking up with the Lyceum's existing four upper boxes. These gave us twenty much-needed extra seats, which when occupied would help to blend the black, rectilinear line of our scaffold seating with the theatre's ornate Edwardian movement beyond. By removing the banqueting tables from the circle, whose rows had been doubled-up in 1947, and forming close-seated rows with the ballroom chairs, we reached, in theory, a capacity of 508 promenaders and 466 seats.

Being an Edwardian theatre, the Lyceum has a steel and concrete roof which, having withstood the rigours of BBC lighting installations and multifarious rock uses, proved substantial enough for Messrs. Unusual Rigging's lighting grid. We conceived this in two parts: an auditorium section running from the second-circle front to just above the proscenium, allowing the moulding to show beneath, and a second overstage section very slightly lower, carrying the main PA speakers safely

(*Programme Notes continued from page 77*)
limbo in a black drum-shaped cage. Satan and Beelzebub escape from the sewers for the Harrowing of Hell and later dispatch the unsaved souls into the giant maw of a waste disposal unit. Christ is resurrected from inside a padlocked magician's cabinet. But the most astonishing effect of all is the vision of writhing souls in torment, for which the black drapes behind God's throne part to reveal a gigantic Ferris-wheel shaped like a globe; and inside this revolving sphere the damned swing from the struts in perpetual agony. This is the most Wagnerian of Dudley's effects and it stuns the senses'.

The temper of serious humour, sometimes black, sometimes benign, that governed the production as a whole, met with much approval, though occasionally its risks puzzled or even scandalised its audiences. Francis King thought that 'the one emotion that is conspicuously absent from the whole undertaking is religious awe'. (*Sunday Telegraph*, 27.1.85) Michael Billington objected that 'when those sitting on the left hand of God are singled out for punishment, the mood is one of faint jokiness; and when a few members of the audience are pitchforked into the waste-disposal hell, it is all a bit of a lark. I believe this should be played with unabashed severity. Without that the whole postulate of the Medieval Mysteries is shaken and the idea of divine redemption diminished'. (*Guardian*, 21.1.85)

Most observers, however, felt an appropriate tone had been established. Christopher Grier (*Standard*, 21.1.85) spoke for many when he wrote: 'William Dudley's pragmatic approach to props and costumes brings together dungarees and crowns, fork-lifts and a wooden donkey, abseiling angels and a post-Crucifixion Jesus (Karl Johnson) in a neat blue suit. That may sound a fearful muddle but it works splendidly, swept along on the impetus of the zestful cast, the breath-taking ingenuity of Bryden and the superb use of demotic music, of song and of dance'.

below the barrier of the proscenium wall, and blessedly just in line with the sound control at the rear of the circle. Reconciling the position of the sound mixer with potential loss of seats and revenue is always a battle! The lower stage grid also gave a sense of perspective (credit to Iain Mackintosh for this idea), in line with Bill Dudley's decision to grade from dark to light the decoration to the front of the scaffold-seating tiers, consisting of works implements and contemporary symbols of leisure, such as brewers' crests and dartboards.

Our centre-stage bandstand was now to be firmly wedged between the end of the side-scaffold seat tiers and the Lyceum's own upstage 'band' proscenium, straddling a 60cm high platform, an 8m band revolve and a portion of the original raked stage not removed in the 1947 dance-hall conversion, and last trod by Sir John Gielgud in 1939 as Hamlet. The Swedish Haki scaffold system in use at that time fortunately provided adjustable legs.

Sufficient headroom for access from beneath the floor was possible only in the old orchestra pit, unused since 1939, and correspondingly airless, as I discovered during several breathless surveys among the rats and thick black spiders' webs. The eleven assorted traps and apertures required in the floor for graves and lighting-effects had to be arranged in a line above the pit, and carefully juggled to avoid the steelwork of the Morrison shelters beneath. The resulting area to which we punched through was in turn sealed with a wall of blockwork, to prevent the spread of accidental fire beneath the whole dance floor. One of the apertures we created was the sewer trap for our drain-dwelling Lucifer, who found added motivation for his entrance at one technical rehearsal when he was ejected by a flood of foul water escaping from a soil pipe that ran from the stalls food kiosk.

The electrical supply had to be extended from an old connection point in the basement (originally installed for 'Come Dancing') to the stage-left fly floor. This provided the only convenient and safe position for the lighting dimmers, as the whole performance area beneath was to be shared by company and public alike. Two main fire exits were situated in the rear stage wall and one pair of public stairs accessing the upper scaffold seats gave access to these via the wings. Fifty or so additional safety lights and exit boxes were installed to cover new seating and to mark routes to the Lyceum's own fire exits.

The whole outline proposal was agreed in principle with the GLC Licensing Electrical and District Surveyor, and the Fire Brigade, at the end of February, prior to final confirmation of the event in April. The use of smoke was conditional on our restoring to full operation the building's Edwardian air-handling plant, a twelve-foot-diameter cast-iron centrifugal impeller, driven by the original and rather handsome motor. This, together with a pair of 1950s extractor fans excavated in the rear wall of the stage, provided sufficient changes of air as required under the licence. But what licence was this? We discovered at the first GLC meeting that of course the Lyceum had only a Music and Dance licence, and hadn't had a Play licence for 46 years. Fortunately, with the GLC owning the freehold and being well disposed to the season, the necessary applications were helpfully sped through, with a momentary pause for the approval of the ruling and opposition political parties at County Hall. Theatre Projects' lease for the season could not be finally granted by Mecca Leisure until the licence had been issued, and my expressed view that we would not receive the final document until the twelfth hour caused much consternation all round, but proved correct: it was not until ten minutes after the published time for the first preview, after the Brigade had 'walked the exits' and indeed found one of many locked (the Bradford Valley Parade football fire having occurred on May 11th, our second day of setting up) that we were permitted to admit the public.

Removal of existing ballroom hangings and a false ceiling over the stage, together with some twenty tons of redundant equipment and waste, had been followed by the complete installation of equipment and fittings to dress-rehearsal condition. All this was achieved in seven days. That this proved possible is a tribute to fellow technicians and the dozen or so contractors involved. The tight schedule hardly allowed for setbacks, which included four floods on the first day, the discovery of some deteriorating asbestos (which delayed the scaffold contract for twelve hours), non-delivery of phones, and a radical reorganization of the circle seating to improve sightlines. Fitting *The Mysteries* into a crumbling if historic theatre never intended for promenade work went beyond a challenge to the verge of something close to recklessness. At the least, however, cast and crew can take pride in having had a small part in drawing the world's attention to the old Lyceum. Doubtful proposals for a casino, preventing future theatrical use, were abandoned, ownership changed, and following restoration, the Lyceum reopened as a live theatre in November 1996.

BILL BRYDEN: PROMENADING THE COTTESLOE

Based on an interview with Ronnie Mulryne and Margaret Shewring

Bill Bryden was asssistant to William Gaskill at the Royal Court Theatre in London. In 1971 he was appointed Associate Director of the Royal Lyceum Theatre in Edinburgh, where he directed many production, including two of his own plays, Willie Rough *(1972; seen in London and later televised) and* Bennie Lynch *(1974; later televised). He also directed* The Three Estates *for the Edinburgh Festival. Invited by Peter Hall to the National Theatre in 1974, he was appointed Associate Director with special responsibility for the Cottesloe in 1975, and directed many productions there, including the landmark* The Mysteries *(Evening Standard and Olivier and Variety Club Awards for Best Director)* Lark Rise to Candleford, American Buffalo *and* Glengarry Glen Ross *(both by David Mamet). Bill joined the Board of Scottish television in 1978 and became Head of Drama for BBC Scotland in 1985. He has directed Opera at the Royal Opera House, written and directed* The Ship *in Glasgow as part of the European City of Culture celebrations (televised 1990) written and directed television and film screenplays, and directed theatre for the Birmingham Rep, the RSC and in the West End. He was awarded the CBE in 1993.*

My appointment to run the Cottesloe was a matter of good fortune. I was very lucky to be in the right place at the right time, and in contact with a circle of creative people whose focus was the Old Vic, the Royal Court and, subsequently, the National Theatre.

I came down from the Royal Lyceum in Edinburgh to do Wedekind's *Spring Awakening*, and joined Peter Hall at his invitation. I also did *The Playboy of the Western World* and John Osborne's *Watch It Come Down* at the Old Vic, the first of which transferred to the Lyttelton and the Olivier and the second to the Lyttelton. The productions also went on tour nationally.

I had previously worked with William Gaskill at the Royal Court, where I was his assistant for a year. We worked together on new writing at the Court with a range of experimental theatre groups, including a season of fringe companies under the title 'Come Together'. So before I joined the National I had some experience of a wide range of plays. I learned from William Gaskill to treat a new play as a classic and a classic as a new play – an approach that stood me in good stead when I came to work at the Cottesloe.

I wasn't really part of the early discussions about the auditoria on the South Bank. I do know that Peter Hall wanted each space to have its own Artistic Director. I accepted Peter's invitation to be the first Artistic Director of the Cottesloe. As things have turned out, I was not only the first but in fact the only Artistic Director with sole responsibility for that theatre.

The Cottesloe never really had a plan or 'mission statement'. It had not been conceived as an auditorium within the original designs for the South Bank complex, or not, at any rate, in any detail. When it was opened up as a

FIG 58 Bill Bryden on the set of *Candleford* (see pp. 94–103).

theatre space, people talked about it engaging with community outreach and education projects. But it also seemed to have, or came to acquire, a role in relation to new plays, especially those plays which would not be commercially safe options in one of the larger auditoria. Yet even *Illuminatus*, a new play and the first piece to be staged in the Cottesloe (in 1977), was not seen as a deliberate statement. It just happened that Peter Hall had wanted for some time to work with Ken Campbell (co-author with Chris Langham of the show), and the production was conveniently available at that moment.

Peter never gave me the brief to 'do new plays'. What he did say was, 'Give the Cottesloe a personality … make it happen.' I was in the fortunate position that he allowed me to develop a team for the Cottesloe, alongside teams for the Olivier and the Lyttelton. The Cottesloe was always 'cushioned', financially, by the larger auditoria, with the privileged role of being financially underwritten but also part of the high expectation, in terms of quality, that went with a National flagship company. Gradually I drew together a creative 'family', including Hayden Griffin (designer), Andy Phillips (lighting designer), John Tams (music), William Dudley (designer), Jason Barnes (production manager), Nobby Clark (photographer), Michael Mayhew (graphic designer and photographer), John Caulfield (stage manager) and Sebastian Graham-Jones (co-director). Thanks to its commercially-cushioned position, and to the financial sacrifice Peter was prepared to make, the Cottesloe was enabled to flourish, drawing the crowds round the corner from the main foyers and into the third auditorium. The Cottesloe became the easiest space in which to have a 'hit', but even a 'hit' could not cover its costs.

Not only was Peter the financial architect of the Cottesloe's success, he never dictated what we had to do, either in play selection or during the rehearsal process. This freedom in turn allowed me to build a large team of front- and back-stage personnel, who saw themselves as part of a very special creative ensemble. Peter always backed what organically grew into an artistic policy.

One of the first things we did was to stage the Crucifixion Play from the York Mystery Cycle on the Terrace outside the South Bank complex. The performance was a great success and drew public attention to the National in general and the Cottesloe team in particular. A strong pool of actors developed – not the great stars but a 'strong mid-field', including Trevor Ray, Brian Glover, Edna Doré, J.G. Devlin, Gawn Grainger and Mark McManus – who formed the group from which any one cast was selected, making allowance for group members to take on television or West End dates, and then come back. The company was not set up as a training ground, but inevitably people did get experience and training in the context of the 'family'. And equally, visitors to the Cottesloe, including famous names like Stacy Keach, Susan Fleetwood and the playwright David Mamet, could rely on the professionalism of the ensemble as a whole.

The Cottesloe space is wonderfully hospitable. Because it was not initially designed as a theatre in the conventional sense, and does not have a designated performance area, it can be 'discovered' in various configurations. All of the Cottesloe team wanted to offer a popular, accessible theatre experience. Bill Dudley discarded the notion of a proscenium arrangement in favour of a flexible promenade space, in which the audience can contribute directly to the vitality of the performance. In this case, it's the responsibility of the designer and the ensemble to give the space its identity for each production. There are no dominant murals in the Cottesloe and no strong architectural forms to divert attention. Instead, the theatre offers the chance to stage both classics and new plays in a flexible mint-new fashion – not in a small, studio-sized setting (as was happening elsewhere in the country at the time) but in a large, unobtrusively 'epic', space in which a whole living environment could be created by artists and audiences alike.

I once described the Cottesloe as 'the Fringe with champagne'. It is part of the National, and physically larger than most if not all 'studio' spaces, but it came to be the hottest ticket in town, even when other National auditoria were struggling. Our programming policy was catholic in comparison with that of other studio theatres, taking in not only new writing but established classics. The audience could see not only our own company, but also visitors such as Sir John Gielgud and Sir Ralph Richardson, in plays (*Half Life* and *Early Days*) that were pre-West End runs. And the ticket prices were fixed, even for these shows, and low. As time went on, Peter Hall had to cope with depressing criticism of the National's expenditure, but he kept faith with the Cottesloe and our work. The guns seemed to be firing from Somerset House (across the Thames), but the Cottesloe appeared, somehow, to be the National's secret weapon in reply.

SEBASTIAN GRAHAM-JONES: THE EARLY DAYS

Sebastian Graham-Jones was assistant to Peter Hall, and trained in film with John Schlesinger, George Roy Hill and Sergio Leone. In 1975, he joined Bill Bryden's creative team at the National Theatre, working mainly in the Cottesloe, where he was Associate Director of (among other plays) The Mysteries. *He has also directed for the Greenwich Theatre, the Donmar Warehouse and the Oxford Playhouse, as well as in Denmark, the USA and Germany. He has directed three major television series for Granada and BBC2 and a series of plays for BBC1. He is Associate Artistic Director of Promenade Productions.*

When Bill Bryden came down to London from Edinburgh to do *Spring Awakening*, I was already in London as a young member of the National company. I had worked with Peter Hall on *No Man's Land* (at the Old Vic, before its transfer to the West End and then to America). I already knew Bill, and on his arrival in London we worked together on *The Playboy of the Western World* and *Watch It Come Down* before our work together in the Cottesloe, as part of the Cottesloe 'family'.

One of the most inspirational things was that Bill, enabled by Peter Hall, made working at the Cottesloe into a shared objective, so that whoever you were you felt honoured to be there – and secure. It's miraculous how Bill allows the whole team to participate in the creative process, making suggestions and trying out their ideas, so that everyone feels absorbed into the total project. The Cottesloe offered us freedom to experiment. It was a space waiting to be discovered. In other words, it did not have a dominant identity – the company could forge an identity for it. Peter Hall understood the importance of this. He was the architect of the opportunity.

At first the general public thought that the National's third auditorium, when it came into being, was going to be like the Bush or the Warehouse, given over to new plays and experimental pieces. But the Cottesloe was never planned as a small-scale experimental theatre. Partly because it was too big for that, but also because its play selection included along with new writing both classical plays and adaptations of classical plays (or fiction), such as *The Mysteries* (Tony Harrison's adaptation of the medieval cycle plays) and *Lark Rise to Candleford* (Keith Dewhurst's adaptation of Flora Thompson's novels). Bill Bryden's directorial approach and Bill Dudley's and Hayden Griffin's designs gave the space its character, allowing the texts to emerge and the room to respond to the living event. If the promenade performances felt improvisational and 'random', this was only the result of a great deal of careful orchestration and planning.

In the Cottesloe in the early days all the tickets were £1.50, pit and first level, £1.00 second level. People came in at the end of a day's work, wanting to be drawn into the world of the play – to share in it. The actors had to invite their audiences into the experience. Because there are galleries in the Cottesloe, the actors had to look up, and open themselves and the space to the audience. They also learned to control the pace of the show. For example, to slow down the tempo during the lunch episode in *Lark Rise*, and so allow a busy, rushed audience to feel at one with the rural world of the play. The pace may have seemed casual, but it was carefully controlled.

I remember Bill talking about Peter Wood's response to *The Mysteries*. Wood had thought the groupings were relaxed and informal until he went into the gallery and looked down. He saw at once that every move was predetermined and choreographed, and that the ensemble controlled the audience with what seemed almost 'Nazi' precision. It was an achievement like this that confirmed Bill's genius in bringing together meticulous rehearsal and creative freedom.

WILLIAM DUDLEY: DESIGNER

Based on an interview with Ronnie Mulryne and Margaret Shewring

William Dudley has designed a huge variety of shows from grand opera to intimate theatre and from environmental performances to television. Born in 1947, he was trained as a landscape painter before working in fringe theatre and at the Royal Court. He has designed work for the Royal National Theatre, the Royal Shakespeare Company and the Old Vic, a well as in Hamburg, in London's West End, and for Glasgow's Cultural Capital of Europe year. His opera designs have included work for the Welsh National Opera, the Metropolitan Opera, the Paris National Opera and the Salzburg Festival, as well as for Glyndebourne, Bayreuth and the Royal Opera House, London.

Stage designers should not be seen as window-dressers, but as artists in their own right, playing a full part in the creative team behind any production. Yet their work is rarely afforded serious analysis, at least by anyone qualified to discuss visual and spatial matters.

The Mysteries were my first show at the Cottesloe. Bill Bryden and I shared the belief that these plays were essentially a popular form of street theatre, and that, as in medieval times, it was crucial to incorporate the audience rather than separate them from the action. The Cottesloe's courtyard seemed to us akin to a medieval town square, in which we could explore the processional mode of story-telling in parallel with the medieval guilds. Working in this way allowed the medieval and modern notions of story-telling to co-exist, so that the audience were not witnessing an historical reconstruction but were complicit in, and interacting with, a living experience.

Our design concept for *The Mysteries* made full use of the height of the Cottesloe. Just as in medieval town squares, we made use of the fact that the floor space is overlooked in the Cottesloe by balconies full of people. We consulted what little evidence there is of medieval performance, including the Fouquet miniature of the torture of St Appollina, which shows a number of balconies, and in addition shows musicians mingling with the crowd. We tried to keep faith with what we discovered of medieval staging, including the use of modern trades-union banners to call attention to the rôle originally played by the craft guilds. We were also conscious in our design of the way in which a person's clothes in medieval times identified that person's social position and craft. The attempt throughout was to offer a three-dimensional portrayal of the medieval plays, using where appropriate modern parallels and analogues. (For more extended discussion of scenic design in *The Mysteries* see pp. 72–80 in this book.)

We went on to develop this sense of three-dimensional space in other promenade productions, notably *Lark Rise* and *Candleford.* Keith Dewhurst's scripts for these plays drew on the vocabulary and habits of expression of ordinary working people of the nineteenth century. These were people who, though living in reduced circumstances, were nevertheless an inherent part of the English pastoral landscape, with its glories as well as its hardships. We tried in our design to co-ordinate all the elements of set, props and costumes to evoke as vividly as possible this non-political evocation of folk memory. We even tried, by the use of a vast sky-cloth and other means, to represent the passing of the seasons from the spring of *Lark Rise* to the winter of *Candleford.* (For detailed description and illustration of the designs for these plays see pp. 94–103 in this book.)

Fig 59 William Dudley's design for *The World Turned Upside Down,* directed by Bill Bryden and Sebastian Graham-Jones, showing the stage used in traverse. The production opened at the Cottesloe on 2 November 1978. The photograph by Michael Mayhew shows Brian Glover (centre, background) as Snapjoint and Trevor Ray (foreground) as Justice of the Peace.

When the Cottesloe opened, it was on an extraordinarily low budget, and worked on a 'resurrectionist' policy of making use of things discarded from the Olivier and the Lyttelton. There had been some active opposition, from the earliest planning meetings, to the creation of a third auditorium, as it was felt that this third space could not hope to sustain the high standards of the other two auditoria. In the event, the simplicity of the Cottesloe's courtyard-style environment, painted in black, proved its greatest asset.

The Cottesloe is sufficiently flexible to host promenade performances, but it also works excellently in traverse. The first use of the space in traverse was for *The World Turned Upside Down,* based on Christopher Hill's book about the Civil War. For this production, the Cottesloe space was employed in allusion to the old House of Commons, a debating chamber with the opposing speakers facing each other at either end. In this way the theatre space offered a physical representation of the play's central question: who rules England? The huge medallion of Cromwell overhead gave the current answer. (See illustration above.)

The Cottesloe derives from the inn-yard spaces of Elizabethan England. It also draws inspiration from the masque designs Inigo Jones prepared for the Banqueting House in Whitehall. We associate Jones with neo-classicism, yet perhaps his greatest skill lay in evoking a mythical dream-world at one end of the relatively small shared space of the Banqueting House, and linking this to the common area at the other, in which the 'revels' dancing, in which everyone participated, took place. Like Jones's arena, the Cottesloe can bridge across from the elevated to the ordinary, from the magnificent to the commonplace. It gives the stage designer some problems but also endless opportunities.

Fig 60 The production team for *The Mysteries* as staged at the Assembly Hall, Edinburgh, August 1980.
Photo: *Nobby Clark*

LIVING SPACES

Ronnie Mulryne, Margaret Shewring, Jason Barnes

THIS SECTION of the book attempts to evoke, so far as this is possible, the experience of attending a Cottesloe performance. We have paid a good deal of attention to design, as well as to direction, acting and (where appropriate) music. We have made free use of published reviews, seeing these as the most readily available source of immediate response to performance. That the reviews are often vividly expressed, but also often register disagreement, seemed to us a source of strength, not weakness. We have also used as many photographs as we could, drawing almost without exception on the photographer appointed by the Company to photograph each show. The name of the photographer is in each case included with the list of directing and technical staff responsible for the production. We are grateful for the professional expertise of both reviewers and photographers, and should like to acknowledge it here. We are also grateful to Nicola Scadding, the RNT's archivist, for her unstinting help in locating relevant material.

Jason Barnes's Technical Summaries provide for each show an indication of the layout of the theatre and the techniques of construction and stage-management peculiar to or characteristic of the production in question. The floor and vertical plans, many of them specially commissioned from Miles King for inclusion here, show visually how the Cottesloe was laid out for each of the chosen shows. In bringing together our account of a production we have made use of the 'Bible Book' drawn up by stage management, an extraordinary document recording almost every aspect of performance, and of the astonishingly complete file kept by Jason Barnes, with its compilation of documents summarising the life of a show before, during and after its production run. Without these sets of documents, and without the National's often richly-researched programmes, we should not have been able to write this section of the book.

The chosen productions are arranged in chronological order. To some extent, therefore, this section chronicles the discovery of the Cottesloe's potential for use in multiple formats. The motive behind our choice of shows was, however, to exemplify that multiplicity by selecting shows which were excellent as theatre, were as varied as possible, and employed each of the main forms of spatial layout. We have had with regret to limit the number of shows we could include, and inevitably have had to omit outstanding instances of writing, performance, design and direction. We wish it could be otherwise.

FIG 61 The surprisingly naturalistic setting for *Half Life*, with its wisteria and 'stunning fall of blossom' (Jason Barnes) in a garden courtyard appropriate for a wealthy Oxford don. The only hint here of the Cottesloe's architecture comes with the gallery-fronts and masking curtain in the top right hand corner of the shot.

HALF LIFE

By Julian Mitchell

The playwright
When *Half Life* was produced at the National, Julian Mitchell had written two stage plays, *A Heritage and its History* (1965) and *A Family and a Fortune* (1975), both adaptations of novels by Ivy Compton-Burnett, as well as numerous television plays, including *Shadow in the Sun, A Question of Degree, Rust* (directed by Waris Hussein), the ITV series *Jennie, Lady Randolph Churchill,* and *Abide With Me,* which won the Monte Carlo International Critics' Prize. He had also written six novels by the age of 32, ten years before the staging of *Half Life,* one of them the recipient of the Maugham Award, but gave up novel writing because he judged the audience small and inward-looking. The topic of *Half Life* presumably owes something to Mitchell's undergraduate days at Wadham College, Oxford, where Sir Maurice Bowra, a supposed prototype for the play's main character, was Warden, and to his interest in archaeology (the source of the term 'Half Life' as used in the carbon-dating process). 'The whole idea of archaeologists uncovering things including, perhaps, themselves,' he told Sheridan Morley (*Times,* 12.11.1977) 'is an intriguing one for a playwright, and I've always liked delving back into the past.' He was not especially pleased with the choice of the Cottesloe for *Half Life*: 'Really I suppose it's a Lyttelton rather than a Cottesloe play, but if it's good enough it'll work in any arena and we can always transfer it later if all goes well. I still somehow yearn for a curtain, even though I know that's against all the Peter Brook open-space rules'. (*Times,* 12.11.1977) The transfer to the Duke of York's provided the kind of auditorium Mitchell was looking for.

HALF-LIFE
Written by Julian Mitchell

Director	*Waris Hussein*
Set Design	*Jane Martin*
Costume Design	*Judy Moorcroft*
Lighting	*Stephen Wentworth*
Sound	*Julian Beech*
Production Manager	*Jason Barnes*
Stage Manager	*John Rothenberg*
Photography	*John Haynes*

Players

Sir Noel Cunliffe	*John Gielgud*
Jones	*Paul Rogers*
Francis Mallock	*Richard Pearson*
Helen Mallock	*Avril Elgar*
Mike Clayton	*Oliver Cotton*
Rupert Carter	*Hugh Paddick*
Barbara Burney	*Isabel Dean*
Prue Hoggart	*Dinah Stabb*

The production opened on 17 November 1977 and ran in repertoire until 7 February 1978 It transferred to the Duke of York's Theatre for a total of 205 performances, previewing from 28 February 1978, and opening on 2 March. The production was subsequently seen at the Royal Alexander Theatre, Toronto, and in Washington DC.

The setting
Audiences and critics had little to say about the stage design for *Half Life,* perhaps because it appeared so familiar in type, if also surprising and even disconcerting when encountered in a theatre-space tagged by the National and by its clientele as 'experimental'. Claire Tomalin in a *Kaleidoscope* broadcast (BBC, 18.11.1977, presented by Sheridan Morley), remarked that she found it 'funny' going into the Cottesloe 'where one expects a sort of tomb-like atmosphere of radical misery' only to be presented instead with 'this bright set, these huge swathes of paper wisteria all over everything'. She thought this 'a considerable bonus', especially since the *Half Life* programme-cover showed a withered tree set in a desolate landscape, which in mid-seventies theatre suggested cataclysm and holocaust. Even so early in its career, the Cottesloe generated expectations which, in this instance, it overturned by employing a set that associated more readily with West End prosceniums than with a studio-size courtyard-type space. The flexibility of the theatre was in the event vindicated by its success in accommodating a theatre-design from a tradition so different from its own.

More prosaically perhaps than Ms Tomalin, Jason Barnes's letter of 14 February 1978 to the Architect to the GLC (copy to the London Fire Brigade), in seeking permission to transfer the show to the Duke of York's, described how 'the setting represents the exterior of a country house, and consists of an FP [fire-proofed] filled cloth cyclorama, black woollen masking and borders rostra forming a patio and garden steps, a criterion cord carpet representing grass, and treated stage gauzes representing Wisteria which surmounts the house'.

B.A. Young thought the set 'handsome' (*Financial Times,* 18.11.1977) and Anne Morley-Priestman described it as 'realistic' (*The Stage,* 1.12.1977), while 'P.A.' in *Q International* (vol. 2 no. 5) considered 'Jane Martin's set is the most florid I've seen in this theatre, and like Judy Moorcroft's costumes, the most evocative'. The anodyne note of these remarks indicates how fully the stage design complemented the structurally unambitious nature of the play, a suitability confirmed by the silence of other reviewers on the matter.

The Director and the Show
Until being offered *Half Life* (after writing to Peter Hall asking for an opportunity to direct) Waris Hussein had worked almost exclusively for film and television. On television his achievements included such notable productions as *Glittering Prizes, Passage to India, Blind Love, Love Letters on Blue Paper,* and *Daphne Laureola,* while on film he had directed *A Touch of Love* (with Sandy Dennis), *Quackser Fortune* (with Gene Wilder)

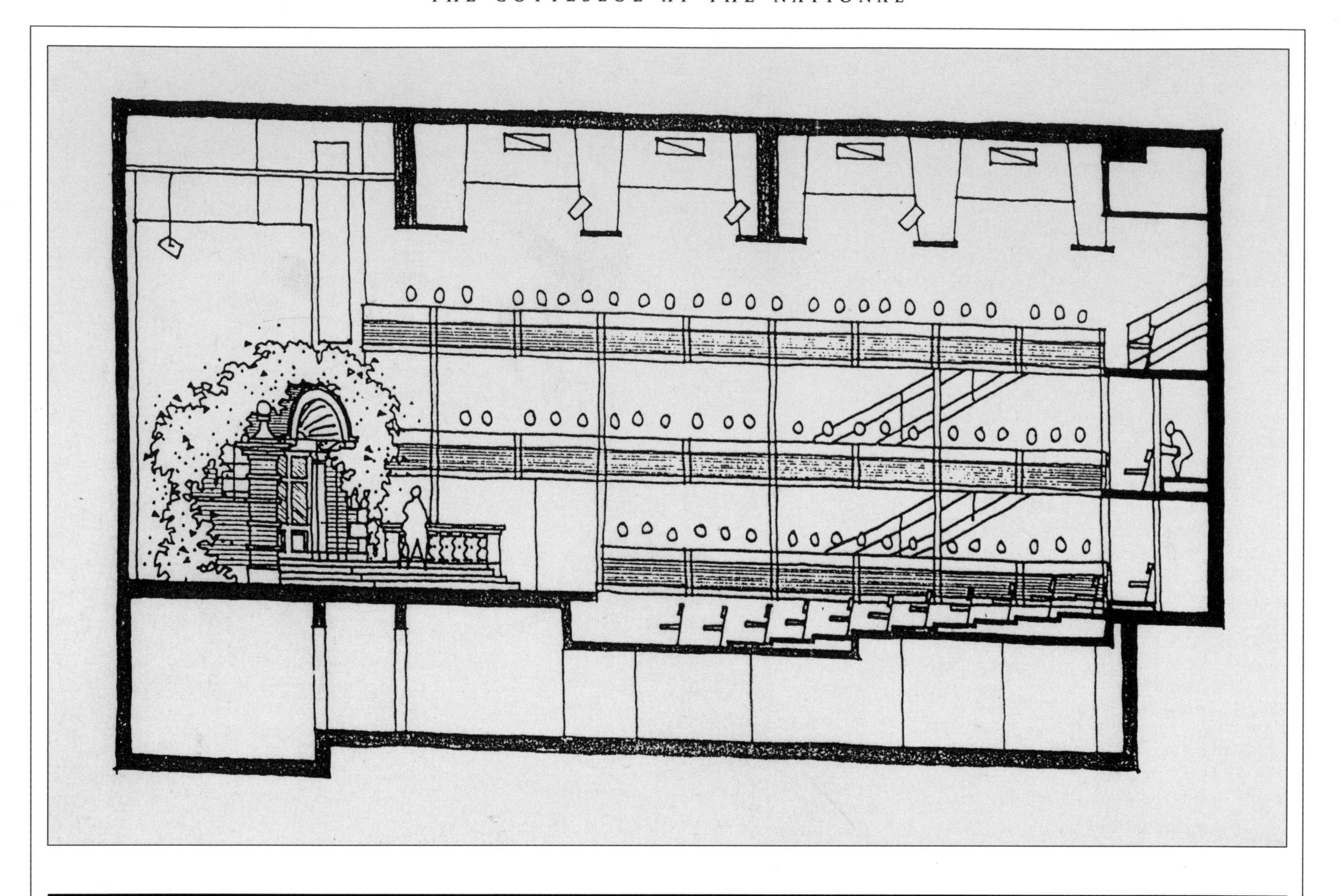

Technical Summary

- One of the few mainly naturalistic exterior settings in the Cottesloe's first twenty-one years. Since this production took place before the introduction in 1986 of the large retractable seating unit, Jane Martin's design used an end-stage format with all eleven rows of seats in the central block below stage level.

- The set comprised a portion of lawn at stage level, accessed stage right through a privet-hedge arch and brick gates, while, up stage left, curved patio steps rose to a paved area and the country villa's Lutyenesque front door.

- Thick trunks of flowering Wisteria attested to the house's sixty or seventy years. The National's painters, highly skilled in fabric and textural techniques as well as paint, created for the wisteria a stunning fall of blossom, thus emphasising the play's naturalistic mode.

- The Cottesloe's side galleries penetrated into the end-stage scenery, and so drew the spectator's eye through into the action.

- The setting was backed by a full wrap-round cyclorama, the first of many used over the years. This called for a special framework to tidy and conceal the edges of the cloth, which are hidden on a conventional proscenium stage.

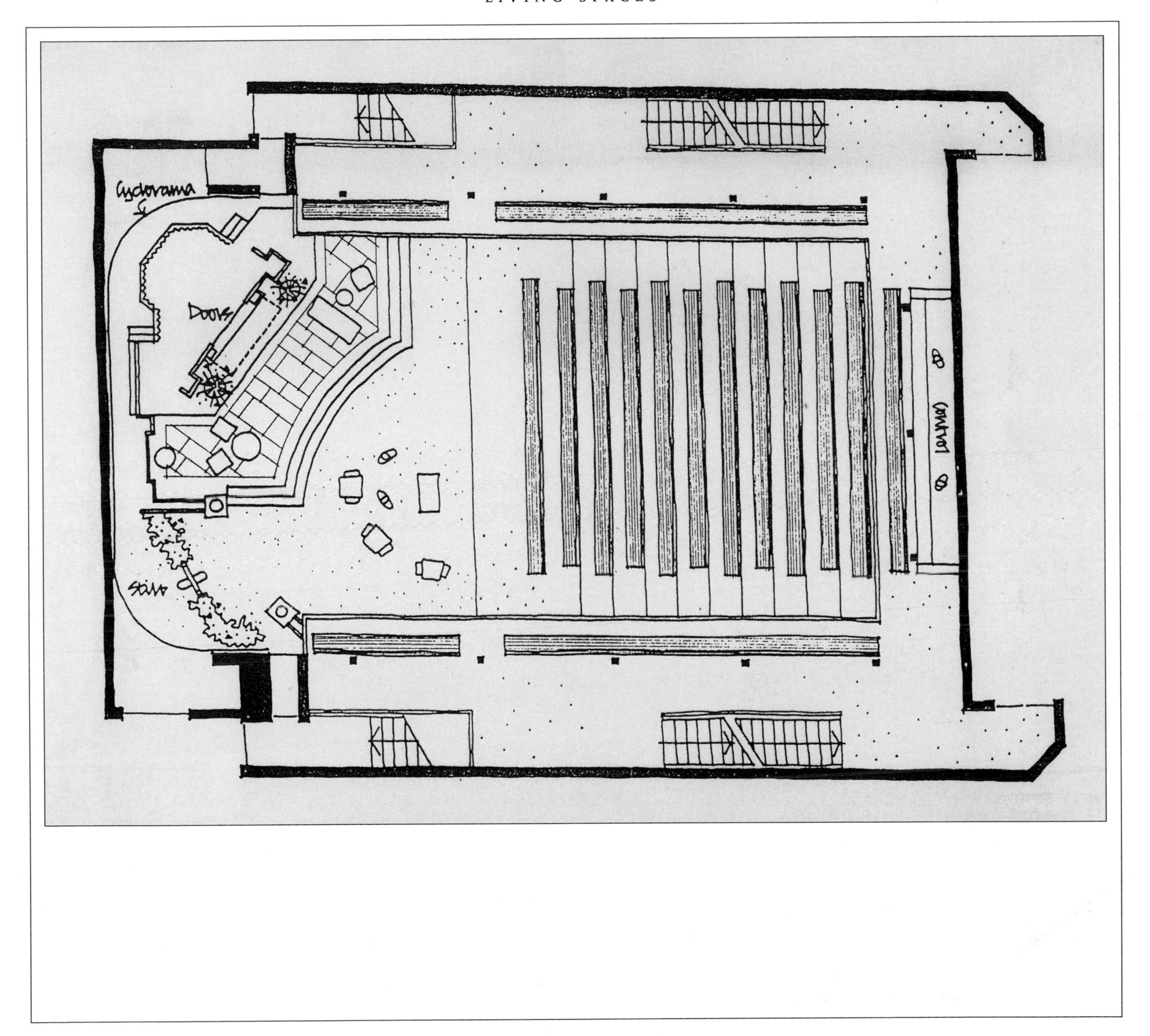
Cyclorama
Doors
Stairs
Control

and *The Possession of Joel Delaney* (with Shirley Maclaine). He had worked with John Gielgud only once previously, on a television version of Shaw's *St Joan*, with Gielgud playing the Inquisitor. 'The attraction of theatre for me', he told Michael Billington (*Guardian*, 2.3.1978) 'is that while in television the work is all the time highly technical, the freedom of the stage by contrast is wonderful, exhilarating.' A product of the Cambridge generation that also produced Ian McKellen, Trevor Nunn, Derek Jacobi, David Frost, Peter Cook, Jonathan Miller and others, he read English at Queens' College before attending the Slade for a year (and deciding not to be a painter) and then becoming a trainee director for the BBC. Conscious of his own status as an assimilated alien (he was born in Lucknow in 1947 and was brought up by his civil servant father as a Muslim) he judged that *Half Life* 'couldn't be more English if it tried'.

The actor

Sir John Gielgud (born 1904) had already played leading roles for the National Theatre (in *Tartuffe*, *Oedipus*, *The Tempest*, *No Man's Land*, *Julius Caesar* and *Volpone*) when Peter Hall asked him to read the script of *Half Life* in 1977. He found the role of Sir Noel Cunliffe demanding: 'I was terribly nervous when it opened at the Cottesloe. It's a long part and I've usually had a try-out tour before London. This time we only had two dress rehearsals. I've had to sweat it out and I've written the part all out … I've done this for a long time. All us senior chaps do'. (Interview with Sydney Edwards and Michael Owen, *Evening Standard*, 24.2.1978) He took the role to be a parody of Oxford dons like Maurice Bowra or Isaiah Berlin, who 'have limited attitudes towards everyday people'.

The central role

Several commentators thought the play no more than a vehicle for Gielgud. Others rebuked the management of the National for its timidity in placing a play with a cast led by such an actor, and with such strong support, in a theatre-space which in this quasi-proscenium arrangement seated just over 300 (307 to be precise), with 75 standing. The reviewer for *Where To Go* (1–7.12.1977), with his eye on the box office, remarked that 'Julian Mitchell's *Half Life* belongs in an ordinary proscenium theatre holding a large audience; any play with a cast as strong as this is

FIG 62 Sir John Gielgud as Sir Noel Cunliffe, the admired and successful but unfulfilled Master of an Oxford College.

FIG 63 Sir John Gielgud with the 'smooth mainchancer' (Bernard Levin) Rupert Carter, played by Hugh Paddick.

FIG 64 Dinah Stabb as Prue Hoggart, a 'middle-class revolutionary' (Marina Warner) with Sir John Gielgud.

wasted in a 300 seat auditorium when the presence of Sir John Gielgud alone would guarantee a West End run' (as in fact happened when the production transferred to the Duke of York's).

Whatever misgivings reviewers might have about the location of the production, there was universal agreement that the part of Sir Noel Cunliffe, the admired and privileged but unfulfilled Master of an Oxford college, fitted Gielgud admirably. Traditional reviewers especially, such as J.C.Trewin, recalling memories of Gielgud in more orthodox spaces, thought the wit, the old-fashioned vocabulary and the suspended cadences of Mitchell's script precisely calculated for Gielgud's eloquent manipulation: 'Sir John will be more familiar with the part verbally as the run proceeds; even so, no one could have matched last night's poise and timing and his delivery of the long and archaeological speech. I do advise young theatregoers to hear him enunciate the name Mycenae'. (*Birmingham Post*, 19.11.1977)

Elocution was not the only grace reviewers perceived, and most were content to overlook Gielgud's lapses of memory in a murderously long role. Frank Marcus commented on his 'style and sardonic loquaciousness' (*Sunday Telegraph*, 20.11.1977), and Robert Cushman on his 'magnificent insouciance' (*Observer*, 20.11.1977). Harold Hobson relished his 'lethal urbanity' (*Drama*, Winter, 1977–78) while Milton Shulman wrote that 'in the person of Sir John Gielgud, dapper, sardonic, superior, this academic ogre certainly justifies his reputation as an unstoppable juggernaut of insults and aphorisms'. (*Evening Standard*, 18.11.1997) Shulman appreciated the return of so much 'polished wit and stimulating reflections' to the English stage, finding the role 'impeccably tailored for Gielgud's grandest manner'.

There was also a theatrical *coup* to applaud: 'The Gielgud moment comes at the end of the second act. We

Fig 65 Sir John Gielgud, Oliver Cotton as Mike Clayton and Isabel Dean as Barbara Burney.

have gone through the banter and the baiting, much of it marvellously funny, and a good deal of revelation. Out of it we suddenly see, and in this performance feel, something new and quite unexpected. The urbane, the malicious, the powerful Sir Noel is made to own up and, in tears, he goes into the house. It is the dramatic turning point of the play, the one where Mr Mitchell takes his greatest gamble and where it needs a great actor to make it pay off'. (Gillian Reynolds, *Plays and Players*, February 1978) Not every reviewer discovered such depths in the play, some finding this moment and the play's relatively optimistic conclusion sentimental. All agreed however on the virtuosity of Gielgud's performance of the central role, with Marina Warner finding under the cruel wit a 'latent gentleness' that only a great actor could expose, a gentleness vindicated by the final redemption which (even if implausible) offered a moment of 'true dramatic power'. (*Vogue*, 18.11.1977)

The Other Roles

There was general agreement among reviewers that this production had been generously cast, with leading actors in every part. Harold Hobson referred to Isabel Dean (playing Barbara Burney) with 'her face as deadly to susceptible hearts as her wit is to everything else' (*Drama* 1977–78) and Benedict Nightingale admired Avril Elgar as Helen Mallock, 'an Oxbridge power-broker with a mean glint in her eye and a pile of bile in her gut'. (*New Statesman*, 25.11.1977). Marina Warner appreciated the performance of Dinah Stabb as Prue Hoggart, who in presenting this middle-class revolutionary 'rounded the character with affection, avoiding an easy fall into satire about "Socialists who love Champers" and thus never losing her humanity'. (*Vogue*, 19.11.1977).

Bernard Levin's characteristically stylish and not altogether favourable review picked out a number of performances to applaud, in addition to Gielgud's: 'Hugh Paddick's smooth mainchancer is appropriately glossy: "Helen," he cries, spotting an old enemy, "this *is* a nice surprise," the accompanying *faux-bonhomme* smile meticulously vanishing on the third word. Paul Rogers, a Jeeves figure, shimmers effortlessly in and out; Avril Elgar, as a disappointed woman, rings true; and Richard Pearson, as a gormandising don ("I've often thought I'd like to be buried in an asparagus bed") strikes real acting roots'. (*Sunday Times* 20.11.1977) Levin's pleasure in the acting skills of all the cast echoed what emerged as the general judgement on a performance that no-one felt was anything less than accomplished.

The script

What seemed to some the awkward fit between the associations of the Cottesloe as an experimental venue and the old-fashioned proscenium-arch characteristics of the play did not prevent most reviewers appreciating the wit of the writing. Some thought there was no more to it than that. Benedict Nightingale, for example, wrote that 'Comedy of manners is, I suspect, Mr Mitchell's real strength, and he hasn't yet discovered how to deepen it into the sombre comedy of morals he was evidently aiming at when he launched *Half Life*'. (*New Statesman*, 25.11.1977) Marina Warner thought otherwise, appreciating first the poise and cleverness of the social observation, but seeing beneath the surface something of greater weight: 'Julian Mitchell works his material with a michievous accuracy of ear and eye. His wit is instantly funny as caricature and lampoon, Osbert Lancaster-style, and there is much rat-a-tat-tat wise-cracking. But he shows greater breadth: his humour bites beyond appearances, like Waugh's'. The observations, she said, 'go beyond the comedy of type into social portraiture that sometimes faces up to solemn issues: the lockjaw of the English establishment, the barrenness of academe.' (*Vogue*, 19.11.1977)

This sense of a depth of implication was shared by Michael Billington who, prompted perhaps by the apparent incongruity of text and venue, detected a tension between the values informing the script and the manner in which they were expressed. 'Julian Mitchell's *Half Life* at the Cottesloe,' he wrote, 'has all the trappings of a conventional West End play. A Wiltshire country-house setting; bucketfuls of Dom Perignon; a good deal of witty banter; and a fat star part for Sir John Gielgud as a retired Oxford archaeologist for whom malice is always aforethought. Yet underneath the Shaftesbury Avenue camouflage there is an interesting idea: that the great dream of liberal education is a myth and that society is none the better for it.' In the climate of 70s moral earnestness, such questioning of establishment values could fit perfectly into an 'experimental' venue such as the Cottesloe, but Billington found the script and the performance compromised by their adoption of the very commitments they apparently attacked: 'Mr Mitchell is an intelligent writer and his play is full of sharp, funny lines. But the flaw is that the attack on liberal humanism is conducted almost entirely in terms of liberal humanism. Running through, round, and underneath the text is a deep, undisguisable love for Oxford, Mycenae, political moderation and good talk on summer afternoons. Debate on the central issue is never really joined because, you feel, Mr Mitchell's heart is not really in it'. (*Guardian*, 18.11.1977)

If the general consensus was that *Half Life* represented a form of theatre outmoded in the seventies world of agit-prop ('a conversation piece such as once might have been seen at the Haymarket some 25 years ago, complete with a stellar cast', Frank Marcus, *Sunday Telegraph*, 20.11.1977), it nevertheless pleased its audiences as a theatrical experience. It was greeted with especial warmth by the older corps of reviewers such as Harold Hobson, who wished to extend the word experimental to take in 'thoughtful' plays such as this: 'Is an experimental play one that uses conventional four-letter words, farts, urination, cunnilingus, fellatio, masturbation, excrement and spitting in the face of the audience to communicate clichés to people who already know them by heart? Or is it also a play that presents, albeit in the suave tones of educated people in Bernard Wetherill clothes in a country garden, unfamiliar ideas that are equally disturbing to those who agree with them and to those who do not?' (*Drama*, Winter 1977–78)

There are echoes here of cultural battles long ago, stilled now in what some would see as the blanketing indifference of the nineties. Perhaps Hobson's view would not have carried general assent even among his seventies readers. What is remarkable is that the Cottesloe proved an accommodating host, on this occasion also, and thus vindicated once more the neutrality and flexibility of its performance space.

FIG 66 The meticulously detailed interior set for *Lark Rise*, with the audience sitting so close that everything had to look authentic.

LARK RISE TO CANDLEFORD

LARK RISE TO CANDLEFORD

Written by Keith Dewhurst, adapted from Flora Thompson's Trilogy, *Lark Rise, Over to Candleford* and *Candleford Green*

DIRECTORS	*Bill Bryden and Sebastian Graham-Jones*
DESIGN	*William Dudley*
LIGHTING	*William Dudley and Laurence Clayton*
MUSIC DIRECTORS	*Ashley Hutchings and John Tams*
SOUND	*Gabby Haynes* (*Lark Rise*) *and Chris Jordan* (*Candleford*)
PRODUCTION MANAGER	*Jason Barnes*
STAGE MANAGER	*John Caulfield*
PHOTOGRAPHY	*Michael Mayhew*

MUSIC BY The Albion Band: Bill Caddick (vocals, guitar, triangle), Howard Evans (trumpet) Michael Gregory (drums), Ashley Hutchings (bass guitar), John Kirkpatrick (vocals, melodeon, concertina), Doug Morter (vocals, guitar), Phil Pickett (woodwinds, tenor horn), Brian Protheroe (vocals, keyboards), Martin Simpson (vocals, guitar, banjo), John Tams (vocals, melodeon, fiddle), Graeme Taylor (vocals, guitar).

Players

Lark Rise

Benedict Beddard or *Paul Davies-Prowles*	Edmund
David Busby	Chad Gubbins, Morris dance
J.G. Devlin	Old David, Dick, Major Sharman
Edna Doré	Mrs Peveril, Queenie
Howard Goorney	Stut, Twister, Tramp Algy
Gawn Grainger or *Derek Newark*	Doctor, Squire, Landlord, Rector
James Grant	Albert Timms
Dave Hill	Bishie, Postie
Morag Hood	Mrs Blaby, Mrs Beamish Garibaldi Jacket
Louisa Livingstone	Martha Beamish, Polly
Kevin McNally	Fisher, John Price
Mary Miller	Emma Timms
Peggy Mount	Mrs Spicer, Old Sally, Mrs Miller, Mrs Andrews
Derek Newark or *Brian Protheroe*	Pumpkin
Bill Owen	Old Price, Grandfather
John Salthouse	Boamer, Cheapjack
John Tams	Cocky Pridham
Valerie Whittington	Laura

Candleford

Benedict Beddard or *Paul Davies Prowles*	Edmund
J.G. Devlin	Matthew
Edna Doré	Zilla
Howard Goorney	Cowman Jolliffe, Mr Coulsdon
Gawn Grainger	Sir Timothy
James Grant	Albert Timms, Mr Wilkins, Tom Ashley
Dave Hill	John (footman) Mr Cochrane
Morag Hood	Dorcas Lane
Louisa Livingstone	Minnie
Kevin McNally	Bavour
Mary Miller	Emma Timms Mrs Macey
Peggy Mount	Mrs Gubbins, Cinderella Doe
Derek Newark	Ben Trollope Looney Joe
Bill Owen	Tho. Brown
Brian Protheroe	Robert
John Salthouse	Bill
John Tams	Solomon
Valerie Whittington	Laura

The Promenade Season of *Lark Rise to Candleford* combined two plays, *Lark Rise* and *Candleford.* It opened on 14.11.1979 and ran until 29.12.1979. *Lark Rise* had previously played in the Cottesloe from 29.3.1978, directed by Bill Bryden and Sebastian Graham-Jones, with a cast including many of those in the Two-Play season, but also including Peter Armitage, Anna Carteret, Brian Glover, Mark McManus, Trevor Ray, Jack Shepherd, Frederick Warder and June Watson. Return performances of *Lark Rise* were staged from 6 to 30 September 1978, and the production was revived from 5.5.1979. *Candleford* was first staged for the Two-Play season in November and December 1979.

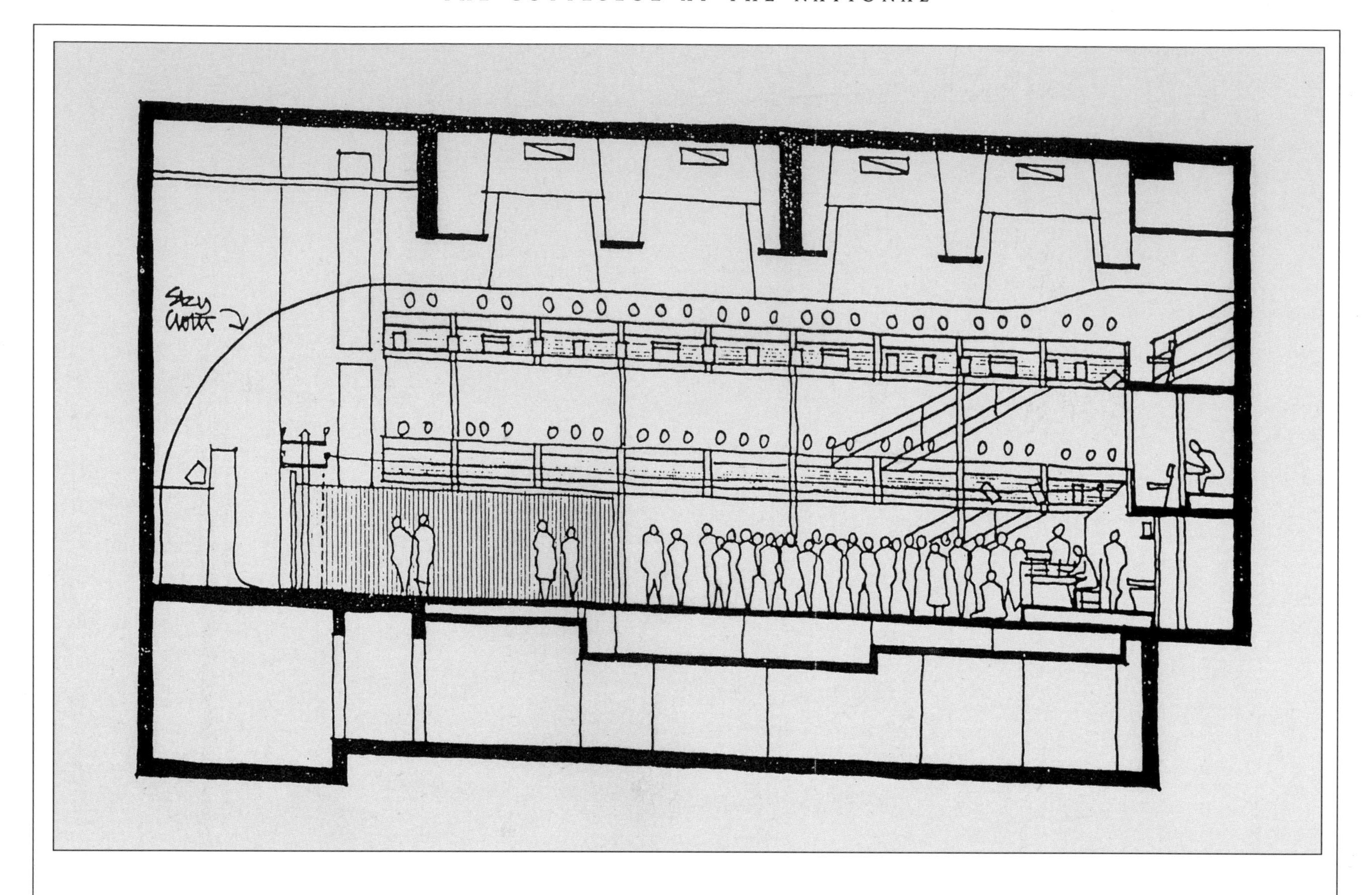

Technical Summary

• For the promenade production, the lower pit area of the Cottesloe was infilled with rostra, providing a clear flat floor throughout the theatre.

• On the main portion of the flat floor (13.75m by 9.9m), serving as field, village green, church, lane, snow-covered landscape or forest, two hundred and fifty promenaders stood, sat, ran and danced throughout the show.

• Both *Lark Rise* and *Candleford* shared a textured corn-coloured floor cloth, heavily covered in *Candleford*, to fit in with the winter's-day setting, with nylon imitation snowflakes (superseded later by paper).

• For *Candleford*, a huge sky cloth representing a frosty woodland scene rose from the back of the stage and, at a height of about 6.5m, covered the entire promenade area. When top lit with 5-kilowatt 'skypan' floods borrowed from Pinewood film studios, this bathed the whole space with a shadowless daylight, when underlit with dark blue it was transformed into a clear evening sky from which projected stars and harvest moon beamed down on the villagers.

• The cottage interior used for *Lark Rise* gave way in

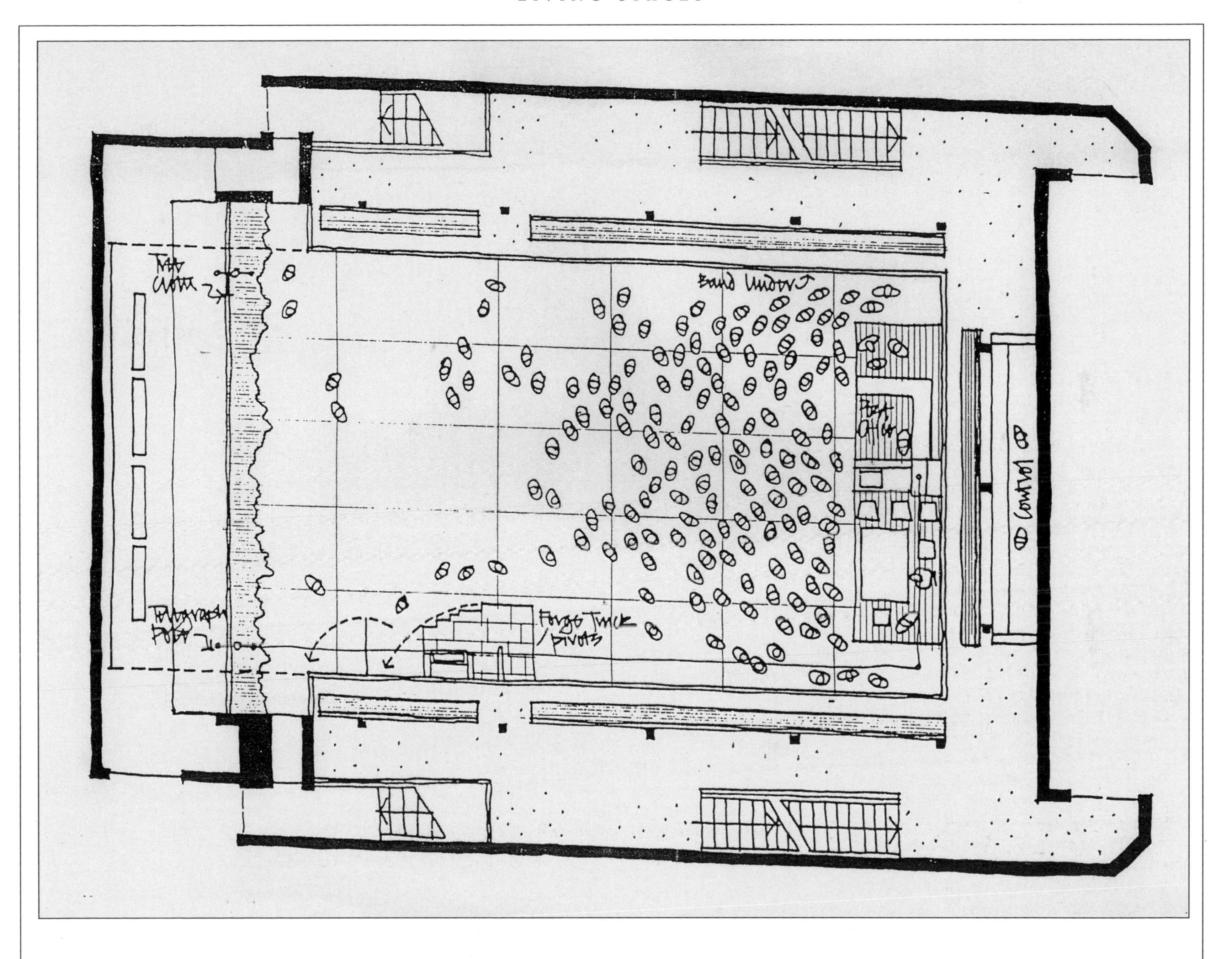

Candleford to a faithfully reproduced double interior representing Laura's Aunt's parlour and the adjacent Post Office. Every effort was made to have these locations authentic, employing such props as a faithfully-reproduced working 'Wheatstone' Telegraph machine.

• For *Candleford,* to stage right wooden doors folded back revealing an apparently working forge complete with bellows (borrowed from the Royal Blacksmiths), forge fire, tools and elm stump.

• Upstage, two stout telegraph poles supported three stretched telegraph wires, carrying a sepia photograph of *Lark Rise* characters on a curtain, which then slid to one side revealing a glistening frosty woodland cut cloth and backing. This provided exits and entrances to the arena.

Promenading the Cottesloe

For both *Lark Rise* and *Candleford*, the Cottesloe was employed as a promenade space, with the lower level made available for spectators to move around freely observing the action, and with the balcony used for seating. This arrangement was greeted with surprise by some audiences, though similar promenade staging had been used the previous year for *The Passion.* Even the veteran theatre-goers invited to review both shows on the BBC arts programme *Kaleidoscope* (Radio Four, 28.11.1979) commented on the novelty of the promenade experience, finding themselves marginally unsettled by what struck them as an unfamiliar relationship to the performance.

A UPI (United Press International) report by Gregory Jensen evoked the excitement and faint sense of danger associated with the promenade form: 'There are no seats and no stage. For two hours without an intermission playgoers shuffle about on a flat floor covered with artificial snow. ... As one scene ends, playgoers find themselves attacked from the rear by a snowball fight outside an authentic village smithy, at another point they have to skitter out of the way of scarlet-clad huntsmen riding (human) horses. All through the play the audience parts like the Red Sea whenever actors in their midst begin a new scene – which seems to happen at random, anywhere at all.' James Fenton, while vividly evoking one memorable incident from *Lark Rise,* questioned whether an effect of the promenade production was to make the actors more, not less, cut off from the feelings of their audiences: 'So here is the Cottesloe company, lined up for a day's reaping, a song on their lips and their scythes at the ready. And here stands the Cottesloe audience, uncomfortably aware that they are about to be reaped. Unblinkingly the actors advance. The scythes sweep. The nerve of the audience cracks, and they retreat before the encroaching blades. Seen from above, the spectators looked for a moment like wheat itself. One felt that if they had dawdled any longer they would certainly have been cut down.' Yet this childlike pleasure in apprehension was transformed during the performance into genuine enjoyment: 'After an hour or so ... I could not deny that I was moved'. (*Sunday Times,* 18.11.79)

The most notable response to the use of a promenade arrangement came in a wryly quizzical review by Peter Jenkins (Spectator, 24.11.1979), poised between appreciation and suppressed annoyance. Theatre, he explained, is the most restrictive of the arts, conventional in being composed of nothing but a stage and an audience. Theatre artists are always trying to escape from this prison: 'They are always captured and returned, for there is no

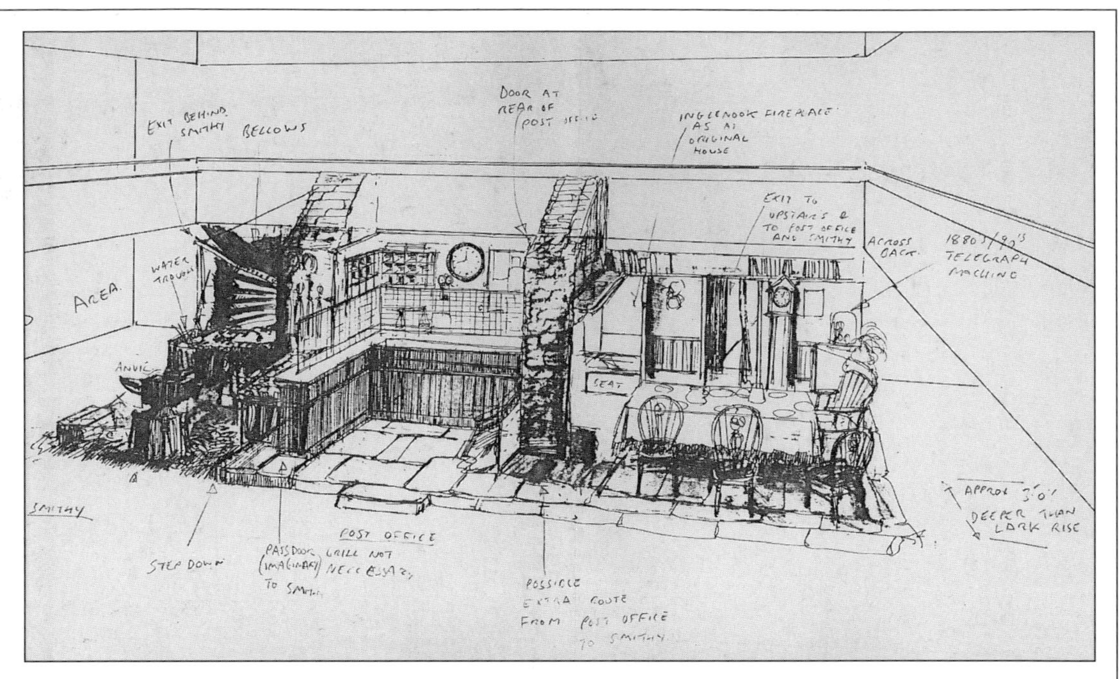

FIG 67 William Dudley's sketch of the smithy, Post Office and living room for *Candleford.* Some details were altered before the set was constructed .

Keith Dewhurst

When Keith Dewhurst adapted the two plays *Lark Rise* and *Candleford* from Flora Thompson's novels, he was best known to audiences as the author of sixteen television plays (one of which, *Last Bus,* had won the Japan Prize in 1968) and as the writer of many episodes of television series, including *Z-Cars.* He had also written nine stage plays, performed on London and provincial stages, including the Royal Court, the Edinburgh Royal Lyceum, the Sheffield Crucible and the Birmingham Rep. His adaptation of Christopher Hill's *The World Turned Upside Down* opened at the Cottesloe in November 1978, some months after the first performance of *Lark Rise.* Dewhurst had also worked as a presenter of BBC arts programmes and as a columnist for the *Guardian.*

Flora Thompson and 'Lark Rise to Candleford'

Remembered almost solely for her trilogy, *Lark Rise, Over to Candleford* and *Candleford Green,* Flora Thompson was born Flora Jane Timms in 1876 at Watford Tunnel Cottage in the hamlet of Juniper Hill in Oxfordshire. The eldest of ten children, six of whom died young, she attended Cottisford school for seven years, and when fourteen became junior assistant to Mrs Whitton, the postmistress of Fringford. She then went to work in the Surrey village of Grayshott where she met and married John Thompson, a post office clerk, by whom she had three children, a daughter, Winifred and two sons, Basil and Peter. John continued in the postal service, becoming sub-postmaster at Liphook, Hampshire, and postmaster at Dartmouth.

Much of Flora's writing directly reflects this biography. Her initial literary efforts were not notably successful, though her love stories and the sketches she wrote on nature sold sufficiently well to pay for school fees. Her autobiographical sketches based on childhood reminiscence were published in 1939 under the title *Lark Rise,* and the other two parts of the trilogy in 1941 and 1943. By the time of her death in May 1947, '*Lark Rise to Candleford* was clearly established as the masterpiece of a lost way of life, an unforgettable impression of the transitional state between the old, stable, work-pleasure England and the modern world.' (Keith Dewhurst in the programme for the 1979 production of *Lark Rise to Candleford.*)

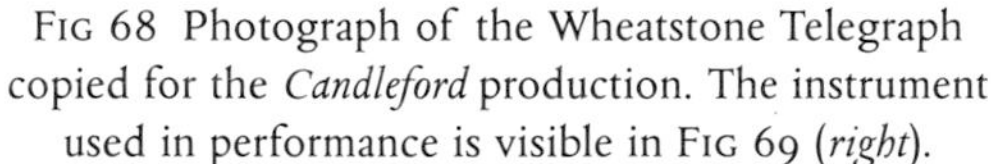

FIG 68 Photograph of the Wheatstone Telegraph copied for the *Candleford* production. The instrument used in performance is visible in FIG 69 (*right*).

FIG 69 Morag Hood (Dorcas Lane) in the Post Office using the copy of the Wheatstone Telegraph.

escape. This is why some go mad, like Artaud. Peter Brook is a borderline case.' 'Short of performing mime plays in a language of grunts on a mat laid out in the middle of the Sahara desert,' Jenkins writes, 'most of the escape bids are of a modest character – the Jacobean aside, the naturalistic illusion, the Brechtian "alienation effect", the "Pirandellian paradox" for examples.' The promenade production, he considered, is another instance of thwarted escapism. 'The theory, presumably, is that by mingling audience and performers the barrier of the theatre is broken down, or at least substantially lowered, that a greater proximity and involvement (in this case the actuality of village life) is achieved, and that humdrum incidents of daily life can be given a theatricality which transcends the absence of plot.' In the event, occupying a seat in the balcony, he was struck by the *distancing* effect of the promenade arrangement ('The crowd-control and self-discipline reminded me of the Open Golf Championship; there was children's behaviour to observe (remarkably good) and pretty girls to gaze at; indeed the amiability of the audience was stronger than the realism of the village scenes depicted'). When he took a place down on the theatre floor, among the actors, his sense of involvement was no greater: 'distracted by the art of their makeup, peering at the props – my feeling was not of being closer to the play but to the actors. It was more like being backstage than *on* stage. The nearer one approached the action the further one was from it.' Yet the total experience, Jenkins found, came across, paradoxically enough, as both fresh and memorable. *Lark Rise* and *Candleford* , he wrote, 'are theatrically original, pleasantly enjoyable, on the whole faithful to the spirit of the book and – hardly necessary to say about the Cottesloe – admirably performed.'

There were some for whom the pleasures of the promenade were qualified by its inconveniences. B.A. Young (*Financial Times*, 15.11.1979) reported that 'the action takes place all over a big stage from which the audience also may view the proceedings, dodging out of the way if ever the players impinge on them. (Bath-night in the barn must give some of them the most intimate full frontals yet seen in the theatre.)' But there was a price to pay. 'When so much happens in the enclosed spaces at one end, only a small proportion of the on-lookers can get a decent view. I saw from my seat in the balcony how many of them at the back of the crowd gave up trying and waited for a scene nearer their area of the stage.' Much the same sense of half-amused frustration comes across from the critic of the *Observer* (18.11.1979), who commented: 'Frankly I got well and truly caught between sitting like a country magistrate in one of the two tiers overlooking the barnyard-style spread of post-office, forge and unmarked country lanes and wandering Blind-Pugh-like among the action and the swirling mass of the audience, most of whom were sold far fewer dummies than I was (I managed on at least four occasions to arrive just as the activity switched to the other end of the auditorium)'.

Adapting the texts

Keith Dewhurst acknowledges in his programme note that the fifteen chapters of *Lark Rise*, each of them devoted to a different aspect of hamlet life, proved a difficult book to adapt for the stage. The solution employed for *Lark Rise* (the play) was to dramatise the events of a single day, with the first day of harvest chosen as 'the richest and most appropriate'. The setting, 'a flat floor and skycloth', he tells us, was suggested by a visit to Flora's birthplace, Juniper Hill. Adapting the remaining two parts of the trilogy for *Candleford* posed a different problem, with the two villages, Fringford in Oxfordshire and the more urbanised Grayshott in Surrey, telescoped into a single location. The solution is again to focus on a single day, in this case the first Saturday in January, when the hunt met, and to concentrate attention on the smithy and the post office.

Laura, the central character, is almost twelve years old in the first play and fourteen in the second. The plays reflect her inner life as well as the life of her place and her historical moment. Both end with a leap forward in time: 'Her journey is one that convinces us of the value of everyday humanity: she herself was strangely lost and lonely'. (From Dewhurst's programme note, 1979)

Dewhurst thought the courtyard arrangement of the Cottesloe particularly appropriate to his kind of play: 'The theatre is a space shared by the audience and the play is an event in that shared space ... The proscenium arch is an alien intrusion – a sheet of glass through which the audience can watch the goldfish cavorting ... None of this is in the English tradition – in Shakespeare, Hamlet actually speaks *to* the audience, there is no proscenium arch'. (Interview with Fenton Bailey, *Isis*, 9.10.1980)

Bill Bryden's stage

Bill Bryden joined the National Theatre while the company was still at the Old Vic. After the move to the South Bank, he directed some of the earliest productions on the Olivier and Lyttelton stages before being appointed director of the Cottesloe on its opening in 1977. Bryden's attachment to the promenade form developed out of his work on *The Passion*, a Tony Harrison adaptation of part of the York Mystery Cycle. The first performances were presented outdoors on the terraces of the National, a space he found 'acoustically terrible but theatrically very exciting' (Interview with Sheridan Morley, *Times*, 24.11.1979) On moving indoors he and his co-director Sebastian Graham-Jones found that 'instead of having the actors move around from place to place, within the Cottesloe it was the audience who would have to walk around between the different acting areas. That was how we got to the concept of "promenade" performances and since then we've never really looked back'. (*Times*, 24.11.1979)

FIG 70 The 1978 production of *Lark Rise*, with John Barrett, Derek Newark, Warren Clarke (on shoulders), Glyn Grain, John Tams and Michael Gough. The panoramic effect of the sky cloth is visible behind the actors.

Bryden, who first made his name as assistant to Bill Gaskill, is also a playwright. His interest in social issues and his skilled command of theatrical detail are evident in his plays *Benny Lynch* and *Willie Rough*, both of them first staged while he was associate director of the Edinburgh Royal Lyceum, and both subsequently brought to London. He has written widely for television. In the theatre, his work as director has characteristically involved ensemble acting, as in *Lark Rise* and *Candleford*, as well as *The Mysteries*. One of his most significant achievements at the National was the establishment at the Cottesloe of a semi-permanent group of actors who worked together on a series of shows, and thus achieved a strong artistic identity. At the same time, Bryden pointed out, the familiarity of the personnel was not allowed to breed staleness: 'The great thing about the Cottesloe,' he said 'is that people don't really know what to expect next: most of the time audiences don't even know if they'll be sitting down or walking around.' (*Times*, 24.11.1979)

Playing, authenticity and social commentary

J.C.Trewin found Thompson's portrait of rural life, and Dewhurst's recreation of it for the stage, appealing and authentic. As previously with *Lark Rise*, he thought the two-play experience moving: 'Again, in a modern poet's phrase, the country habit has us by the heart; it is a vanished England summoned with unsentimental honesty (as Flora Thompson's readers will recognise) under the wintry skycloth of the Cottesloe Theatre'. (*Birmingham Post*, 15.11.1979) This is a view largely shared by Charles Spencer (*Evening Standard* 15.11.1979). The two plays 'offer a

FIG 71 Men in the fields with scythes, *Lark Rise*, 1978.

moving and beautifully observed view of humanity at both its humorous best and hard-hearted worst' evoked in 'lovingly detailed and often joyful productions'. There are lessons, he believed, to be learned: 'Beyond the grinding poverty and monotony, there is a real and unsentimental feeling for values which we have possibly lost today – good fellowship, the satisfaction of a job well done, and unspoken love of the land which provides the food'.

For some, the plays hovered near the borderline that separates fact from sentiment. Surprised by the huge success of *Lark Rise* with its audiences, Dewhurst himself thought the plays' appeal due at least in part to the emotional climate of the seventies: 'I think *Lark Rise* caught the nostalgia boom, but there is also a genuine wish by people these days to find out how people lived in the past'. (Interview with P.J.B., *Advertiser*, 21.11.1979) The Cottesloe company thought it appropriate to absorb as much of the atmosphere of Thompson's Oxford villages as lingered into the present. As visitors to Juniper Hill and Fringford, they saw in the latter the old post office and smithy where much of the action of *Candleford* is set and noted 'where the horses stood under the tree waiting to be shod'. Learning country crafts – lace-making, the techniques of wielding a scythe, the arts of the blacksmith – formed a significant part of rehearsal, so that mimes would be accurate. Undoubtedly, such preparation as this paid dividends in the actors' adoption of their roles and in the sense most audiences had of a lovingly detailed stage-world. Only a few commentators thought the attempt at authenticity turned the performance, in Peter Jenkins's words, into 'a period-piece version of the Archers'. (*Spectator*, 24.11.1979)

Irving Wardle described the play and its staging as 'a beautiful piece of work'. Social observation, he considered, was supported and enhanced by accuracy of language: 'A cross-section of the community, from the destitute and crazed to the passing gentry, is built up in tiny flint-hard scenes, punctuated with dances, games, songs ... and, above all, work routines. Dialogue is partly invented (supplying a coarse masculine side to village life), but most of it is an immensely skilful collage of direct and reported speech from the book'. The temper of this recreation of Flora Thompson's life and times was 'in the best sense puritanical: sober virtue, warmth, satisfaction in small tasks perfectly performed'. Paradoxically, Wardle thought, a sense was achieved of a life both familiar and remote, an effect (it could be argued) to parallel the Cottesloe staging. The piece was performed, he wrote, 'in such a way as ... to hold the modern audience at 100 years' distance, for all their physical proximity'. (*Times*, 15.11.1979)

The Company

The nature of the show, with a great many double and triple roles, was such as to lay emphasis on ensemble work rather than individual performances. Nevertheless, the playing of the young actress Valerie Whittington as Laura, the Flora Thompson figure ('a beautifully grave performance', *Sunday Telegraph*, 18.11.1979) was widely praised, as were 'Peggy Mount's pugnacious old postwoman, J.G.Devlin's grizzled foreman smith, and Tony Haygarth's gentle village idiot (his last in a series of splendidly rounded small parts)' (Irving Wardle, *Times*, 15.11.1979) Most comment went, however, to the production's success in evoking a vigorously-diverse rural community. Yet the risk of offering nothing but caricatures was avoided. In the midst of the bustle of events and the multiplicity of characters, James Fenton for example discovered 'a reserve in the playing, a sense of dignity and privacy which is pleasing' (*Sunday Times*, 18.11.1979), a tribute to the persuasiveness of the actors' full possession of their roles.

Music

Music and dance contributed both to the story-line and to the audience's sense of participation and enjoyment: 'plenty of folk music, song and dance woven into the action, and a rousing finish to both plays with the audience joining in the final country dance'. (Patricia Leman, *Morning Star*, 29.11.1979) Edward Haber particularly welcomed the integration of the music and dance with the action: 'in this context one can perceive the traditional song in the social context from whence it comes', he wrote. He instanced 'Martin Carthy leading the harvesters while singing "All in a Row", Carthy singing a solo song while the farmers are gathered at a pub, a fruit seller singing an almost music-hall song while selling his fruit, David Busby performing a Morris step dance'. But the musical pieces were not mere inserts, having at times a role in enlarging the emotion of the script, or serving as dramatic irony: 'thus, John Tams (of the Albion Band) and Carthy duet in a moving unaccompanied version of "John Barleycorn"

while one of the characters, Major Sharman, is being taken to the workhouse against his will. Here the almost pathetic picture of senility is counterbalanced by a song which portrays life as an ongoing process – both death and birth'. (*New York Pinewoods Folk Music Club Newsletter*, December, 1978) The show's music was issued in December 1980 as a 33 rpm recording under the title *Lark Rise to Candleford: A Country Tapestry*.

The Albion Band under Ashley Hutchings had twice performed with the National before becoming involved with *Lark Rise* – in *The Passion* and in *Sir Gawain and the Green Knight*, a show principally aimed at children. Hutchings had the assistance of Martin Carthy and Shirley Collins, together with other members of the Albion Band, a group with much success in recording and concert tours behind them. Some reviewers objected to the lack of authenticity in the instruments used, the *Sunday Telegraph* commenting that 'electric guitars are surely an unforgivable anachronism in what is supposed to be a village band at the turn of the century'. (18.11.1979) B.A.Young in the *Financial Times* (15.11.1979) took much the same view, writing that 'with great pains a true Victorian country atmosphere is created. In such a circumstance, electronically amplified music, either for voices or instruments, kills the illusion at once. Our hair is just about to stand on end as little Martha goes to cut the witch-elm and see if it bleeds human blood when there is a cadenza of electric guitar notes and we are jerked back to Waterloo in 1979'. Hutchings' answer to such criticisms was to insist on the interpretive role of the music, a role integral to the effect of the production from its first rehearsals. 'A concertina and acoustic guitar cannot draw the real drama out,' he argued. 'No one says we should have cowboy films without music just because there wasn't any *actually* being played in the old Wild West.' (Interview with Tony Jasper, *The Stage and TV Today*, 30.3.1978)

Design

William Dudley's design drew little comment, perhaps because under the huge skycloth it was so detailed and complete as to be virtually imperceptible as design. Michael Billington wrote that 'it would be difficult to fault the detail of William Dudley's set with its Victorian engravings on the post-office walls and Hume's *History of England* on the parlour shelf'. (*Guardian*, 16.11.1979) This kind of authenticity, in sets, props and costumes, was achieved as the result of extensive research by Dudley

FIG 72 J.G. Devlin as Matthew, with cast and audience.

FIG 73 The Albion Band, who performed in both *Lark Rise* and *Candleford* in 1979.
Seated: Bill Caddick, Michael Gregory, Doug Morter, Ashley Hutchings. Standing: Howard Evans, Phil Pickett, Brian Protheroe, John Tams.

and by members of the production staff, and props buyers and makers. The post office, living room, smithy and farmyard were meticulously designed on the basis of period furnishings and artefacts, including farmyard implements (such as the scythes), household objects and personal belongings (period crockery, food, tables and chairs), an inglenook fireplace, a detailed reconstruction of an anvil, bellows and forge and, among the paraphernalia of the post office, a precise copy of a Wheatstone telegraph. The list of Running Props extended to something like 130 separate items and groups of items (e.g. 2 Beaded Covers for milk and ale; 15 hymn books; bee veil, bee gloves, 1 coal shovel and spoon for Queenie to tang for the bees; lace making equipment). The Food Running List included 'to be kept in good supply' 1 bag brown flour, 1 jar of jam, 1 packet margarine, 1 lb carrots, 2 packets Benson and Hedges Mellow Virginia Pipe Tobacco, assorted fresh fruit and vegetables and 1 large sprig of rosemary. 1 John Dory Fish and 3 large Bloaters were 'to be fresh for each performance', though they 'may last more than one depending on smell'. The vast skycloth, covering the whole playing area, needed proofing (because of the lights). On the insistence of the fire authorities, this proofing had to be renewed after each twenty performances.

FIG 74 Paul Jones as Macheath with some of the cast of whores in Richard Eyre's production of John Gay's *The Beggar's Opera,* designed by John Gunter. The photograph conveys something of the energy and the sleaze of the performance. The footlight oil-lamps used (among much else) to evoke the aura of the eighteenth century are visible in the foreground.

BEGGAR'S OPERA

By John Gay

The Director's Cut

Many of those who went to the first performances of the Cottesloe's *The Beggar's Opera* had in mind the huge success of Richard Eyre's Olivier musical *Guys and Dolls*. Many of the cast of the earlier show stayed with Eyre for the new venture, so that comparison was inevitable. Michael Billington thought the success was comparable: 'Richard Eyre's fine production at the Cottesloe succeeds for much the same reason as his now-legendary *Guys and Dolls*: it treats it as an integrated work in which the drama carries as much weight as the songs that punctuate it.' (*Guardian*, 2.7.82) Sheridan Morley, quoting Kenneth Tynan's remark that *Guys and Dolls* was *The Beggar's Opera* of Broadway, thought that the National Theatre had taken advantage of the embarrassment of riches available to it: 'a lot of people shamefully underused in *Guys and Dolls*, not least the amazing Imelda Staunton (who manages to play Lucy Lockit like Bette Midler imitating Judy Holliday, and that is no mean achievement) come into their own as musical stars.' (*Punch*, 14.7.82) Milton Shulman (*Standard*, 2.7.82) was pleased: 'Richard Eyre's direction has the vitality and bite of a Cruikshank cartoon but never allows social significance to get in the way of the fun. The National Theatre has, indeed, found a fitting companion piece to run in tandem with its joyous production of *Guys and Dolls*.'

Cottesloe productions do not exist in a theatrical vacuum, however much a Cottesloe audience anticipates freshness and innovation. Many audience members and reviewers saw the current production in the context of other revivals, each of them dedicated to making the dry bones of text and music live. Michael Coveney (*Financial Times*, 2.7.82) thought Eyre had succeeded: 'No revival can nowadays make much of the attacks on the government, the allusions to the informer Jonathan Wild, the rivalry between Walpole's wife and mistress invoked in the warring arias of Polly Peachum and Lucy Lockit. What can be achieved and is achieved in Richard Eyre's beautiful, smokily Hogarthian production for the National Theatre, is a free flow of expressively emotional content between the brief musical items and the spirited dialogue and a coherent, colourful picture of Newgate society where the transaction of a life is as casually undertaken as the sale of a piece of cloth.' Bernard Crick was elated:

THE BEGGAR'S OPERA
By John Gay

Director	*Richard Eyre*
Designer	*John Gunter*
Music adapted by	*Dominic Muldowney*
Dances by	*David Toguri*
Lighting	*Peter Radmore*
Staff Director	*David Penn*
Dialect Coach	*Joan Washington*
Production Manager	*Jason Barnes*
Stage Manager	*John Caulfield*
Deputy Stage Manager	*Sarah Parkin*
Sound	*Caz Appleton*
Photography	*John Haynes*

Cast in order of speaking:

Beggar	*William Armstrong*
1st Gentleman	*Norman Warwick*
Pickpocket	*Kevin Williams*
2nd Gentleman	*Kevin Quarmby*
Fence	*David Ryall*
Irish Cockney	*Harry Towb*
Pimp	*Paul Jones*
Peachum	*Harry Towb*
Filch	*Kevin Williams*
Mrs Peachum	*June Watson*
Polly Peachum	*Belinda Sinclair*
Macheath	*Paul Jones*
Ben Budge	*Larrington Walker*
Matt of the Mint	*Richard Walsh*
Jemmy Twitcher	*William Armstrong*
Crook-Fingered Jack	*Norman Warwick*
Wat Dreary	*Kevin Williams*
Nimming Ned	*Kevin Quarmby*
Harry Paddington	*Vincent Pickering*
Drawer	*Vincent Pickering*
Jenny Diver	*Fiona Hendley*
Mrs Coaxer	*Gail Rolfe*
Mrs Vixen	*Rachel Izen*
Molly Brazen	*Imelda Staunton*
Dolly Trull	*Belinda Sinclair*
Suky Tawdry	*Sally Cooper*
Mrs Slammekin	*June Watson*
Lockit	*David Ryall*
Lucy Lockit	*Imelda Staunton*
Mrs Trapes	*June Watson*
Gaoler	*Kevin Quarmby*

Musicians: Rory Allam (*clarinet*), Robin Jeffrey (*guitar/mandolin*), Tim Laycock (*concertina*), Roderick Skeaping (*violin/psaltery*)

The production opened at the Cottesloe Theatre on 1.7.82 and continued in repertoire until 10.10.82. It transferred to the Theatre Royal, Bath in June 1983, and to the Grand Theatre, Wolverhampton in October 1983. It was recorded in the Cottesloe for television in November, 1982.

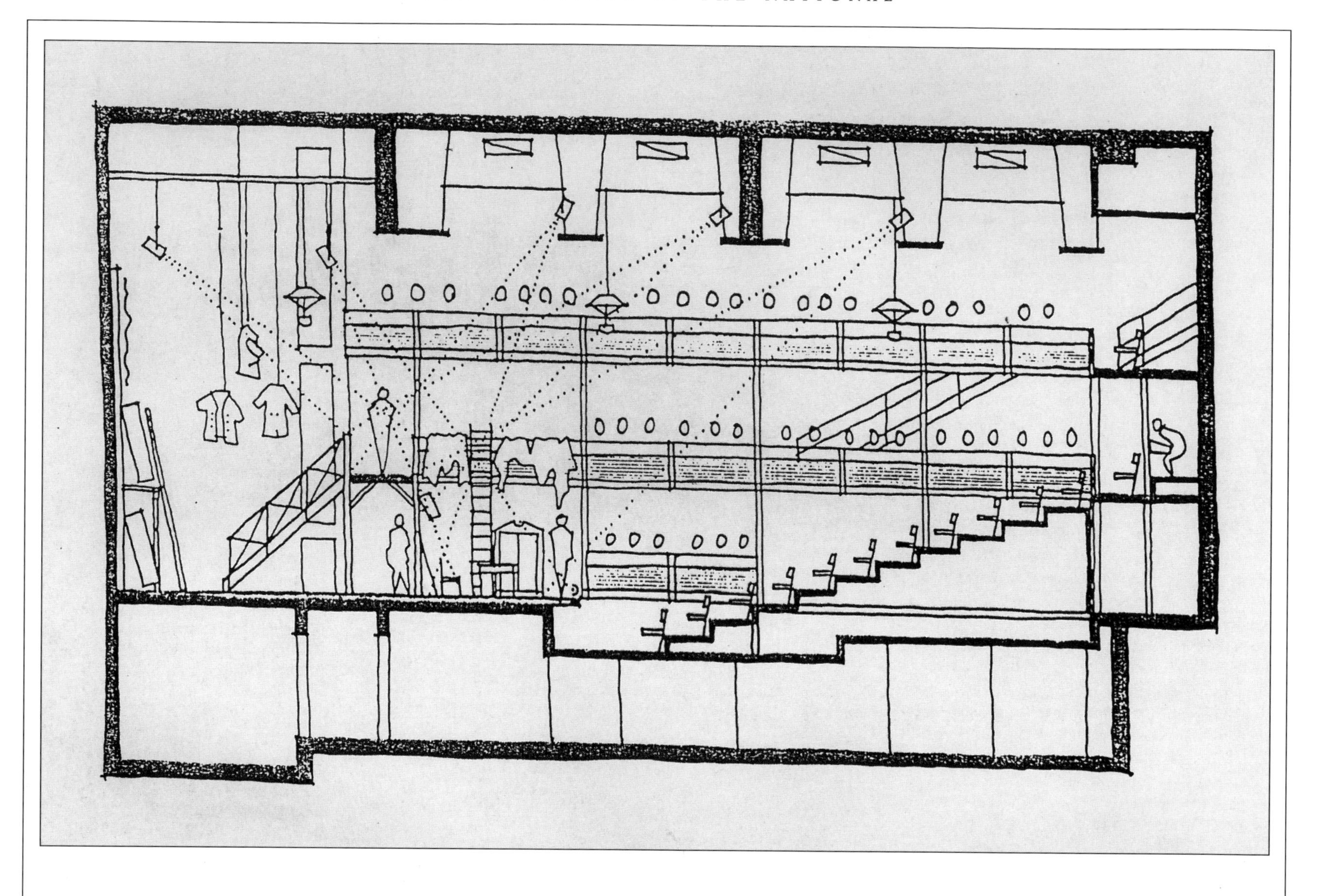

Technical Summary

• This production used an end-stage configuration, with the front row set down 94cm.

• John Gunter's design drew directly on the architectural nature of the theatre itself, in that it employed an existing bridge, and a one-level 'fourth wall' (as originally envisaged by Iain Mackintosh and realised by William Dudley for the first of the *Mysteries*) in order to create a mid-Victorian workhouse.

• The audience entered a smoky, galleried room lit by gaslight overhead, and peopled by the beggars, whores and pimps celebrated in ballads contemporary with the play's (or musical's) author, John Gay (1685–1732).

• A coarsely boarded forestage area, 3.3m deep by 9.9m wide, was variously furnished for the Peachum and Lockit dwellings, and for the tavern and goal.

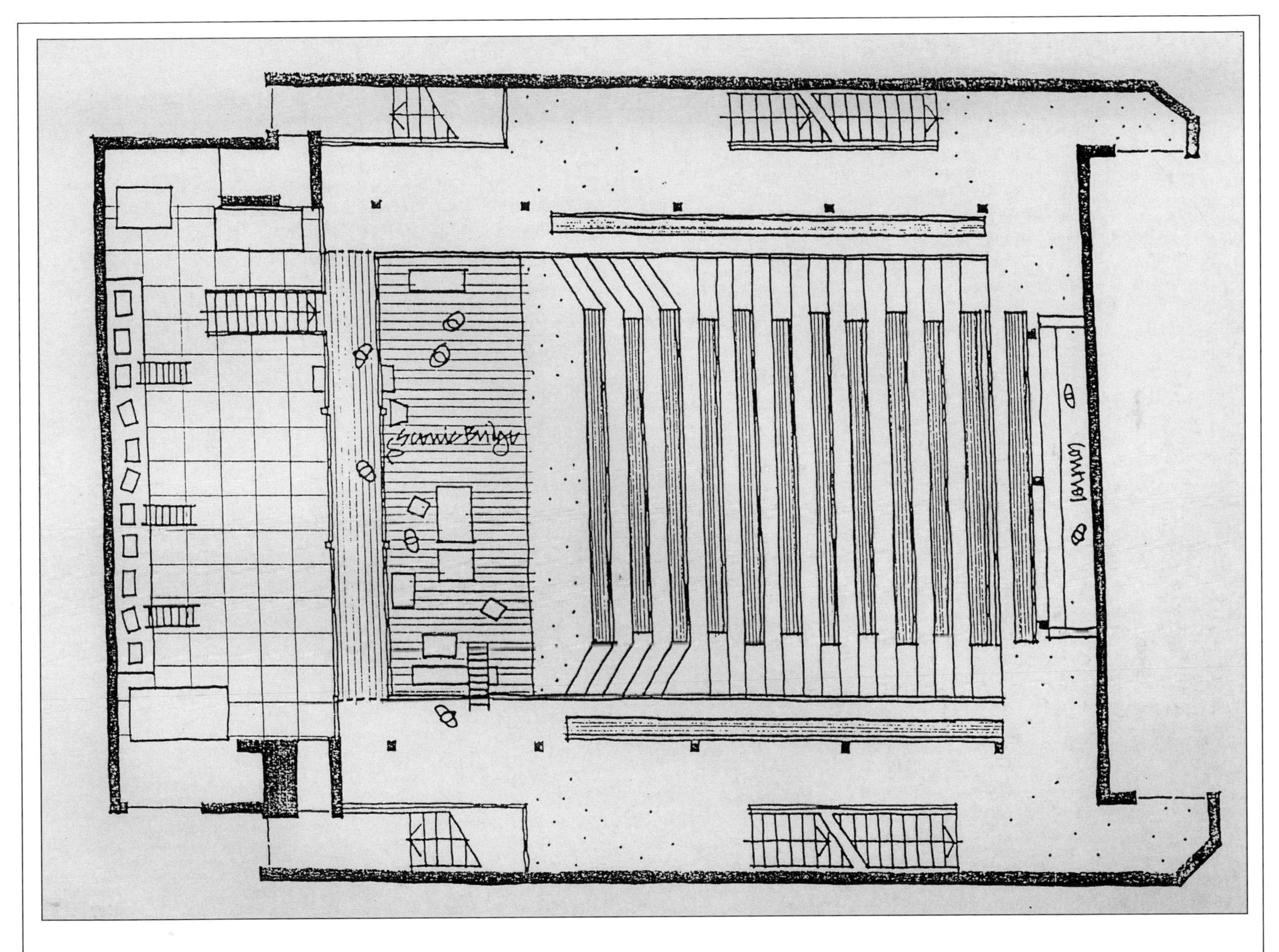

• This gave way upstage to a musicians' area (upstage right) and to a rear wall of poorhouse sleeping boxes, stacked three high and accessed by ladder, gently seething with grubby humanity throughout.

• Overhead hung the poorhouse occupants' clothing, hauled up in historically authentic fashion with the line clung to in order to avoid theft.

• A collaboration with Warner Communications led to the first television recording to be made wholly within the Cottesloe itself. All the necessary recording equipment was installed behind the raised pit tier seating, with the cameras accommodated in front of the acting area by decking-over the front seating rows. Recording started at 8.00a.m. each day, with the theatre reverting to live performance each evening.

'Richard Eyre's National Theatre production is neither definitive nor perfect, but it is very very good: lively, vigorous and with actors full of joy and love for the play. I went out bouncing almost as if I had seen it in 1728 for the first time rather than in 1982 for the tenth.' (*Times Higher Education Supplement*, 23.7.82) Ned Chaillet was almost equally delighted by Eyre's recovery of the spirit of the original: 'What a glorious thing, then, to see the play roughened and stripped of formal accretions. It could never be exactly the play that Gay gave to the English theatre in 1728, but with Richard Eyre's direction and the adapted music that Dominic Muldowney has turned back to its folk and popular roots, it is a play that now dances forward with great energy and great wit. It is a fine success that beautifully partners its remote descendant elsewhere in the National Theatre, *Guys and Dolls*.' (*Times*, 3.7.82)

There were some reservations. John Barber (*Daily Telegraph*, 2.7.82) complained that 'We are hardly made aware ... that Macheath's gang stand for the freehearted and generous aristocracy, and that the gaoler Lockit and the fence Peachum represent the money-grubbing Whig middle-classes. But it is clear enough that all are motivated – except perhaps for the doting women – by a cynical self-interest.' A few reviewers were worried by what seemed the excessive grimness of it all. John Fuller thought the production sacrificed some of the opportunities for irony of Gay's text, and in particular criticised the final chorus for its lack of humour: it was 'here presented by the assembled company directly facing the audience in a suddenly stark and admonitory stance, singing in strident staccato, as though it were the Chorale of the Poorest of the Poor from *Die Dreigroschenoper*.' (*Times Literary Supplement*, 16.7.82) Francis King made something of the same point: 'Realistic squalor is the keynote of Richard Eyre's production of John Gay's *The Beggar's Opera* (Cottesloe). Macheath is not so much a debonair and romantic highwayman as a Gorbals trickster; Lucy Lockit is a strident termagent; and the women of the town are so gaunt and bespotted that they are clearly in the ultimate stages of syphilis. Such an approach amplifies to the full Gay's yelp of social protest; but it also destroys the piquancy of the contrast between, on the one hand, the crudeness and ugliness of the characters' behaviour and, on the other, the delicacy and prettiness with which they express themselves in the airs of the time.' (*Sunday Telegraph*, 7.2.82) 'The whole thing', said Robert Cushman succinctly, 'reeks of gin and bitterness'. (*Observer*, 9.7.1982)

Bernard Crick's concern, amidst his delight, was different: 'I cannot tear myself away from this wonderful spectacle without commenting that, as usual, the ladies of the town were hideously overdone. Do producers think that Gay was a queer trying to put men off women? Excess breeds excess. Richard Eyre needs reminding that a single flash of an inch of gartered thigh is more erotic than constant exposure to (if gallantry did not forbid) two aging drooping bosoms. I say this in the interests of proper prurience, not public decency.' (*Times Higher Education Supplement*, 23.7.82) Few reviewers were so sophisticatedly fastidious. At other points in his review, Crick

The Author

John Gay was born in Barnstaple in Devon in 1685, and went to London as apprentice to a silk merchant. In 1712 he became 'domestic steward' to the Duchess of Monmouth, and in 1714 secretary to the Tory Lord Clarendon. His early efforts at dramatic writing were unperformed or failures. His interest in literary sincerity is shown in his farce *The What D'Ye Call It* (1715), which satirises the high-flown sentiment of both heroic tragedy and fashionable comedy. His *Trivia, or the Art of Walking the Streets of London* (1716) vividly depicts the conditions of life, especially low life, in the capital. Both strands are combined in *The Beggar's Opera* (1728). This ballad opera produced by the impressario John Rich, manager of the Lincoln's Inn Fields Theatre, proved an instant success which, it was said, 'Made Gay rich and Rich gay'. As a satire on corruption, and an account of the values shared by the privileged and the down-and-out, it proved controversial when it was interpreted as an attack on the current government of Sir Robert Walpole. The offence caused led to the banning from the stage of Gay's much less effective sequel *Polly* (1729), set in the West Indies (though it was published by subscription), and may have influenced the introduction of Walpole's Licensing Act (1737), an Act that gave powers to the Lord Chamberlain that were finally surrendered only in 1968.

Gay's apparent sympathy for the impoverished may arise from his own lack of financial success and ill luck (at least as he saw it). Though he raised a considerable sum from the sale of his *Poems on Several Occasions* (1720), he lost it all again in the disastrous 'South Sea Bubble', when the investment company failed. At the same time, he had friends in high places, not only aristocrats but also the arbiters of current literary taste, Pope and Swift, his fellow members in the Scriblerus Club. (Swift may have suggested the idea of *The Beggar's Opera* when he wrote to Pope (in 1716) asking 'what think you of a Newgate pastoral among the whores and thieves there?') Gay was capable of wide sympathy for all kinds of people – and of a mordant wit, as when he wrote his own epitaph (he died in 1732), now inscribed on his tomb in Westminster Abbey: 'Life is a jest and all things show it;/I thought so once and now I know it'.

The Music

The use of ballad tunes in *The Beggar's Opera* to create a new type of music theatre proved a notable success. Gay was himself a musician (a flautist). His association with the musical establishment is suggested by the invitation he accepted to write the libretto for Handel's *Acis and Galatea*. But his sources for the ballad tunes of *The Beggar's Opera* were by and large more popular. As Adrian Mitchell remarks in the Cottesloe programme, 'Most of them were the common street tunes of the time – all his audience would recognise most of them. These were interspersed with a few from more remote sources, most of them from France. Gay drew on songs from the six volumes of Tom D'Urfey's *Wit and Mirth, or Pills to Purge Melancholy* and also on the Scottish songs in William Thompson's *Orpheus Caledonius*. Another source was Playford's *Dancing Master*. But Gay equipped the traditional tunes with new and brilliant words.'

Gay's wish to have the songs performed unaccompanied was vetoed by his aristocratic patroness, the Duchess of Queensberry, whose opposition led to the appointment of the German composer Dr Pepusch to orchestrate the music and to write an overture. His setting for two violins, two oboes, a tenor and a cello, is recalled in the sparseness of the orchestration (by Dominic Muldowney) for the Cottesloe revival, though not in terms of its sound quality or musical writing (Pepusch had the two violins and two oboes play in unison). Muldowney's adaptation, praised by John Fuller (*Times Literary Supplement*, 16.7.82) as 'discreet, low-key, a subtle aura of concertina and psaltery', in fact used clarinet, guitar, mandolin, concertina, violin and psaltery to achieve its effects. *The Beggar's Opera* has inspired a number of musical adaptations and revivals, including a notable score from Benjamin Britten, and the Kurt Weill music for Brecht's *Dreigroschenoper* (*The Threepenny Opera*).

FIG 75 The stage setting and audience for *The Beggar's Opera*. The clothing of the workhouse inmates can be seen hoisted on ropes above the stage.
PHOTO: *Jason Barnes*

FIG 76 Some of the numerous properties that conveyed the realism of setting in *The Beggar's Opera*: 'a marvellous clutter of ledgers, aspidistras and overflowing wardrobes' (John Fuller, *Times Literary Supplement*, 16.7.82)
PHOTO: *Jason Barnes*

appreciated the subtlety of Eyre's interweaving of weighty comment and light touch: 'the trio of Lockit, Peachum and Mrs Trapes were sublimely comic. Comic, yes, but as Irlin Hall sang the fat brothel keeper's last line, "Lip to lip while we're young, then the lip to the Glass", she shuddered with a Dr Johnson-like *memento mori*, old mortality crept in behind the gin fumes – that was a fine touch. The laughter of life and the fear of death are so close together in Gay's world.'

The Cottesloe as Workhouse

In place of the eighteenth-century world of Gay's music theatre, the Cottesloe was set out for *The Beggar's Opera* as a nineteenth-century workhouse. As Richard Eyre explained on a Radio 4 *Kaleidoscope* programme (2.7.82, presented by Sheridan Morley), John Gunter's setting was intended to refer to a late nineteenth-century beggars' doss-house, evoking the hard-bitten world of petty criminals and vagrants without saddling itself with the forced contemporary parallels that would have resulted from complete up-dating. Michael Billington (*Guardian*, 2.7.82) approved: 'It is amazing how well the text suits the time-shift and it gives John Gunter the chance to come up with a highly atmospheric set dominated by a massive timbered bridge. From under its smoke-ridden arches emerge a group of Mayhewesque vagrants to put on a show for the swells on a gas-footlights stage. It is an excellent idea that enhances the central irony: that the rich are patronising an entertainment that attacks their own values.' The stage-set was complemented, Billington noted, by costume design and a multiplicity of props that re-enforced the apparent authenticity of the piece: 'Everyone is rooted in some precise world so that Lockit becomes a Victorian gaoler-cum-fence retreating to his aspidistra-filled lair where his dusty wardrobe bulges with stolen goods. As so often in the theatre, a closely-observed realistic background gives life to events in the foreground.'

John Fuller (*Times Literary Supplement*, 16.7.82) amplified Billington's remarks: 'Eyre's is a more purely theatrical space [than the Britten version], compounded of Charenton, Mayhew, Brecht's Soho and the all-purpose timber of Bart's *Oliver!* John Gunter's Dickensian set is a marvellous clutter of ledgers, aspidistras and overflowing wardrobes. When David Ryall's morose Lockit puts on his boots, the putting on of the boots becomes an absorbing activity. When a bosom is bared or soup splashed about, these things become more than theatrical symbols, they are tangible necessities. The production absorbs, eclectically, every suggestion from Cruikshank to Toulouse-Lautrec appropriate to the moment. The dust, the sour erotic grimace, the sweat, the saucers of tea, the juggling, the bad teeth: excellent characterization is accompanied by an inventive and patient realism (and beautifully-timed stage-business) which roots Gay's moral insights in an actual world of shabby ambition and pathetic acquisitiveness.'

Benedict Nightingale, while very favourably disposed to the production, joined critics quoted above in thinking the grimness of the Victorian setting sometimes overdone: 'just once or twice the production over-emphasises the tawdriness of its setting and society. Surely Macheath, who "always loved to have his ladies well dressed", would not allow himself to be caught in company quite so mucky as that provided by the National's Molly Brazen, Suky Tawdry et al, with their tacky dresses, over-ripe underclothes, exposed bosoms, and general air of cackling all the way to a collective death by syphilis.' (*New Statesman*, 9.7.82) It was a point picked up by Bernard Crick, who found the production 'too uniformly Swift and Brecht, not gay enough'. Yet Crick considered the show offered its own corrective, in costume and design terms, to this tonal emphasis: 'The stage of the Cottesloe was Peachum's lock or warehouse. Its wooden galleries and rafters blended into the side galleries of the theatre itself, a splendid unity of design. My fears arose that clever tricks were afoot when the beggars wandered in wearing late Victorian rags amid fog and dim gaslight; but when Peachum began to sing, he put on a green velvet early eighteenth-century frock coat, just as Macheath appeared in scarlet above his Victorian rags. Then all was well. The trick was vindicated. The time change gave us a more familiar Mayhew world of poverty, and these beggars then played their grand old opera: the first thorough-going alienation effect. They even set up oil lamp footlights (Peachum, Lockit or Robin of Bageshot, alias Black Bob, must have had a word with the GLC's safety officers).' (*Times Higher Education Supplement*, 23.7.82) He added: 'There is dark Swiftian misanthropy in it, but also great shafts of gaiety and light. The class war is there and the sex war too, not just the predatory Macheath – "I must have Women ... Money is not so strong a Cordial for the Time" – but also the brutally affable yet cruelly habitual tyranny of father over daughter.'

The Music of the Times

Richard Eyre's direction was praised especially for discovering an idiom that blended music with speech. As Eyre himself explained on *Kaleidoscope*, the Company began from the premise that the songs were extensions of the dialogue, and that the play's language must flow seamlessly from dialogue to song and back again. He compared Gay's 'opera' to Brendan Behan's *The Hostage* and to Joan Littlewood's shows. (Broadcast on Radio Four's *Kaleidoscope*, presented by Sheridan Morley, 2.7.82) Ned Sherrin, while placing Gay's work 'eight leagues above *The Threepenny Opera*' had even more homely analogies: 'It was the *Anyone for Dennis?* of its day, set to the current top twenty (or top fifty-odd)', though he conceded that Gay's show is, in contrast to our own trivia 'a survivor'. (*Plays and Players*, August 1982) Michael Billington, while considering that 'the problem ... always lies in the music' thought (in terms that are reminiscent of Eyre's own) that the production had solved or almost solved the difficulty: 'treat the work as an opera and you are in trouble because these sawn-off popular melodies don't have the weight for arias. But here there are only four musicians (on clarinet, guitar, concertina and violin) and the songs adapted by Dominic Muldowney seem like an extension of the dialogue. Thus Polly's sung "What I did you must have done," is followed without pause by Mrs Peachum's spoken "Not with a highwayman", and the gang's "Fill every glass" is not a bit of thigh-slapping roistering but something that grows gradually from a quiet injunction into a noisy assertion of life. Instead of numbers, the songs become a continuation of drama by other means.' (*Guardian*, 2.7.82) John Fuller agreed: 'The singing, and the relationship between singing and speaking (so hard to manage), are first rate. All in all, Gay would be intrigued and amazed at the rich texture of this production.' (*Times Literary Supplement*, 16.7.82)

FIG 77 Imelda Staunton as Lucy Lockit, Paul Jones as Macheath and Belinda Sinclair as Polly Peachum.

Bernard Crick's long and enthusiastic review appreciated the decision to use actors not singers: 'the director chose to have actors singing rather than singers acting. Now classical singing is not part of the training or acquired talents of most modern actors, so here is a crucial option: but even bad classical singing is closer to a beggar's opera than the horror of an over-orchestrated score and of trained singers trying to act low, as if in pantomime (the Scottish Opera Company did just such a memorably awful version last year).' It was in this context that he assessed some of the leading performances, and the shaping of the opera's text: 'Macheath (Paul Jones) marvellously played as a handsome but vulgar Glaswegian street-seducer, simply couldn't sing well enough. (Yes, I know *the* Paul Jones; but the former rock star couldn't get the grace notes, when folk melody satirizes opera.) Lucy Lockit (Imelda Staunton) could – by god she could! – a pocket volcano of anger, some comic effects but some pregnant and real enough to create a shudder for ruined woman's lot: so they left her all her songs and gave them full musical value, except that the slanging match with Lucy (the satire of two divas going at each other) had to be simplified. Polly even lost her most famous "Oh, ponder well" and, even more astonishing, her duet with Macheath, "Oh what pain it is to part". Inherently beautiful and touching, they had to go. And they got through possibly the loveliest love duet in the native repertory, "Were I laid on Greenland's Coast/And in my arms embrac'd my Lass" as quickly as they could, flattening every note, just crooning to each other "naturalistically". Again, this misses the irony. Gay contrasts the natural and the artificial. The satire of "Italian opera" of that period can surely extend to a type of opera of every period.' (*Times Higher Education Supplement*, 23.7.82)

There was appreciation for Dominic Muldowney's adaptation of the original ballad-music. Michael Coveney wrote that 'The great virtue of Dominic Muldowney's arrangements is two-fold: the monotonously predominant triple time of each snippet is cleverly disguised by interesting rhythmic variants; and the threadbare tedium of the traditional fiddle and harpsichord accompaniment quite banished in the ingeniously deft colourations for clarinet, mandolin, guitar, concertina, [violin] and psaltery.' (*Financial Times*, 2.7.82) What emerges from virtually all the comment is a sense of the sheer enjoyment – lusty, toe-tapping, rambunctious – that was generated by Muldowney's up-dating of tunes that for the most part go deep into the subsoil of popular music.

The Players not the Play

Whatever reservations were expressed about the temper of the show or the treatment of the music, there was almost universal admiration for the acting, and for Richard Eyre's success in eliciting wonderfully energetic performances from a talented cast. Paul Jones as Macheath, essaying a new career, and Imelda Staunton as Lucy Lockit (fresh from taking over from Julia MacKenzie the starring role of Miss Adelaide in *Guys and Dolls*) drew most comment. Jack Tinker was struck by the performance of Paul Jones as 'a mean-eyed Glaswegian chauvinist, who takes his pleasure where he may, and gives his lusts the urgency of a man who knows full well his days may be numbered.' 'It is,' Tinker adds, 'a powerfully judged performance, which he stands and delivers.' (*Daily Mail*, 2.7.82) Michael Billington similarly relished a gutsy piece of playing: 'Paul Jones's Macheath (Scots incidentally) is no dashing swaggerer but a pimp playing a highwayman in dirty scarlet coat and mud-covered spats; and his sexual voracity ("I must have women") comes to seem less like rampant jollity than an ungovernable obsession.' (*Guardian*, 2.7.82) Graham Hassell (*London Arts Magazine*, 13.7.82) overcame his expectations of the former rock star to end up admiring his performance: 'The surprise ... is how good a Macheath Paul Jones is. His voice has a grittiness that enhances his canny Scots captain. I expected him to sing everyone else off stage, as he did, and it's here one wished the songs were more than one verse long and not so often in a minor key. But Mr Jones's accent holds good too and his portrayal of the tacky, unchivalrous chauvinist highwayman, with one eye on women and two on self-interest has a squalid charm that like his singing strikes just the right note.'

Lynne Truss was among those dazzled by Imelda Staunton's performance as Lucy Lockit: 'Outstanding, even alongside other very good performances, is Imelda Staunton's Lucy Lockit, for which she received two SWET award nominations. Small, dark and intense, her Lucy is a comic termagent who hurtles about the stage, belting out her songs. When she rests from her rages she stands threateningly close to people, panting, her face glaring up into theirs. Miss Staunton says that she thinks of Lucy as "a tiny, pregnant, *mad* woman". (*Times Educational Supplement*, 15.7.82) Lucy Hughes-Hallet saw something of the same edge and passion: 'she erupts on to the stage like a small but dangerous tornado. She sings with a voice that is as expressive as it is powerful and fighting Polly Peachum, her rival for the highwayman's love, she blends a ferocious, anarchic, comic style with something more subtle and disturbing, an edge of painfully undignified passion.' (*Standard*, 14.1.83) Michael Billington found that 'Imelda Staunton makes a ferocious impact as a mob-capped, heavily pregnant Lucy Lockit unable to remember, when entertaining Polly, which of two teacups she has filled with ratsbane.' (*Guardian*, 2.7.82)

John Fuller was almost alone in thinking the full-bloodedness of the playing sacrificed opportunities for irony. 'As Polly,' he suggested, 'Belinda Sinclair is a tall red-head, with a striking bone-structure. She sits on the arm of her father's chair as bold as you please, whereas we should feel shocked to hear her parents call her 'slut' and 'baggage' simply because she has married for love. Similarly, the Macheath of Paul Jones exhibits not those high-born pretensions that would lend a shocking yet engaging edge to his reckless sexuality, but something more like the slightly dazed aggressiveness of a Rangers supporter determined against the odds to have a good night out.' (*Times Literary Supplement*, 16.7.82) A similar footballing analogy occurred to Benedict Nightingale, making a similar point within a general appreciation for the achievements of the production: 'strong, vivid, unsentimental performances ... we get in some abundance. Harry Towb's canny Ulster Peachum; David Ryall's sly and swinish Lockit; Imelda Staunton, a tiny bruiser, stamping and pummelling her way through the part of Lucy Lockit; above all, Paul Jones's Macheath, less the down-market matinee idol than the prototype of those sweaty, menacing Glaswegians you find every other May in London, roaming the West End and reeling towards Wembley Stadium, flags tied round their waists. The last actor I saw in the part looked as if he'd find it hard to break an egg, let alone a head, and, given his genteel tones, might as well have been called Fitzmansion or Plantation-Smythe. This one is a plausible highwayman, a true Mac*heath*.' (*New Statesman*, 9.7.82)

FIG 78 June Watson as Mrs Peachum and Kevin Williams as Filch.

It was this whole-heartedness that appealed to most reviewers and audiences. Bernard Crick took the view that 'It was meet, right and proper that so many of the cast of the current "smash hit" *Guys and Dolls* should be transported from the Olivier into the Lilliputian Cottesloe for the *Beggar's Opera*, though by design as well as good fortune they neither guyed it nor dolled it. For Gay's *Beggar's Opera* is the mother of them all: ballad operas, music dramas, dramas with song and the modern musical. And until the work of Benjamin Britten, it was our truly national "opera", both in the beauty and vitality of the folk melodies and in the satire of obsessive social class.' (*Times Higher Educational Supplement*, 23.7.82) It was something of a triumph that Richard Eyre's cast succeeded in carrying off so convincingly this up-dated version of a national classic.

FIG 79 Jennifer Hall as Miranda and Michael Bryant as Prospero in *The Tempest*. The textures of the sanded floor can be seen behind them.

SHAKESPEARE LATE PLAYS

The Director and his Legacy

It was inevitable that Peter Hall's decision to stage Shakespeare's Late Plays as his final set of productions as Director of the National should lead the media to extended comment on the achievements of his tenancy, and to drawing analogies between the plays and Hall himself. Headline writers tried every variation on 'Swansong' and 'Hall and Farewell', and reviewers wrestled with alleged parallels between the retiring director and *The Tempest's* Prospero, whose action in breaking his staff has been traditionally and sentimentally interpreted as Shakespeare's farewell to the stage. The fact that Hall's Prospero (Michael Bryant) was characterised chiefly by irascibility and a compulsion to look back in anger did not deter but on the contrary provoked some reviewers to search out fancied autobiographical references. Hall's decision to cast his daughter Jennifer in the rôle of Prospero's daughter Miranda invited further comment. Rehearsal-room and other troubles sharpened public awareness of the shows: the veteran actor Robert Eddison dropped out claiming Sir Peter was trying to teach an old dog new tricks, Sarah Miles, herself a replacement for Wendy Morgan, withdrew as Innogen amidst a blaze of press speculation (to be replaced by Geraldine James), Jennifer Hall left a short way into the run against a supposed background of family disharmony, and postponement of the opening of *Cymbeline* was followed by the cancellation of two public previews of *The Tempest*. Even academic niceties, such as the re-naming of Imogen as 'Innogen', in line with current editorial opinion, provoked widespread remark. Long anticipation of the productions, and the intensive media commentary that surrounded them, made it almost impossible for Cottesloe audiences to respond to these three plays without interpreting them in a heightened and sometimes distorting context.

The Late Plays represented not only the culmination of Hall's career at the National but also formed part of *End Games*, described by Nicholas Snowman, artistic director of the South Bank Centre, as 'a celebration of the mature, distilled poetry of the later works of major artists' (*Daily Telegraph*, 15.4.88) The twelve-week Festival, comprising in addition to the Late Plays forty-two concerts, twenty-one films and art exhibitions, literature and dance, may not have realised Snowman's ambition to forge 'something of a community' out of the disparate artistic interests of the South Bank, but it did provide yet an-

SHAKESPEARE LATE PLAYS

The Winter's Tale, The Tempest, Cymbeline

DIRECTOR	*Peter Hall*
DESIGNER	*Alison Chitty*
MUSIC	*Harrison Birtwistle*
LIGHTING	*Gerry Jenkinson and Ben Ormerod (The Winter's Tale)*
MOVEMENT	*Elizabeth Keen*
ASSOCIATE DIRECTOR	*Alan Cohen*
STAFF DIRECTOR	*Robert Clare*
STAGE MANAGER	*Ernest Hall*
PRODUCTION MANAGER	*Jason Barnes*
PHOTOGRAPHY	*John Haynes*

Main rôles in order of speaking:

The Winter's Tale
Archidamus *John Bluthal*
Camillo *Basil Henson*
Polixenes *Peter Woodward*
Leontes *Tim Pigott-Smith*
Hermione *Sally Dexter*
Mamillius *James Goodwin* or *William Puttock*
Paulina *Eileen Atkins*
Emilia *Janet Whiteside*
Antigonus *Tony Church*
Cleomenes *Robert Arnold*
Dion *Michael Carter*
Old Shepherd *Michael Bryant*
Clown *Jeremy Flynn*
Time *Michael Carter*
Autolycus *Ken Stott*
Florizel *Steven Mackintosh*
Perdita *Shirley Henderson*
Dorcas *Jennifer Hall*
Mopsa *Jenny Galloway*

The Tempest
Shipmaster *Daniel Thorndike*
Boatswain *Michael Beint*
Alonso *Robert Arnold*
Antonio *Ken Stott*
Gonzalo *Tony Church*
Sebastian *Basil Henson*
Miranda *Jennifer Hall* (later: *Shirley Henderson*)
Prospero *Michael Bryant*
Ariel *Steven Mackintosh*
Caliban *Tony Haygarth*
Ferdinand *Peter Woodward*
Trinculo *Tim Pigott-Smith*
Stephano *John Bluthal*
Iris *Jenny Galloway*
Ceres *Steven Mackintosh*
Juno *Sally Dexter*

Cymbeline
Queen *Eileen Atkins*
Posthumus *Peter Woodward*
Innogen *Geraldine James*
Cymbeline *Tony Church*
Cloten *Ken Stott*
Iachimo *Tim Pigott-Smith*

Belarius *Basil Henson*
Guiderius *Steven Mackintosh*
Arviragus *Jeremy Flynn*
Leonatus *Daniel Thorndike*
Jupiter *Michael Carter*

Other parts in *The Winter's Tale* (in order of speaking) were played by Ian Bolt, Michael Beint, Alex Hardy, Doyne Byrd, Peter Gordon, Daniel Thorndike, Michael Carter, Michael Bottle, Simon Scott; in *The Tempest* by Michael Carter, Paul Ashby, Ian Bolt, Michael Bottle, Doyne Byrd, Judith Coke, Peter Gordon, Alex Hardy, Simon Scott, Janet Whiteside; and in *Cymbeline* by John Bluthal, Janet Whiteside, Robert Arnold, Simon Scott, Judith Coke, Peter Gordon, Jenny Galloway, Alex Hardy, Doyne Byrd, Michael Bottle, Michael Beint.

Musicians for the three shows were: Martin Allen (*Music Director/percussion*), Philip Alexander (*wind*), Andrew Byrt (*viola*), Ann Morfee (*violin*), Ingrid Perrin (*cello*), Colin Rae (*trumpet*), Christopher Tombling (*violin*).

The Winter's Tale opened on 18.5.88, *The Tempest* on 19.5.88 and *Cymbeline* on 20.5.88. The productions toured to the Soviet Union (Moscow and Tbilisi) and Japan (Tokyo) before returning to the Cottesloe in July 1988, and transferring to the Olivier in August.

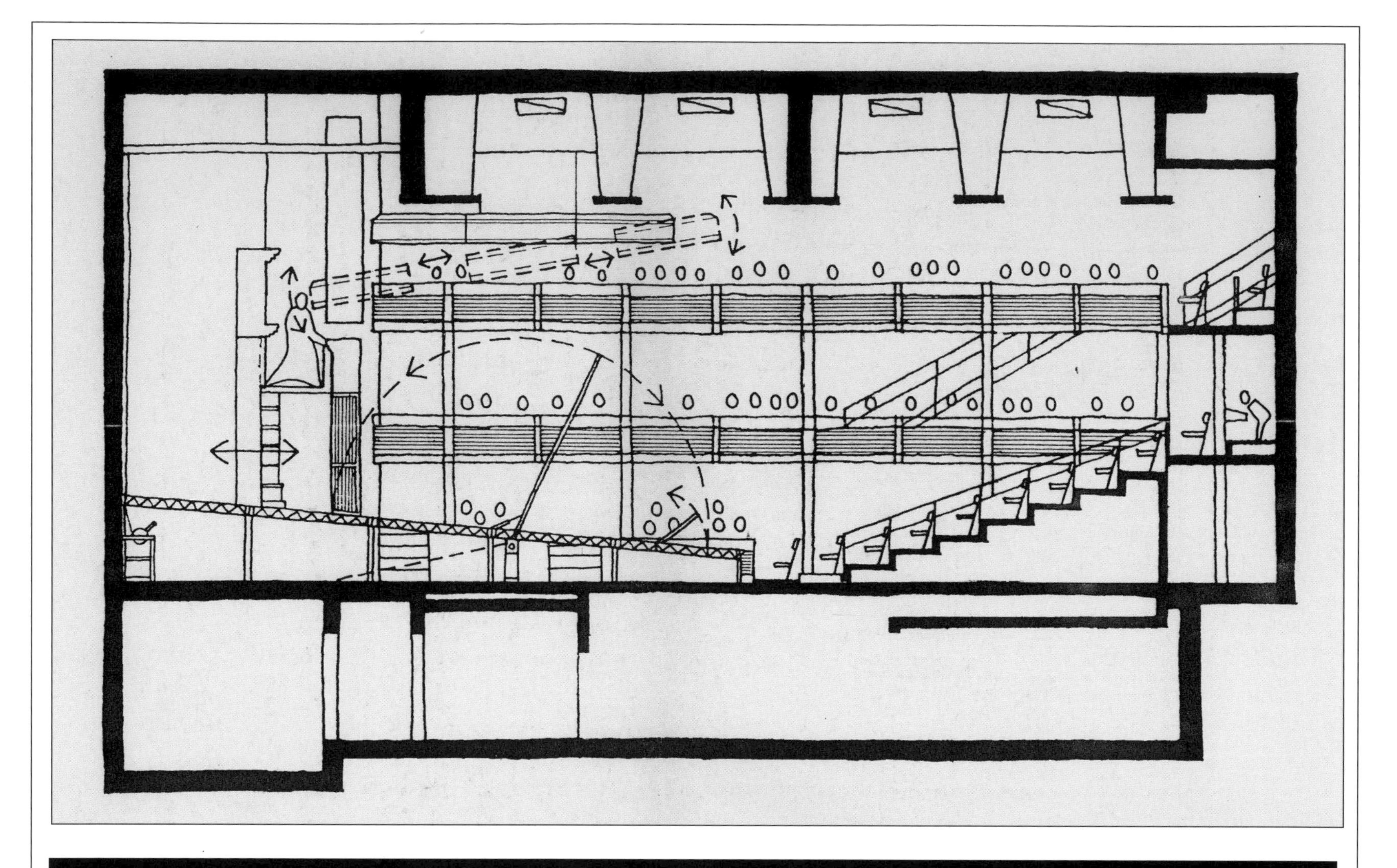

Technical Summary

• The three Late Shakespeares – *The Winter's Tale, The Tempest* and *Cymbeline* – were designed by Alison Chitty for the Olivier repertoire, following an opening season in the Cottesloe and visits to Moscow, Tbilisi and Tokyo.

• A steeply-raked boarded stage (1:12), raised 60cm at the front and rising to 1600cms at the rear, gave the impression of a Jacobean indoor playhouse. The stage thrust out into the auditorium, leaving only nine of the normal eleven pit rows.

• The main floor, 9.4m wide, almost filled the Cottesloe's stage-space, and widened upstage to 12m.

• 2.8m beyond the main floor a corniced, pilastered wall, painted with *trompe l'oeil* clouds, gave lighting designers Jerry Jenkinson and Ben Ormerod a canvas which responded to projected enhancement as exterior sky or warm cover for interiors.

• Three vertical sliding panels each side of a central pair of imposing double doors allowed both a variety of entrances and the introduction of scenic elements from the handling passage behind the wall (particularly statues for Leontes' palace in *The Winter's Tale*).

• A Copernican 'heaven' surmounted the acting area. This comprised a deep circular steel disc faced with golden mesh, backed with glowing blue silk and featuring at its centre a flaming golden sun, flaring outwards to a ring of stars, and at its perimeter the signs of the Zodiac.

• Both floor and 'heaven' concealed articulated elements which varied the setting for each of the three plays.

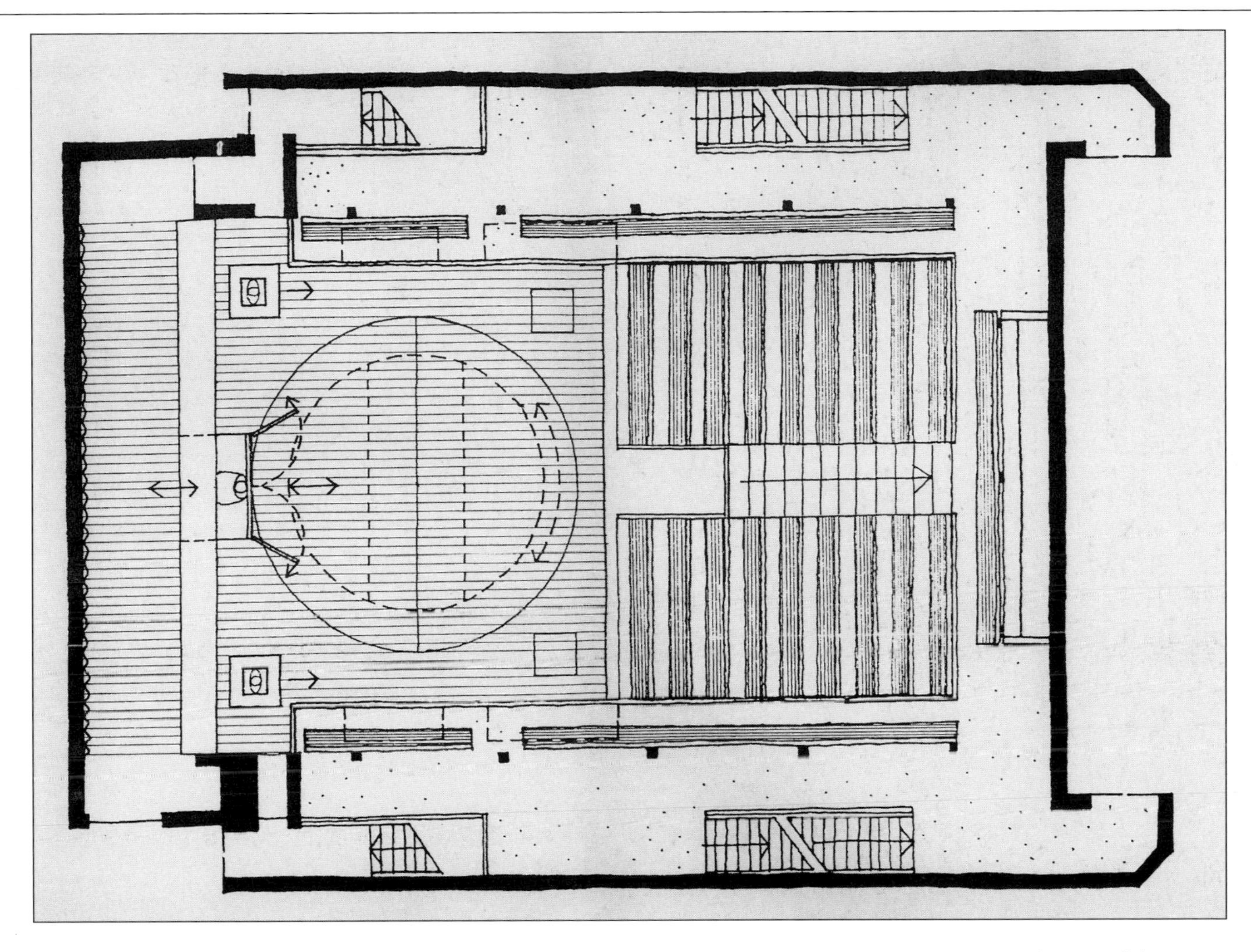

• To each side of the downstage-centre access steps, the floor held a 3.4m run of sealed-beam PAR lights. Driven up electrically on a hinge when in use, they quickly became known as the Porsche headlights.

• Upstage of the lights a 7.6m diameter disc was cut into the floor. The surface of this continued the boarded stage, but was divided, across-stage, into semicircles. The upstage semicircle turned over along its diameter, revealing a further circular surface of meadow for Bohemia in *The Winter's Tale,* and a rocky landscape for the British exteriors (and, by hinging down a further upstage semicircular panel, the Welsh cave) in *Cymbeline.*

• For *The Tempest,* the whole incised circle was lowered and filled with pale silver sand. The rear double doors slid downstage to allow a high balcony position for Prospero, or opened below to reveal his study cell.

• The 'heavens' cylinder, driven by electric motors, split into three parts along two chords. Through the spaces thus created the flown actors descended: Ariel on a single line and steel stirrup, Iris with her rainbow, Ceres and Jupiter in *The Tempest* and Jupiter in *Cymbeline.*

• The raised stage (which was also reached by two stepped entrances each side) provided space for the hydraulically-articulated floor and route to the cave in *Cymbeline,* and manual winches for the statues.

• The actors were flown using hydraulic power, as the more traditional method of counter-weights could not be used. This was because of the position of the seating galleries which flank the first half of the Cottesloe's end stage. Hydraulic packs were sited in the stage basement to prevent noise transmission, with the hoses fed up to the top level stage-right gallery, which, when not seated with audience, regularly serves as a control and fly gallery.

• The overseas tour encountered difficulties when, despite lengthy negotiations in Moscow, the company was offered only refrigeration vehicles for the transfer of the equivalent of three truckloads of scenery to Tbilisi. The trucks from Britain were eventually allowed to make the journey, heavily escorted by KGB officials, only to arrive towards the end of the last performance. The company performed with props and costumes borrowed from the Georgian Opera Company, and with no scenery.

other frame for viewing Hall's productions. Hall himself saw analogies between the late Shakespeares and the final works of some of the greatest artists, though his perspective may have had a personal tinge. 'The late works of our abiding geniuses,' he wrote, 'are not generally drenched in nostalgia and regret. They are more likely, if we look at them unsentimentally, to be questing and restless creations, posing new problems with an urgency, even a rage. For time is short. Hence the reckless virtuosity of Beethoven's last quartets, or the magnificent last sculptures of Michelangelo, hardly deigning to struggle out of their marble.' (*Daily Telegraph*, 19.1.88)

In this light, Hall was unlikely to interpret the plays as 'Romances'. Instead he saw 'the horror and brutality that surrounds their comedy'. Even 'the magical coincidences and golden pastorals that resolve their tragedy' do not absolve us from pain. Instead, 'their partially happy endings are all achieved with effort and ambiguity'. (*Daily Telegraph*, 19.1.88) 'These three plays,' he said in interview, 'came out of the same head at the same time. The idea of doing them is to examine the man's imagination and his obsessions.' (Peter Lewis, *The Observer*, 7.5.88) That the impulse to do them was a matter of his own imagination and his own preoccupations he readily accepted in another interview (*The Independent*, 23.4.88): 'Common sense would dictate that my last production at the National should be a star-packed, safe sort of thing. But I've wanted to do these three plays for years'.

The Text and the Space

Hall identified the Cottesloe as the ideal space for his exploration of these plays, seeing it as analogous to, and sharing the dimensions of, the Blackfriars, the indoor theatre for which Shakespeare primarily imagined his work after 1608, and which his company had wished to use from as early as 1599 (though they continued even after 1608 to use the Globe for summer, outdoor, performances, a practice in which Hall saw an analogy for the transfer of his own productions to the Olivier). 'The Blackfriars, I believe,' Hall claimed, 'dictated the aesthetic of these late plays, with fables more "gothick" containing more music, more spectacle and more emphasis on the *way* the thing is done rather than *what* is done.' (*Daily Telegraph*, 19.1.88) It is an emphasis that accords well with Hall's reputation as a meticulous director of script, enquiring into the phrasing of every speech – Michael Billington praised in the Late Shakespeares 'the hard analytical light they bring to the texts' (*Guardian*, 31.5.88) – and with his experience as a director of grand opera.

John Peter found the verse speaking in the Late Plays sometimes mannered, 'often self-conscious, oddly archaic and, quite simply, difficult', but he judged these plays 'the majestic end to one of Hall's careers': 'Hall's great achievement is to weld a complicated narrative ... and a brisk but profound characterisation rather like the rapid, magisterial brush-strokes in Titian's late paintings, into an organic breathing whole. It is done with an assurance, a miraculous consistency of tone, which are fully equal to these difficult, enchanting and profound plays.' (*Sunday Times*, 22.5.88) It's a judgement with which Peter Kemp agreed, in drawing attention to what he called the 'messy physicality' of *Cymbeline*: 'These bloody interludes [as when 'Iachimo slaveringly licks the sleeping Innogen's hand to make her bracelet slip over it'] serve Hall's intention of getting you to look at the plays in a new and fiercer light. He rejects the notion that they are serene acts of farewell and thus nicely suitable for his valediction to the National Theatre. But it's hard to see how he could have made a grander finale than with these productions of high finish'. (*Independent*, 23.5.88)

FIG 80 Alison Chitty's design, showing the circular 'heaven' and the stage in its plainest form. The circular opening in the stage floor, divided into semicircles, which could be lowered for the sandpit in *The Tempest*, or turned over along the circle's diameter for outdoor locations in *Cymbeline* and *The Winter's Tale*, is clearly visible.

The Designer and the Design

Alison Chitty (see interview, pp. 63–64 in this book) designed both the settings and the costumes for the Late Plays. Vera Lustig admired the late-Jacobean or neo-Caroline elegance of the costume design: 'Not only are the costumes designed by Alison Chitty mouth-wateringly beautiful (soft apricots, coffees, plums and creams) and exquisite in their detail (filigree lace at throat and wrists, shot fabrics delicately encrusted with jewels, a sensuous harmony in every grouping) but her designs illuminate the text'. (*Drama Quarterly*, vol.3, August 1988) On a wider front, John Peter traced that illumination of the text to Hall's and Chitty's knowing 'all about acting space' and in particular to their perfect grasp of the flamboyant idiom of the Jacobean private theatre, a theatre that 'could be highbrow and popular at the same time'. Peter specified the visual appeal of what he saw as an attractive and versatile design: 'Over the stage Chitty has suspended a golden disc of the post-Copernican sky, and this is mirrored below by an earthly circle which turns into a sandpit ("Come unto these yellow sands") in *The Tempest*, the rocky countryside in *Cymbeline*, and, rather awkwardly, into a village green in *The Winter's Tale*.' (*Sunday Times*, 22.5.88) Irving Wardle drew attention to the raked floor, 'a clean expanse of unpainted timber, with a downstage bridge leading straight into the house' and thought that with this layout 'the stage confronts you at once as a chessboard set out for a grand masters' game, and as a machine for projecting dramatic action with the utmost force.' (*Times*, 20.5.88) Vera Lustig appreciated the changing textures and the practicality of *The Tempest's* sand: 'In the middle, a circle of fine white sand, deep enough to change its contours as the actors tread and ruffle its surface, but not so deep that they flounder.' (*Independent*, 11.5.88)

Occasionally, a reviewer had reservations about the settings for the Late Plays. Jane Edwards found the 'trimmings' of the set, particularly in *The Tempest*, 'irritating': 'The doorway unnecessarily creaks backwards and forwards; a hinged circular turf lands with a thud; the astrological disc stutters open in order for Ariel and the gilded characters of the masque to descend; there is the constant sound of footsteps as the actors prowl behind the audience; and swamped in dogs heads they fall over themselves as they pursue Stephano and Trinculo.' (*Time Out*, 25.5–1.6.88) But majority opinion thought the set-

Fig 81 (*above*) Prospero (centre, in elevated position) watches the reapers' dance in *The Tempest*. The actors, apart from Miranda and Ferdinand, are masked

Fig 82 (*right*) Tony Haygarth as Caliban.

Fig 83 Steven Mackintosh as Ariel.

Fig 84 Tim Pigott-Smith as Leontes (foreground) with Sally Dexter (upstage centre) as Hermione and members of the Company in *The Winter's Tale.*

tings both significant and practical. Peter Kemp enjoyed the attractively colour-coded costumes of *The Winter's Tale*: 'The cast ... wear clothes that are picturesquely colour-coded: shades of russet, cinnamon and scarlet for Leontes and his Sicilian entourage, tints of green for Polixenes and his Bohemian retinue. Sometimes pleasingly mingling, sometimes starkly separated, these two sets of colours keep you constantly aware of the preoccupation with union and division running through this drama of meeting opposites: youth and age, court and country, destructiveness and fertility.' He also remarked how 'the archetypal seasonal patterns in a tale moving from wintery devastation to the blooming of new vitality and a final harvesting of the fruits of maturity are resplendently made apparent in the alternation of autumnal and vernal hues.' (*Independent*, 20.5.88)

Michael Billington was another reviewer who appreciated both the attractiveness and the clarifying logic of the design, this time in *Cymbeline*: 'One of the pleasures of this *Cymbeline* is the physical excitement of the staging. The separate ingredients of Alison Chitty's set here reflect the play's diversity. The suspended astrological ceiling becomes the natural vehicle for Jupiter in his earthly descent. The bare stage boards open up to disclose a rough, uneven hillside. At one point, the back blue-and-white panels part to reveal the Roman and British armies in massed formation: I normally get confused as to who is fighting on whose side in this play but Hall's formalised battle scenes make everything clear.' (*Guardian*, 23.5.88) Alison Chitty, with characteristic modesty, saw the visual effects of the design as subordinate to the performances: 'These plays need magic at some times, and they don't at others. Sometimes the best thing in the world is Michael Bryant standing there in the middle of the stage speaking to you.' (reported by Vera Lustig, *The Independent*, 11.5.88) It's a judgement very much in keeping with Chitty's aim of 'holding' the actors in the space (see the interview in this book).

Michael Bryant and the Questioning of Prospero

There was common consent that, against all the odds, Peter Hall had pulled off not only an extraordinarily ambitious undertaking in staging all three Late Plays with a single company of players (and in managing, just, to open all three on consecutive nights), but had succeeded in discovering new readings within texts too often seen in a cosily reassuring light. Some reviewers thought certain rôles were miscast (owing largely to the complex cross-casting imposed by the project as a whole). But there was almost universal admiration for Michael Bryant's discovery of a much harsher Prospero within the lines than has usually been supposed. Jane Edwardes (*Time Out*, 25.5–1.6.88) suggested that 'it will never again be possible to accept Prospero as a magisterial old man with a beard after Bryant's restless portrayal, prone to bouts of fury and self-doubt and anxiously anticipating retribution for dabbling in the world of black arts until forgiven by the applause of the audience'. Irving Wardle understood how this Prospero, 'peremptory, urgent, and subject to fits of blind fury', one for whom 'the very name of Antonio ... chokes him with hatred', is nevertheless capable of 'repose' as he stands above his humiliated enemies: 'Conscience then strikes, and the great renunciation speech changes from a farewell to art into a confession of blasphemy. There is no luxuriating in the great verse paragraphs. "Graves at my command Have wak'd their sleepers", he whispers, as though expecting a thunderbolt to fall on him.' (*Times*, 20.5.88) Stephen Wall too saw the doubleness in the portrayal, revenger and victim: 'Bryant brings out finely not only Prospero's pride in and emotional dependence on his "rough magic", but also his terror at the thought of having opened graves and waked their sleepers.' (*Times Literary Supplement*, 10–16.6.88)

It was the suppressed, or at least postponed, anger that most reviewers drew to attention. John Peter remarked that 'Michael Bryant's performance, which is one of the towering achievements of the trilogy, makes clear that there is nothing saintly about the exiled magus; he's tough, choleric and irascible. To have his enemies in his power gives him huge satisfaction; and his final forgiveness is the generosity of the strong. At the same time it is far from certain that his forgiveness is accepted or deserved.' (*Sunday Times*, 22.5.88) Under the headline, 'A storm of temper', Peter Kemp wrote of this Prospero that 'Michael

Bryant infuses him with ferocious cantankerousness. Real rage erupts even in speeches about what happened twelve years earlier: "Of temporal royalties/ He thinks me now incapable", he fumes, red-faced with fury, of his perfidious brother. Wielding his staff like a martial arts stave, he's tetchy and hectoring to Miranda. Rarely can the expletives that pepper the old man's speeches – "malignant things", "hagseed", "posionous slave" – have been delivered with such spitting explosiveness.' (*Independent*, 21.5.88) The power and the detail of Bryant's performance gave *The Tempest* a less than still centre, and set the standard and the tone for the whole trilogy of plays.

Tim Pigott-Smith: Changing Rôles

If there was comment among reviewers about the difficulties encountered by members of the company in taking on a variety of rôles, there was much interest in, and by and large approval of, Tim Pigott-Smith's performance of three important and varied parts, Leontes, Trinculo and Iachimo. Of his Leontes, John Peter remarked: 'The performance is piercingly effective because Pigott-Smith knows that Leontes appears both tragic to himself and terrifying and slightly absurd to others. He goes through that baptism of fire called life – except that he gets a second chance. The ending is a kind of beginning, a surge of life darkly qualified by a sense of past wrong-doing which cannot be forgiven, only understood.' (*Sunday Times*, 22.5.88) Charles Osborne (*Daily Telegraph*, 20.5.88) also appreciated the depth of a performance that had to reconcile opposites: 'Tim Pigott-Smith's Leontes is impressive from improbable beginning, with the character's all-too-sudden eruption of jealousy, to ambiguous end, with the muted joy of reunion, his concentration never faltering despite the daunting proximity of the audience'.

When it came to assessing the three rôles, Osborne (*Daily Telegraph*, 23.5.88) thought the marks earned varied, but greeted the overall achievement with some enthusiasm: 'Tim Pigott-Smith triumphed as Leontes, sank into professional competence as Trinculo, and soared to the heights again as a lively, plausible, convincingly Italianate Iachimo, squeezing Posthumus Leonatus's breast with a sensuous hatred as he describes Innogen's similarly placed mole, or falling to the ground to lie suggestively on his back as he recollects the ceiling of that lady's bedchamber.' Michael Billington found Iachimo's lust in Imogen's chamber brilliantly observed: 'He frantically unbuttons as if he means to rape the sleeping heroine. Inspection of her left breast once more inflames him. And the removal of her bracelet becomes a fantastically tricky operation involving the moistening of her palm: a gesture at once practical and erotic and the kind of detail that gives the scene internal life.' (*Guardian*, 23.5.88) Michael Ratcliffe wrote that Pigott-Smith's 'Iachimo is an Italian arriviste with a fancy accent and a body which moves with the ingratiating vulgarity of a gigolo still defining his pitch.' (*Observer*, 22.5.88) Christopher Edwards relished Pigott-Smith's Iachimo even more keenly, and thought it the culmination not only of the three-play series, but of the actor's career to date: 'One thinks particularly of Tim Pigott-Smith's Iachimo – a dangerous, smiling Italian playboy whom this actor inhabits from the inside. His Trinculo in *The Tempest* was a funny clown with a Michael Crawford voice, but it was layered in technique, as was his Leontes. For Iachimo, he transforms himself utterly and is riveting. It must be the best thing he has ever done.' (*Spectator*, 28.5.88)

Fig 85 A striking juxtaposition of Peter Woodward as Posthumus Leonatus and the tilting 'heaven' (in *Cymbeline*) designed by Alison Chitty.

Other Players, Other Rôles

Perhaps the most warmly received performance was that of Geraldine James, who came into the company at a very late stage to replace Sarah Miles in the rôle of Innogen. She was not regarded until this performance as a Shakespearean actress, and a general wish was expressed that she should take on this new direction in her work. Michael Billington wrote that 'Geraldine James's Innogen emerges superbly as a tough, strong-jawed woman full of irony and anger.' (*Guardian*, 23.5.88) Michael Coveney considered that 'This wonderful Innogen is a woman who grows up matching words to a great range and variety of experience. … She has a fine musical voice and a deeply sympathetic personality, both prerequisites for the rôle.' (*Financial Times*, 23.5.88) Christopher Edwards considered that 'She has the beauty, wit, poise and dignity of a true Innogen. At the same time, she has a completely contemporary manner. Her delivery of the verse is rich with intelligence, spontaneity and understanding.' (*Spectator*, 28.5.88) Her own reaction to being cast at such short notice for this second-largest of Shakespeare's female rôles (as she told Angela Brooks, *Daily Mail*, 21.5.88) was comprehensive failure of nerve: 'I have been like a blinkered horse for the whole of the rehearsal period. I have lived, eaten slept and thought nothing but this part. All of me is frightened – from head to toe.' The adrenalin rush that must have accompanied this fear led to a performance universally admired.

Other performances drew laudatory comment, often due to their unexpected accenting of familiar rôles. B.A.Young (*Financial Times*, 1.6.88) remarked that 'Tony Haygarth's Caliban is a man, not a fish, his back cruelly scarred with the marks of the lash. There is no suggestion that he is a poor, bullied subject; he is a monster, a comic unpolitical one.' Michael Ratcliff judged that 'Haygarth's naked, blood-stained Calilban, his genitals muzzled like a dog, is outstanding: fierce, sensual and ecstatic, the artist exiled in his own land.' (*Observer*, 22.5.88) Francis King developed the paradoxical nature of this Caliban: 'Tony Haygarth's Caliban, his mouth crowded with fangs and his body smeared with excrement and blood, has none of the pathos and nobility which some other actors have recently found in the rôle. He speaks the verse with unexpected beauty, providing a lesson to some of his colleagues, and makes his jubilation on changing masters extraordinarily moving.' (*Sunday Telegraph*, 22.5.88)

Another performance to draw praise was Ken Stott's Autolycus. As Francis King put it, 'Ken Stott's unusually tart, even malevolent Autolycus is a strong creation.' (*Sunday Telegraph*, 22.5.88) John Peter described this Autolycus as 'a ruthless con man with shifty, red-rimmed eyes and a wolfish smile' (*Sunday Times*, 22.5.88), Michael

FIG 86 Geraldine James (centre) as Innogen, with Steven Mackintosh (Guiderius) and Jeremy Flynn (Arviragus) in *Cymbeline.*

Coveney called him 'ferociously disaffected' (*Financial Times*, 23.5.88) and Michael Ratcliffe referred to 'an Autolycus who roams Arcadia like a slippery-tongued gargoyle – pallid, unsleeping and red-eyed' (*Observer*, 22.5.88). Christopher Edwards appreciated another of Stott's characterisations: 'Ken Stott's Cloten completes a fine threesome of parts for this accomplished actor and sweet singer (he also plays Autolycus and Antonio). Stott has that special, risky presence whenever he steps on stage. Even with the doltish, absurd Cloten you sense a strong wilful intelligence.' The same reviewer thought Peter Woodward's three performances, as Polixenes, Ferdinand and Posthumus 'first-class', a judgement shared by Peter Kemp who wrote of 'Peter Woodward completing a brilliant set of performances with a forceful, finely characterised Posthumus.' (*Independent*, 23.5.88)

The other male – some said androgynous – rôle to draw a good deal of comment was Steven Mackintosh's Ariel. Charles Osborne wrote that 'the delicate Ariel is given a performance by Steven Mackintosh in which other-worldly strangeness and adolescent charm are engagingly blended. ... This Ariel is allowed a touching moment of human feeling when he tentatively returns Prospero's embrace before his final dismissal to the elements.' (*Daily Telegraph*, 21.5.88) Peter Kemp found this Ariel disturbing: 'Ariel, spoken in a sexless alto by Steven Mackintosh, seems eerily dispassionate – staring at the mortals' unruly behaviour with the cold fascination of a child who has a quick intelligence but no empathy with adult emotions.' (*Independent*, 21.5.88) Michael Billington thought the performance notable even if, by the most demanding standards incomplete: 'Steven Mackintosh plays the spirit as a metamorphosing Ovidian gender-bender who can turn at will into a sea-nymph with long blonde locks and bulging mammaries. But I missed within him that yearning hunger for freedom constantly thwarted by the imposition of one more task; and his final release has none of the emotional impact of the Strehler production where the flying Ariel was unhooked and sped like lightning through the auditorium.' (*Guardian*, 21.5.88)

There was less comment on the female roles aside from Innogen. Jennifer Hall was noticed as Miranda, Milton Shulman commenting, perhaps not without mischief, that this Miranda 'seemed less starstruck by the sight of a man than the usual run of Mirandas but was, appropriately enough, in genuine awe of her father.' (*Evening Standard*, 20.5.88) Michael Coveney (*Financial Times*, 20.5.88) was among those who appreciated 'Jennifer Hall's girlish but naturally exotic Miranda'. Eileen Atkins, whose inclusion in the company was much advertised in advance by the media, drew favourable attention from reviewers including Stephen Wall (*Times Literary Supplement*, 10–16.6.88) who praised Paulina as the work of an actress who 'effortlessly combines subtle characterization with purity and authority of diction'. Charles Osborne, judging Paulina to be 'the most rewarding of roles', particularly relished Atkins's performance of 'the scene in which she defends the innocent Queen'. (*Daily Telegraph*, 20.5.88) Christopher Edwards had much to say in praise of Sally Dexter as Hermione: 'Hermione's ... generous smile, her frank, open nature and the delight she takes in hearing of her husband's boyhood with Polixenes – all this puts her beyond the suspicion of anyone who is not mad with jealousy. ... And when Hermione [in the statue scene] does come alive, the sight of Sally Dexter's gracious, mature beauty – lined with hurt as well as age – is very moving. We have a powerful sense of the cost of Leontes's psychotic jealousy.' (*Spectator*, 28.5.88)

Words and Music

Peter Hall's reputation as a scrupulous master of text made audiences and reviewers listen more attentively than usual. There was a good deal of comment on verse-speaking in the three plays. John Peter took time out to explain the growing complexity of Shakespeare's verse as it reached his last period: 'his phrases over-ran his lines, setting up an internal rhythm which works against the beat of blank verse like a kind of counterpoint.' He had reservations about Hall's emphasis on the structure of the verse: 'Hall makes his actors just perceptibly pause at the end of some lines, as if to remind us: "Danger! Verse being spoken!" Sometimes this is effective. In Hermione's trial scene, Sally Dexter, superbly dignified, can convey her shock and pain with these abrupt breaks; and they help Geraldine James's Innogen, both a regal princess and an eager girl, to suggest grief and outrage. Elsewhere the effect is often self-conscious, oddly archaic and, quite simply, difficult: some actors are defeated by it.' (*Sunday Times*, 22.5.88) Michael Billlington partially disagreed: 'the production [*Cymbeline*]also works because Shakespeare's densely packed verse is spoken with wit and relish. Good verse-speaking is not a matter of recitation but of highlighting antitheses and finding the key word that unlocks character.' (*Guardian*, 27.9.88, referring to the Olivier revival)

Michael Coveney found a harmony between the verse-speaking and the lively pacing of *The Tempest*: 'It is spoken lightly and quickly, played without an interval on a magic circle of sand beneath Alison Chitty's permanent tilting celestial gold coronet.' (*Financial Times*, 20.5.88) Reviewing the three productions in retrospect, Coveney repeated his admiration for the enunciation of the verse (and prose): 'If nothing else, the productions offer a rare chance to hear every single word uttered with skill and intelligence. They bind the worlds of artifice and experience, of lost time and spent passion, in an ingenious recreation of Jacobean stage conditions. There may be other, more contemporary styles in which to cast the late plays. But that is not Hall's concern.' (*Financial Times*, 23.5.88)

As with words, so with music, at least in several reviewers' appreciation of the Harrison Birtwistle compositions. Michael Ratcliffe referred to '*The Tempest* – luminous, lucid, and greatly enhanced by Harrison Birtwistle's sensuous and seductive score.' (*Observer*, 22.5.88) Michael Coveney relished the music while deploring its presentation, at least in one respect: 'Harrison Birtwistle's song settings are tautly ethereal, but I loathe Ariel's miming of them to a recorded voice.' He nevertheless saw in the presentation of the masque of Juno and Ceres 'the glittering decorum of Sir Peter's Glyndebourne Monteverdi productions', a tribute surely to the musical idiom as much as the visual style. (*Financial Times*, 20.5.88) Charles Osborne had a divided and perhaps faintly patronising response: 'Harrison Birtwistle's music in *Cymbeline* is almost as splendid as it was in *The Tempest*. Only his setting of "Hark, hark the lark at heaven's gate sings" is disappointing, melody not being this composer's strong suit.' (*Daily Telegraph*, 23.5.88) For the most part, however, audiences and reviewers considered that Birtwistle's music fully supported the exquisite and hard-edged experimentalism of Hall's three productions.

Stephen Wall went further: 'Harrison Birtwistle's music is so good that one wishes there were more of it: his attractive settings of Ariel's songs (post-synched by the actor to an uncredited counter-tenor) ought surely to be published separately.' (*Times Literary Supplement*, 10–16.6.88)

After the Cottesloe

Among the many tours out of the Cottesloe (see Jason Barnes's listing, pp. 187–191 in this book) the Late Plays tour and its vicissitudes remain vivid in many participants' minds. The difficulty of transferring the shows to Tbilisi at a time of political tension in the USSR proved particularly memorable. Michael Billington's account for the *Guardian* (15.6.88), detailing the practical problems (in particular the drastically unsuitable transport arrangements from Moscow, and the discovery of gallons of water in the diesel fuel of the British trucks when these were substituted for the Russian replacements), led on to a celebration of the inherent strengths of the shows and the capacity of the actors to improvise in the absence of sets and costumes (which did not arrive until the final performance was almost completed). The result of the difficulties, Billington wrote, 'was a staggering demonstration of what theatre is about: the primacy of acting and language over spectacle and design.' 'It would be sentimental,' he conceded, 'to pretend that what we saw was perfect. In *Cymbeline* – played in the middle of a violent storm with hailstones coming through the Rustaveli Theatre roof onto the stage – I missed the vital scenic distinction between court and country. But *The Winter's Tale*, mounted in the 300-seat Rustaveli Upstairs, emerged with startling clarity and power. The great discovery, however, was *The Tempest*. Stripped of the original visual clutter, the play acquired a headlong momentum (it was seven minutes shorter than at the Cottesloe) and worked intensely on the imagination.' Billington remarked how a simple sheet in place of the elaborate tarpaulin under which Caliban and Trinculo hid in the Cottesloe production allowed the actors to improvise 'an instant pantomime horse', how 'Steven Mackintosh as Ariel spoke his songs on stage while Shirley Henderson sang them off-stage in eerie counterpoint' and how 'the actors transformed themselves into spirits, elves, nymphs and even dogs without the help of masks but through simple body-movements.' The result, Billington declared, was that 'the performance that night was the most exciting *Tempest* I have ever seen. In the Cottesloe Peter Hall's production seemed to be weighed down with too much baroque opera invention: one suddenly realised how much more moving it is if Ariel simply walks onto the stage rather than being flown in like a Monteverdi goddess.' The actors, he added, 'also seemed gloriously uninhibited by the lack of costume'. Declaring that 'I am not anti-designer,' Billington nevertheless went on to say: 'Tbilisi has made me – and I suspect many of the National Theatre company – into a theatrical Luddite'. It is something of an extreme position, which Billington would no doubt want to qualify in other circumstances. What the Tbilisi experience demonstrated, it could less controversially be said, was not only the skill and versatility of the Late Plays company, but the essential strengths of Hall's reading of the playscripts.

FIG 87 The richly elaborate properties of peasant society in the 1992 production of *Fuente Ovejuna.*
Clive Rowe, (Mengo) left; Anthony Walters (A Boy) on shoulders; Dominic Rickhards (Second Alderman) right.

FUENTE OVEJUNA

Written by Lope de Vega

FUENTE OVEJUNA
Written by Lope de Vega
New version by Adrian Mitchell
Literal translation by Gwenda Pandolfi

Director	*Declan Donnellan*
Design	*Nick Ormerod*
Music	*Paddy Cunneen*
Lighting	*Mick Hughes*
Movement	*Jane Gibson*
Fight Director	*John Waller*
Sound	*David E Smith*
Production Manager	*Jason Barnes*
Stage Manager	*Alison Rankin*
Staff Director	*Kenneth Mackintosh*
Photography	*Robert Workman and John Haynes* (revival)

Principal Cast Members

The Rulers

Commander Fernando Gomez de Guzman	*James Laurenson*
The Grand Master of Calatrava	*Mark Lockyer*; *Karl Collins* (revival)
Captain Flores	*David Beames*, *Mark Strong* (revival)
Queen Isabella of Castile	*Ellen Thomas*; *Mona Hammond* (revival)
King Ferdinand of Aragon	*Jon Rumney*

People of Fuente Ovejuna

Laurencia	*Rachel Joyce*
Pascuala	*Joy Richardson*, *Pamela Nomvete* (revival)
Frondoso	*Wilbert Johnson*
Esteban	*George Harris*, *Ben Thomas* (revival)

Other parts were played in the 1989 production by Jim Barclay, Ivan Kaye, Nicholas Blane, Trevor Sellers, Oliver Beamish, Jo Stone-Fewings, Jonathan Cullen, Clive Rowe, Tam Dean Burn, George Harris, Gilbert Wynne, Sandy McDade, Timothy Matthews, Sandra Butterworth, Laura Shavin, Glyn Pritchard, David Schneider, Merlin Shepherd and John Fitzgerald-Jay and in the revival by David Hounslow, Stephen Hattersley, Nigel Leach, James Kerr, Aaron Shirley, Dominic Taylor, Jo Stone-Fewings, Clive Rowe, Michael Gardiner, Ben Thomas, Stefan Kalipha, Helen McCrory, Thomas Murrill, Anthony Walters, Clara Onyemere, Teresa McElroy, Ignatius Anthony, Ben Miles, Dominic Taylor and Dominic Rickhards.

The production opened on 10 January 1989, and remained in repertoire until 28 August 1989. It was revived at the Cottesloe on 14 May 1992, and ran in repertoire until 30 July 1992. It toured to the Teatro Lope de Vega for Expo 92 (2–6 June 1992) to Derry in N. Ireland (from 17 June 1992) and to the 1992 Edinburgh Festival, where it played in the Assembly Hall using a specially constructed traverse stage.

Fuente Ovejuna and the Cottesloe space

Press comment on the production of *Fuente Ovejuna* by Declan Donnellan and his designer Nick Ormerod drew particular attention, unusually, to Donnellan's and Ormerod's bold re-ordering of the Cottesloe space. 'Mr Donnellan's staging,' wrote Michael Billington, 'exactly matches Lope's political ambivalence. He splits the Cottesloe in two to create a traverse stage with Ferdinand and Isabella permanently enthroned at one end (to remind us who is boss) and the people embenched at the other. But he also uses the central space intelligently to give the village scenes a pulsating life.' (*The Guardian*, 12.1.1989) Jeremy Kingston found the staging such as to cast the audience, Brecht-like, as spectators of a theatre of politics: 'Declan Donnellan transforms the great rectangle of the Cottesloe into a long yard resembling the prints of Stuart parliaments with thrones at one end and the audience sitting in rows down the sides. Without his marvellous feel for grouped crowds the play would not hold our attention for long'. (*The Times*, 11.1.1989)

Other reviewers thought the staging reminiscent of the original conditions for which the play was written. Michael Coveney observed that the Cottesloe for this production 'except for the significant absence of daylight and fresh air, resembles a Spanish *corral* in the Madrid of the Golden Age.' He went on to explain: 'We have the rectangular courtyard, the covered rows of *gradas*, the galleries and swagged boxes, the jutting apron on which sit King Ferdinand and Queen Isabella', and what he discerned as the allusion in their costuming to the Spanish court black of a Velasquez painting. (*The Financial Times*, 11.1.1989). Robert Hewison associated the staging with a royal tennis court anywhere in Europe, in which Ferdinand and Isabella watch the action 'rather as Queen Elizabeth may have watched *Twelfth Night*' (*The Sunday Times*, 15.1.1989). Michael Ratcliffe remarked on the intersecting perspectives of an audience observing both from each side and above. Thus, he considered, 'The theatre is part throne room, part plaza, part galleried courtyard inn, and provides a wide and intimate space for a masterpiece of class rebellion and collective courage that never relaxes its grip for nearly two hours.' (*The Observer*, 15.1.1989)

Whatever the historical analogy adopted by individual reviewers, it was a matter of common consent that the spatial arrangement created by Donnellan and Ormerod flexibly complemented the characteristics of this play as human drama and political parable. The potential of the Cottesloe for both intimacy and detachment was it seems successfully revealed. The various historical analogies offered by the reviewers, set alongside the immediacy of the experience, also marked out the ambivalent nature of

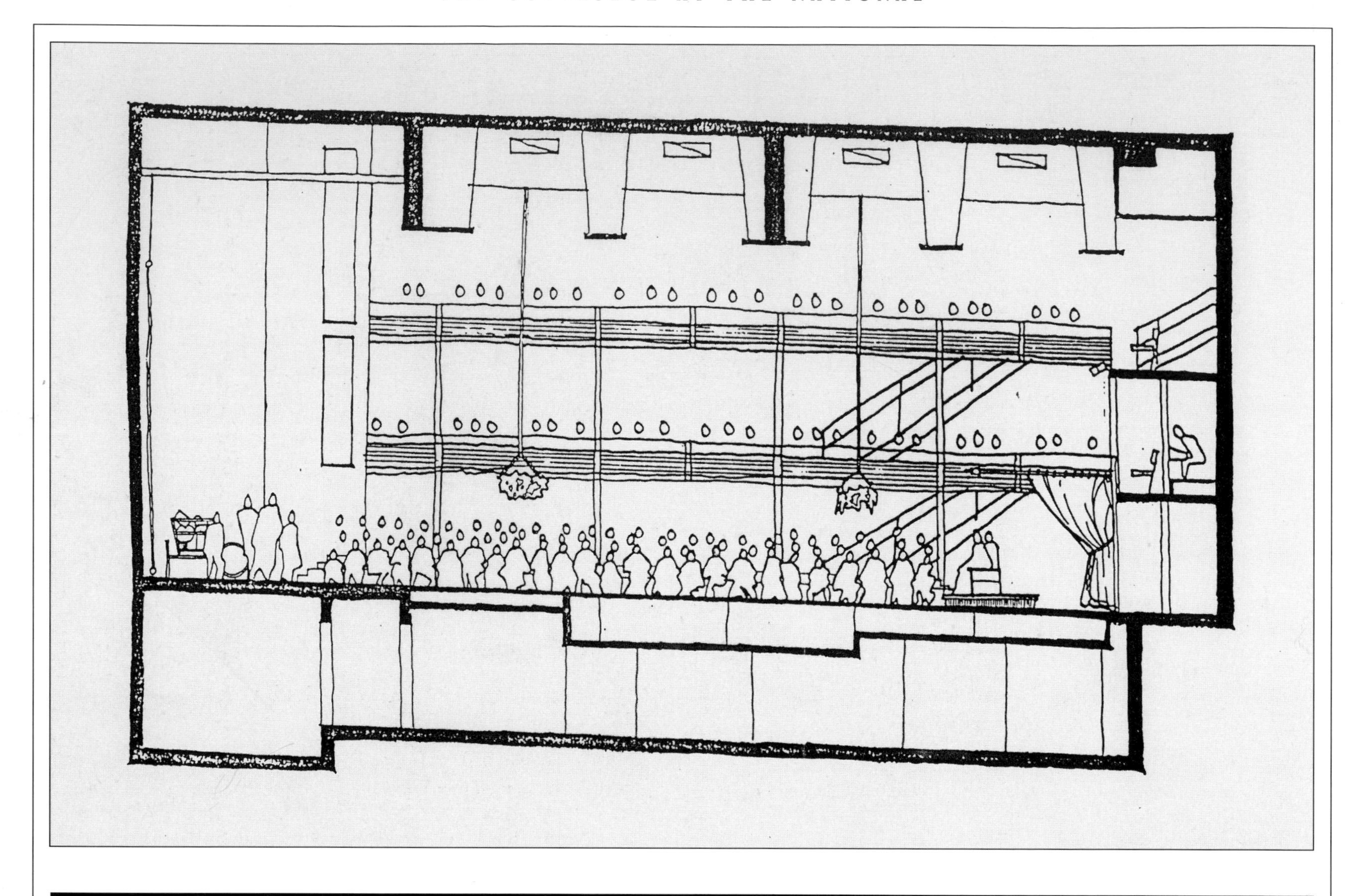

Technical Summary

- Until *Fuente Ovejuna's* first production at the beginning of 1989, Long Traverse staging had not been seen at the Cottesloe since the seasonal non-repertoire installation of 1978 and 1979 for *The World Turned Upside Down, Has Washington Legs* and *Dispatches*, plus performances of *The Putney Debates*, which made use of the debating chamber layout of *The World Turned Upside Down*.

- *Fuente Ovejuna* differed from these previous traverse productions in that it had to be changed over in repertoire. The three rows of 25 seats which bounded each long side of the playing space were raised by only 35cms at the rear, and were formed using a new arrangement of inexpensive, single-linking chairs mounted on a recently-introduced platform system. This marked the beginning of the Cottesloe's ability to vary the staging layout from play to play within a season's repertoire.

- The playing space, 19m long by 6m wide, reinforced the strength of the Cottesloe down its length, underpinning the confrontation between protagonist groups ranged at each end.

- The front-row audience for the 1989 production sat on stage level, their feet on the arid Spanish red-earth floor. In the revival of 1992, when Declan Donnellan wished the play to be performed as if at court, the feet of the front-row audience rested on the floor boards of the royal Chamber, in which Ferdinand and Isabella (having led in the entire Company of Knights of Calatrava

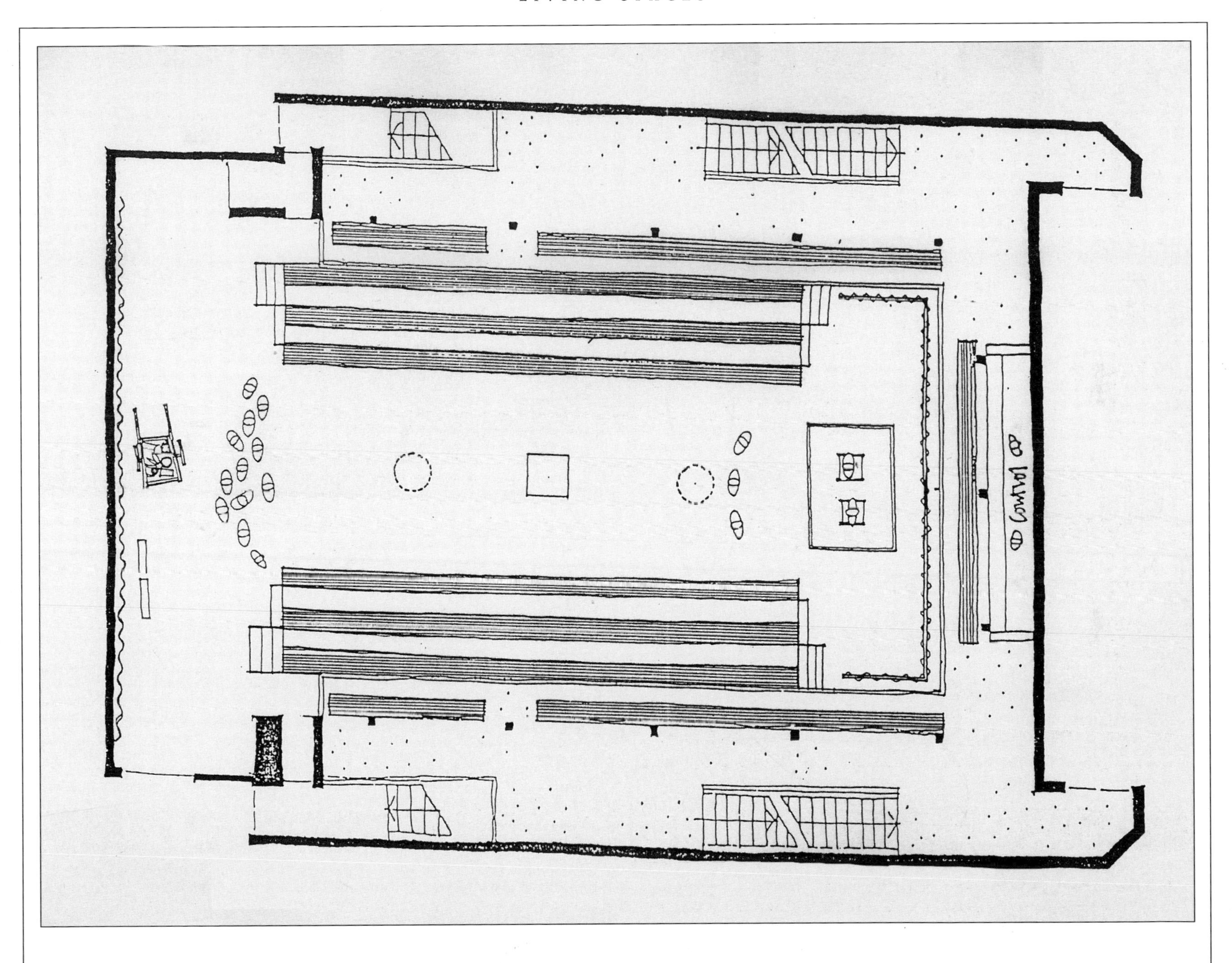

and villagers of Fuente Ovejuna) sat enthroned throughout, stepping down from their black-velvet-hung dais only to take part in a scene.

• At the opposite end of the stage, the villagers began the action, and reinforced the sense of a play-within-a-play, by raising Ormerod's landscape backcloth, which filled the whole space with a parched vista punctuated with scrubby bushes.

• Scenes were set with minimal furniture, from a selection of chairs, tables and a cart kept upstage. The wedding scene.was staged by lowering two floral garlands strung between the long galleries at second level.

Fuente Ovejuna, as of all great classics, as a document of the past and of the present simultaneously.

Stage Life

Reviewers remarked on the physical vigour of the production. Jane Gibson's choreography of crowd movement, released by the freeing of the theatre space, drew much appreciative comment. The *coup de théâtre* of the opening scene was recalled by Michael Ratcliffe: 'the loud bang of a trap door flung open, through which the villagers climb into the light. Muffled drums are followed by dissonant trumpet fanfares of piercing beauty, and the first of many raw songs and stamping dances pound down the centre of the stage. The play shouts for justice and the floor actually shakes beneath the audience's feet.' (*The Observer*, 15.1.1989) Michael Coveney found in this version of Lope's play an energy that is 'lyrical, vital and rude', one that invested the peasants with a Breughelesque life. (*The Financial Times*, 11.1.1989) 'Work,' noted Michael Billington, picking up on the physical realism of the production, 'is a reality as the women pound the ground with their washing and the men grind corn. So also is festivity.' (*The Guardian*, 12.1.1989)

FIG 88 *Fuente Ovejuna* in performance, 1989, showing the stage lay-out and audience seating.
PHOTO: *Jason Barnes*

Lope de Vega

Fuente Ovejuna is the best known and most frequently revived of Lope de Vega's plays. Of the fifteen hundred scripts Lope claimed to have written by the end of his working life, more than three hundred survive. The most esteemed as well as the most prolific of the Spanish Golden Age dramatists, Lope (1562–1635) lived a full life that included living in poverty, two marriages (one with a noblewoman the other with a rich butcher's daughter) at least eight children, numerous love affairs, a range of sexual adventures, service on the Spanish Armada, ordination as a priest and the practice of extreme forms of self-abasement. All of this was in addition to writing not only an extraordinary number of plays but also novels, verse epics and vast quantities of ballads, verse epistles and sonnets. By a vicious irony the experience in Lope's life that came closest to the subject matter of *Fuente Ovejuna*, the rape of his daughter by the son of a nobleman, came twenty years or so after the play was written (around 1613) and fifteen years after its publication in 1619.

The Spanish Golden Age

Spanish Golden Age plays were staged in playhouses or *corrales* that developed piecemeal within the courtyards of existing buildings, on the initiative of charitable brotherhoods and under the usually benevolent supervision of the municipal authorities. With a rectangular apron stage at one end the yard was surrounded by (eventually) three tiers of galleries, one section of which (the *cazuela* or 'stew pot') was specifically reserved for women. A popular theatre catering for a wide social range and accommodating perhaps two thousand spectators, the *corrales* are in structure reminiscent of the Elizabethan innyards and arena theatres while contrasting with them in their founding and in their relationship with the authorities. *Fuente Ovejuna* would speak plainly as a human and social-political document to the socially-stratified, sexually-divided and sometimes boisterous audiences of early seventeenth-century Spain.

The Plot

Fuente Ovejuna tells the real-life tale of the revolt in April 1476 of peasantry from the Cordoban village of Fuente Ovejuna (or Sheep Well) against the feudal authorities of their area. It also portrays their subsequent acceptance of the supreme power of the Spanish rulers Ferdinand of Aragon and Isabella of Castile. The human events behind the peasant revolt concern the tyrannical behaviour of the military commander, Fernando Gomez de Guzman, who interrupts the wedding of a local girl, Laurencia, abducts and rapes her and has her father beaten. She taunts the peasantry into rising against him and murdering him. An investigator sent to discover the culprits only elicits the proud cry 'Fuente Ovejuna did it'. The final acceptance of the authority of Ferdinand and Isabella resulted, though the play does not say so, but as Lope's initial audience may have known or believed, in the total destruction of the village.

Donnellan and Ormerod found ways of creating, through ensemble playing and through costume, lighting, props and gesture, the vigorously robust life of a community responsive both to the natural features of their world (evoked in part by Ormerod's backdrop of a rural landscape) and to the physical, moral and social threats of repressive politics. As Peter Kemp put it: 'Vivid, boisterous scenes bring out the peasants' humane humour which increasingly contrasts with the inhuman hauteur of the Knights. As warm as the light glowing down on them, these interludes are ripe with bucolic banter and a kind of mellow poetry. Into this world of wholesome seasonal rhythms, the Commander, stiff with pride and priapism, ferociously thrusts himself.' (*The Independent*, 12.1.1989) John James, relishing the way in which 'from beginning to end the production teems with life', drew attention to Mick Hughes's 'chiaroscuro lighting' that 'pulsates with Spanish heat' and particularly noted the way in which 'in one of Donnellan's strokes of genius two lovers, centre stage, react seismographically to the sounds of the unseen torture of their loved ones, harrowing in its intensity.' (*Times Educational Supplement*, 20.1.89)

Whatever their differing emphases, reviewers reacted with enthusiasm to a production that employed all the resources of a strong company, and of design, lighting and movement. Central to many comments were the rape scene and its aftermath, played with extraordinary force by James Laurenson and Rachel Joyce. Jeremy Kingston was particularly struck by the playing of the victim-heroine: 'Rachel Joyce gives a performance that is ordinary only until the astonishing scene where she reappears, raped, before the town council and stalks the length of the table with her skirts up to show her bleeding bruises'. 'It is a scene,' he reflects, 'politically unthinkable and emotionally beyond the capacity of Jacobean playwrights, Shakespeare included.' (*The Times*, 11.1.1989) There was wide agreement that, in Sheridan Morley's words, 'The Cottesloe has not seen such a triumph of the company spirit since the great days of Bill Bryden's miracle plays, performed there almost a decade ago.' (*Punch*, 3.2.1989).

The Cottesloe Version

Fuente Ovejuna was seen at the Cottesloe in a version by Adrian Mitchell, based on a literal translation by Gwenda Pandolfi. Most comment responded favourably to

FIG 89 James Laurenson in Velasquez-like costume for his role as Commander of the Order of Calatrava.
PHOTO: *Robert Workman*

FIG 90 Dance of the people of Fuente Ovejuna, 1989 production.

Mitchell's 'earthy yet lithe translation of Lope's text' (Paul Preston, *Times Literary Supplement*, 20–26 January 1989). Michael Billington found it 'a text that is springy, alive and free of translatorese'. He offered an example of its qualities: 'In William Cornford's American version, someone says of Laurencia, "I'll bet the priest poured on the salt in fistfuls when he christened her." Here we are simply told, "She is tough as leather and cold as scandal": less literal but more pungent.' (*The Guardian*, 12.1.1989)

Even allowing for Michael Coveney's reservations about 'the failure of Mitchell's text to indicate Lope's rich polymetrical variety. No sign, for instance, of Laurencia's great sonnet before the torture commences' (*Financial Times*, 11.1.1989), there was broad agreement that Mitchell's text was both richly playable and faithful to the spirit of the original. Mitchell's work has been described by John Berger as characterised by 'a kind of revolutionary populism, bawdiness, wit and the tenderness sometimes to be found between animals', qualities patently appropriate to the translation of *Fuente Ovejuna*. (Quoted by Michael Horowitz, *The Weekend Guardian*, 25–26.2.1989) Nurtured by his work for Peter Brook on *Marat Sade* (1964) and *US* (1966), Mitchell subsequently adapted two plays by Lope's contemporary Calderon, *The Mayor of Zalamea* for the National and *Life is a Dream* for the RSC, and by the time of *Fuente Ovejuna* (in Horowitz's words) his work showed he understood 'the common language of creativity as solidly as Shakespeare did his wooden O'.

The Cheek By Jowl Style

Donnellan's *Fuente Ovejuna* marked the Cottesloe debut of a director who with his designer Nick Ormerod had

FIG 91 Wilbert Johnson as Frondoso (1992 production).

already made a name as the founder of the highly successful experimental touring company Cheek By Jowl. The performing and technical Company playing in the Cottesloe were recruited specifically for *Fuente Ovejuna,* but several had already worked with Donnellan and Ormerod. Described by Kenneth Rea as 'one of Britain's boldest and most exciting theatre groups' of the '80s (*The Weekend Guardian,* 10–11.12.1988) Cheek by Jowl based their success on Donnellan's beliefs that theatre is the actor's art and that actors must in performance vigorously acknowledge their own bodies. Choreographed movement and dance are therefore prominent features of his shows.

Donnellan stresses improvisation as a rehearsal technique, and based his preparation for *Fuente Ovejuna* on a series of physical and vocal experiments: 'We started with exercises, building up through improvisation, and didn't get to the text until a few days in. All of which is very frightening if you are an actor used to the read-through on the first day, then blocking round the model. But I think actors want to work in this way.' (Interview with Alex Renton, *The Independent,* 11.1.1989) 'I never start with a read-through, but with the *dance* of the play', as he said on another occasion. (Interview with Andy Lavender, *City Limits,* 1.12.88). Taken together with Donnellan's reputation as a director of political plays, and his conviction that theatre has a profoundly political role in society, these attitudes and practices clearly underlie the powerful theatricality of the Cottesloe *Fuente Ovejuna.*

There was grumbling on the BBC Radio Three programme, *Critics' Forum* (14.1.89), about some of the stage action, with unflattering comparisons to Morris Dancers and Thomas Hardy, together with some objections to what was taken to be the inappropriate political updating of a sixteenth-century play. But the critical response from audiences and media generally was almost uniformly favourable, with Paul Preston claiming *Fuente Ovejuna* as 'a work of stark contemporary relevance', and reminding us that 'in 1932, an almost exact repetition [of the events recorded in the play] took place at the village of Castilblanco in Extremadura. Lorca [the play's director on this occasion], perhaps inevitably, used modern dress when he took *Fuenteovejuna* on tour to the villages of the south in the following year.' (*The Times Literary Supplement,* 20–26 January 1989) Donnellan's production, though not in modern dress, thus followed in a tradition of revivals that have spoken effectively to an audience distant in time and place from the script's violent events, but nevertheless sharing its human concerns and anger.

FIG 92 Carol Woods-Coleman, the American singer and actress (Ma Rainey) at the microphone. Her 'imperious and mesmerizing presence' (Matt Wolf, *Wall Street Journal*, 3–4.11.1989) and powerful voice were memorable features of the production. "You don't sing to feel better; you sing 'cause that's a way of understanding life." (*From the script*)

MA RAINEY'S BLACK BOTTOM

By August Wilson

August Wilson

By the time *Ma Rainey* was staged at the Cottesloe, the forty-four-year-old black dramatist August Wilson was already the author of highly acclaimed plays dealing with black experience in twentieth-century America. *Fences* won a Tony Award for best play, the New York Drama Critics' Circle Award and the Pulitzer Prize for drama (1987), *The Piano Lesson* was to win a second Pulitzer in 1990 and *Joe Turner's Come and Gone* won the New York Drama Critics' Circle Award (1988). All were widely toured across America. *Ma Rainey's Black Bottom* opened on Broadway in October 1984, winning the New York Drama Critics' Circle Award and receiving widespread critical applause.

Wilson first came to notice when in 1981 the manuscript of one of his plays was identified as promising by Lloyd Richards at the Eugene O'Neill Theater Center in Waterford, Connecticut. Richards, Dean of the Yale School of Drama, formed a strong working relationship with Wilson. He directed much of Wilson's playwriting, first at Yale and then on Broadway, winning a Tony Award as best director for *Fences*.

Wilson and Black Music

Wilson's programme note for the Cottesloe production describes how in the sixties, living in Pittsburgh, he first became aware of Black popular music of the 30s and 40s. Among a pile of cheap 78 rpm records he discovered a pirated copy of Bessie Smith's *Nobody in Town Can Bake a Sweet Jellyroll Like Mine*. 'It is difficult to describe what happened when I put it on the turntable. For the first time, someone was speaking directly to me about myself and the cultural environment of my life. I was stunned.' The experience led him to involvement in the debate about Black culture: 'I felt it a duty and an honour to participate'. Writing *Ma Rainey's Black Bottom* followed from listening to Gertrude ('Ma') Rainey on a Milestone album and thinking that 'through her I might explore the economic exploitation of the early Black performers'.

MA RAINEY'S BLACK BOTTOM
Written by August Wilson

Director	*Howard Davies*
Designer	*Bob Crowley*
Lighting	*Mark Henderson*
Music Director	*Neil McArthur*
Sound	*Scott Myers*
Dialect Coach	*Joan Washington*
Photography	*Richard Mildenhall*
Production Manager	*Jason Barnes*
Stage Manager	*Trish Montemuro*

Players

Ma Rainey	*Carol Woods-Coleman*
Dussie Mae	*Jacqueline de Peza*
Levee	*Hugh Quarshie*
Sylvester	*Lennie James*
Sturdyvant	*Tom Chadbon*
Irvin	*William Hoyland*
Cutler	*George Harris*
Toledo	*Clarke Peters*
Slow Drag	*Tommy Eytle*
Policeman	*Sean Gascoine*

The play previewed from 19 October 1989, opened on 25 October 1989 and ran in repertoire until 24 March 1990. It also played at the Hackney Empire (in London) for a short season in February 1990.

Instrumental coaching for the performers was provided by Richard Allen (bass), Neil McArthur (piano), Jonathan Small (trumpet) and Pete Beachill (trombone). Live music during the interval was performed by Carol Woods-Coleman, with Pete Hurt, Keith Jenkins, Henry Lowther and Chris Pyne.

'Ma' Rainey

Gertrude Rainey was born on 26 April 1886 in Columbus, Georgia. Her singing career began at the age of 14. By the time of recording her version of the dance number 'Black Bottom' for Paramount in December 1927 she had become a highly respected figure, working with such famous artists as Louis Armstrong and Tommy Ladnier. Her marriage to Will 'Pa' Rainey in 1904 led to a touring show billed as 'Ma and Pa Rainey, the Assassinators of the Blues', the title of 'Ma' sticking to her in her character as 'Mother of the Blues'. Her warm and powerful voice ideally suited the melancholy of a form 'which combined the cries of the cottonfields with the tough saloon music of the cities' (Paul Oliver). Her only serious rival as a woman singer in this mode was the beautiful Bessie Smith, whom she may have introduced to the blues form, and who went on to record for the national company, Columbia.

Described by Paul Oliver as a 'short, dark-skinned, wild-haired, bi-sexual woman', Gertrude Rainey remained the darling of the black audience, especially in the South. She became in addition a leading figure among the numerous black professional musicians and singers of Chicago. Her allegiance to her Southern roots helped to stir rivalries among black performers, many of whom were beginning to despise the barnstorming southern troupes with which Ma often worked, preferring a new professionalism signalled by the ability to read music and the wearing, as in the production, of natty clothes, including smart snap-brim hats and expensive shoes. Ma's biography, including the recording session of December 1927 (which the play recreates), epitomises the racial tensions of the time, including the far from perfect economic and cultural assimilation of blacks, and the exploitation by whites of black skills. It also spells out the stresses within the black community itself.

This account draws on Paul Oliver's detailed note in the programme for the Cottesloe production.

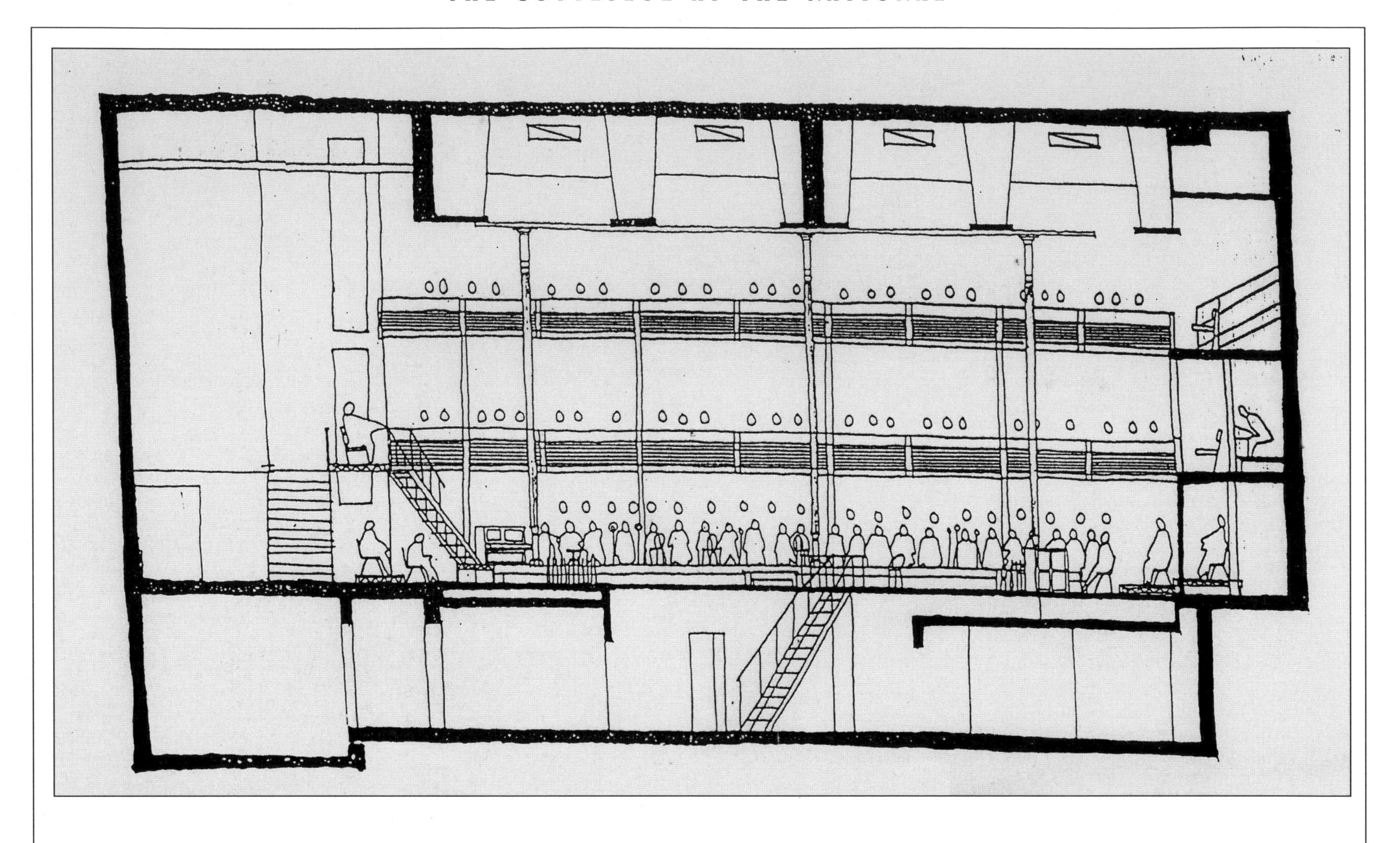

Technical Summary

• Bob Crowley's setting used the whole performance space to evoke a 1920s loft building in Chicago, pressed into service as a recording studio.

• The theatre's fourth side (normally the end stage) was bridged across, linking the existing seated galleries at first level (2.575m high). Such a bridge had been used as playing space in both *The Passion* and *The Beggars' Opera*, but for *Ma Rainey* it provided audience seating for the first time for two thirds of its length, the remaining third being occupied by the recording booth. This produced a rectangular room bounded on four sides by seats at floor level, mid level and at the top level on three sides.

• Repertoire changeover restrictions prevented a seated gallery at the top level, but a hanging false gallery-front matched the handrails of the side galleries, and completed the architecture.

• The playing space of 8.12m wide, by 10.87m long, was split by two long diagonal steps leading to a triangle occupying half the acting area, and raised by 0.4m. The whole floor was boarded, and three 'cast-iron' fibreglass pillars marked the diagonal.

• There were entrances at the four corners, with additional entrances via a stair linking the recording booth gallery to the main playing area, and from the Cottesloe's sub-stage via a stair through the 1986 pit elevator.

• Simple overhead design features can increase the 'room' feel, and for this show Bob Crowley ran blue and pink neon zigzags diagonally across the roof.

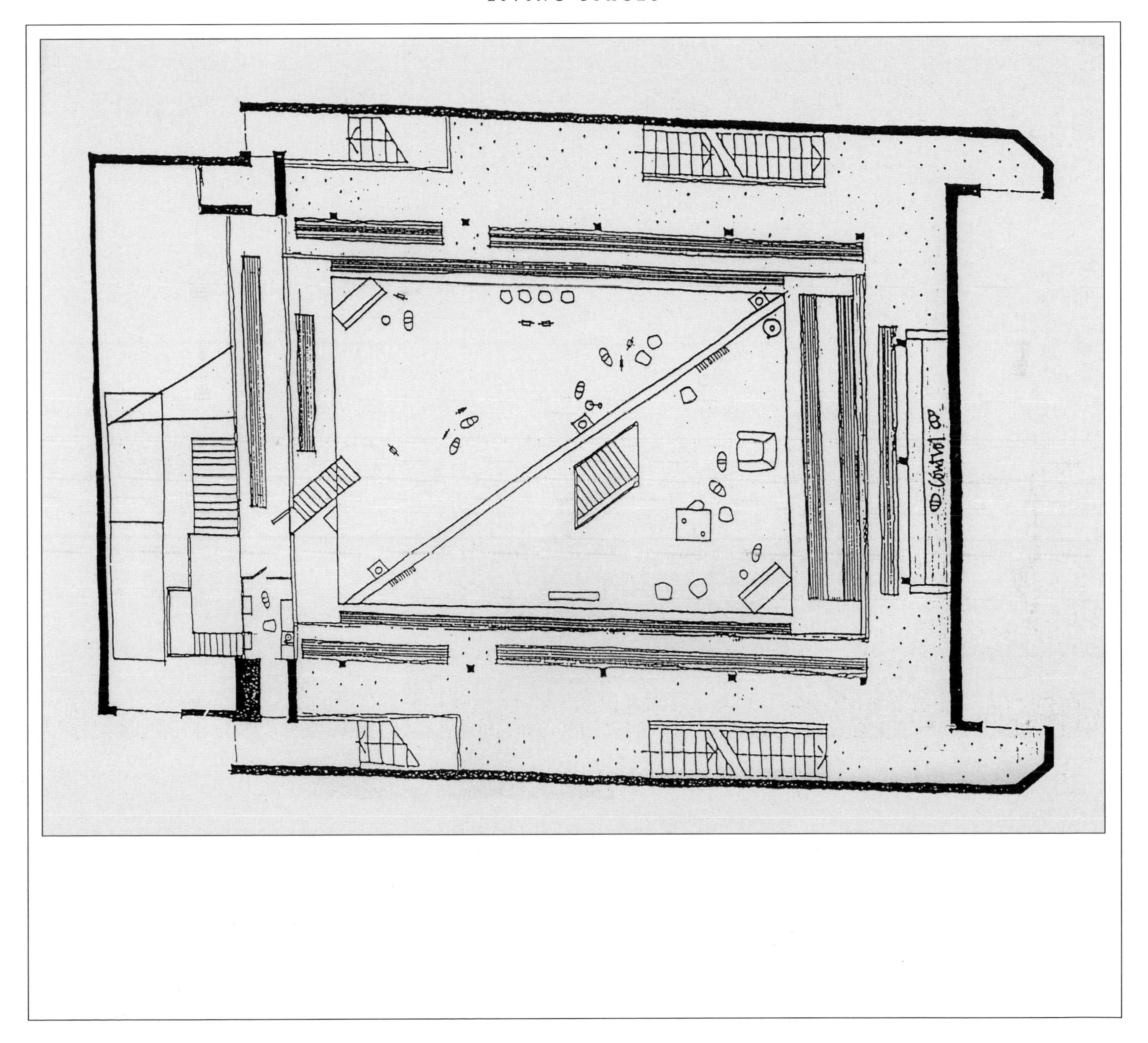
Control

FIG 93 (*left*) Lennie James (Sylvester) and Jacqueline de Peza (Dussie Mae), with one of the carefully crafted 'wrought iron' pillars and period telephone.

FIG 94 (*above*) Bob Crowley's setting, meticulously detailed and authentic, occupied almost the whole of the Cottesloe's floor-area, with two steps bisecting the space diagonally. A balcony area was used as the control room.

The Cottesloe as Recording Studio

For this production, any resemblance of the Cottesloe to a proscenium or end-stage theatre was abolished. As Kate Kellaway noted, for *Ma Rainey* 'the Cottesloe has been transformed: Bob Crowley has captured the centre of the theatre and filled it with spacious, sanded floors on different levels. The audience is made marginal by this generous design, the performers are central and there is an exciting sense that we are spying on a rehearsal'. (*Observer*, 29.10.1989) The set entirely took over the theatre space, 'a huge, loving re-creation of a Chicago recording studio in 1927. There are elderly radiators and bentwood chairs, dinky upright pianos, and, on the balcony, a recording booth hung with demure pin-ups from *Photoplay*'. (Rhoda Koenig, *Punch*, 10.11.1989) John James appreciated especially the way in which the set and costumes freed the cast to perform a compellingly realistic piece of theatre: 'Bob Crowley's marvellously authentic setting ... fills the Cottesloe, establishing in detail – from the left-over nickel in the public telephone to the water escaping from a radiator – a cheap recording studio in Chicago, 1927. This loving attention to life's minutiae ... shows itself also in Crowley's costume designs ... leaving a brilliant cast free to act in a play as rich and varied as life itself'. (*Times Educational Supplement*, 17.11.1989)

Most reviewers were struck by the visual authority of the design, and by its social implications. Jane Edwardes referred to 'Bob Crowley's atmospheric design sprawling across a vast playing area with cast-iron pillars, hissing radiators and scruffy pianos', and noted how 'up above in the control room the white men who hold the purse strings periodically descend to have it out with the troublesome niggers'. (*Time Out*, 1.11.89)

Comparing the Cottesloe theatre-in-the-round performance with the play's original proscenium staging on Broadway (1985), Michael Billington commented that 'In a proscenium theatre, the band-room and the recording studio are simply stage left and right; here they are on slightly different levels with characters constantly descending from the cable-strewn chaos of one to the dusty sub-world of the other. We share the same space as the actors'. The result was a production that in Billington's view made the play 'more engrossing, less melodramatic'. (*Guardian*, 27.10.1989)

There were reservations. Steve Grant thought the Broadway proscenium set 'much clearer'. Poor acting in that production, it was true, hampered the performance of 'Wilson's vibrant, punchy text'. Here, 'on Bob Crowley's set, which resembles the kind of trendy Diner that has sprung up in Central London recently, the words are lost by the actors' need to face away from the majority of the audience at certain periods and the rather excessive use of music to point up certain scenes, which drowns out key exchanges'. (*Twenty/Twenty*, December, 1989) Most reviewers, however, viewed the staging arrangements as integral to what one called 'the coming-of-age of black theatre in Britain'. (John James, *Times Educational Supplement*, 17.11.1989)

FIG 95 The recording session in progress.

The Music

More than for most productions at the Cottesloe, music sat close to the heart of this one, exemplifying the ways in which 'musical and social history are intertwined, and how jazz in particular has always had to fight to escape the shackles of show business'. (*Stage*, 2.11.1989) Perhaps most remarkably — almost incredibly — the performers had to learn their instruments as part of the rehearsal process. As Michael Billington noted approvingly, 'Three months ago, none of the actors were instrumentalists. Under Neil McArthur's musical direction, they play together with just the right rigid tempo of a back-up band'. (*Guardian*, 27.10.1989)

Graham Hassell interviewed Clarke Peters, the performance's pianist, keen to know how the actors felt about their level of competence. He was anxious that the show's music might send Ma Rainey, whatever her preference for 'grass roots' over 'city slick', spinning in her grave. Peters responded, 'Well, it sounds difficult, sure. But in reality it's only two numbers and we've been working on them since the end of July. [It was by now October.] You have to remember also that this is theatre, not a concert. The music has ulterior motives and takes on other dimensions. It doesn't have to stand alone. ... Often, too, we play only snatches which get interrupted by the dialogue, or which fade and become background only. So we handle it that way. Anyway it's our job as actors to make it look like we've been doing it for years.' He went on to link the pleasures and perils of on-stage performance to the adrenalin-promoting essence of theatre itself: 'Believe me, we've got it to a point now where we may even go jamming in the pub afterwards. We can improvise. At first everything was done pedantically. I'd read the music and be told exactly where my finger should be for each note on each line. Now I've discarded the sheet music and I'm finding chords I know from guitar playing. There's still a risk of drying though. Although I've made the songs personal party pieces I found even at home the other day that the right hand suddenly forgot where to go. It made me real nervous. But that's all part of being in the theatre and it's my responsibility to make sure it comes out right on the night'. (*What's On*, 28.10.1989).

With few exceptions, the reviewers seemed comfortable with the musical skills of Hugh Quarshie, a 'stroppy, strident trumpet player' (Jack Tinker, *Daily Mail*, 1.11.1989), George Harris as the hack-musician trombonist Cutler, Tommy Eytle on double-bass as Slow Drag 'an ancient relic of an older Black culture' (Dominic Gray, *What's On*, 1.11.1989) and Clarke Peters himself as the pianist Toledo. All were agreed on the formidable presence and voice of the Broadway star Carol Woods-Coleman who as Ma Rainey 'dominates regally and sings resoundingly'. (Kate Kellaway, *Observer*, 29.10.1989) One reviewer went so far as to prefer the musical to the verbal abilities of the actors: 'They work together like musicians long familiar with each other and the amazing thing is that they can even play. If I have any reservations about the piece, it is that one keeps hoping they will stop talking and start making music.' 'The whole play,' he concludes, 'stays in the mind for days afterwards like a great piece of jazz, always drawing you back for a second hearing.' (Hugo Williams, *Sunday Correspondent*, 5.11.1989)

The Players

There was general agreement about the stage-filling presence of Carol Woods-Coleman 'looking like a small dirigible in red velvet' (Milton Shulman, *Evening Standard*, 26.10.1989), an 'Amazonian presence ... belting out her big number or fighting her corner against white producers with queenly disdain'. (Jack Tinker, *Daily Mail*, 1.11.1989) She emerged as 'a powerhouse when she talks and a joy when she sings', according to Rhoda Koenig (*Punch*, 10.11.1989). Her first entry proved memorable: 'Ma Rainey appears after 45 minutes, sweeping down the steps from gallery level in a froth of indignation and a full-length fur, an entourage of pretty girl, burly young man and angry cop in tow. It is quite an entrance'. (Martin Hoyle, *Financial Times*, 26.10.1989) Another reviewer was equally impressed: 'Preceded by a bow wave of expectant commotion, she sails in, rouged-faced and fur-coated, trailing an ingenue lover, a stuttering nephew, a traffic cop and their attendant cacophony. This mother of the blues is larger than life ... the only one who car-

FIG 96 Costume sketch by Bob Crowley for Ma Rainey's costume.

Fig 97 Jacqueline de Peza as Dussie Mae 'a pretty thing in red flounces and marcelled hair' (Rhoda Koenig, *Punch*, 10.11.1989), surrounded by the band instruments and a period lamp.

ries any weight with the Paramount bosses'. (Graham Hassell, *Plays and Players*, March 1990)

The 'pretty girl' made an impression of another kind. Jacqueline De Peza as Dussie Mae 'looks wonderfully meek as Ma's gal, a pretty thing in red flounces and marcelled hair, but Wilson gives her little to do besides sashay around and show her garters'. (Rhoda Koenig, *Punch*, 10.11.1989) Kate Kellaway read the sexual signals too, seeing 'the delicious, sloe-eyed' Dussie Mae as a woman 'who wriggles in her dress, suggesting an eagerness to get out of it; testing her sex appeal as if it were a form of market research'. (*Observer*, 28.10.1989)

Hugh Quarshie 'who plays Levee like a black Brando' (Charles Osborne, *Daily Telegraph*, 27.10.1989) offered a convincing complement to Dussie Mae's sexuality, being 'magnetic' 'a sharp dresser, a sweet talker ("They don't call me sweet lemonade for nothing") and a go-getting song-writer'. (Kate Kellaway, *Observer*, 29.10.1989) 'Brilliantly touchy and virile' (Milton Shulman, *Evening Standard*, 26.10.1989), Quarshie played Levee 'as a riveting mixture of strutting cockiness, complacent stupidity and fight-picking defensiveness'(Paul Taylor, *Independent*, 27.10.1989), one whose dandified self-esteem and proclaimed musical sophistication (he's the only one with serious aspirations as a jazz musician) couldn't save him from self-destruction.

'Clarke Peters's attractive Toledo,' noted Paul Taylor, is 'the group's self-appointed consciousness-raiser and the only one who can read. Humanisingly, he is not as dexterous with ideas as he thinks'. (*Independent*, 27.10.1989) George Harris as Cutler, 'the gentle giant trombonist' (Irving Wardle, *Times*, 26.10.1989) 'balancing exploited worker with a sense of value in what he is doing' (Dominic Gray, *What's On*, 1.11.1989), and Tommy Eytle as Slow Drag 'a grizzled bass player of legendary erotic powers' complete a trio of players 'who invest the parts with an extraordinary depth of personal biography'. (Irving Wardle, *Times*, 26.10.1989)

The Script

Judged by Matt Wolf as 'an astonishing piece of writing, at once exhilarating and elegiac, melodious and mournful, and one that its admirers might have thought to be uniquely American in its rhythms and patois' (*City Limits*, 2.11.1989), *Ma Rainey* translated with extraordinary effectiveness to the Cottesloe stage. Several reviewers commented on the vitality of the language. 'Wilson's ear for the poetry of everyday language is extraordinary, his didactic purpose tempered by the unusual ability to create believable characters whose views are entirely at odds with his own'. (Paul Anderson, *Tribune*, 3.11.1989) Steve Grant saw sources and parallels for the language of this 'passionate, angry piece': 'Wilson's heightened realistic style seems like a mix of Beckett or Pinter with the aural felicities of a David Mamet; like the former he shows powerless individuals frittering their lives on petty squabbles and trivialities, arguments about shoes, women, music, money. Like Mamet his grasp of dialect and speech-rhythm is uncanny'. (*Time Out*, 11.10.1989)

Some had hesitations. Several found the opening act slow, while others judged it 'naturalistic'. Michael Billington offered a mixed response: 'The play has a loose-limbed anecdotal quality and occasionally drifts off into reminiscence. But it grips one's attention because it is about something important: music as an instrument of power as well as self-expression'. (*Guardian*, 27.10.1989) Rhoda Koenig thought the piece dramatically inconsequential but nevertheless significant. She concluded 'if *Ma Rainey* doesn't amount to much more than ambience, it's a thick, juicy slice, and its rich suggestive language takes much of the despair out of Wilson's tale of rats in a trap who eat one another. "Life!" says Levee, considering the poor stuff of his, "life ain't nothin'. Now, death – death got some *style*!". (*Punch*, 10.11.1989) Style was a quality the reviewers unanimously agreed could aptly be discerned in both script and production.

Fig 98 Hugh Quarshie as Levee, 'a sharp dresser, a sweet talker' (Kate Kellaway, *Observer*, 29.10.1989). Quarshie played the role as 'a riveting mixture of strutting cockiness, complacent stupidity and fight-picking defensiveness'. (Milton Shulman, *Evening Standard*, 26.10.1989)

FIG 99 Bob Crowley's cruciform set for David Hare's *Racing Demon*, directed by Richard Eyre. Michael Bryant as the Rev. Harry Henderson at the apex of the cross. Notice how, in Jason Barnes's words, 'lighting designer Mark Henderson cut his coverage tightly to the cross shape, which shone with a pale glow in contrast to the black auditorium'.

RACING DEMON

By David Hare

The Issues

It was perhaps inevitable that, given David Hare's track record as social critic, comment on the production should focus principally on the assessment it offered of one of the remaining institutions bolstering the hierarchy-ridden structure of English society – the Church of England. No longer (as several reviewers remarked) the Tory Party at prayer, the Church nevertheless appeared to provide opportunities for satirical comment on social attitudes, and on a privileged if no longer comfortable social status. One reviewer even concluded that the dated but still-potent influence of the Church had the effect of drawing into the Cottesloe an audience peculiarly suited to the enjoyment of its rituals – a conclusion that would in equal measure alarm and amuse the playwright, and, if true, would offer a wry comment on the power of the Cottesloe to operate on the cutting edge of contemporary culture. Rhoda Koenig reported (in *Punch*, 23.2.90) that 'If the audience at *Racing Demon* was not what you would expect for a David Hare play, it was exactly what you would expect for a play about the problems of vicars in the Church of England. Twinsets, hairnets, and sensible shoes were out in force. One lady so attired remarked to me at the interval how life-like she found the play. 'Well," I said, to be polite, "I hope no one's going to come around with a collection plate." "Oh, my," she said, repeating the remark to her friend and chuckling gently, "that's quite as funny as anything in the play."' 'So now you know,' Koenig sourly added, 'just how funny *Racing Demon* is.'

There is no independent audience survey to back Koenig's observations, but reviewers divided sharply into those who found the play a penetrating analysis of a crumbling institution, and those who thought it the work of a writer poorly qualified to hold any opinion at all on its overt subject-matter, the present state of religion and its social context. Perhaps in taking either stance reviewers were unconsciously betraying their own commitments and origins. At the very least, Hare and the Cottesloe could reflect that they had stirred up controversy. James Christopher (*Time Out*, 14.2.90) took the play as cogent social analysis: 'David Hare's gripping play, set on Bob Crowley's spare, cruciform set, is a compelling portrait of the contentious problems that afflict London's inner-city parishes. By distilling the arguments, Hare subtly caricatures the weaknesses of the Anglican Church: its comfy clubbiness, its banal inadequacy in dealing with social realities and the constant compromises – pertinently over women clerics and homosexuals – that constitute its unfashionable liberal flexibility.' Michael Coveney was inclined to agree, but pushed the play into a rather more precarious area of debate: 'Hare concocts potent drama, and a text of whiplash pertinence, without once resorting to the tritely blasphemous. This is much more a serious play about religion than an irreligious one about Christianity.' (*Observer*, 11.2.90) Michael Billington (*Guardian*, 10.2.90), in slightly re-defining the play's 'fundamental question', was nevertheless disposed to take it on a similarly serious level: 'David Hare's bracingly intelligent and highly entertaining *Racing Demon* at the Cottesloe ... asks a fundamental question: can the church be taken seriously if it divorces itself from ritual and sacrament and operates as a branch of the social services?'

There were those who thought Hare in no position to hold opinions on such matters. Christopher Edwards (*Spectator*, 17.2.90) saw the objections and offered a partial response: 'he is clearly an outsider himself. He sees, and dramatises, the contemporary "image" of the Church without being in a position to grasp the sort of active faith and spiritual struggle that still exists beyond the Church's contemporary agenda. The play lacks an historic and individual dimension, that probably makes it seem both patronising and ignorant to many. Hare could fairly retort that an assiduous search by an intelligent and inquisitive outsider has found little evidence of this precious dimension.' Chris Peachment (*Sunday Correspondent*, 18.2.90) was more direct (if scarcely gram-

RACING DEMON
Written by David Hare

DIRECTOR	*Richard Eyre*
DESIGNER	*Bob Crowley*
LIGHTING	*Mark Henderson*
MUSIC	*George Fenton*
STAGE MANAGER	*Trish Montemuro*
PHOTOGRAPHY	*John Haynes*

Players

The Rev. Lionel Espy	*Oliver Ford Davies*
The Rt. Rev. Charlie Allen	*Richard Pasco*
Frances Parnell	*Stella Gonet*
The Rev. Tony Ferris	*Adam Kotz*
Stella Marr	*Joy Richardson*
The Rev. Donald Bacon	*David Bamber*
The Rev. Harry Henderson	*Michael Bryant*
Heather Espy	*Barbara Leigh-Hunt*
Ewan Gilmour	*Ewan Stewart*
Tommy Adair	*Paul Moriarty*
The Rt Rev. Gilbert Heffernan	*Malcolm Sinclair*
Head Waiter/Server	*Paul Moriarty*
Waiter/Server	*Andrew Woodall*

The production opened on 8.2.90 and ran in repertoire until 18.7.90. It transferred to the Lyttelton in November 1991 and toured to Newcastle, Canterbury, Bath, Bradford and Nottingham in November and December 1991.

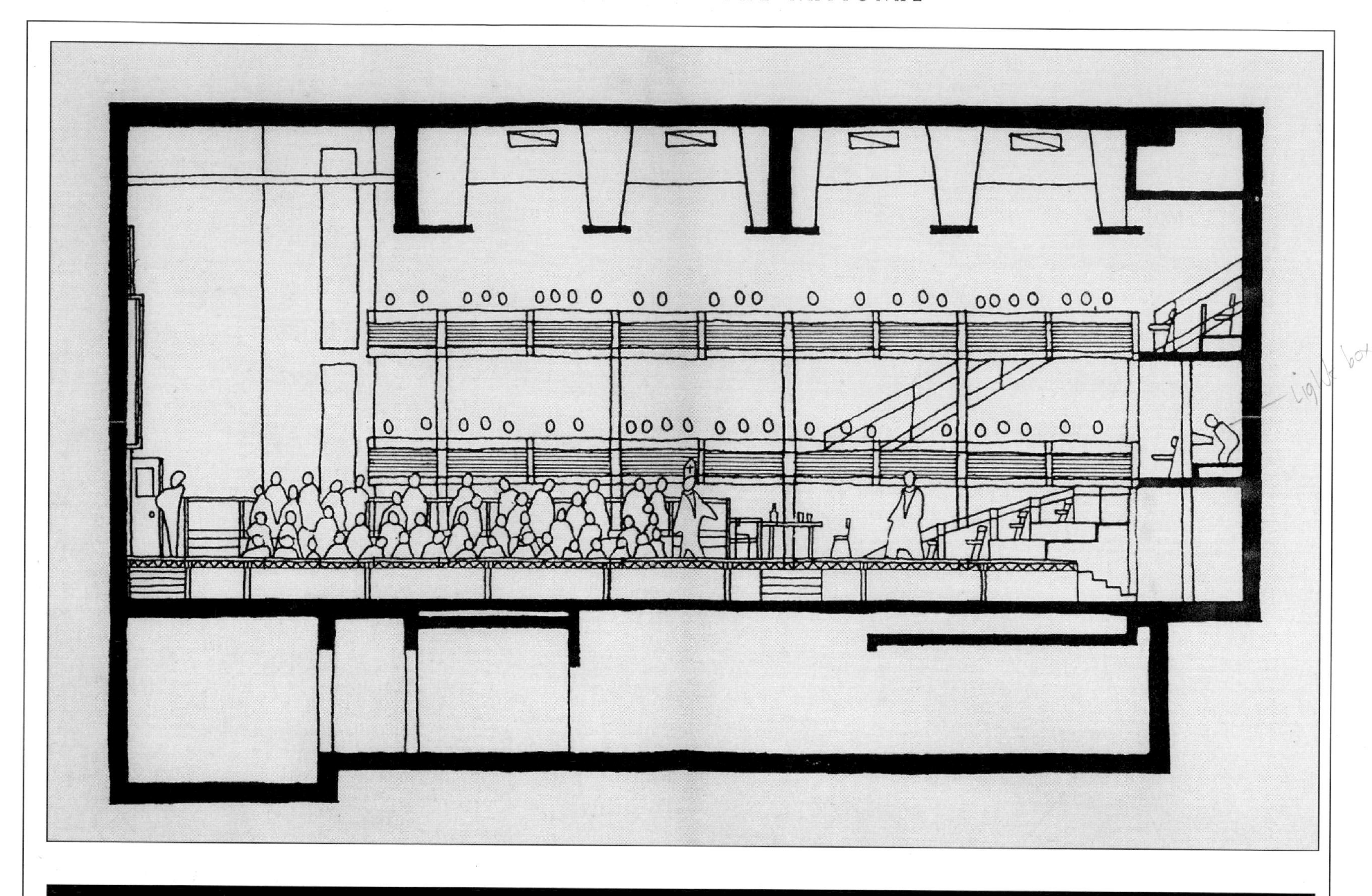

Technical Summary

• A year after *Fuente Ovejuna* reintroduced the long traverse, Richard Eyre and his designer Bob Crowley wanted to examine the form again. The installation of steeply-raked bleacher seating in 1986 made it possible to change auditorium layouts as well as the physical settings of plays during any repertoire changeover. *Fuente Ovejuna, Richard II, The Ends of the Earth* and *King Lear* accommodated the retracted pit seating unit under the rear auditorium gallery, where, by pushing the two halves apart, a centre entrance could be made.

• Bob Crowley designed a cruciform platform, with access to the foot of the cross at the upstage end of the space via a walkway from each side, and to the wings of the cross via steps from the centre of the auditorium.

• In order to make the seat storage space available for performance (and given the very narrow acting area required of 3.66m), it proved possible to use the four sections of bleacher seating, turned through 90°, for the upstage seating which flanked the leg of the cross. Angled rows of seats were placed each side of the head of the cross.

• At the lower pit level, the platform was raised 60cm above the front rows, themselves already 30cm above the normal stage level beneath. This gave an improved relationship with the middle and upper galleries, which were seated along the whole length of the theatre, and produced a strong dynamic. It also permitted high seat numbers (316).

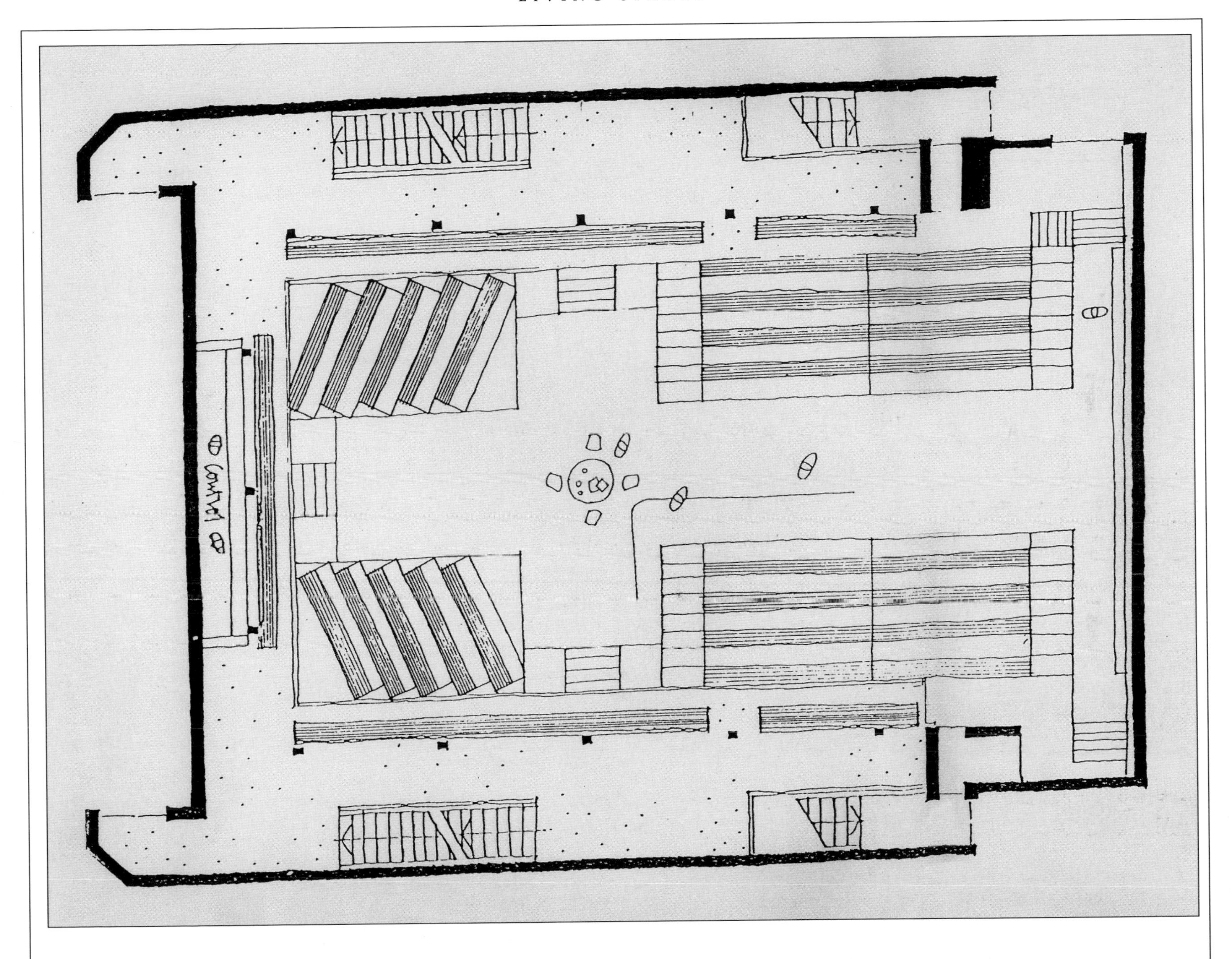

• The whole platform was covered with pale grey carpet. Lighting designer Mark Henderson cut his coverage tightly to the cross shape, which shone with a pale glow in contrast to the black auditorium.

• Mounted on the far end wall of the theatre was a 9m high advertising hoarding with revolving flats, one face of which was black, the other carrying a Calvin Klein *Obsessions* model.

• Interiors were staged centrally, with furniture rapidly introduced from the sides. The setting for the Savoy cocktail bar featured a glowing neon line set within the floor surface.

FIG 100 Adam Kotz (The Rev. Tony Ferris), David Bamber (The Rev. Donald 'Streaky' Bacon) and Michael Bryant (The Rev. Harry Henderson) on the plain-carpeted set.

DAVID HARE's pedigree in British theatre runs from the early days of the Fringe in the 1960s to something like Establishment status when he was appointed an associate director of the National Theatre in 1984 and became the author of one of the most successful play series ever staged at the National, including *Plenty* (1978) *Pravda* (1985; with Howard Brenton) *Racing Demon* (1990) *Murmuring Judges* (1991) *The Absence of War* (1993) and *Skylight* (1995). He was co-founder with Tony Bicat of Portable Theatre (1968–72), and began with this company his satirical account of British society and the evils of capitalism which has continued throughout his work. He was resident dramatist at the Royal Court in 1970–71, and at Nottingham Playhouse in 1973. He was a founder member of Joint Stock, the experimental company which launched the careers of a number of influential figures in recent theatre, and for whom he wrote *Fanshen* (1975), his play about the Chinese Revolution (it played at the Cottesloe in 1988). Another play by Hare, *Brassneck* (1973; with Howard Brenton) about corruption in local government also enjoyed considerable national success. Hare is a director as well as author and has directed a number of shows for the National Theatre, including Howard Brenton's *Weapons of Happiness.*

matical): 'Hare's knowledge of the inner workings of the Church is about as persuasive as was his knowledge of Fleet Street in *Pravda* – hardly at all.' Benedict Nightingale thought the same thought but more pungently: 'how can he satisfactorily analyse the Church of England, for all that institution's faults, when he clearly thinks the idea of Someone Up There is a delusion and distraction, a folly and snare?' (*Times*, 9.2.90) Clifford Longley, in the same issue of *The Times*, was clearly well clued up: 'Of the Church as an institution it is only a mild caricature, but of the Christian faith it is, it must be whispered, rather a mockery. … Even in the Church of England, a faith which dislikes enthusiasm, the landscape which lies between *Te Deum* and *Dies Irae* is more interesting and more dangerous than *Racing Demon* dares to hint at.'

It is rare for even a Cottesloe piece to set the reviewers debating such spiritual issues. Perhaps the final word on spiritual matters has to lie with the Rt. Rev. Richard Harries, Bishop of Oxford, writing, appropriately enough, in *The Times* (19.2.90): 'I think there *is* something religious to be found in the play. … In short, this is a play that hints at the *via negativa* of St John of the Cross, and of Eliot in *The Four Quartets*. There is a deliberate link between the apparent absence of God disclosed in the prayer and the sense of something beyond our conceiving or imagining, apprehended in the quiet personal disclosures of Lionel and Frances.' The David Hare of 1990 might have been disquieted at being recruited for such a stance, but who are we, or the reviewers, to know the secrets of the heart? At least, that is the sort of question, and the sort of phrasing, the responses to the play prompt. Michael Coveney, in sharing Rhoda Koenig's church-associations, nevertheless managed to balance irreverence and admiration in a neat paradox: 'In elegantly considering the Church's crisis, and in skating round all the positions with poise, *Racing Demon* religiously refuses to sermonise. The Cottesloe has been made like a church, and I found myself last Thursday night fumbling for small change in case there was a retiring collection by the door.' (*Observer*, 11.2.90) On the other hand, Coveney perhaps ought to know that in 1990 or 1998 small change is not what the Church wants.

The Performance

There were those who dismissed the play as little short of juvenile. Chris Peachment (*Sunday Correspondent*, 18.2.90) thought it 'all very sixth-form debate-ish'. Others thought it ill-informed about, for example, the position of the liberal wing in the Church of the 1990s. Rhoda Koenig, big on fashion metaphors, considered it 'a woolly cardigan of a play, all muffled anguish and thumping clichés.' (*Punch*, 23.2.90) But the common opinion was that Hare had written, in Michael Billington's words, a 'bracingly intelligent and highly entertaining' play. (*Guardian*, 10.2.90) Paul Taylor (*Independent*, 10.2.90) found the play 'a powerful study of liberalism at bay'. Edward Pearce (*Sunday Express*, 11.2.90) thought it 'a play of vast quality'. In a somewhat daring judgement he told us: 'What we have is didactic Wilde', in unconscious rebuttal, perhaps, of Chris Peachment's judgement that Hare is 'the Terence Rattigan of his generation.' (*Sunday Correspondent*, 18.2.90) Sheridan Morley could scarcely contain his enthusiasm: 'Unquestionably the best new play it has staged in the five years since his *Pravda*, the National Theatre's new production of David Hare's *Racing Demon* is a truly wonderful start to the British drama of the 1990s. ... Not since the epilogue to Shaw's *Saint Joan* have we had such a spirited debate about church versus state. It is in the very best sense a moral thriller.' (*Herald Tribune*, 14.2.90)

If there was division of opinion about the merits of the play, there was virtual consensus about the excellence of the playing. Michael Billington found the performances refreshingly unprejudiced: 'It is also rare to see English actors play clerics so unpatronisingly. Oliver Ford Davies is superb as Lionel: a shaggy, distracted man with a sad-spaniel countenance but a fierce tenacity when cornered. Michael Bryant as Harry is all sports-jacketed probity, David Bamber as Streaky brims over with pastoral passion and Richard Pasco as the Bishop exudes the security of power. Adam Kotz has a hard task reconciling one to the perfervid Tony but Stella Gonet as his rejected girl friend puts the rationalist case with real style.' (*Guardian*, 10.2.90)

There was praise too for Barbara Leigh-Hunt: 'Prickly, defeated, and palpably walled-up in neglect, Barbara Leigh-Hunt as [Lionel's] wife Heather seems to be the victim not just of his crippling pastoral workload, but also of his knotted, over-scrupulous introspection.' (Paul Taylor, *Independent*, 10.2.90) Maureen Paton described her as 'almost unbearably poignant as the embittered wife'. (*Daily Express*, 12.2.90) For Graham Hassell 'the strongest part, and certainly the one Hare most empathises with, is Lionel, a sack of crumpled benevolence whose sympathetic demeanour has continually smothered a razor mind. Oliver Ford Davies gives us a bemused humanitarian besieged by the machinations of zealots and dogmatists for whom his meek but practical holiness is too humble by half.' (*What's On*, 14.2.90) It says something for the depth of Hare's writing that another reviewer, Jack Tinker, located Hare's sympathies elsewhere: 'Though one suspects that his instincts and sympathy lie with the radiant Stella Gonet, who loves and loses the evangelical curate only to flee to a place where God has never been heard of, he nevertheless allows us to comprehend the anguish of

FIG 101 Richard Pasco as the Rt Rev. Charlie Allen and Oliver Ford Davies as the Rev. Lionel Espy. Mark Henderson's lighting is again both atmospheric and precise.

those who struggle to serve an impossible master.' (*Daily Mail*, 9.2.90) John Gross, one suspects, found his instincts drawn to another role again: 'David Bamber's Streaky is a study worthy of Trollope or Barbara Pym; Michael Bryant brings his usual authority to the role of the Reverend Harry – and his attempts to cope with a slice of hot apple pie from McDonalds are a joy.' (*Sunday Telegraph*, 11.2.90)

Design and Direction

It is no doubt a tribute to the aptness of the settings and the authority of the direction that few reviewers took time off from debating the play's issues to comment on Bob Crowley's work or Richard Eyre's. Yet the Long Traverse/Cruciform set devised for the production, as Jason Barnes's technical summary makes plain, was a considerable innovation or at least development in the use of the Cottesloe space. Reading the reviewers one has the sense that the elevated stage, well related to the embracing galleries, provided just the arena for the working-out of conflicting views that the play demanded. One reviewer only found the set positively unhelpful: 'Bob Crowley's set, a platform stage in the shape of a crucifix which makes it difficult for patrons seated along one arm to see what's going on down one of the others, and which presents some of them with the distracting sight of a bank of spectators facing them from ten feet away.' (Rhoda Koenig, *Punch*, 23.2.90) Others, less self-conscious, described the set as 'stark' or 'spare'. Lyn Gardner (*City Limits*, 15.2.90) was reminded of Church interiors, though the visual allusions of the grey-carpeted floor might in this case be more non-conformist than Anglican (this was not, in that sense, one of the Cottesloe's atmospheric productions): 'Theatres frequently resemble churches – cold, forbidding, removed from the real world and distressingly empty. The ritual of church services – baptisms, marriages and funerals – are often the closest most of us come to theatre in our daily lives. The NT's Cottesloe theatre has been transformed into a church (courtesy of Bob Crowley's breath-takingly simple cruciform set) for David Hare's stupendous new play about faith in the inner city.'

Richard Eyre's direction drew widespread, if unspecific, praise. Lyn Gardner wrote that 'Richard Eyre's marvellously acted production brings out all the passion and pain in a play that is hilariously funny, intellectually rigorous and awash with non-chastising humanity. A genuinely uplifting evening.' (*City Limits*, 15.2.90) Irving Wardle (*Independent on Sunday*, 18.2.90) was equally laudatory: 'Played on a traverse stage in

FIG 102 Barbara Leigh-Hunt as Heather Espy 'prickly, defeated and palpably walled-up in neglect' (Paul Taylor, *Independent*, 10.2.90).

FIG 103 Richard Pasco as the Rt Rev. Charlie Allen, 'an ineffably smooth Bishop of Southwark' (Sheridan Morley, *Herald Tribune*, 14.2.90).

the form of a nave and transept, Richard Eyre's production makes goodness visible. It is a most perfectly cast show, placing religious identity in piercing and often hilarious contrast with personal character.' Benedict Nightingale, even if he thought the play 'fatally flawed', nevertheless remarked that 'The play is cleanly and sparely staged by Richard Eyre on what looks, presumably deliberately, like a vast empty cross.' (*Times*, 9.2.90) The remark about the emptiness of the cross is unique among the reviewers, and perhaps demonstrates the fertility of meaning the spectator can read into the visual signals of staging. Martin Hoyle (*Financial Times*, 9.2.90) endorsed and amplified the general view: 'On the thrust cruciform stage Richard Eyre's production evokes lovely ensemble playing and exploits the play's dying fall.' Paul Taylor wrote about 'Richard Eyre's focused, lucid production' and called it 'generally excellent'. (*Independent*, 10.2.90) The high degree of satisfaction represented by these and other reviewers' comments offers testimony to the compelling qualities of a production that ran in the Cottesloe for 66 performances before going on a highly successful national tour.

FIGS 104 and 105 David Threlfall as Henry Bolingbroke and Fiona Shaw as Richard. The production made much use of the physical and facial similarities of the two actors.

RICHARD II

By William Shakespeare

Theatre Space

For Warner's *Richard II* the Cottesloe was adapted to a traverse arrangement, with audience above and on both sides of the stage area. Paul Taylor saw this as both playable and significant: 'Hildegard Bechtler's set – a beautiful, long, narrow, wood and gold traverse stage which bifurcates the Cottesloe with the audience sitting on either side in what could be cathedral stalls or jury boxes – has been rightly praised for the way it heightens a sense of the play's formal patterning and imparts a vivid, sport-like urgency to the aborted tournament at Coventry. What it also eerily evokes, though, is a corridor, a no-man's land (bounded by an eavesdropping audience): this is a resonantly apt location for a play where people are endemically betwixt and between states of mind, allegiance and being.' (*Independent*, 14.6.1995)

Warner herself endorsed the spatial significance of the stage arrangement, and underlined its contemporary meanings: 'It's a corridor play, between well-defined spaces. And I think that's an incredible late twentieth century state, that's where most of us are.' (Interview with Barbara Norden, *Everywoman*, August 1995) John Lahr responded not to the socio-psychological dimensions of the set but to its atmospheric evocation of a distant time, of lavishness and of danger: 'You enter Deborah Warner's thrilling London production of Shakespeare's *Richard II* … to the chanting of Latin, the flicker of candles, and the smell of incense. Here in the medieval murk … the audience looks down into an oblong corridor as if onto a bull run … On each side of the narrow alley, cordons protect seven silver stands on which miniatures (a crystal ball, a golden coin, a tiny dagger) are set out … The gilt walls and floors of the court space hint at the King's lavishness; but Shakespeare's drama and Warner's marvellous interpretation of it are about the waste of inner, not external, resources.' (*The New Yorker*, 10.7.1995)

Some found aesthetic contradictions in the set. Matt Wolf thought that 'Hildegard Bechtler's blanched-wood set at first evokes a trendy London restaurant rather than a pomp-laden medieval world.'

RICHARD II
Written by William Shakespeare

Director	*Deborah Warner*
Designer	*Hildegard Bechtler*
Music	*Arturo Annecchino*
Lighting	*Peter Mumford*
Voice Work	*Patsy Rodenburg*
Sound	*Freya Edwards*
Production Manager	*Jason Barnes*
Stage Manager	*Alison Rankin*
Photography	*Neil Libbert*

Principal Players

Richard II	*Fiona Shaw*
Henry Bolingbroke	*David Threlfall*
John of Gaunt	*Graham Crowden*
Thomas Mowbray	*David Lyon*
Queen Isabel	*Brana Bajic*
Duke of York	*Michael Bryant*
Duke of Aumerle	*Julian Rhind-Tutt*
Duchess of Gloucester	*Paola Dionisotti*

Other parts played by John Rogan, Jonathan Slinger, Jem Wall, Henry Ian Cusick, Nicholas Gecks, Struan Rodger, Richard Bremmer, John McEnery, Danny Sapani, Jude Akuwudike, Elaine Claxton.
Music performed by Eleanor Alberga (*music director*), Rebecca Arch and Irita Kutchmy, with Elaine Claxton (*soprano*)
The production opened on 2 June 1995 and ran in repertoire until 17 February 1996. It toured to the Bobigny Theatre, Paris, and to the Salzburg Festival, 1996.

At the same time he appreciated its diversity and practicality: 'Elegantly lit by Peter Mumford, the design bisects the adaptable Cottesloe space while using every bit of it, from traps underneath the stage serving as graves and prisons to a gilt-edged balcony from which Richard at one arresting moment slides his crown down a sheet.' (*Variety*, 12–18.6.1995) Bechtler is noted for minimalist rather than realistic sets, complementing Warner's unwillingness to be limited by fixtures and fittings: 'She wants a playing space which is free enough for her and the actors to invent in.' (Interview with Tiffany Daneff, *Daily Telegraph*, 2.6.1995) Most reviewers and audiences admired the multiple locations Warner and Bechtler fitted into the relatively restricted spaces of the Cottesloe, finding space for the Coventry lists, the various interior locales and the geographically far-flung parts of England where the action takes place. They also succeeded in stretching the visual dimensions of the space from the stage surface to the underfloor spaces representing Richard's prison (picked out by sunken spotlights) and the elevated balcony high on one wall.

Warner and the Space of Theatre

Deborah Warner's sensitivity to theatre space as a component of theatrical meaning is strongly marked. Her celebrated *King John* for the Royal Shakespeare Company (1988) wholly occupied Stratford's small-scale The Other Place, imaginatively reducing a large-scale play to the dimensions of a studio, while her *Titus Andronicus* for the same company (for which she received Olivier and Evening Standard awards for Best Director) adapted even the strongly positive personality of the Stratford Swan to the needs of Shakespeare's arguably darkest play. Almost concurrently with her *Richard II*, she directed the St Pancras project, with Bechtler as designer, in which the former (but by now empty) Midland Grand Hotel was offered as an 'experience' through which members of the public were invited to walk at ten minute intervals. The building was only minimally prepared for the event. 'I thought

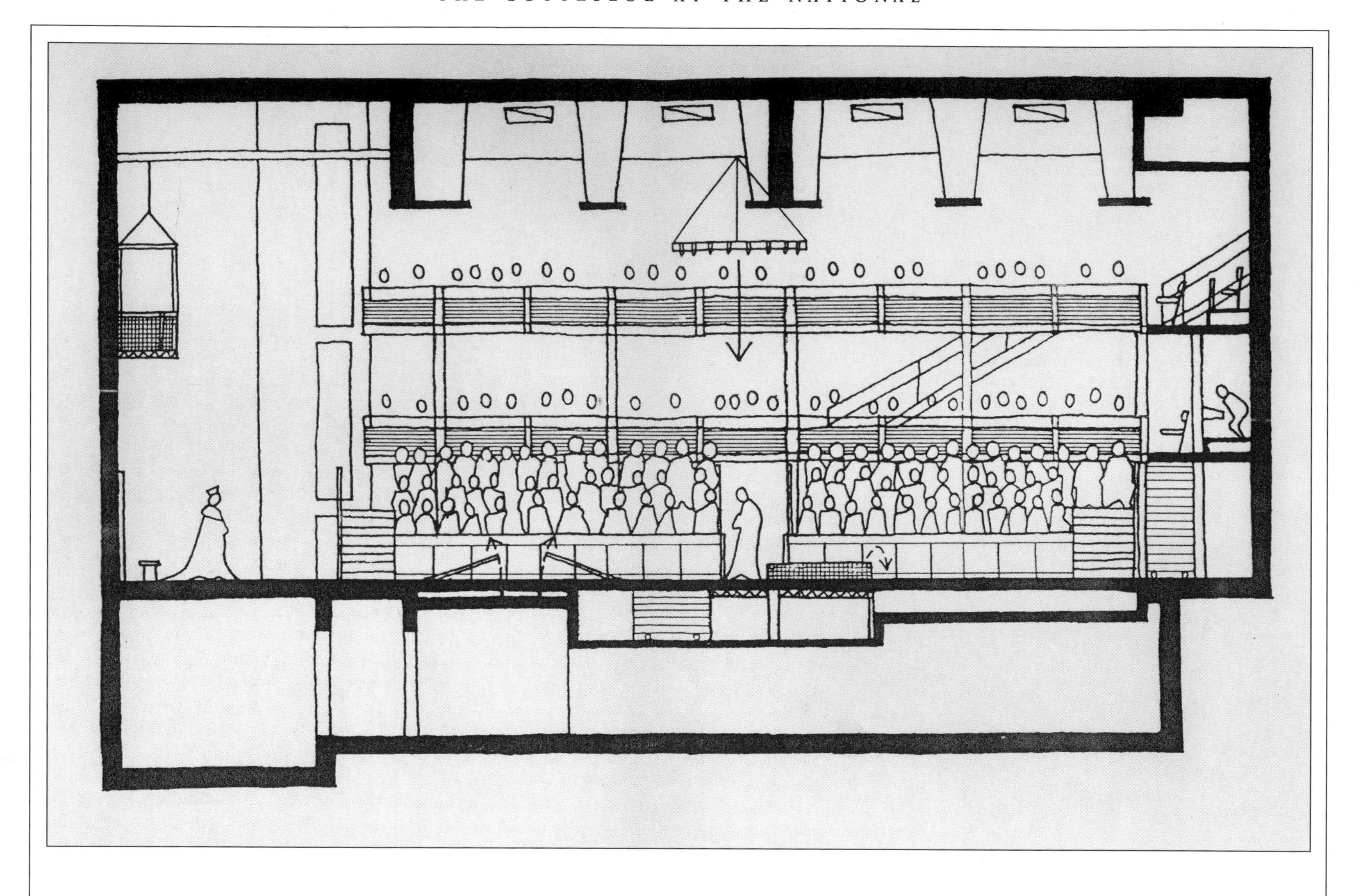

Technical Summary

• The Cottesloe's pit elevator was lowered and in-filled, and the end-stage bleacher seating retracted, to produce a flat floor throughout, on which a 'long traverse' acting area of 18.75m by a narrow 4.5m was flanked by three rows of tiered seats on each side, split by a centre vomitory entrance for actors only.

• The seat banks were faced with natural wood handrail panels. Cottesloe designs have often avoided potential alienation of the audience by separating them from the action. In this case the steep terraces and the resulting jousting area or 'list' proved an effective and non-alienating lay-out.

• Matching wooden floor panels were interspersed with brass, worn to a dull finish in the centre area, and to the rear left fully burnished and glinting like molten gold. Each end of the long space was bounded by felt sliding-door panels, inset with brass.

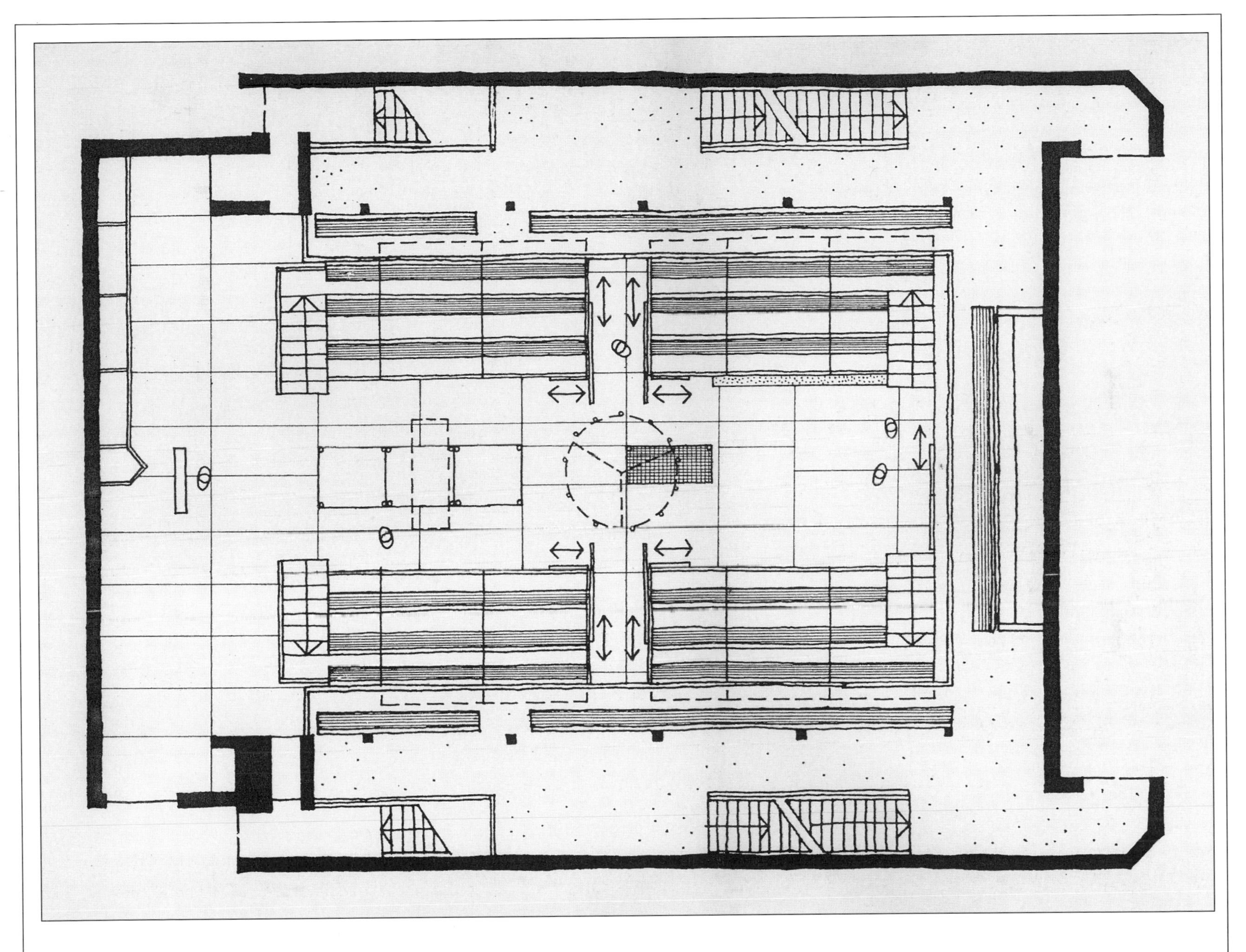

- The centre area and vomitory entrances could be closed off in each direction with wooden panels drawn across by the cast.

- Upstage, against the theatre's black brick wall hung a dull gold bridge, accessed from a small fly gallery upstage left, at a height of 5m.

- A brass meshed sunken trap let into the in-filled pit area provided the prison cell and a source of light for other scenes.

- The graceful slim avenue formed between the seat banks shimmered with the light of candles and torches, evoking a church setting, and with the selective introduction of furniture lent itself to interiors as well as exteriors, including a garden and a castle courtyard.

- The use of incense enhanced the ritual feel of the performance.

about putting a piece of theatre in it,' she said, 'then I began to see the folly of that. The building itself is a far bigger event than any play I could do.' (Interview with Sarah Hemming, *Financial Times*, 11.6.1995) Asked about the possibility of following Richard Eyre as director of the National, Warner demurred, calling herself 'a rogue and a vagabond'. But she added: 'If I were given the go-ahead to strip out the seating in the Lyttelton, and turn that into a flexible space, then I'd think again.' (Interview with Barbara Norden, *Everywoman*, August 1995)

Costume

Costumes for the *Richard II* production were mostly in subdued colours, though sometimes elaborately devised, as in the head-dresses inspired by Holbein and Dürer. The costume for Richard unsurprisingly drew most comment. Jane Edwardes referred to the 'pixie-faced, close-cropped Richard II wrapped in white bandages as though dressed by Issy Miyake.' (*Time Out*, 7.7.1995). Charles Spencer saw less *haute couture* than inappropriate history: Shaw, he said, 'wears a preposterous costume in which Richard is swathed in bandages, like an Egyptian mummy.' (*Telegraph*, 5.6.1995) Richard Hornby was more appreciative, responding to the design's practicality as well as sense of period, saying that the costumes are 'mostly plain long tunics in gray, brown or black, which set off the actors' faces wonderfully, recalling paintings by Breughel or Bosch.' Even he, however, complained of Richard's 'doublet hanging open over a loose hidden shirt, and long wrinkled slacks' a garb he thought 'hardly kingly attire'. (*Hudson Review*, Winter 1996)

The capacity of this production to dismay as well as enliven carried through its every aspect from casting and interpretation to spatial design and costume.

Reading the Production

The production drew attention in the media chiefly as a result of the casting of Fiona Shaw as Richard. There was a good deal of frothy prose in broadsheets as well as tabloids dealing with gender-bending, transexualism and related topics, as well as widespread competition to display a knowledge of cross-casting in both early theatre and modern. It was generally agreed that, while getting heated, there was nothing to get heated about. Reviewers reminded readers of Sarah Bernhardt (repeatedly) and of Frances de la Tour (as Hamlet). They remarked on the cross-dressing of Elizabethan boy actors and on Adrian Lester playing Rosalind in Declan Donnellan's *As You Like It*. The recollection of Felicity Kendal taking a boy's role in Stoppard's *On the Razzle* led one reviewer (a woman)

FIG 106 The Duke of York (Michael Bryant) and the Duchess of Gloucester (Paola Dionisotti) at the memorial patch of earth for the Duke of Gloucester.

Director, Actress, Designer

Previous stage collaborations between Deborah Warner and Fiona Shaw included Sophocles' *Electra* (1988 for the RSC), Brecht's *The Good Person of Sichuan* (1989 at the National), Ibsen's *Hedda Gabler* (1991 at the Gate Theatre, Dublin) and Beckett's *Footfalls* (1993 at the National). The Sophocles and Beckett brought Shaw Best Actress prize in the Olivier Awards, and the Ibsen won a director's prize in the same awards for Warner. Hildegard Bechtler had previously worked with Warner and Shaw on *Electra, Hedda Gabler* and *Footfalls*. Her exposure to German theatre led to an interest in 1970s German minimalism. Her training in design was at the Central School of Art and Design in London.

Shakespeare and Richard II

Written about 1595, Shakespeare's *Richard II* comes relatively early in the playwright's career, though it follows other histories such as the three-part *Henry VI*, as well as *Richard III* and *King John*. Itself the first of the group of histories that includes *Henry IV* parts 1 and 2 and *Henry V*, the play has been politically controversial since its early performances. It was revived in 1601 at the request of the followers of the Earl of Essex to accompany the Earl's abortive rising against Queen Elizabeth, when its sponsors thought its staging of a royal abdication might stimulate rebellious notions in the minds of the populace. Controversial again in its performances after the Restoration, it has remained in the theatre repertoire until today, chiefly perhaps because of the opportunities it offers the actor of Richard. A production opening in 1974 at the Royal Shakespeare Theatre had Richard Pasco and Ian Richardson exchange the roles of Richard and Bolingbroke for each performance, a device that offers a parallel to the look-alike casting of Fiona Shaw and David Threlfall for the Cottesloe production.

FIG 107 The coffined body of Richard is delivered to Bolingbroke's court.
The Bishop of Carlisle (John Rogan) kneels in prayer.

to quote a director saying of cross-casting: 'Men find it wild and women also find it attractive. It can of course be simply effete. When it works, it heightens the mystery of theatrical sexuality.' (Georgina Brown, *Independent*, 26.5.1995) Despite displays of scholarship and sexual sophistication, a good many reviews, perhaps representative of audience comment generally, responded too often not to the production as a whole but to the spectacle of a woman, gifted actress as she is, playing a man's part.

It fell to Warner and Shaw to raise the level of the discussion, abetted by some of the more thoughtful commentators. Confessing herself disappointed by the critical reaction to her production in London ('I think this Richard is an infinitely more serious and fascinating experience than they – the London critics –were willing to tackle' (*Guardian*, 2.2.1996)) Warner agreed that the casting, on a simple level, reflected the familiar perception that Richard is 'somewhat feminine' but yet 'not effeminate'. The casting decision, she asserted, was aesthetic not polemical, and yet was in tune with the times. Ten years previously it would have been read as a feminist statement. In 1995, in Shaw's words, it sat close to the heart of one of the concerns that could renew the theatre: 'we're on the brink of something ... we are the gender generation. We have no statement to make, but we're sounding a gong.'

Shaw found it a privilege to play the role: 'What is fantastic, as a woman, is being allowed to play with the existential contradictions of the universe: being the supreme nothing and the supreme something. To be playing with the theatre of mankind rather than just with joy or grief; with the idea that salvation is one's relationship to death rather than to marriage. There's nothing in the theatre for women that addresses that so directly.' (Interview with Claire Armistead, *Guardian*, 31.5.1995) There were difficulties in the role, 'something about the vocabulary, a texture, that's male: all that talk of glory'. At the same time, the cross-gendering could in another perspective seem enabling: 'someone who isn't a man, playing someone who isn't a man'. (Interview with Simon Fanshawe, *The Sunday Times*, 14.1.1996)

Shaw thought that in *Richard II* the gender distinctions remain in place, but not as decisive or exclusive definitions: 'I suppose I'm playing into the notion that this pupa has been so fed royal jelly that it has no beard, is soft and female from a life of never having to function as a human being, either male or female.' 'I play Richard not from my gender center but from my imaginative center.' (Jack Kroll, *Newsweek*, 15.1.1996) The script, she thought, itself needed a renewing production such as the Cottesloe's: 'The play has become worn out on the issue of [Richard's] effeminacy. If you put a woman in it she doesn't waste half her energy trying to be feminine.' (Interview with Christian Tyler, *Financial Times* 9.12.1995) 'Maybe sometimes,' Shaw reflected, 'by withdrawing certain colors you see a painting more clearly. The joy of being the wrong sex is that you meet the play as a new play.' (Interview with Carole Woddis, *London Theatre News*, August 1995)

The insistent note in Warner's comments and Shaw's on the positive aspects of cross-casting reflects an irritation with shallow responses to the production's novelty. No-one denied that the director-and-actor team, for whom this was a sixth collaboration, had once again, if controversially, revealed a new play latent within the shell of an old. There was, however, a division of opinion about the success of the interpretation and the detail of Shaw's playing. Theatre director Deborah Paige (*Guardian*, 22.1.1997) remarked in retrospect that she 'never for a moment questioned her [Shaw's] gender – it just didn't matter. What I love about her is that there is absolutely no separation between her thinking and her acting. It was a simple and profound performance ... Her work is so uncluttered, the imagery so deceptively plain. That afternoon in the almost religious atmosphere of the Cottesloe I fell in love with theatre all over again.' John Lahr, recognising that *Richard II* is 'as much about the perception of power as about the seizing of it' almost equally relished Shaw's incorporation of the title role: 'Her hair is cropped short. She stands wide-eyed, blinking, sometimes even pigeon-toed before us; her smile is tight with uncertainty, and there is a boyish spring to her step. Smooth-faced and soft-skinned, Shaw eliminates the effeteness with which Richard is often played; her feminine qualities hint instead at the coddled, pristine, almost mutant unreality of the boy king.' (*New Yorker*, 10.7.1995)

For others, the unquestioned detail of Shaw's observation of the role led distractingly to overstatement. John Gross described how 'she simpers, glances at a hand mirror, smiles inanely, lets her attention wander in all directions ... she fidgets, shifts from foot to foot, makes her

exit dancing a jig ... Richard is meant to be an inadequate king ... but this one is such a hopeless flibbertigibbet that there is no possibility of tragedy at all.' Yet he conceded that the last act brought its rewards in Richard's meditative and movingly-played prison-house reflections on his own identity. (*Sunday Telegraph*, 11.6.1995) Alastair Macaulay shared something of a similar division of mind. Appreciating Shaw's 'intensity, audacity, imagination, eloquence, wit' he at the same time found 'her utter lack of repose when either speaking or listening becomes maddening.' Reluctantly he reached the conclusion that her 'exaggerations cancel out her expressiveness.' (*Financial Times*, 6.6.1995)

By contrast, John Peter found Richard's mannerisms an illuminating commentary on the script's personal and political significance, taking them to represent 'the insecurity of somebody spiritually immature who likes to reassure himself by turning his daily behaviour into a series of performances.' 'You may think,' he wrote, 'that Shaw is giving a fidgety, exhibitionistic, self-absorbed performance; in fact she is portraying a fidgety, exhibitionistic, self-absorbed and hyperactive man, and does so without the tactful compromises some actors like to make so that their public would still like them.' (*Sunday Times*, 11.6.1995) In a highly positive review, Paul Taylor took a similar line, referring to 'Fiona Shaw's dazzlingly discomforting impersonation of Richard' as essential to the production's purposes. (*Independent*, 14.6.1995)

An unorthodox 'Richard'

Disagreement among critics and audiences was inevitable given the challenges to orthodox readings offered by Warner's production. More interesting was the degree to which such a division could be seen as complementary to the production's insights. Speaking with Carole Woddis (*London Theatre News*, August 1995) Shaw gave her view that 'Contradiction is at the heart of this play, everything is in opposition! ... We are a post-deconstructive society now and it's fun to endlessly play with it.' Division among the critics lay, it could be argued, between those who could accept a playful postmodern reading and those for whom inhabiting a fully-imagined and consistent playworld remains a theatrical necessity.

FIG 108 Fiona Shaw as Richard cradles David Threlfall as Bolingbroke, drawing attention to their similarities of facial appearance and suggesting their shared experience and mutual understanding.

Kate Clanchy perceived a contradiction between Shaw's playing and that of the rest of the cast: 'Deborah Warner is after realism, naturalism, emotional truth ... Everyone on Warner's stage is real, troubled, complex ... And Shaw is not ... It is a remarkable performance: intelligent, literate, varied, casting line after line in a fresh light ... But it remains, because of Shaw's gender, a performance, the sole artifice in the naturalistic world Warner has created.' (*Scotsman*, 6.6.1995) But just such a duality might be seen, at least until the episode in prison, as essential to the play's meanings. Both Shaw and Warner commented in interview on the oppositions that sit at the heart of the play, and reviewers like John Mullen (*Times Literary Supplement*, 16.6.1995) saw these oppositions as integral to the performance. The standard Elizabethan and earlier notion of the king's two bodies, as Jack Kroll also noted (*Newsweek*, 15.1.1996), allows Richard to be 'a gripping study in self-delusion, a king who's been seduced by the medieval idea of divine right, and who learns that he is flawed and mortal.' Carl Miller (*Plays International*, July 1995) developed the same point, noting how Richard's self-division made for 'a disastrous love affair with kingship' and exposed how his 'need for – and resentment of – father figures John of Gaunt and the Duke of York is just one of the contradictions deftly explored' in the play.

FIG 109 Michael Bryant as the Duke of York, 'an avuncular politician, shrewd and watchful' (John Peter).

Mirroring

The image of the mirror, both in the script and as stage-prop, gave division and doubling a theatrical presence. Warner took this perception into casting by choosing David Threlfall as Bolingbroke to play opposite Shaw, a look-alike *doppelgänger* who mirrored Shaw's appearance especially when wearing the crown. One reviewer at least read this psychologically: 'The programme cover shows Shaw and Threlfall in a near smooch, and there's more than a whiff of sexuality and co-dependency', he found, in their performance. (Carl Miller, *Plays International*, July 1995) Paul Taylor, noting the moment before his banishment when Richard embraced Bolingbroke intimately, saw the device in more rounded terms: 'the near-twinship, as well as kinship, and the haunted mutual fascination, brings out the way these characters inversely reflect each other, both [of them] the placings of a curiously under-willed fate, like figures on escalators moving in opposite directions' – a modern make-over of the script's reference to the two figures as buckets in a well. According to Taylor, the Shaw-Threlfall casting was not just factitious but genuinely integral to the production's insights. It complemented Shaw's playing: 'From Fiona Shaw's deliberately uncomfortable, continuously compelling performance, all these ideas radiate and derive their validity. The masterly production lives up to her.' (*Independent*, 14.6.1995)

Other Meanings

Given the high-profile casting of Shaw as Richard and her unquestionable skills as an actress, comment was bound to focus on her role. There was however some appreciation of the production's other interests and some discussion of other roles. (*The Guardian*, 5.6.1995) remarked on the play as 'a long-range study in social disintegration' and assessed it as 'a national tragedy about a land going into freefall decline'. John Peter saw the inbred nature of the play's politics: 'it is important to remember that this whole thing is a claustrophobic family affair: the principal allies antagonists and neutrals are all cousins, brothers and uncles, and between them, behind the splendours of court ceremony, they prepare to shed each other's blood and settle the destiny of England.' (*Sunday Times*, 11.6.1995) Such perspectives were rare, however, despite the play's stage-history down the centuries as a politically controversial piece.

There was generous comment on a number of performances, notably on Michael Bryant's Duke of York: 'a magnificent performance: ... an avuncular politician, shrewd and watchful, who manages to be both a consummate operator and a bastion of traditional loyalty.' (John Peter, *Sunday Times*, 9.7.1995) Other reviewers praised 'Paola Dionisotti's shrivelled monkey of a Duchess [of Gloucester] tottering on two sticks with a vindictiveness great as her grief' (Rhoda Koenig, *Independent*, 5.6.1995) and several commented with appreciation on Struan Rodger's 'craggy' Northumberland. (Nicholas de Jongh, *Evening Standard*, 5.6.1995). In general, however, this was most widely perceived as Warner's, Shaw's and Bechtler's remarkable re-making of a teasingly theatrical play, one which is, it could be said, 'of all Shakespeare's history plays ... arguably the most difficult to accommodate on the twentieth century stage' (Margaret Shewring, *Richard II*, Manchester, 1996, p.2.)

Fig 110 Anna Chancellor (Patricia Preece) 'fierce, willowy and angularly beautiful like a killer heron' (John Peter) and Antony Sher (Stanley Spencer) 'a brilliant impersonation of the physical man'.

STANLEY

Written by Pam Gems

The Cottesloe as Work in Progress

Tim Hatley's ambitious and detailed design for *Stanley* invited the Cottesloe audience to inhabit a replica of the artist's workspace, complete with scaffolded galleries and embellished with work-in-progress paintings referring to the Cookham Resurrection and the Glasgow shipbuilding series. The design also evoked Spencer's wish for a comprehensive artistic vision 'solemnising and celebrating' his life: 'I like my own life so much that I would like to cover every space on a wall with it'. (*Quoted by Judith Collins in the Cottesloe programme*)

Benedict Nightingale found the spatial experience remarkable: 'The Cottesloe can never have looked so exotic. Tim Hatley has transformed its stage into a blend of artist's studio, tacky living room and church, with spectators in pews stretching from three sides towards an easel, an old chair, an oil stove. But it is what is painted on the theatre's walls and beneath its balconies that grabs the eye: a vast mural of bulbous labourers and roly-poly grocers, askew arms and oddly angled legs, nuts and screws, buckets and piping. It is unmistakably the work of Stanley Spencer in high Cookham mode'. (*Times*, 3.2.1996)

The design seemed to some reviewers to have direct implications for reading the script. 'Caird and his designer, Tim Hatley,' wrote Sheridan Morley, 'have hung and lit reproductions of Spencer's paintings all over the Cottesloe so that we don't forget the conflations of sacred and profane that inform all of Stanley's self-justificatory speeches, perorations of such ego-ridden carelessness that the laughter they generate has a kind of gobsmacked admiration.' (*Spectator*, 10.2.1996) Paul Taylor saw similar deliberate contradictions in the set design: 'With the colossal *Resurrection* (not yet finished) on the back wall, tiers of scaffolding and part of the audience in pew-arrangement seating, the Cottesloe is transformed into a sort of secular cathedral. While Stanley and his second wife choose sexy underwear in a posh shop, a swelling church organ in the background acts like a cheeky aural pun. The spirituality of Bach steals over scenes that would give a devout Lutheran a heart attack'. (*Independent*, 3.2.1996)

William Feaver thought the set facilitated Spencer's eccentric social behaviour and notorious garrulity: 'Spencer liked charades and would have loved the notion of the Cottesloe transformed into a scene-painter's vision of the Church House, with *The Resurrection, Cookham* under scaffolding, strips of Clydeside shipbuilding down the sides, Bach on the organ and lots of space in which to talk and talk'. (*Observer*, 4.2.1996)

Most reviewers and in all probability most audiences found the comprehensively designed environment conducive to a full experience of the play, thoroughly complementing and enriching Pam Gems's script. Its remarkable persuasiveness as a pastiche of Spencer's work represented a triumph for the National Theatre's painting workshop, where much effort and talent were brought to bear on the steep task of reproducing the work of a major artist without caricature and without sentiment.

STANLEY

Written by Pam Gems

DIRECTOR	*John Caird*
DESIGN	*Tim Hatley*
LIGHTING	*Peter Mumford*
SOUND	*Freya Edwards*
DANCE	*Jane Gibson*
MUSIC	*Ilona Sekacz*
VOICE	*Patsy Rodenburg*
DIALECT COACH	*Jeannette Nelson*
PRODUCTION MANAGER	*Jason Barnes*
STAGE MANAGER	*Angela Fairclough*
PHOTOGRAPHY	*Sasha Gusov*

Players

STANLEY	*Antony Sher*
HILDA	*Deborah Findlay*
PATRICIA	*Anna Chancellor*
DOROTHY	*Selina Cadell*
AUGUSTUS	*David Collings*
HENRY	*Pip Torrens*
GWEN	*Nicola King*
DUDLEY	*Richard Howard*
ELSIE	*Stephanie Jacob*
MRS CARLINE	*Avril Elgar*
BRIAN	*Nicholas Deigman; Daniel Forster Smith*
TIM	*Robbie Morton; Robert Smythson*
PIANIST/KEYBOARDS	*Walter Fabeck*

The production opened on 1 February 1996 and continued in repertoire until 17 August 1996. It transferred to the Circle in the Square, New York, for a limited season from 4.2.97 to 27.4.97 (press night, 7.2.97), and was nominated for four Tony awards.

Tim Hatley, Designer

Hatley won an Olivier award for his design for *Stanley*. He tried by way of homage, he said, to do Spencer's work for him, creating 'the feeling of being in the artist's studio, with Spencer's paintings interspersed throughout the auditorium'. It was his wish 'to create a space that actors could inhabit, that could evolve over rehearsals'. (*Design Week*, 21.2.1997) Trained at the Central St Martin's College of Art and Design, Hatley had already won the *Plays and Players* Best Designer award for 1991, a 1992 *Time Out* Award and represented Britain at the Prague Quadrennial Exhibition in 1995. His work for Théâtre de Complicité included the award-winning *The Three Lives of Lucie Cabrol* and *Out of a House Walked a Man* (a co-production with the National). Hatley has designed plays for the RSC, Nottingham Playhouse, the Traverse, Almeida and Gate theatres, opera for Opera North, Scottish Opera and D'Oyly Carte, and dance for Rambert and Northern Ballet Theatre.

Hatley was included by Lyn Gardner in a round-

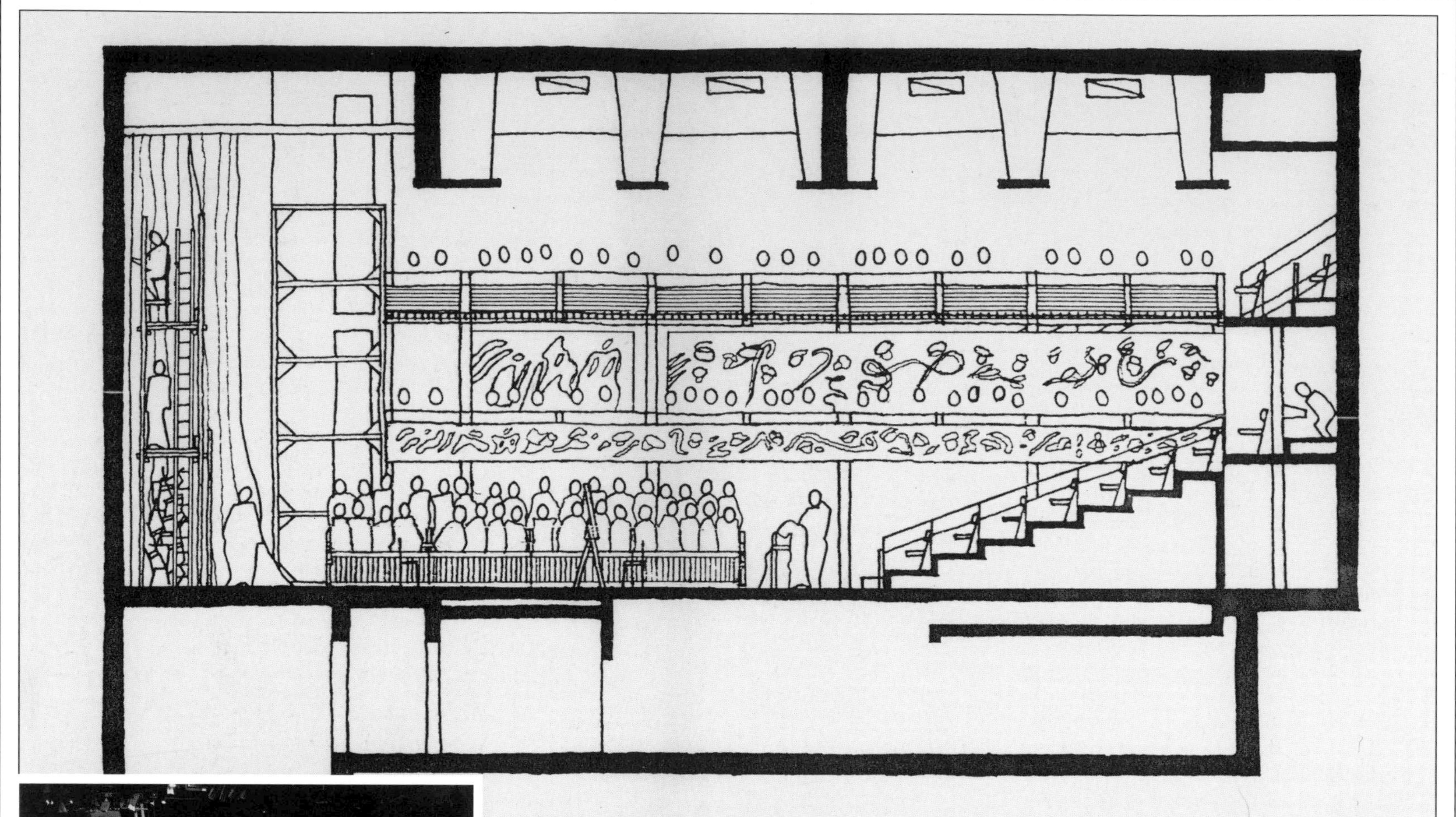

The lay-out of the Cottesloe in preparation. The photograph (by Philip Carter) shows the paintings (from the *Cookham Resurrection* and the Glasgow series) being put in position, with the scaffolding and ladders that formed part of the stage set. The church pews used as seating on each side of the stage were also part of Tim Hatley's design, intended to evoke the atmosphere of reverence with which Spencer regarded his artistic work. Problems of comfort, sight-lines and latecomers had all to be coped with, given this unconventional seating arrangement.

Technical Summary

• The Cottesloe space as 'environment'. Designer Tim Hatley wanted to reflect Spencer's obsession with decorating whole ecclesiastical buildings, an obsession largely realized with the memorial commission at Sandham Chapel in Old Burghclere, Berkshire. Hatley's original design was based on the layout and content of murals at the chapel, so we visited Burghclere with the National Theatre's painters, who were proposing to re-create the necessary paintings. The design however failed to obtain the blessing of Spencer's daughters, who controlled the copyright. While retaining the chapel layout, therefore, we reproduced other Spencer paintings, with permission from their copyright holders, chiefly the Imperial War Museum and the Tate Gallery.

• Two thirds of the theatre's length was used scenically in plan, giving an acting depth of 13.3m, while leaving seven rows of the end-stage bleacher seating available for audience use.

• The 6.2m wide acting area was paved with flagstones, providing a suitably neutral floor for the many locations. Furniture was introduced from storage positions on the perimeter of the space, and the scaffolding 'dressed' with church furnishings and painting materials, including Spencer's own easel.

• Stage right and upstage the acting area was bounded by three-level scaffolding. This provided access to our

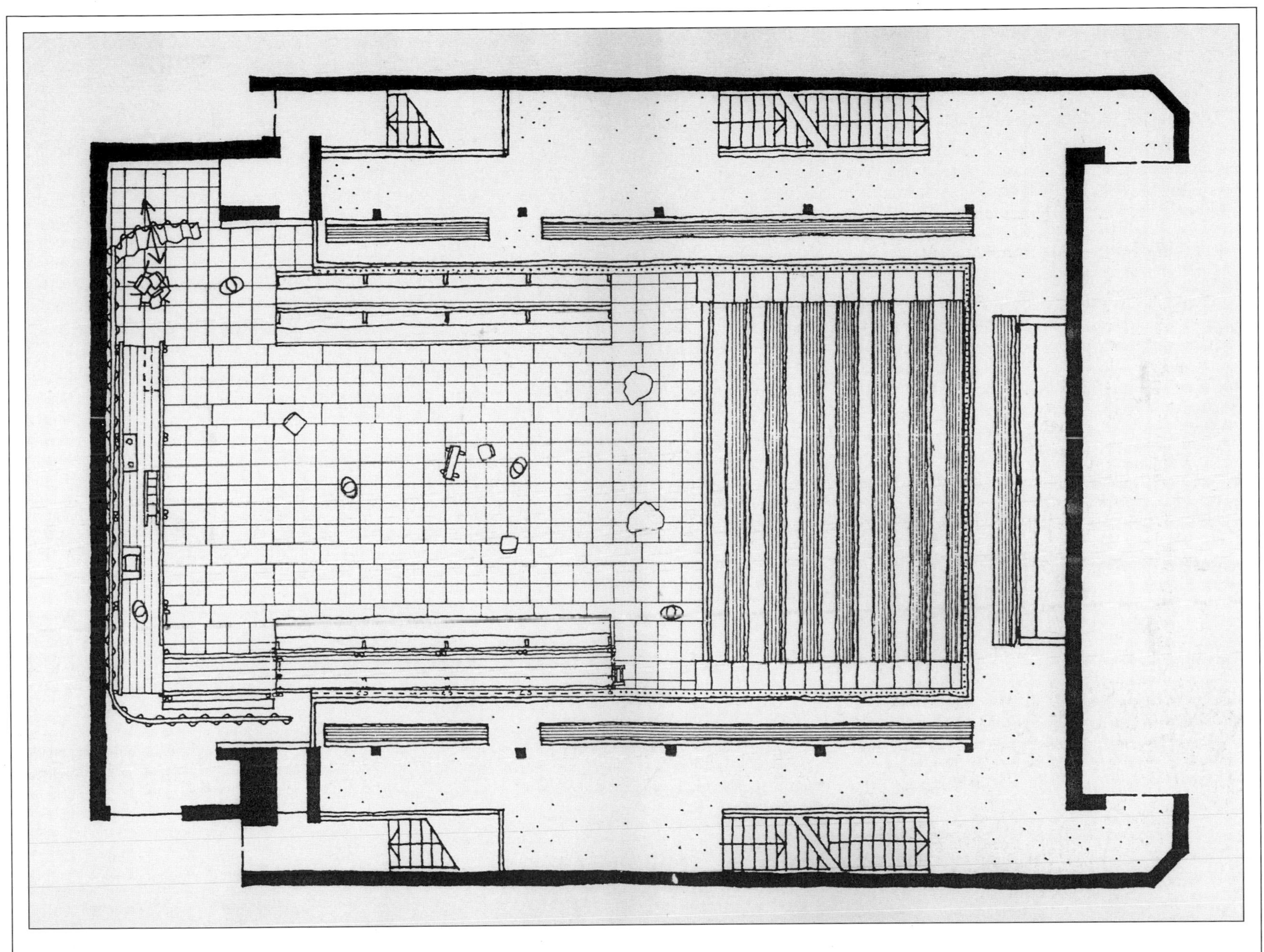

reproduction of Spencer's 'The Resurrection at Cookham', which Antony Sher (playing Spencer) worked on during the action.

• The scaffolded levels gave way to seated galleries surrounding the space on three sides. To each side of the playing space at stage level further seating was provided in (real) Victorian church pews, with some allowance for comfort offered by padded seat squabs and backrests decorated with cross motifs. The matchboard 'pine' pew-fronts continued along the front surface of the bleacher seating downstage of the action.

• Scenic elements comprising reproductions of Spencer's 'Glasgow' series, painted by the National's scenic artists, hung in front of the middle-level seat galleries on each side, and, for the first time at the Cottesloe, behind the audience in these positions. The run of paintings on each side measured 14.25m.

• Rough-sawn timber frames and vast dust sheets completed the 'Chapel under decoration' theme.

up of the new generation of British designers, in what she saw as a quiet renaissance in theatre design. (*Guardian*, 26.2.1997) 'Against the odds,' she wrote, 'theatre design is on a roll.' 'You only have to go abroad,' designer Bob Crowley is quoted as saying, 'and see what is happening there to recognise the incredible vitality of design in this country'. Hatley's, Gardner says, is a 'deceptively rich, multi-layered style', nurtured by his work for Complicité, and fully displayed in the Cottesloe.

For *Stanley*, the design echoed Spencer's mind by creating a studio setting alluding to a range of work from different periods of the artist's life. A list prepared for the production department shows almost forty paintings, or parts of larger works, considered for reproduction in-house for use on set. In the event, there were fewer sources, largely because of copyright problems, with the Glasgow shipbuilding series and 'The Resurrection, Cookham' the main works referred to. On-stage paintings in the style of Spencer were created by Antony Sher, an accomplished painter himself, using oils, like Spencer, and employing white spirit for cleaning brushes during the performances, a decision that needed careful monitoring from a safety angle.

Pam Gems

When *Stanley* was presented at the National, Pam Gems had already had numerous plays professionally staged in Britain and abroad, including the immensely successful *Piaf* for the RSC, with transfers to the West End and Broadway (1978, revived 1993-4), *Queen Christina* (RSC, 1978), *The Danton Affair* (RSC, 1987) and *The Blue Angel* (RSC, 1991). She had also written versions of four Chekhov plays and published two novels. A late starter as a playwright, after bringing up four children, her marked interest in women's issues has always been close to the centre of her writing.

In a programme note for *Stanley*, Gems explained she was drawn to the painter during an enforced stay in France. Spencer offered her an art that excited her interest and a biography that compelled her attention. Biographical drama attracted her: 'there is an advantage in starting with a known milieu, or familiar characters. Then one plays a different game, pulls the rug, for drama is by its nature subversive, it seeks to influence indirectly. You use known data as a springboard. Or a lure.' Theatre and its performances, she felt, should compensate for the absence of glamour in daily lives impoverished by dull work-patterns: 'our anxieties are in free fall, and our imaginations, urban and suburban, deprived of air and trees, birds, weather, water and animals, stultified'. Plays open

FIG 111 Antony Sher as Stanley Spencer at work on the scaffolding during performance. Sher's own skills as a painter served him well in the continuous business of finishing the 'work-in-progress' as the run of performances went on. Sher decided to use oil paints and white spirit (for cleaning his brushes) for reasons of authenticity. This gave its own olfactory sense of the authentic, as the smell of oil paint wafted through the auditorium. The use of white spirit (readily inflammable) had to be strictly controlled for safety reasons.

windows on richer prospects: 'It used to be fashionable to say that art changes nothing. I don't believe that. We modify all the time. We respond to stimuli. What those stimuli are comes back to the quality of art. If we are lucky, the best. Like, for example, the painting of an English genius, Stanley Spencer'.

Stanley Spencer

Spencer was born in the Berkshire village of Cookham in 1891 and died there in 1959. His devotion to the village, a place which in his own words offered 'a rich religious significance', is expressed in many of his paintings, culminating in the very large canvas known as The Resurrection, Cookham, completed in 1927 and sold to the Tate. This painting inspired much of the dècor for the Cottesloe set. In it, mingling Spencer's religious and physical-erotic interests, the dead inhabitants of the village are shown rising from their tombs wondering at the balmy pleasures of the May air.

A parallel impulse lay behind Spencer's acceptance, and completion after five years' work, of the commission to paint mural decorations for a chapel erected at Burghclere, Berkshire, in memory of Lieutenant Henry Sandham, who contracted a fatal illness on active service in Macedonia. Spencer had also served there in the Royal Army Medical Corps, witnessing appalling carnage. In an assessment of Spencer that evokes the effect of the Cottesloe design, Richard Cork has written that 'much depends, at Burghclere, on the overwhelming impact of paintings covering the walls from eye-level to ceiling in a relatively confined space. Their intensity recalls the collective effect of the frescoes Giotto executed in the Arena Chapel at Padua, which Spencer enthusiastically adopted as his principal inspiration.' Cork judges the chapel 'a triumphantly individual *tour de force*, deserving to be ranked among the supreme achievements of twentieth-century British art'.

Spencer's conviction that life offered a force of goodness sufficient to redeem its evil, a conviction celebrated in The Resurrection, joined with visions of sexual liberality, not always sensibly handled. His daily reading of the Bible, a practice learned from his organist father, William, in no way inhibited his interest in erotic fulfilment. To the contrary, his Christianity combined with a life-long interest in physical sexuality, including a study of Indian temple sculpture, where he understood the acrobatic coupling of the sculpted figures as a metaphor for divine intercourse between God and worshipper, a mystical experience he sought to replicate in his own life.

Spencer's marriage in 1925 to Hilda Carline, a fellow student from the Slade School of Art and a successful painter and scholar of art history in her own right, 'foundered in a welter of frustrated fantasies about free love'. (Richard Cork) His second marriage, in 1937, to the socialite Patricia Preece, seems to have been less fulfilling, in every respect, than he wished and dreamed. The two marriages, together with the lesbian alliance between Preece and Dorothy Hepworth, form the essential material for Gems's play. The *leitmotif* of his painting, a combination of 'angels and dirt', survived against all the odds to the end of his creative life, being incorporated even in his late work, including the Government-commissioned Clydeside shipbuilding series copied in the Cottesloe design.

Spencer's nature was a complex one. Skilled admirer and performer of the music of Bach and an exceptionally gifted painter, he was also, in ways Gems's play brings out, an aggressive egotist. As Elizabeth Rothenstein puts it, his nature had in it 'something of the saint, something of the seer, majestic and formidable, but also something mean and quarrelsome, bitter and nasty, reminding one of the sparrow fighting in the dust.'

This account draws on contributions to the Cottesloe programme

by Judith Collins, Curator of Modern Collections at the Tate Gallery, and Richard Cork, Art Critic for 'The Times'. The Elizabeth Rothenstein quotation comes from 'Stanley Spencer, the Man: Correspondence and Reminiscences', edited by John Rothenstein.

Sher as Stanley, Stanley as Sher

Antony Sher's distinguished acting career represents only one of his multiple talents. As well as being the on-stage creator of such roles as the Fool in *King Lear*, Tamburlaine, Titus Andronicus, Astrov in *Arturo Ui* and numerous parts in contemporary plays, Sher has acted widely in films and on television, and achieved recognition as the author of a number of books. He is also a painter of distinction with exhibitions at the Barbican and the National to his credit. Michael Coveney thought Sher's success in the role was directly associated with his insights and practices as a painter: 'Sher's oil and charcoal figures have always been lumpen and fleshy, hovering sensuously between the styles of Beryl Cook and Lucian Freud; his onstage impersonations often bear traces of his own drawing board. In another trick of physical transformation, he now becomes the priapic mystic of Cookham, Stanley Spencer'. (*Observer*, 4.2.96)

Costume and gesture assisted this process of transformation: 'Sher has acquired a convincing hairpiece, as well as the right spectacle frames, corduroy trousers and scuffed shoes. His inimitable style of busy, penetrative character acting brings the artist alive while suggesting another sort of volcanic, alien energy, the anguish behind Spencer that transcends Cookham and the Bible and invests him with a Blakean, visionary wildness'. (Michael Coveney, *Observer*, 4.2.96) Nicholas de Jongh found the vocal mannerisms equally revealing: 'as he bounds about Tim Hatley's design of a two-tiered, scaffolded artist's studio, chattering in Cookham brogue to his wife (Deborah Findlay), who poses half-nude, there's an air of the earnest Slade school art student about him', a characteristic naîveté that fully consorts in this 'eternal adolescent' with a 'most persuasive portrayal of the artist as terminal egotist'. (*Evening Standard*, 2.2.96) Michael Billington thought Sher's portrait of 'the peculiar childlike nature of Spencer's genius ... the most moving thing he has done'. (*Guardian*, 3.2.96)

FIG 112 Spencer's erotic attachment to his first wife Hilda seems to have had some unusual features. Here Deborah Findlay as Hilda poses for Spencer's (Antony Sher's) artistic attention.

John Peter responded admiringly to Sher's assumption of Spencer's physical and psychological characteristics: 'Sher's performance is a brilliant impersonation of the physical man, achieved with virtually no help from the make-up department; but what makes it unforgettable is his spiritual and psychological understanding of Spencer. ... Sher has the cocky but stolid walk of villagers, shy but aggressively pigeon-chested, standing with his legs bent slightly outwards like a donkey observing a friendly stranger'. (*Sunday Times*, 11.2.96) Robert Butler thought the caricature so shrewdly observed as to be comic: 'Antony Sher is superbly skilled as the bespectacled, snorting painter scurrying up ladders in his corduroy trousers and ill-fitting jacket, or blinking sweatily as he runs his hand up skirts. In the bumbling, innocent manner in which he mucks up people's lives he emerges as a comic creation'. (*Independent on Sunday*, 4.2.96)

John Gross found Sher's portrait not entirely persuasive, though he conceded the actor's remarkable artistry: 'do you also believe that he is Stanley Spencer? Not really; but then the kind of biographical fiction that has flourished in recent years almost always involves a degree of travesty. This latest example is probably less misleading than most'. (*Sunday Telegraph*, 4.02.'96) For Charles Spencer, in contrast, the circle closed, and performance became identity: with Sher 'blinking myopically behind his specs, quivering with a disconcerting mixture of lust and spirituality, and rabbiting on ceaselessly, you genuinely believe you have encountered the artist himself'. (*Daily Telegraph*, 5.2.96)

FIG 113 'Spencer's secondary love, the lesbian painter Patricia Preece, slinkily impersonated by Anna Chancellor, removes her clothes, or flaunts herself in black lingerie, as a forbidding counterpart in Stanley's true devotion.' (Michael Coveney) The dust-sheeted stage, at this point in the action, projected both the environment of the artist's studio and the emptiness of the relationship between the two figures.

The Women

The trio of Deborah Findlay as Hilda, Anna Chancellor as Patricia and Selina Cadell as Dorothy drew virtually unanimous praise. The sexual chemistry between Stanley and Hilda, and in a less orthodox way between Patricia and Dorothy, and Patricia and Stanley, offered plenty of material for comment. Michael Coveney perceived in Stanley's artistic observation of Hilda a pronounced if deviant erotic charge: 'Sher as Spencer lies prostrate, squirming on top of his own erection, as he paints his wife Hilda's inner thighs'. Patricia Preece's gestures and motives were, he thought, scarcely more innocent: 'Spencer's secondary love, the lesbian painter Patricia Preece, slinkily impersonated by Anna Chancellor, removes her clothes, or flaunts herself in black lingerie, as a forbidding counterpart in Stanley's true devotion. ... The actress lopes through Stanley's fantasies, her voice carefully conveying destructive devotion in a long whining caress'. (*Observer*, 4.2.96)

Robert Butler, like others, saw Hilda as the play's near-saintly heroine: 'As played with rich and intelligent sympathy by Deborah Findlay, she emerges as the wounded emotional centre of the play, the victim of two appallingly selfish people'. (*Independent on Sunday*, 4.2.96) John Peter, while holding back from advising Pam Gems on how to write her play, nevertheless thought her portrait of Stanley 'would have been more balanced and more shocking if she had paid more attention to Hilda'. (*Sunday Times*, 11.2.96) David Nathan saw the painful doubleness in Dorothy, the butch lover of Patricia: 'Selina Cadell ... beautifully conveys the dilemma of a woman in sexual thrall to a creature she despises'. (*Jewish Chronicle*, 9.02.'96) John Peter appreciated this as 'an apparently calm but quiveringly sensitive performance full of wariness and weariness and anxiety'. He identified Cadell's artistry: 'Decency can be the most difficult but also the most rewarding thing to impersonate'. (*Sunday Times*, 11.2.96)

Most comment went to Anna Chancellor's 'shockingly perceptive' evocation of 'the frightful Patricia', the practising lesbian who blew apart the Spencers' marriage: 'fierce, willowy and angularly beautiful like a killer heron, she exudes narcissistic selfishness, sexual maladjustment, snobbish gentility, and a cold calculating meanness from every pore'. (John Peter, *Sunday Times*, 11.1.96) So virulent was the portrait that in some reviewers' eyes it bordered on the grotesque: 'The petulance, the whining egotism, the transparent greed are all hilariously and mercilessly exposed'. (Charles Spencer, *Daily Telegraph*, 5.2.96) For others, the cruelty of the characterisation almost defied an audience's tolerance: 'Patricia sees Spencer as "a dreadful little oik" who paints "vulgar and deranged pictures" but who might be useful when it comes to meeting famous people or buying expensive lipstick. She proceeds to deny him her body, exclude him from everywhere but the kitchen and, in effect, steal his house while somehow regarding herself as the victim of a cruel world. The wincing preciosity Anna Chancellor brings to the task of embodying Patricia's narcissism is enjoyably awful; but you do wonder if the woman hasn't a defence

FIG 114 The lesbian relationship between Patricia Preece (Anna Chancellor) and Dorothy Hepworth (Selina Cadell). Cadell movingly projected 'the dilemma of a woman in sexual thrall to a creature she despises'. (David Nathan)

FIG 115 Anna Chancellor and Selina Cadell as the lesbian pair on a painting expedition. Though neither had anything approaching Spencer's talent, Dorothy Hepworth (Selina Cadell) was at least a painter to take seriously. The National's props department provided an array of authentic objects to document the performances, including the painting easels shown here.

worth hearing'. (Benedict Nightingale, *Times*, 3.02.'96)

The Script

Some reviewers experienced resistance to the *genre* to which *Stanley* belongs. Robert Butler commented that 'Pam Gems has written the latest artist-as-an-awful-person play, which presents Sir Stanley Spencer … as wheedling, randy, nerdish, spoilt, childish and cruel. Fans, be warned'. (*Independent on Sunday*, 4.2.96) Alastair Macaulay could not be reconciled to the play's content or attitudes. Finding the narrative reminiscent of the 'good old woman's movie from the Hollywood of the 1930s and 40s', he was unmoved by what he saw as the sentimentality of the play's more positive moments and more than irritated by the play's language and its 'tabloid mentality, staying on the social and gossip pages'. Even the dècor and the music offended: 'The Cottesloe Theatre has Spencerian murals-in-progress (in his most Giottoish vein) on three sides and puts some of the audience in English church pews. Because Spencer liked Bach, the play is accompanied by chunks from Bach's Greatest Hits. Trying to identify each chunk is as good a way to pass the time as any'. (*Financial Times*, 4.2.96)

There were other negative comments on aspects of the play, especially in a divided response to the ending (which some found sentimental), and in occasional questioning of the accuracy of the portrait of bohemian society and of references to Freud. Charles Spencer was troubled by what he saw as a fashionable approach to documentary history, even if written in a generous spirit: 'The current obsession of biographers with the sex lives of their subjects seems to reach its apotheosis here. The play is an unashamed, at times novelettish, account of love among the bohemians, in which Gems paints her portrait of the artist with the broadest of dramatic brushstrokes. It is, however, a gutsy and often touching work, at times clumsy and cliché-ridden, undoubtedly too long, but written with the kind of emotional generosity that Spencer espoused in his own art'. (*Daily Telegraph*, 5.2.96)

Yet in general the response was strongly positive, not only in relation to the playing of Sher and the three principal women, but also to what was perceived as a remarkable feat of social and artistic recreation, set in an evocative space. Paul Taylor found Gems's 'very funny and affecting play' wonderfully illuminating about the extraordinary Cookham world: 'What the play makes you understand … is that Stanley's selfish purblindness to the needs of nearest and dearest is somehow part and parcel of the paradoxically monomaniacal generosity of his art. In its charmed universe, where Christ relives his career in Cookham and lumpy, clumsy creatures achieve the levity of transfiguration, everyone is saved at the last judgement. Which is both charitable of Stanley and not exactly lacking in blinkered ego either'. (*Independent*, 3.2.96) Generous and monomaniacal, charitable and egotistic, these are the opposites which define Spencer's life and art and which Gems captured in her remarkable dramatic biography.

FIG 116 Lear (Ian Holm) cradles Codelia (Anne-Marie Duff) in the agonised Pietá that concludes the performance. Edgar (Paul Rhys), 'the clear-eyed compassionate revenger' (John Peter) hovers over the tableau.

KING LEAR
By William Shakespeare

Downscaling?

Despite the undoubted critical success of some other small-scale *Lears* (such as the performances at Stratford's The Other Place directed by Cis Berry), there were reservations on the part of some reviewers and audiences about Richard Eyre's decision to closet what Michael Billington called 'Shakespeare's impossible masterpiece' (*Guardian*, 29.3.97) in the Cottesloe. Many on the other hand appreciated what they saw as the implicit, and detailed, 'domestication' of the tragedy's preoccupations. Robert Butler, for one, found the playing space exactly appropriate to Eyre's insights and intuitions: 'In the studio-sized Cottesloe, we get a close domestic *Lear*. The audience sits on three sides, bringing the intensity of an arena to these rapidly unfolding antagonisms. The intimacy is important and so is the width. We are in the middle and our sympathies flick back and forth.' (*Independent on Sunday*, 30.3.97) Sheridan Morley tended to agree, though he felt domesticity was an inadequate concept to apply to the huge world of *Lear*: 'To call this *Lear* domesticated would be to undervalue its infinite pity and compassion; yet by allowing the intimate dictates of the Cottesloe to condition what is effectively a studio production, Eyre has managed to celebrate the space and the play and the actor without any of the modernist gimmicks which have all too often marred previous attempts at downscaling.' (*Spectator*, 5.4.97) Alastair Macaulay saw the advantages to the spectator of the courtyard space in substituting detail for grand effect: 'The director, Richard Eyre, has placed it in the intimate Cottesloe Theatre, so that – whereas we have grown used to having *Lear* oracularly hurled at us across some mighty distance – we here are easily encompassed by its volcanic flow of detail.' (*Financial Times*, 1.4.97)

John Peter, in the course of a highly positive review, regretted the use of the Cottesloe, preferring to think of this production in an altogether grander physical environmnent: 'Eyre's production is set in a long oblong acting area with the audience sitting in banked rows on either side. I do not warm to this at all: it is not as if the play were a tournament. Its monstrousness and its subtleties go far deeper than that. … I hope that when the Cottesloe run is over, Eyre will move *King Lear* to the Olivier, which is the natural home for the huge political and emotional scale of the play and for the overwhelming moral magnificence of this production.' (*Sunday Times*, 6.4.97) Peter's reservations about the space employed were shared by Michael Billington, who felt the absence of what he calls the script's 'paradoxical absurdity': 'It is set by Bob Crowley on a traverse stage that neatly bisects the audience. This has the advantage of bringing us close to the action, but the disadvantage of making it difficult to evoke cosmic disturbance and the idea of wounded Nature. It even raises the question of whether Lear really is a studio play. I'm not asking for operatic spectacle, but there is something about the scale and intensity of the suffering that demands distance and perspective.' (*Guardian*, 29.3.97)

Richard Eyre was himself in no doubt about the rightness of the Cottesloe as the one space in which he could realise the meanings of the play as he saw them at this point in his career (see the interview printed in this book, pp.••••• above). The power of the performance, in the experience of many in the audiences, endorsed the view that this was one of the memorable explorations of an extraordinarily rich play, made possible by the scale and layout of the playing space.

KING LEAR
Written by William Shakespeare

DIRECTOR	*Richard Eyre*
DESIGNER	*Bob Crowley*
MUSIC	*Dominic Muldowney*
LIGHTING	*Jean Kalman*
SOUND	*Simon Baker*
FIGHTS	*William Hobbs*
ASST. DIRECTOR	*James Kerr*
STAGE MANAGER	*John Caulfield*
PRODUCTION MANAGER	*Jason Barnes*
PHOTOGRAPHY	*John Haynes*

Principal Players

LEAR	*Ian Holm*
GLOUCESTER	*Timothy West*
EDMUND	*Finbar Lynch*
GONERIL	*Barbara Flynn*
REGAN	*Amanda Redman*
CORDELIA	*Anne-Marie Duff*
EDGAR	*Paul Rhys*
FOOL	*Michael Bryant*
ALBANY	*David Lyon*
CORNWALL	*Michael Simkins*
BURGUNDY	*Nicholas Bailey*
FRANCE	*Adrian Irvine*
OSWALD	*William Osborne*

Other parts played by Martin Chamberlain, Paul Benzing, Harry Jones, Daniel Coonan.

The production opened on 27.March.1997, and ran in repertoire until 10 September 1997. It toured to the Istanbul Festival, playing in the sixth-century Basilica of St Eirene, and to Thessaloniki (European City of Culture, 1997) where it played in a converted Custom House building. A televised recording was made for the BBC in December 1997 for transmission in 1998.

Design

Bob Crowley's stage was for the most part plainly dressed with two large tables (which could be run together as one), chairs and a few domestic props around which the cast established their relationships. The effect of this sparing design-concept was to underline the bleak detail of the script. William Fiennes (*Punch* 5.4.97) found himself reminded of the austerity of Eastern visual design: 'The stage is on a long terracotta-coloured track running through the middle of the confined space of the Cottesloe, with sheer banks of spectators rising up on either side. It

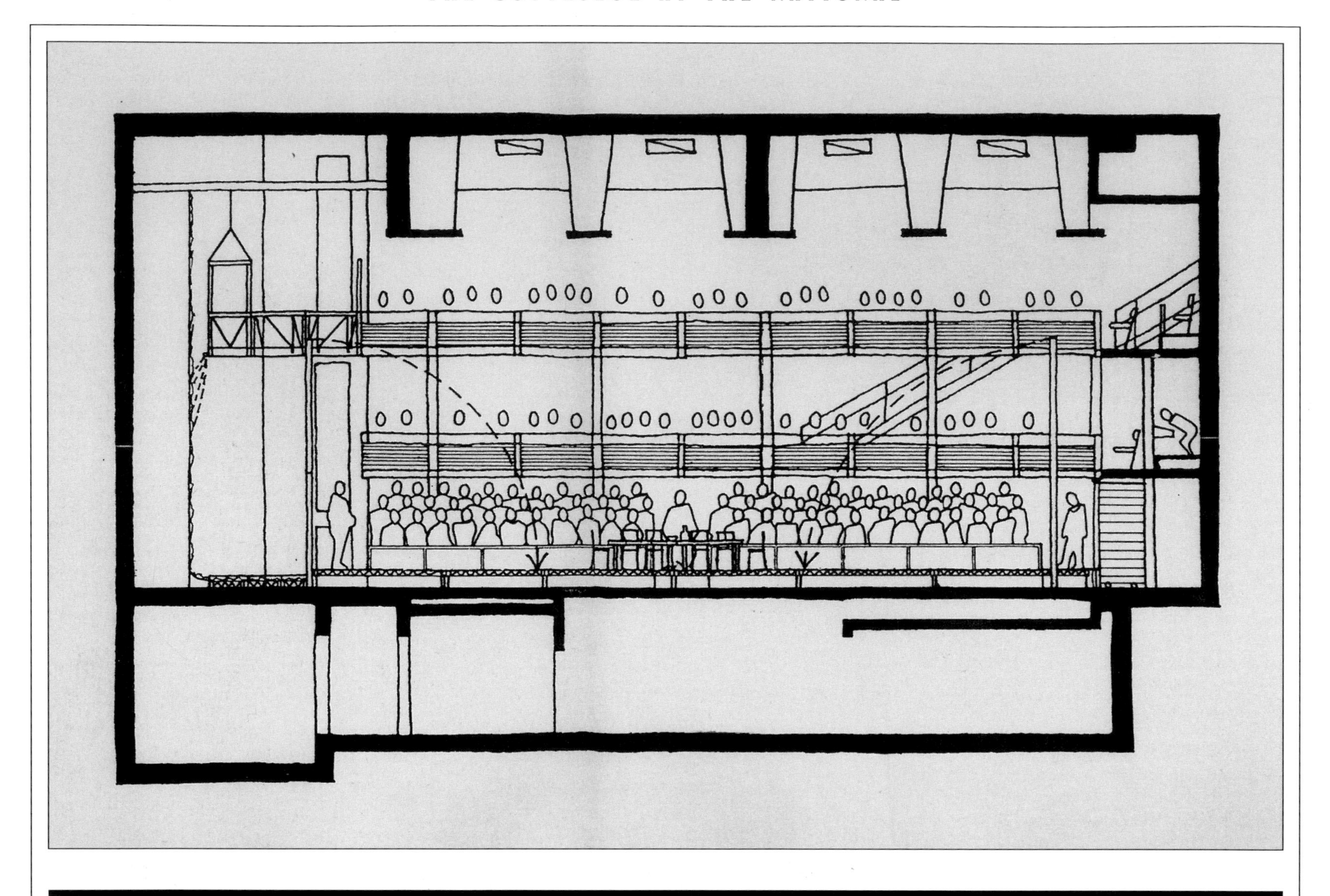

Technical Summary

• Richard Eyre and Bob Crowley wished to create a strong visual and physical contrast between the early interior scenes and Lear's subsequent self-imposed removal from court and family life.

• Interiors were established by the economic use of a common set of two tables, which could be paired as one long one, and upright chairs, all with changeable covers in red and off white.

• A rich earth-red platform 4.8m wide by 9.8m long, raised 35cm, ran up the theatre in long traverse, terminated at each end by 4.8m-high pannelled red walls, punctured with double doors opening out of the space.

• Walkways half-way down each side allowed further entrances, and doubled as audience access to the three rows of seating which flanked the floor at pit (lower) level.

• The decision to raise the performance space (as in *Racing Demon*) was taken early on, in order to maintain sightlines for those seated at pit level. A good view to the floor was required, particularly during the hovel scene, and for the final scene, where the bodies of Goneril, Regan and eventually Cordelia and Lear himself were piled on a low cart. Steep row rises, which would also provide an improved view, were avoided, given the need to maximise seat numbers and to save the space that would be required for additional access steps.

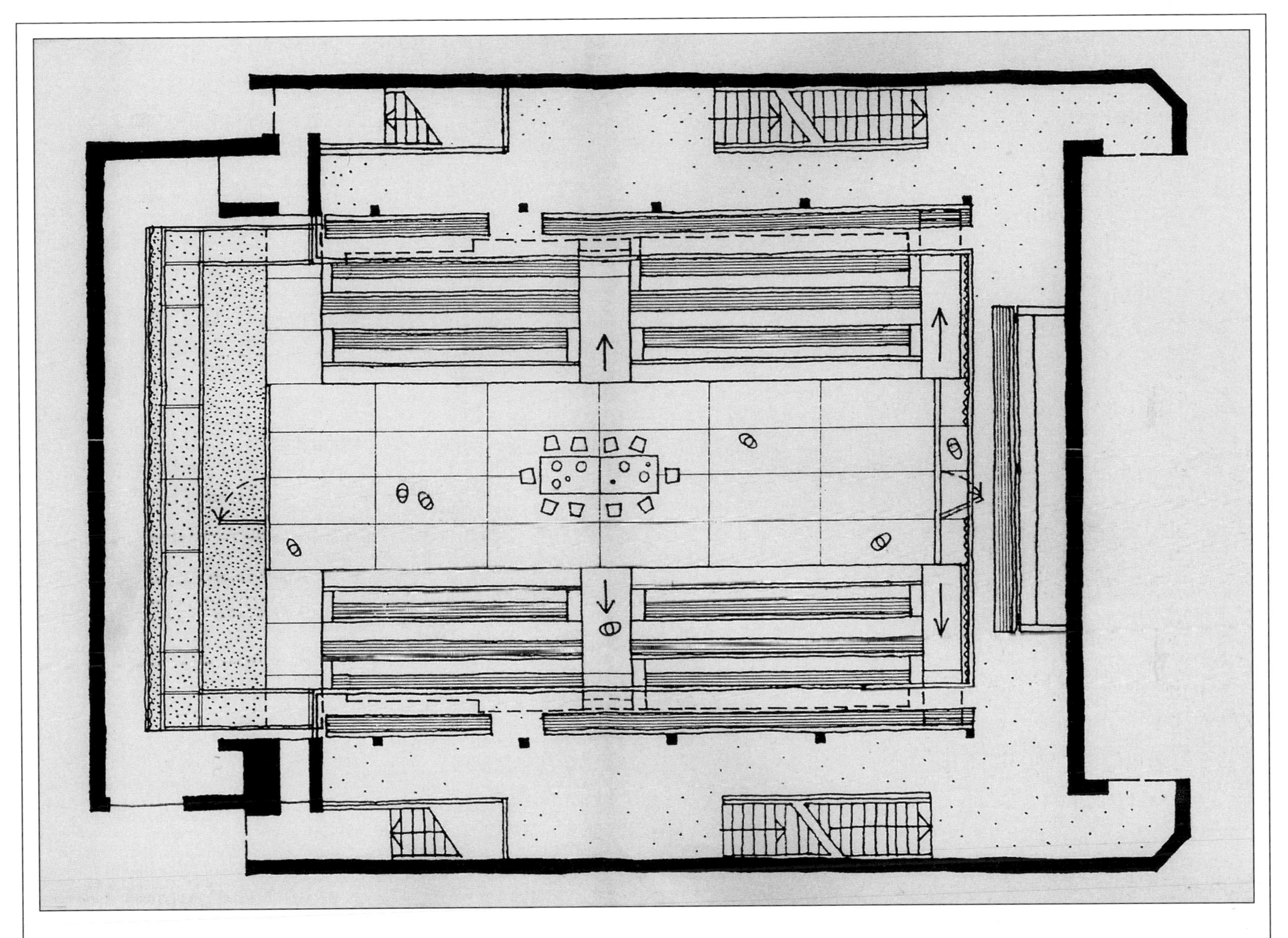

• At the height of the storm both end walls hinged over in free fall, within 40cm of the front row of audience. As a result of demonstration and discussion with both the licensing authority and the National's own safety department, a solid handrail was fixed in place, bearing appropriate warnings, to protect the audience and to deflect the considerable air blast.

• In designing the doors, the requirement for a balance between rigidity and weight led design engineer Mike Barnett to a combination of aluminium frames with aluminium honeycomb and fibreglass sheets known as aerolam (a material used in aircraft flooring). This structure ensured that the weight did not exceed a quarter of a ton, yet gave enough strength to the reverse side of the walls to allow them to serve, after the walls' collapse, as the actors' stage-surface for part two of the performance. Equally, the walls were of the right weight to allow them to 'float' over as they fell, buffered on a cushion of air trapped in the recessed panels forming the structure.

• As the walls fell into the performance space they revealed at the far end up-stage a rain-drenched rock face rising from a sea of mud. Above the mud surface, an overhead balcony linked the permanent top-level balconies, providing a high-level performance space and a structure to brace the falling walls. It also offered a position for the emphatic rain effects. Non-peat compost (for the mud) proved inert when mixed with water, an important health consideration as the muddy tank remained in the theatre for up to ten days at a time.

FIG 117 Ian Holm as Lear, 'the brutal, bullet-headed old man' who is also 'a shrill, wounded small boy ... who has grown old but has not grown up'. (John Peter)

The Play

Written, it seems likely, around 1605–6, *King Lear* has come to be regarded as Shakespeare's most profound tragedy. It may be that Shakespeare himself, as well as modern critics and audiences, considered the play of special importance, since in contrast (so far as we know) to his other plays, the script appears not only to have been reviewed and 'corrected' (as was the case for instance with *Hamlet*) but to have undergone searching and extensive revision, in all probability by the author himself, some time between its initial publication in 1608 and its printing in the First Folio in 1623. The result is two separate play texts, between the readings of which modern directors have to choose.

Most productions have emphasised the metaphysical dimensions of the tragedy, making use of large theatres, or even the virtually unlimited spaciousness of film (as in Peter Brook's celebrated re-making of his stage version with Paul Scofield), to complement the greatness of the play's reach. Richard Eyre's choice of the Cottesloe allowed the exploration of the tragedy in another perspective, laying stress on the family relationships that compose its narrative, but by no means blinking the pain which in earlier times (as in Nahum Tate's 1681 adaptation) has on occasion led to the re-writing of its ending in the direction of sentiment and consolation (in Tate's case preserving Cordelia alive).

looks like a strip of clay along the bottom of a gorge. Bob Crowley's design, with its black robes and sandals, has an uncluttered elegance redolent of Buddhist monasteries and Japan'.

Costumes drew little comment, except for the lookalike garments of King and Fool, a visual effect authorised by suggestions in the script. The visual absurdity of these costumes clearly unsettled some observers, prompting references to garden ornament: Michael Bryant's fool was said to be one who 'needs only to add a fishing rod to his conical hat, white beard and padded beige paunch to look like an antique garden gnome.' (Benedict Nightingale, *Times*, 29.3.97) For Kate Bassett, likewise, 'In soiled quilted jerkin and pointy cap, Bryant looks like one of Father Christmas's gnomes sporting a straitjacket, while the pixieish-looking Holm is an eccentric King with a twinkle in his eye.'(*Daily Telegraph*, 31.3.97) The deliberate contrast between the relative austerity of the main group of costumes and the eccentricity of mad King and Fool seems to have passed some observers by.

The theatrical device which, unsurprisingly, drew most comment (and played a major part in the preparations for the show – see the Technical Summary below) was the collapsing walls that bounded both ends of the stage area. The shock of their sudden descent emphasised in very physical fashion the danger and fear that underlay the apparent domesticity of Lear and his extended family, and threw into relief the two arenas, indoor-domestic and exposed-cosmic that formed the environment of this production. Michael Coveney reported that 'The end walls of a blood-red courtroom flap down to form a blasted heath.' (*Observer*, 30.3.97) Robert Butler explained the effect a little more fully: 'When Holm heads out into the storm, the orange walls that stand at either end of Bob Crowley's set tip forward to reveal rain pouring down a black sheet: a spectacular moment that provides its own chilly draught.' (*Independent on Sunday*, 30.3.97) (In fact, the rain effects were confined to one end of the Cottesloe, the upstage end farthest from the foyer entrances). The audience was warned, before entering the auditorium, that elements of the scenery would collapse – a sensible caution, given the force of the effect, both in terms of the wind it generated and the apparent danger to the front row of spectators.

Ian Holm: Playing the King

Holm's Cottesloe performance of Lear marked his return to Shakespeare after a long period of absence. Struck down by stage fright during a preview of Eugene O'Neill's *The Iceman Cometh* in 1976, Holm made his career in film and television until his return to live theatre with Pinter's *Moonlight* (1993), written for him by a writer with whom he had had a productive working relationship going back to 1965. Holm's earlier Shakespeare was mainly at Stratford, where he had worked for five years before Peter Hall established the Royal Shakespeare Company in 1960, and cast Holm in leading roles such as Puck, Ariel, Prince Hal, Henry V and Richard III.

Holm found Lear mentally 'a fairly easy progression', with the king a 'reactor' rather than an instigator, but physically 'mountainous'. (Interview with William Russell, *Glasgow Herald*, 30.8.97) Recognising that 'at my height, I obviously can't bring grandeur or stature to the part' (Interview with Michael Owen, *Evening Standard*, 9.4.97) he nevertheless infused it with a personal force that drew on every facial and physical gesture learned over years of film-making. As Jasper Rees, referring to 'Holm's ineffably doomy face' phrased it: 'In an immensely subtle performance, every wrinkle that time has chiselled into his physiognomy is made to pull its weight, every trademark twitch and muscular tic to speak of his immense burden of sadness'. (*Telegraph*, 23.8.97) Always an understated, naturalistic actor (Kenneth Branagh encapsulated his style as 'Anything you can do I can do less of'), Holm found the Cottesloe a congenial space: 'When you do Shakespeare on a big stage you have to go on twice every time. You enter, then you have to hit the back of the theatre. Here you go on immediately.' (*Glasgow Herald*, 30.8.97) He characterised the note of the production as 'disturbing', paying tribute to Richard Eyre's discovery of a coherent emotional idiom within the complex changes in direction of the play's narrative.

Incorporating the King

Comment on Holm's Lear repeatedly drew attention to the physical distinctiveness the actor brought to the rôle. Sheridan Morley saw him as 'a little, angry bearded gremlin', one who seemed 'to defy all the preconceptions about the King as he pads about the stage, mannered and mad and majestic by turn, but always letting us into the inner workings of his increasing self-destruction'. (*Spectator*, 5.4.97) Michael Billington saw a similarly accessible and pungent figure: 'Stocky, grizzled and bullet-headed like a George Grosz *junker*, he captures very well Lear's patriarchal whimsicality … This is Lear seen, unsentimentally, as a capricious tyrant.' (*Guardian*, 29.3.97) Others too saw the double image incorporated by Holm, physically insignificant but with a powerful presence: 'Even when

FIG 118 Gloucester (Timothy West) and Lear. West's 'magnificent' Gloucester showed him as suffering 'a tragedy no less moving or demanding of sympathy than Lear's' (Sheridan Morley)

FIG 119 The figures of Lear and the Fool (Michael Bryant), backed by the wall which collapsed as a notable stage-effect during the action.

reduced to a shufflingly infirm captive, this king – short, crop-haired, bushy-bearded – can send out, in daunting flashes, reminders of his former fierce authority.' (Paul Taylor, *Independent*, 29.3.97)

The emotional energy which left the actor drained by the end of the evening came across to Robert Butler as a combination of regal vanity ('Each slight to his status catches him on the blindside') aggression ('He bangs the table with his ivory-handed whip, and then, when he perceives the mistake is of his own making … bangs it with his forehead') and incipient insanity ('Madness looms as a daunting possibility: he speaks of it in a level, sincere way … As it unseats him, bit by bit, Holm paws at his cropped hair, tugs at his beard and chokes on words.') (*Independent on Sunday*, 30.3.97) Nicholas de Jongh noticed Holm's progressive incorporation of a physical as well as mental decline: 'This is a portrait of the royal autocrat sent humiliated to the lower depths … The way this Lear jumps atop that table or intentionally bangs his head upon it suggests the impetuous fury to which he is prone …Then the darkness of rejection falls upon him and he changes entirely – brisk step into shuffle, voice choked and quavering as madness becomes dread not threat.' (*Evening Standard*, 1.4.97) In many ways, the knowledge of insanity lay at the very centre of Holm's interpretation of Lear. As Alan Franks commented in his interview with Holm (*Times* 17.8.97), the line 'O let me not be mad, not mad sweet heaven' 'draws from within him the deepest feelings imaginable'.

Inside the supremely vigorous caricature of a blind and mad king, several commentators found a richly developed personal portrait. John Peter noted that 'Within the brutal, bullet-headed old man with his bushy, grizzled beard, a shrill, wounded small boy appears, a boy who has grown old but has not grown up, crying out indignantly against the cruel women from whom he expected warmth, kindness and shelter.' (*Sunday Times*, 6.4.97) Holm and Eyre, he went on, had analysed Lear's self-perception with acute precision: 'Lear enters like the star of the event he obviously likes to be. Holm portrays a truculent little man who watches people, not so much to find out what they think or feel, as to see what effect he is having on them. The distinction is subtle but crucial'. Benedict Nightingale appreciated that such complex effects had come from a mastery of the detail of playing: 'Those who want telling detail will find it in the look of panic that crosses his face when Goneril first suggests he sacks his knights, or the embarrassingly unstoppable tics of his head that undermine his vows of revenge, or his rigid shoulders and white-hot glare when, madly dressed in flowers and patchwork, he declares himself "every inch a king".' (*Times* 29.3.97)

Technically, there was a great deal to admire. Alastair Macaulay argued that 'the marvel of his performance is the way it lives in the line – the way it makes you feel anew the surprising developments of Shakespeare's thought in every word, and yet makes these sound spontaneous, new-minted.' (*Financial Times*, 1.4.97) This mastery of the word, taken together with physical possession of the role, led John Peter to a notable accolade: 'This is a historic moment. With his granite performance as King Lear, Ian Holm has entered a special hall of greatness. It is reserved for actors who have conquered this physically and spiritually exhausting role and left on it their personal imprint.' (*Sunday Times* 6.4.97)

Exposure

It may be that the Cottesloe provided the appropriate arena for a feature of the production that drew a good deal of press comment, not all of it mature: the nakedness of the King on the heath. Holm claimed the idea as his own: 'That was my idea. The whole play is about disrobing and stripping off.' (Interview with Michael Owen, *Evening Standard*, 9.4.97) The poignance of Holm's incorporation of ageing and physical decline sat near the heart of the production, intensified by the intimate closeness of the audience's presence.

The naked King and the near-naked Edgar, who in Robert Butler's words 'cling like lost souls' in the heath scenes (*Independent on Sunday*, 30.3.97), seemed to many observers to incorporate the stinging pathos the production laid bare in the play's relationships. 'Holm,' said Benedict Nightingale, 'strips completely and, a blanket half-hiding the bare, forked animal he now is, he cradles Poor Tom as he once cradled his daughters. It is a searingly intimate moment, perhaps the most unsettling of a great performance.' (*Times*, 29.3.97) For Paul Taylor, likewise, the nakedness was not marginal but central, giving expression to emotional and moral as well as physical truths: 'Exposure is crucial to *King Lear*, physical exposure to the

FIGS 120 and 121 The Fool and Lear in the *outré* costumes that gave rise to some comment.

FIG 122 Anne-Marie Duff as Cordelia 'a severe and innocent young woman' (John Peter)

storm on the heath and exposure of the heart to the sufferings of the most wretched. Holm's king impulsively strips stark naked in compassionate emulation of Paul Rhys's agonised Edgar/Poor Tom. I've never seen the relationship between this pair conveyed with such a mutually fascinated moving tenderness.' (*Independent*, 29.3.97) It is by no means certain that this tenderness would survive as a central aspect of the audience's experience in a more distancing theatre environment – as indeed it did not in a film version that literally and figuratively cloaked the king's nakedness.

Other Performances

If Lear took centre stage in most reviewers' comments, there were other roles that received appreciative notice by both reviewers and audiences. William Fiennes noted that 'Michael Bryant's Londoner Fool really does seem to be the alter ego of the King. When he calls Holm "Lear's shadow", the two men stare at one another, contemplating their matching silver beards, not quite sure who is who: Lear seems to be looking at some aspect of himself.' (*Punch*, 5.4.97) Paul Taylor referred to 'Michael Bryant's ancient Cockney Fool, a musical hall Big Ears look-alike who is a wonderfully elusive mixture of involvement and detachment.' (*Independent*, 29.3.97) John Peter amplified both these descriptions: 'In theory, I am against the Fool being played as an old man, but Bryant's haunting performance as Lear's alter ego, his innocent but shrewd conscience and the tenacious, pitiful voice of his fracturing sanity, brushes aside pedantic criticism.' (*Sunday Times*, 6.4.97)

There were other pairings to complement the central one of Lear and Fool. Sheridan Morley thought that 'in Paul Rhys and Finbar Lynch we have, for the first time in my recollection, an Edgar and an Edmund who could in real life be bastard half-brothers, so alike are they in looks and bearing.' (*Spectator*, 5.4.97) For Nicholas de Jongh, Rhys as Edgar was 'absolutely definitive' in his emphasising of the production's dedication to the exposure of moral truths: 'the young man exiled from his home and father, here becomes Lear's surrogate son and the play's saving grace. It is this bookish Edgar, emerging from what looks like a mental breakdown as the king goes into his, who sounds the play's clear notes of consolation. Rhys, a dazed smile playing upon his lips, presents not the usual madly emoting Edgar, but a wracked, shorn survivor of cruelty who, begrimed and naked, struggles to put the world back in balance.' (*Evening Standard*, 1.4.97) John Peter, too, saw Edgar as 'one of the moral connecting threads of Eyre's production', offering a performance that showed how 'in the world of power-politics, otherworldliness is a fatal handicap'. 'Rhys's final emergence' he went on, 'as the clear-eyed compassionate avenger is one of [the production's] great abiding images, shining and moving in its hard simplicity.' (*Sunday Times*, 6.4.97)

Robert Butler (*Independent on Sunday*, 30.3.97) referred to 'David Burke's impressively pugnacious Kent' who, in common with so many others in this interpretation 'has his own absorbing trajectory' of self-discovery. John Peter saw this role as one of the central moral discoveries of the production: 'Kent, too, is exhausted by the end: David Burke draws a majestic portrait of self-denying loyalty in action, and his destruction, for that is what it is, is one of the bitterest indictments against the king.' (*Sunday Times*, 6.4.97) Oswald (William Osborne) came in for praise from the same critic: 'stately, ingratiating, excellent'. For Sheridan Morley, 'Timothy West's magnificent Gloucester is there all the time to remind us, by example and nobility, that his is a tragedy no less moving or demanding of sympathy than Lear's, perhaps more so in that he unlike his king has done nothing to bring it on.' (*Spectator*, 5.4.97)

The play's women received less comment, perhaps, but there were discoveries in the performances here too. Anne-Marie Duff's Cordelia, for example, seemed to Sheridan Morley 'at times … no less manipulative' than her sisters, 'the baby daughter accustomed to being

FIG 123 The Fool (Michael Bryant) perched on the long banquet-table as Lear's roistering knights wreak havoc.

FIG 124 Members of the cast including Goneril (Barbara Flynn), 'a strong woman … cold but not frigid' and Regan (Amanda Redman) 'blonde and panther-like … a first-class hostess and an expert manipulator'. (John Peter)

spoiled and only too late aware that she, too, has a journey shortly to go'. (*Spectator*, 5.4.97) John Peter concurred, seeing in Anne-Marie Duff's 'deeply impressive Shakespearean debut' 'a severe and innocent young woman, with that schoolmistressy righteousness that tends to go with total and impersonal goodness'. (*Sunday Times*, 6.4.97) Amanda Redman as Regan appeared to Morley as a woman 'who starts out as a high-society hostess, forever encouraging Lear's faintly disturbing paternal passion for her, only to disintegrate into illness and death in a journey which seems to mirror that of her father.' (*Spectator*, 5.4.97) John Peter thought Goneril (Barbara Flynn) 'a strong woman, an authoritarian manager of great estates; today she would be a high-flying executive, cold but not frigid, and using her femininity ruthlessly both to cajole and to intimidate'. Regan he saw as 'blonde and panther-like: a trophy-wife who is probably a first-class hostess and an expert manipulator.' 'I shall never,' he adds, 'forget Redman's wolfish look of expectation and relief when, near the end, she looks at her dying husband.' (*Sunday Times*, 6.4.97)

Royal Politics

If most commentators saw domesticity in the production and personal suffering, others traced relationships outwards into the world of politics. John Peter, in particular, identified the hard political consequences flowing from action by privileged people: 'It is Shakespeare's ruthless perception of political responsibility, as much as anything else, that makes *King Lear* an indestructible tragedy'. Identifying Lear as a portrait with uncomfortably clarifying lessons for the absolutist King James I and 'his equally capricious and authoritarian son Charles', he found in Holm's playing a cogent portrait of the absolute ruler whose 'attention will not be trivialised'. 'The topicality of this play', he sums up, 'is astonishing. The status of Renaissance and baroque kingship is incomprehensible to us today … But Shakespeare had a perception of political power, and its effect on people who hold such power, which still grips 400 years on.' (*Sunday Times*, 6.4.97)

The sense of this production's contemporaneity was such that it even drew a (biased?) leader from *The Times*: 'It is, eminently, a play for today. The exploration of betrayal, the depiction of female power, the unhappy consequences of arbitrary division of a nation and the unreliability of heirs are all themes which engage with contemporary concerns.' (*Times*, 29.3.97) Others, less grandly, praised the 'transparency' of the production 'very rare in Shakespeare today' (Alastair Macaulay, *Financial Times*, 1.4.97) or the terrible immediacy of the central performance: 'Convincing you that he has travelled to the limits of experience, Holm's Lear leaves you feeling both glutted and gutted'. (Paul Taylor, *Independent*, 29.3.97) For John Peter, the greatness of the production was that it achieved contemporaneity by bridging the centuries: 'Shakespeare extracts every ounce of suffering, as if to say: you think you have seen as much as you can bear? No, you have not: here is more. In our frightful century, it is not surprising that this great play becomes even greater and inspires performances such as Holm's: timelessly classical, harrowingly modern and unforgettable'. (*Sunday Times*, 6.4.97)

THE CHRONOLOGY

Compiled by Jason Barnes

The Cottesloe Theatre Chronology attempts to include every production mounted at the Cottesloe between the theatre's opening with Ken Campbell's *Illuminatus* on 4th March 1977 and the Tenessee Williams *Not About Nightingales*, which concluded the theatre's twenty-first year in March/April 1998. Details are given of the staging configuration and the type of play, along with the names of the author (or adapter), the directing and main design staff, the producing company, the stage manager and the dates and number of performances and number of seats. A key (overleaf) explains the abbreviations used.

The Tour and Transfer Chronology gives as much information as is readily available about tours out from the Cottesloe, and transfers to other London theatre spaces, including the Lyttelton and Olivier Theatres at the National. This table is not exhaustive, due to the number and variety of Cottesloe tours and transfers.

Please note that full details of a production are given only on the first occasion on which it was mounted in the Cottesloe.

KEY TO STAGING

END End Stage. Uses the main acting area at the stage end of the theatre, and the main seating bank together with side galleries at both levels, but not over the stage itself.

3 S Three Sides. This is a truncated form of Long Traverse using up to three rows of seats across the rear end of the auditorium.

PR Promenade. No seats at ground floor. 250 members of the audience share the space with the cast and technicians. The two gallery levels are seated, with further standing places behind.

RND Theatre in the round, or usually 'square'. The acting space is smaller, and is flanked on two sides with seven rows of seats, and usually three rows on the other two.

THR Thrust. Similar to end stage, but with two pit level rows removed, giving a deeper stage of 11.5 metres. Often used for simpler staging demanding an epic layout.

LT Long traverse. Acting area runs the full length of the theatre flanked on each side by up to four rows of seats, on simple terraces.

KEY TO TYPE OF SHOW

N New play

NV New version

C Concert

V Visitor

R Revival

LN Late Night

P Poetry

RN Revival of National Theatre Production

Cottesloe Theatre Chronology

Play	Staging	Type of Play	Author	Director	Designer Setting	Designer Costume	Designer Lighting	1st preview	Opening or Press Night	Last Performance	Producer	Stage Manager	No of Perfs	No of Seats	Music
Illuminatus	END	NV	Ken Campbell and Chris Langham from Books by Robert Shea and Robert Anton Wilson	Ken Campbell and Chris Langham	Bill Drummond	Bill Drummond	Mike Hurst		04-Mar-77	27-Mar-77	Science Fiction Theatre of Liverpool	John Caulfield / Frank Nealon	13	319	Terry Canning Camilla Saunders Fergus Hambleton
Strawberry Fields	END	N	Stephen Poliakoff	Michael Apted	Di Seymour	Di Seymour	Stephen Wentworth	31-Mar-77	05-Apr-77	09-Jul-77	NT	John Caulfield	35	309	
Passion	PR	NV	The company with Tony Harrison	Bill Bryden & Sebastian Graham-Jones	William Dudley	William Dudley		19-Apr-77	21-Apr-77	28-Apr-77	NT	John Caulfield	65	400	
Albion Dance Band	PR	C							04-May-77	04-May-77			1	311	Ashley Hutchings
Sell Out	END	V	Roger Smith and Tom Kempinski	David Scase	David Cockayne	David Cockayne	Michael Williams		09-May-77	14-May-77	Manchester Library Theatre	Sean O'Neill	8	327	MD Liza Martin
Four to One	RND	N	Gawn Grainger	Sebastian Graham-Jones	John Halle	John Halle	Laurence Clayton	17-May-77	18-May-77	30-May-77	NT	John Caulfield	6	294	
To Those Born Later	END	NV	Bertolt Brecht. Devised by Michael Kustow & John Willett	Michael Kustow	Peter Mumford	Peter Mumford	Peter Mumford	01-Jun-77	09-Jun-77	02-Jul-77	NT	John Caulfield	9	311	
Old Movies	END	N	Bill Bryden	Bill Bryden	Geoffrey Scott	Geoffrey Scott	Peter Radmore	15-Jun-77	16-Jun-77	31-Aug-77	NT	John Caulfield	22	311	
Camilla Ringbinder Show	END	N LN	Trevor Ray with Richard Mangan and the Company	Sebastian Graham-Jones	Sue Jenkinson	Sue Jenkinson	Stephen Wentworth		01-Jul-77	20-Jul-77		John Caulfield	10	339	
Camilla Ringbinder Show	END	R	Trevor Ray with Richard Mangan and the Company	Sebastian Graham-Jones	Sue Jenkinson	Sue Jenkinson	Stephen Wentworth		01-Jul-77	30-Jul-77	NT	John Caulfield	6	311	
Entracte (Discourse III) part of Bow Down	THR	NV	Erik Satie/Hene Clair/Harrison Birtwistle/Tony Harrison	Walter Donohue Music Director Dominic Muldowney	Jennifer Carey	Jennifer Carey	Stephen Wentworth	04-Jul-77	05-Jul-77	13-Jul-77	NT	John Caulfield	9	339	Dominic Muldowney
Repertoire, part of Bow Down	THR	NV	Mauricio Kagel	Music Director Dominic Muldowney	Jennifer Carey	Jennifer Carey	Stephen Wentworth	04-Jul-77	05-Jul-77	13-Jul-77	NT	John Caulfield	9	339	Dominic Muldowney
Kemp's Jig	END	V	Chris Harris & John David	John David	Louise Belson	Louise Belson			11-Jul-77	16-Jul-77	Chris Harris	John Caulfield	4	349	
East	END	V	Steven Berkoff	Steven Berkoff			John Gorringe	18-Jul-77	19-Jul-77	23-Jul-77	London Theatre Group	John Caulfield	8	311	Neil Hansford
Metamorphosis	END	V	Steven Berkoff	Steven Berkoff			John Gorringe		29-Jul-77	02-Aug-77	London Theatre Group		5	311	
Judgment	END	R	Barry Collins	John Russell Brown	John Bury	John Bury	Brian Ridley	09-Aug-77	11-Aug-77	20-Oct-77	NT	Frank Nealon	15	311	
For The West	END	NV	Michael Hastings	Nicholas Wright	Anne-Marie Schone		Steve Whitson	13-Aug-77	15-Aug-77	18-Aug-77	English Stage Company	Vandra Edwards	5	311	
Sir Is Winning	END	N	Shane Connaughton	Christopher Morahan	Sue Jenkinson	Sue Jenkinson	Brian Ridley	24-Aug-77	25-Aug-77	29-Oct-77	NT	Jackie Harvey	17	311	
The Passion	PR	RN							26-Sep-77	26-Oct-77	NT	John Caulfield	15	400	
Metamorphosis	END	V							21-Oct-77	24-Oct-77	London Theatre Group	John Caulfield	4	339	
Albion Dance Band	PR	C							27-Oct-77		NT	John Caulfield	1	400	
Fall of the House Of Usher	END	V	Edgar Allan Poe, adapted by Steven Berkoff and Terry James	Steven Berkoff			John Gorringe		01-Nov-77	03-Nov-77	London Theatre Group	John Rothenberg	3	339	David Ellis
Lavender Blue	RND	N	John Mackendrick	Sebastian Graham-Jones	William Dudley	William Dudley	Brian Ridley & William Dudley	07-Nov-77	10-Nov-77	29-Dec-77	NT	John Rothenberg	18	226	

Cottesloe Theatre Chronology

Play	Staging	Type of Play	Author	Director	Designer Setting	Designer Costume	Designer Lighting	1st preview	Opening or Press Night	Last Performance	Producer	Stage Manager	No of Perfs	No of Seats	Music
Half Life	END	N	Julian Mitchell	Waris Hussein	Jane Martin	Judy Moorcroft	Stephen Wentworth	15-Nov-77	17-Nov-77	07-Feb-78	NT	John Rothenberg	32	307	
Babel's Dancer	END	V	Geoff Moore (conceived by)	Geoff Moore	Peter Mumford	Pamela Moore	Peter Mumford		22-Nov-77	26-Nov-77	Moving Being	John Rothenberg	8	291	
The Groucho Letters	END	NV LN	Groucho Marx, Adapted Derek Newark	Michael Kustow					02-Dec-77	26-Jan-78			6		
Richard III, Part 2	END	V	David Pownall	Edward Adams	Bettina Reeves	Bettina Reeves			05-Dec-77	10-Dec-77	Paine's Plough	John Rothenberg	4	339	
Motocar	END	V	David Pownall	Edward Adams	Tot Brill	Tot Brill			06-Dec-77	10-Dec-77	Paine's Plough	John Rothenberg	4	339	
Hunchback of Notre Dame	END	N	Victor Hugo, adapted by Ken Hill	Michael Bogdanov & Giles Block	Paul Bannister	Paul Bannister	Peter Radmore	20-Dec-77	21-Dec-77	14-Jan-78	NT	John Rothenberg	16	288	
But You're a Woman	END	N	Paul Henley	Paul Henley			Laurence Clayton		07-Jan-78	28-Jan-78	NT Contact Department	Anthony Godel	4	311	
Robert Lowell, American Poet	END	P	Ian Hamilton & Michael Kustow Devised	Michael Kustow			Paul McLeish		20-Jan-78	21-Jan-78	NT Opened US Embassy 14.12.77		3	311	
Love Letters on Blue Paper	END	N	Arnold Wesker	Arnold Wesker	Bernard Culshaw	Bernard Culshaw	Stephen Wentworth	11-Feb-78	15-Feb-78	03-Apr-78	NT	John Caulfield	21	301	
Vamp Till Ready	END	N	Gawn Grainger	Sebastian Graham-Jones	Sue Jenkinson	Sue Jenkinson	Paul McLeish		17-Feb-78	18-Feb-78	Workshop Production	John Caulfield	2	301	
Four Weeks In The City	END	N	William Martin	Giles Block	Sue Jenkinson	Sue Jenkinson	Alan Bell		24-Feb-78	25-Feb-78	Workshop Production		5	301	
Last Summer in Chulimsk	END	NV	Alexander Vampilov, adapted by Paul	John Russell Brown with Paul Thompson					02-Mar-78	02-Mar-78	Workshop Production	John Caulfield	1	301	
Lark Rise	PR	NV	Keith Dewhurst from Flora Thompson's book	Bill Bryden and Sebastian Graham-Jones	William Dudley	William Dudley	William Dudley & Laurence Clayton	23-Mar-78	29-Mar-78	27-Apr-78	NT	John Caulfield	104 inc. revivals	400	MD Ashley Hutchings
Don Juan Comes Back from The War	END	NV	Odon von Horvath, adapted by Christopher Hampton	Stewart Trotter	Tanya McCallin	Lindy Hemming	Brian Ridley	14-Apr-78	18-Apr-78	10-Jun-78	NT	John Caulfield	19	291	
Lost Worlds	END	N	Wilson John Haire	Robert Kidd	William Dudley	William Dudley	William Dudley & Laurence Clayton	12-May-78	25-May-78	17-Jun-78	NT	John Caulfield	26	311	
Jews/Arabs	END	N	Ron Huchinson	Nickolas Simmonds	Sue Jenkinson		Nick Hurran		01-Jun-78	12-Jun-78	Workshop Production	Mark Taylor	2	311	
American Buffalo	END	R	David Mamet	Bill Bryden	Grant Hicks	Grant Hicks	Andy Phillips	22-Jun-78	28-Jun-78	02-Aug-78	NT	John Caulfield	34	309	
Mayor of Zalamea	END	NV	Calderon de la Barca, adapted by Adrian Mitchell	John Russell Brown					21-Jul-78	21-Jul-78	Workshop Production	Jondon Gourkan	1	270	
The Passion	PR	R	Tony Harrison with the Company	Bill Bryden and Sebastian Graham-Jones	William Dudley	William Dudley	Stephen Wentworth	08-Aug-78	09-Aug-78	02-Sep-78	NT	John Caulfield	23	400	MD Ashley Hutchings
Lark Rise	PR	R	Flora Thompson, adapted by Keith Dewhurst	Bill Bryden & Sebastian Graham-Jones	William Dudley	William Dudley	William Dudley with Laurence Clayton		06-Sep-78	29-Dec-78	NT	John Caulfield	see above	400	Ashley Hutchings
American Buffalo	END	NR	David Mamet	Bill Bryden	Grant Hicks	Grant Hicks	Andy Phillips		05-Oct-78	21-Oct-78	NT	John Caulfield	18	309	
World Turned Upside Down	LT	NV	Keith Dewhurst from book by Christopher Hill	Bill Bryden & Sebastian Graham-Jones	William Dudley	William Dudley	Brian Ridley	27-Oct-78	02-Nov-78	06-Feb-79	NT	John Caulfield	36	346	MDs Ashley Hutchings and John Tams
Has Washington	LT	N	Charles Wood	Geoffrey Reeves	William Dudley	Pamela Howard		22-Nov-78	29-Nov-78	08-Jan-79	NT	Frank Nealon	16	284	
Herod	END	N	Paul Mills	Sebastian Graham-Jones	Sue Jenkinson	Sue Jenkinson	Stephen Wentworth	08-Dec-78	11-Dec-78	17-Jan-79	NT	John Caulfield	22	290	

Cottesloe Theatre Chronology

Play	Staging	Type of Play	Author	Director	Designer Setting	Designer Costume	Designer Lighting	1st preview	Opening or Press Night	Last Performance	Producer	Stage Manager	No of Perfs	No of Seats	Music
Putney Debates	LT	NV	Jack Emery, Devised and adapted	Sebastian Graham-Jones	William Dudley	William Dudley	Paul McLeish	01-Dec-78	24-Jan-79	31-Jan-79		John Caulfield	3	346	
Long Voyage Home Moon of the Caribees Bound East for Cardiff In The Zone	END	R	Eugene O'Neill	Bill Bryden	Hayden Griffin	Hayden Griffin	Andy Phillips	14-Feb-79	20-Feb-79	15-Mar-79	NT	John Caulfield	26	302	John Tams
Beowulf		V	Lawrence Butler	Christopher Leith					20-Mar-79	23-Mar-79	Christopher Leith puppets, scheduled for 20.3.79 but cancelled because of industrial action, performed at St George's Theatre Tufnell Park		6		
The Passion	PR	RN	The Company with Tony Harrison	Bill Bryden and Sebastian Graham-Jones	William Dudley	William Dudley		17-Apr-79		28-Apr-79	NT	John Caulfield	11	400	
Lark Rise	PR	RN	Flora Thompson, adapted by Keith Dewhurst	Bill Bryden and Sebastian Graham-Jones	William Dudley	William Dudley	William Dudley & Laurence Clayton		05-May-79	22-May-79	NT	John Caulfield	see above	400	
Dispatches	LT	NV	Bill Bryden and the Company	Bill Bryden	William Dudley	William Dudley	Andy Phillips	02-Jun-79	06-Jun-79	28-Jul-79	NT	John Caulfield	49	286	John Tams
Wings	END	R	Arthur Kopit	John Madden	Andrew Jackness	Andrew Jackness	David Hersey	09-Aug-79	15-Aug-79	29-Sep-79	NT	John Caulfield	44	291	
Lark Rise	PR	R	Flora Thompson, adapted by Keith Dewhurst	Bill Bryden and Sebastian Graham-Jones	William Dudley	William Dudley	William Dudley & Laurence Clayton	15-Oct-79	14-Nov-79	29-Dec-79	NT	John Caulfield	see above	400	MDs Ashley Hutchings and John Tams
Candleford	PR	NV	Keith Dewhurst from Flora Thompson's book	Bill Bryden and Sebastian Graham-Jones	William Dudley	William Dudley	William Dudley & Laurence Clayton	07-Nov-79	14-Nov-79	29-Dec-79	NT	John Caulfield	33	400	MDs Ashley Hutchings and John Tams
A Country Calendar	PR	NV	Flora Thompson						29-Nov-79	30-Nov-79	NT		2	400	
The Long Voyage Home	END	R	Eugene O'Neill	Bill Bryden	Hayden Griffin	Hayden Griffin	Andy Phillips	08-Jan-80	10-Jan-80	13-Feb-80	NT	John Caulfield	14	302	John Tams
Hughie	END	R/LN	Eugene O'Neill	Bill Bryden	Hayden Griffin	Hayden Griffin	Andy Phillips	18-Jan-80	20-Jan-80	16-Feb-80	NT	John Caulfield	20	302	John Tams
The Iceman Cometh	END	R	Eugene O'Neill	Bill Bryden	Hayden Griffin	Hayden Griffin	Andy Phillips	26-Feb-80	04-Mar-80	05-Apr-80	NT	John Caulfield	34		
Early Days	THR	N	David Storey	Lindsay Anderson	Jocelyn Herbert	Jocelyn Herbert	Nick Chelton	11-Apr-80	22-Apr-80	21-Jun-80	NT	Jennifer Smith	62	255	Alan Price
Schools on the South Bank Wicked Women, Displaced Persons, Our Town, Matchgirls	END	V							01-Jul-80	05-Jul-80		Frank Nealon	7	275	
A Lesson from Aloes	END	V	Athol Fugard	Athol Fugard	Douglas Heap	Vanessa Cooke	Mannie Manim	03-Jul-80	10-Jul-80	06-Aug-80	Market Theatre Johannesburg	John Caulfield	25	285	
Line 'Em	END	N	Nigel Williams	Christopher Morahan	John Bury	John Bury	John Bury	12-Aug-80	18-Aug-80	13-Sep-80	NT	Jennifer Smith	28	268	
The Passion Part One Creation to Nativity	PR	NV	The company with Tony Harrison	Bill Bryden and Sebastian Graham-Jones	William Dudley	William Dudley	William Dudley and Laurence Clayton	19-Sep-80	23-Sep-80	17-Oct-80	NT	John Caulfield	16	400	Ashley Hutchings and John Tams
The Passion Part Two Baptism to Judgment	PR	R	The company with Tony Harrison	Bill Bryden and Sebastian Graham-Jones	William Dudley	William Dudley	William Dudley and Laurence Clayton	20-Sep-80	24-Sep-80	18-Oct-80	NT	John Caulfield	10	400	Ashley Hutchings and John Tams
The Crucible	END	R	Arthur Miller	Bill Bryden	Hayden Griffin	Deirdre Clancy	Rory Dempster	25-Oct-80	30-Oct-80	10-Dec-80	NT	John Caulfield	39		John Tams
The Nativity	PR	RN	The Company with John Russell Brown, Jack Shepherd, Tony Harrison	Bill Bryden	William Dudley	William Dudley	William Dudley & Laurence Clayton		16-Dec-80	28-Jan-81	NT	John Caulfield	36	400	Ashley Hutchings and John Tams
The Ticket-of-leave	END	R	Tom Taylor	Piers Haggard	Robin Don	Robin Don	Leonard Tucker	05-Feb-81	12-Feb-81	21-Feb-81	NT	John Caulfield	39	271	Matthew Scott
Don Juan	THR	NV	Moliere adapted by John Fowles	Peter Gill	Alison Chitty	Alison Chitty	Rory Dempster	02-Apr-81	07-Apr-81	17-Oct-81	NT	Rosemary Beattie	58	273	George Fenton

Cottesloe Theatre Chronology

Play	Staging	Type of Play	Author	Director	Designer Setting	Designer Costume	Designer Lighting	1st preview	Opening or Press Night	Last Performance	Producer	Stage Manager	No of Perfs	No of Seats	Music
Sergeant Musgrave's Dance	THR	R	John Arden	John Burgess	Peter Hartwell	Pamela Howard	Rory Dempster	10-May-81	27-May-81	15-Sep-81	NT	Jennifer Smith	36	269	Roderick Skeaping
One Woman Plays	END	NV	Dario Fo & Franca Rama, adapted by Olwen	Michael Bogdanov	Sue Jenkinson & John Bury	Sue Jenkinson & John Bury	Andrew Torble & Michael Bogdanov	11-Jun-81	26-Jun-81	02-Jul-83	NT	Jennifer Smith	69	273	
The Mayor of Zalamea	END	NV	Calderon de La Barca, adapted by Adrian Mitchell	Michael Bogdanov	Stephanie Howard	Stephanie Howard	Andrew Torble & Michael Bogdanov	04-Aug-81	12-Aug-81	24-Nov-81	NT	Howard Kingston	56	273	John White
Caritas	END	N	Arnold Wesker	John Madden	Andrew Jackness	Andrew Jackness	Rory Dempster	01-Oct-81	07-Oct-81	12-Jan-82	NT	John Caulfield	35	259	MD Kevin Leeman
True West	END	R	Sam Shepard	John Schlesinger	Grant Hicks	Grant Hicks	Rory Dempster	03-Dec-81	10-Dec-81	31-May-82	NT	Frank Nealon	58	272	
Summer	END	N	Edward Bond	Edward Bond	Hayden Griffin	Hayden Griffin	Rory Dempster	21-Jan-82	27-Jan-82	19-Jun-82	NT	John Caulfield	60	273	
The Prince of Homburg	THR	NV	Heinrich von Kleist, adapted by John James	John Burgess	Alison Chitty	Alison Chitty	Stephen Wentworth	16-Apr-82	22-Apr-82	14-Aug-82	NT	Frank Nealon	46	273	John White
The Beggar's Opera	END	R	John Gay	Richard Eyre	John Gunter	John Gunter	Peter Radmore	24-Jun-82	01-Jul-82	10-Oct-82	NT	Sarah Parkin	124	273	Adapted by Dominic Muldowney
The Caucasian Chalk Circle	END		Bertolt Brecht, adapted by James and Tania Stern, with	Michael Bogdanov & Justin Greene					02-Aug-82	19-Aug-82	Educational Workshop Presentation	Jennifer Smith	6	273	Joss Buckley
Don Juan	THR	R	Moliere adapted by John Fowles	Peter Gill	Alison Chitty	Alison Chitty	Rory Dempster		18-Aug-82	28-Sep-82	NT	John Caulfield	72	273	George Fenton
The Spanish Tragedy	END	R	Thomas Kyd	Michael	Chris Dyer	Chris Dyer	Leonard Tucker	04-Sep-82	22-Sep-82	04-Mar-83	NT	John Caulfield	51	273	Henry Brown
Other Places. 3 Plays. Family Voices	END	R	Harold Pinter	Peter Hall	John Bury	John Bury	John Bury	09-Oct-82	14-Oct-82	19-Mar-83	NT	John Caulfield	46	267	
Victoria Station	END	R	Harold Pinter	Peter Hall	John Bury	John Bury	John Bury	09-Oct-82	14-Oct-82	19-Mar-83	NT	John Caulfield	46	267	
A Kind of Alaska	END	N	Harold Pinter	Peter Hall	John Bury	John Bury	John Bury	09-Oct-82	14-Oct-82	19-Mar-83	NT	John Caulfield	46	267	
A Midsummer Night's Dream	THR	R	William Shakespeare	Bill Bryden	Bob Crowley	Deirdre Clancy	William Bundy	19-Nov-82	25-Nov-82	29-Mar-83	NT	John Caulfield	35	400	MD John Tams
Kick for Touch	THR	N	Peter Gill	Peter Gill	Alison Chitty	Alison Chitty	Stephen Wentworth	09-Feb-83	15-Feb-83	02-Jun-83	NT	John Caulfield	26	262	
Small Change	THR	R	Peter Gill	Peter Gill	William Dudley	Alison Chitty	Stephen Wentworth	19-Feb-83	23-Feb-83	10-Sep-83	NT	John Caulfield	54	262	
One Woman Plays	THR	RN							26-Apr-83	30-Jun-83		Ernest Hall	11		
Macbeth	END	R	William Shakespeare	Michael Bogdanov with Justin Greene & Alan Cohen					16-May-83	23-Jun-83	NT Workshop Presentation following an Education Tour	Sally Forrest	13	400	
The Fawn	END	R	John Marston	Giles Block	Poppy Mitchell	Poppy Mitchell	Rory Dempster	07-Jul-83	14-Jul-83	20-Oct-83	NT	Sarah Parkin	30	293	David Bedford
Glengarry Glen Ross	END	N	David Mamet	Bill Bryden	Hayden Griffin	Hayden Griffin	Andy Phillips	15-Sep-83	21-Sep-83	20-Mar-84	NT	John Caulfield	149	285	
Two Inches of Ivory	END	NV	Jane Austen. One woman performance Geraldine	Richard Digby Day					05-Oct-83	05-Oct-83	NT		2	285	
Antigone	THR	R	Sophocles adapted by	Peter Gill and John Burgess	Alison Chitty	Alison Chitty	Stephen Wentworth		13-Oct-83	05-Jan-84	Workshop Production	Ernest Hall	29	246	Terry Davies
Master Harold and the Boys	END	V	Athol Fugard	Athol Fugard	Douglas Heap	Robyn Lewis	Mannie Manim	18-Nov-83	24-Nov-83	13-Feb-84	Market Theatre of Johannesburg	Sarah Parkin		295	
Strider - The Story of a Horse	3S	R	Mark Rozovsky from Tolstoy, adapted by Peter Tegel	Michael Bogdanov	Christopher Dyer	Christopher Dyer	Paul McLeish	20-Jan-84	26-Jan-84	18-Jul-84	NT	Diana Boddington	48	299	

Cottesloe Theatre Chronology

Play	Staging	Type of Play	Author	Director	Designer Setting	Designer Costume	Designer Lighting	1st preview	Opening or Press Night	Last Performance	Producer	Stage Manager	No of Perfs	No of Seats	Music
Captain Stirrick	END	V	James Taylor & David Scott	Jeremy James Taylor & Mark PattEnden	Chris Richardson	Sheila Darlington	Peter Walters and Tony Roper		11-Mar-84	11-Mar-84	Children's Music Theatre	Simon Lupini	2	291	Richard Brett
Animal Farm	THR	NV	George Orwell, adapted by Peter Hall	Peter Hall	Jennifer Carey	Jennifer Carey	John Bury	17-Apr-84	25-Apr-84	04-Sep-84	NT	Sarah Parkin	43	228	MD Matthew Scott
Antigone	THR	R	Sophocles, adapted by C.A.Trypanis	John Burgess & Peter Gill	Alison Chitty	Alison Chitty	Stephen Wentworth	15-May-84	17-May-84	11-Oct-84	NT	Ernest Hall	26	246	Terry Davies
Anton Chekhov	THR	NV	Michael Pennington Devised		Alison Chitty	Alison Chitty	Paul McLeish	04-Jul-84	05-Jul-84	22-Sep-84	NT	Sally Forrest	28	266	
As I Lay Dying	THR	R	William Faulkner	Peter Gill	Alison Chitty	Alison Chitty			26-Jul-84		NT Studio presentation of work in progress	Trish Montemuro	1	266	
Bit A' Business	THR	N	Brian Hall & Tunde Ikoli	John Burgess	Alison Chitty	Alison Chitty			30-Aug-84		NT Studio presentation of work in progress	Trish Montemuro	1	266	
Carrington	THR	N	Christopher Hampton	John Burgess & Peter Gill					13-Sep-84		NT Studio presentation of work in progress	Trish Montemuro	1	266	
Fool for Love	THR	R	Sam Shepard	Peter Gill	Alison Chitty	Alison Chitty	Stephen Wentworth	27-Sep-84	04-Oct-84	31-Jan-85	NT	Trish Montemuro	54	264	
Garden of England	THR	N	Peter Cox & the Company	John Burgess, Tim Flywell & Peter Gill	Alison Chitty	Alison Chitty			23-Oct-84		NT Studio presentation of work in progress	Trish Montemuro	1	266	
Up For None	THR	N	Mick Mahoney	Peter Gill	Alison Chitty	Alison Chitty			19-Nov-84		NT Studio presentation of work in progress	Trish Montemuro	1	266	
Lottery of Love	THR	R	Marivaux. Version by John Fowles	Stephen Unwin	Alison Chitty	Alison Chitty			07-Dec-84		NT Studio presentation of work in progress		1		
The Nativity, Part 1 of The Mysteries	PROM	R	The Company with Tony Harrison	Bill Bryden	William Dudley	William Dudley	William Dudley and Laurence Clayton	12-Dec 84	19-Jan-85	20/04/1985 Last in Cottesloe before transfer	NT	John Caulfield	29	400	MD John Tams
The Passion, Part 2 of The Mysteries	PROM	R	The Company with Tony	Bill Bryden	William Dudley	William Dudley	William Dudley and Laurence	18-Dec-84	19-Jan-85	20-Apr-85	NT	John Caulfield	24	400	
Doomsday, Part 3 of The Mysteries	PROM	NV	The Company with Tony	Bill Bryden	William Dudley	William Dudley	William Dudley and Laurence	00 Jan-05	19-Jan-85	20-Apr-85	NT	John Caulfield	24	400	
A Twist of Lemon Double Bill with In the Blue	THR	N	Alex Renton	Peter Gill	Alison Chitty	Alison Chitty	Laurence Clayton		18-Mar-85			Trish Montemuro	1	256	Terry Davies
In The Blue Double Bill with A Twist of	THR	N	Peter Gill	Peter Gill	Alison Chitty	Alison Chitty	Laurence Clayton		18-Mar-85			Trish Montemuro	1	256	Terry Davies
Festival of New Plays	THR		See Individual Plays						23-Sep-85			Trish Montemuro		256	Terry Davies
The Murderers	THR	N	Daniel Mornin	Peter Gill	Alison Chitty	Alison Chitty	Stephen Wentworth		23-Sep-85	30-Sep-85	Part of the Festival of New Plays	Trish Montemuro	9	256	Terry Davies
True Dare Kiss	THR	N	Debbie Horsfield	John Burgess	Alison Chitty	Alison Chitty	Stephen Wentworth		03-Oct-85	11-Oct-85	Part of the Festival of New Plays	Trish Montemuro	11	256	Terry Davies
As I Lay Dying	THR	NV	William Faulkner & Peter Gill	Peter Gill	Alison Chitty	Alison Chitty	Stephen Wentworth		15-Oct-85	22-Oct-85	Part of the Festival of New Plays	Trish Montemuro	8	256	Terry Davies
Command or Promise	THR	N	Debbie Horsfield	John Burgess	Alison Chitty	Alison Chitty	Stephen Wentworth		24-Oct-85	02-Nov-85	Part of the Festival of New Plays	Trish Montemuro	11	256	Terry Davies
Up For None 1	THR	N	Mick Mahoney	Peter Gill	Alison Chitty	Alison Chitty	Laurence Clayton		06-Nov-85	28-Nov-85	Part of the Festival of New Plays, Five Play Bill	Trish Montemuro	10	256	Terry Davies

Cottesloe Theatre Chronology

Play	Staging	Type of Play	Author	Director	Designer Setting	Designer Costume	Designer Lighting	1st preview	Opening or Press Night	Last Performance	Producer	Stage Manager	No of Perfs	No of Seats	Music
Bouncing 2	THR	N	Rosemary Wilton	Peter Gill	Alison Chitty	Alison Chitty	Laurence Clayton		06-Nov-85	29-Nov-85	Part of the Festival of New Plays, Five Play Bill	Trish Montemuro	10	256	Terry Davies
Sunday Morning 3	THR	N	Rod Smith	John Burgess	Alison Chitty	Alison Chitty	Laurence Clayton		06-Nov-85	30-Nov-85	Part of the Festival of New Plays, Five Play Bill	Trish Montemuro	10	256	Terry Davies
Twist of Lemon, A 4	THR	N	Alex Renton	Peter Gill	Alison Chitty	Alison Chitty	Laurence Clayton		06-Nov-85	01-Dec-85	Part of the Festival of New Plays, Five Play Bill	Trish Montemuro	10	256	Terry Davies
In The Blue 5	THR	N	Peter Gill	Peter Gill	Alison Chitty	Alison Chitty	Laurence Clayton		06-Nov-85	02-Dec-85	Part of the Festival of New Plays, Five Play Bill	Trish Montemuro	10	256	Terry Davies
The Garden of England	THR	N	Peter Cox & The Company, Edited	John Burgess	Alison Chitty	Alison Chitty	Ian Williams		14-Nov-85	23-Nov-85	Part of the Festival of New Plays	Trish Montemuro	11	256	Terry Davies
The Cherry Orchard	THR	NV	Anton Chekhov, adapted by Mike Alfreds with Lilia Sokolov	Mike Alfreds	Paul Dart	Paul Dart	Paul Dart	03-Dec-85	10-Dec-85	19-Apr-86	NT	John Rothenberg	45	248	Ilona Sekacz
The Road to Mecca	END	RN	Athol Fugard	Athol Fugard	Douglas Heap	Douglas Heap	Rory Dempster	14-Dec-85	16-Dec-85	19-Jul-86	NT	Courtney Bryant	68	297	
Hamlet	END	R	William Shakespeare	Cicely Berry	Chris Dyer	Chris Dyer		09-Jan-86	10-Jan-86	27-Feb-86	NT Workshop presentation and education tour	Sally Forrest	19	334	Terry Davies
Torquato Tasso	THR	R	Goethe, adapted by Alan Brownjohn	Stephen Unwin	Alison Chitty	Alison Chitty			27-Jan-86		NT Studio presentation of Work in Progress		1	248	
Not About Heroes	END	N	Stephen MacDonald	Michael Simpson	Alison Chitty	Alison Chitty	Stephen Wentworth		13-Feb-86	19-Jun-86	NT	John Rothenberg	19	256	Nigel Hess
The Futurists	THR & CABARET	N	Dusty Hughes	Richard Eyre	William Dudley	William Dudley	Peter Radmore	08-Mar-86	17-Mar-86	14-Jun-86	NT	Courtney Bryant	46	285	Dominic Muldowney
The Women	END	N	Clare Boothe Luce	Peter Gill & John Burgess	Alison Chitty	Alison Chitty			24-Mar-86		NT Studio presentation of Work in Progress		1		
Act of Faith	END	N	Terry Heaton	Tim Fywell	Alison Chitty & Eve Stewart with Peter King	Alison Chitty & Eve Stewart with Peter King			21-Apr-86		NT Studio presentation of Work in Progress		1		
Only Fourteen Lines	END	R	Devised by Frances de la Tour & David	David Leveaux			Mark Seaman		25-Apr-86	26-Apr-86	NT	John Caulfield	3	266	
Down Cemetery Road	END	P	Philip Larkin, devised by Patrick Garland	Patrick Garland			Ian Williams		01-May-86	05-May-86	NT	Angela Fairclough & Sue Millin	5	321	
Venus and Adonis	THR	P	William Shakespeare	Bardy Thomas for Art Depot					16-Jun-86		NT Studio presentation of work in progress		1		
Neaptide	THR	N	Sarah Daniels	John Burgess	Alison Chitty	Alison Chitty	Stephen Wentworth	26-Jun-86	02-Jul-86	04-Oct-86	NT	Courtney Bryant	42	256	Terry Davies
The American Clock	THR	R	Arthur Miller	Peter Wood	Timothy O'Brien	Stephen Brimson Lewis	Robert Bryan	31-Jul-86	06-Aug-86	27-Nov-86	NT	Ernest Hall	40	256	Arr Robert Lockhart
A Matter of Life and Death	END	N	Anthony Clark and Di Trevis from Lorca	Di Trevis	Bunny Christie with Pamela Howard	Bunny Christie with Pamela Howard	Ian Williams		19-Aug-86	19-Aug-86	NT	Elizabeth Markham	1	266	Dominic Muldowney
The Bay at Nice, Double Bill with	END	N	David Hare	David Hare	John Gunter	John Gunter	Rory Dempster	04-Sep-86	09-Sep-86	03-Jan-87	NT Double Bill	Diana Boddington	64	278	Nick Bicât
Wrecked Eggs, Double Bill with The	END	N	David Hare	David Hare	John Gunter	John Gunter	Rory Dempster	04-Sep-86	09-Sep-86	03-Jan-87	NT Double Bill	Diana Boddington	64	278	Nick Bicât
Long Time Gone	THR	N	Catherine Hayes	Peter Gill	Alison Chitty with Ashley Martin-Davis	Alison Chitty with Ashley Martin-Davis			04-Dec-86	08-Dec-86	NT Studio presentation of work in progress	Anglea Bissett, Frances Ford, Eddie Keogh	4	256	

Cottesloe Theatre Chronology

Play	Staging	Type of Play	Author	Director	Designer Setting	Designer Costume	Designer Lighting	1st preview	Opening or Press Night	Last Performance	Producer	Stage Manager	No of Perfs	No of Seats	Music
The Mother	END	R	Bertolt Brecht, adapted by Steve Gooch	Di Trevis	Bunny Christie	Bunny Christie			11-Dec-86	20-Dec-86	NT education workshop presentation	Peter Tansley	8	260	MD Stephen Warbeck
Bopha	END	V	Percy Mtwa	Percy Mtwa			Mannie Manim	06-Jan-87	08-Jan-87	07-Mar-87	Market Theatre of Johannesburg	Smal Ndaba Courtney Bryant John Caulfield	23	302	
Three Men on a Horse	END	R	John Cecil Holm and George	Jonathan Lynn	Saul Radomsky	Saul Radomsky	Robert Bryan	15-Jan-87	22-Jan-87	27-Jun-87	NT	John Caulfield	48	288	Bob Burns Quintet
A Yorkshire Tragedy	THR	R	Anon	Stephen Unwin	Ashley Martin-Davis & Alison Chitty	Ashley Martin-Davis & Alison Chitty			27-Jan-87		NT Studio presentation of work in progress		1		
A View from the Bridge	END	R	Arthur Miller	Alan Ayckbourn	Alan Tagg	Alan Tagg	Mick Hughes	06-Feb-87	12-Feb-87	28-Sep-87	NT	Courtney Bryant	72	302	
Travelling Time	THR	N	Rosemary Wilton	John Burgess	Alison Chitty & Ashley Martin-Davis	Alison Chitty & Ashley Martin-Davis			10-Mar-87		NT Studio presentation of work in progress		1	256	
Yerma	3S	NV	Federico Garcia Lorca, version by Peter Luke	Di Trevis	Pamela Howard with Bunny Christie	Pamela Howard with Bunny Christie	Gerry Jenkinson	19-Mar-87	26-Mar-87	17-Sep-87	NT	Elizabeth Markham	57	340	Dominic Muldowney
Macbeth	THR	R	William Shakespeare	Peter Gill & John Burgess	Alison Chitty & Ashley Martin-Davis	Alison Chitty & Ashley Martin-David			14-Apr-87		NT Studio presentation of work in progress		1		
Rosmersholm	THR	NV	Henrik Ibsen, version by Frank McGuiness	Sarah Pia Anderson	Roger Glossop	Roger Glossop	Paul Denby	30-Apr-87	06-May-87	27-Aug-87	NT	Trish Montemuro	37	228	Mike Figgis
Black Poppies	THR	N	John Burgess and the Company, Edited	John Burgess	Alison Chitty & Ashley Martin-Davis	Alison Chitty & Ashley Martin-Davis			28-May-87		NT Studio presentation of work in progress		1	256	
Effie's Burning	END	N	Valerie Windsor	Susan Mayo	Phil R Daniels	Phil R Daniels	Paul McLeish		29-Jun-87		Library Theatre Company, Manchester, Studio Night		1		
Mean Tears	THR	N	Peter Gill	Peter Gill	Alison Chitty	Alison Chitty	Stephen Wentworth	16-Jul-87	22-Jul-87	02-Dec-87	NT	Trish Montemuro	37	260	
Ting Tang Mine	RND	R	Nick Darko	Michael Rudman	Carl Toms	Lindy Hemming	Len Tucker	10-Sep-87	23-Sep-87	30-Jan-88	NT	Alison Rankin	41	294	Matthew Scott
Entertaining Strangers	PROM	N	David Edgar	Peter Hall	William Dudley	William Dudley	Gerry Jenkinson	09-Oct-87	15-Oct-87	24-Mar-88	NT	Ernest Hall	69	400	Dominic Muldowney Mellstock Band MD David
Space	THR	N	David Spencer	Nick Ward	Fred Pilbrow	Fred Pilbrow	Andrew Torble		28-Oct-87		NT Studio presentation of work in progress		1	256	
Down Cemetery Road	Prom / sitting on Entertaining Strangers	P	Patrick Garland, devised from Philip Larkin's poetry	Patrick Garland			Ian Williams		19-Nov-87	21-Nov-87	NT	Angela Fairclough Sue Millin	3 This revival	227	Sidney Bechet
Love Songs of World War Three	Prom / sitting on Entertaining Strangers	P	Adrian Mitchell	Adrian Mitchell	Jenni Gregory & Sasha Mitchell		Paul McLeish		11-Jan-88	12-Jan-88	NT	Elizabeth Markham	2	227	

Cottesloe Theatre Chronology

Play	Staging	Type of Play	Author	Director	Designer Setting	Designer Costume	Designer Lighting	1st preview	Opening or Press Night	Last Performance	Producer	Stage Manager	No of Perfs	No of Seats	Music
The Rain Gathering and Darkening Fields	THR	N	Jeremy Raison Tim Fywell	Jeremy Raison Peter Gill					02-Feb-88		NT Studio presentation of work in progress		1	256	
A Place with the Pigs	END	N	Athol Fugard	Athol Fugard	Douglas Heap	Susan Hilferty	Paul Pyant	06-Feb-88	16-Feb-88	14-Apr-88		Alison Rankin, Elizabeth	38	302	
Committee, The	END	V	Julia Bardsley and the Company,	Julia Bardsley		Emma Gibson	Ian Williams & Martin Perry		22-Mar-88		Middlesex Polytechnic Students		1		
Fanshen	END	R	David Hare	Les Waters	Bunny Christie	Bunny Christie			31-Mar-88	05-Apr-88	NT Workshop presentation	Rosie Wakley	6	270	
The Winter's Tale	3S	R	Willliam Shakespeare	Peter Hall	Alison Chitty	Alison Chitty	Gerry Jenkinson & Ben Ormerod	02-May-88	18-May-88	30-Jul-88	NT	Ernest Hall	24	298	Harrison Birtwistle
The Tempest	3S	R	William Shakespeare	Peter Hall	Alison Chitty	Alison Chitty	Gerry Jenkinson	25-Apr-88	19-May-88	30-Jul-88	NT	Ernest Hall	23	298	Harrison Birtwistle
Cymbeline	3S	R	William Shakespeare	Peter Hall	Alison Chitty	Alison Chitty	Gerry Jenkinson	10-May-88	20-May-88	29-Jul-88	NT	Ernest Hall	22	298	Harrison Birtwistle
The Strangeness of Others	THR	N	Nick Ward	Nick Ward	Fred Pilbrow	Fred Pilbrow	Fred Pilbrow	10-Jun-88	21-Jun-88	27-Sep-88	NT	Elizabeth Markam	46	333	Richard Heacock
Mrs Klein	THR	N	Nicholas Wright	Peter Gill	John Gunter	Stephen Brimson-Lewis	Mark Seaman	05-Aug-88	10-Aug-88	30-Nov-88	NT	Angela Fairclough	58	254	Terry Davies
When We Were Women	THR	N	Sharman Macdonald	John Burgess	Alison Chitty	Alison Chitty	Iain Dewar		15-Sep-88	22-Sep-88	NT	Brewyeen Rowland	5	254	
Russell of the Times	THR	N	Devised by James Hayes		Alison Chitty	Alison Chitty			04-Oct-88	05-Oct-88	NT Education presentation in association with the NT Studio	Lesley Walmsley	3	254	
Roots	END	R	Arnold Wesker	Simon Curtis	Bunny Christie	Bunny Christie	Christopher Toulmin		19-Oct-88	25-Apr-89	NT Education presentation	Matthew Lynch, Becky Webb	41	260	
The Father	END	NV	August Strindberg, version by John	David Leveaux	Annie Smart	Annie Smart	Christopher Toulmin	17-Oct-88	26-Oct-88	25-Feb-89	NT	John Caulfield	48	276	Giles Swayne
Making History	END	V	Brian Friel	Simon Curtis	Julian McGowan	Martin Chitty	Christopher Toulmin	03-Dec-88	05-Dec-88	18-Jan-89	Field Day Theatre Company	Lizzi Cocker	20	260	
Fuente Ovejuna	LT	NV	Lope De Vega, version by Adrian Mitchell	Declan Donnellan	Nick Ormerod	Nick Ormerod	Mick Hughes	15-Dec-88	10-Jan-89	28-Aug-89	NT	Alison Rankin	95	294	Paddy Cunneen
Bed	END	N	Jim Cartwright	Julia Bardsley	Peter J Davison	Peter J Davison	Christopher Toulmin	04-Mar-89	08-Mar-89	02-Apr-89	NT	Courtney Bryant	32	298	John Winfield
Tango Varsoviano	END	V	Alberto Felix Alberto	Alberto Felix Alberto	Alberto Felix Alberto				24-May-89	27-May-89	Teatro del Sur - Buenos Aires		5	302	Carlos Stella & Alberto Felix Alberto
The Voysey Inheritance	RND	R	Harley Granville Barker	Richard Eyre	William Dudley	William Dudley	Mark Henderson	10-Jun-89	27-Jun-89	18-Jan-90	NT	Ernest Hall	70	358	John Woolrich
The Long Way Round	THR	R	Peter Handke, version by Ralph Manheim	Stephen Unwin	Bunny Christie	Bunny Christie	Paul Jozefowski		06-Jul-89	22-Jul-89	NT Studio presentation of work in progress	Courtney Bryant	12	262	
Schism in England	THR	R	Calderon de la Barca, version by John Clifford	John Burgess	Alison Chitty	Alison Chitty	Ben Ormerod		26-Jul-89	09-Aug-89	NT Studio presentation of work in progress	Ray Bingle	12	262	
Man Beast and Virtue	END	NV	Luigi Pirandello, version by Charles Wood	William Gaskill	Annie Smart	Annie Smart	Mick Hughes	01-Sep-89	07-Sep-89	12-Dec-89	NT	Alison Rankin	54	292	
The Magic Carpet	3S	N		Stephen Unwin	Emma Fowler	Emma Fowler	Tim Bray & Iain Dewar		25-Sep-89	14-Oct-89	NT Education production	Paul Quinn & Brewyeen	19	180	

Cottesloe Theatre Chronology

Play	Staging	Type of Play	Author	Director	Designer Setting	Designer Costume	Designer Lighting	1st preview	Opening or Press Night	Last Performance	Producer	Stage Manager	No of Perfs	No of Seats	Music
Ma Rainey's Black Bottom	RND	R	August Wilson	Howard Davies	Bob Crowley	Bob Crowley	Mark Henderson	19-Oct-89	25-Oct-89	24-Mar-90	NT	Trish Montemuro	89	291	MD Neil McArthur
Five Guys Named Moe	V LN	V LN	Clarke Peters with Rosalind Hickson, Devised	Clarke Peters with Rosalind Hickson					19-Jan-90		Carmeltree presentation (Late-night)		1	291	
Racing Demon	LT / Cruciform	N	David Hare	Richard Eyre	Bob Crowley	Bob Crowley	Mark Henderson	01-Feb-90	08-Feb-90	18-Jul-90	NT	Trish Montemuro	66	316	George Fenton
Abingdon Square	THR	V	Maria Irene Fornes	Nancy Meckler	Lucy Weller	Lucy Weller	Stephen Watson	28-Mar-90	29-Mar-90	24-Apr-90	Shared Experience / Soho Theatre	Sue Millin	19	260	
Tartuffe	END	NV	Moliere, version by Jatinder Verma from Literal by P	Jatinder Verma	Magdalen Rubalcava	Magdalen Rubalcava	Brian Knox		18-Apr-90	31-May-90	NT Education Mobile Production	Imamul Ameen, Richard Reddrop	17	270	V Chandran
Berenice	RND	NV	Jean Racine, version by Neil Bartlett	Tim Albery	Antony McDonald	Antony McDonald	Charles Edwards	03-May-90	09-May-90	01-Sep-90	NT	Elizabeth Markham	46	280	Orlando Gough
After The Fall	END	R	Arthur Miller	Michael Blakemore	Haydon Griffin	Tanya McCallin	Rory Dempster	15-Jun-90	20-Jun-90	05-Sep-90	NT	Courtney Bryant	36	288	Barrington Pheloung
Piano	3S	NV	Trevor Griffiths after Chekhov	Howard Davies	Ashley Martin Davies	Ashley Martin Davies	Chris Parry	02-Aug-90	08-Aug-90	19-Jan-91	NT	Elizabeth Markham	59	277	Dominic Muldowney
Once in a While the Odd Thing Happens	THR	N	Paul Godfrey	Paul Godfrey	Stephen Brimson-Lewis	Stephen Brimson-Lewis	Paul Pyant	13-Aug-90	18-Sep-90	01-Dec-90	NT	Alison Rankin	29	260	
Tartuffe	END	RN	Moliere, version by Jatinder Verma	Jatinder Verma	Magdalen Rubalcava	Magdalen Rubalcava	Brian Knox		25-Sep-90	24-Oct-90	NT Education Mobile Production	Imamul Ameen, Richard Reddrop	14	270	
More Tales from the Magic Carpet	3S	N	Chris Barton, Devised	Chris Barton	Emma Fowler	Emma Fowler	Tim Bray		02-Oct-90	15-Nov-90	NT Education	Paul Quinn	11	180	
The Shape of the	RND	N	David Edgar	Jenny Killick	Dermot Hayes	Dermot Hayes	Paul Pyant	02-Nov-90	08-Nov-90	06-Apr-91	NT	Trish Montemuro	55	280	Ian Dearden
Tectonic Plates	RND	V	Conceived by Robert Lepage and Company	Robert Lepage	Michael Levine & Robert Lepage	Michael Levine & Robert Lepage	Lucie Bazzo & Robert Lepage		06-Dec-90	13-Dec-90	Tramway co-production produced by Cultural Industry Ltd & Theatre Repere (Quebec) in assoc. with Festival des Ameriques	Alan Roy	9	297	
Accidental Death of An Anarchist	THR	NV	Dario Fo, version by Alan Cumming & Tim Supple	Tim Supple	Ashley Martin-Davis	Ashley Martin-Davis	Ben Ormerod	04-Jan-91	07-Jan-91	28-Feb-91	NT Education Department Mobile Production	Angela Bissett	19	330	
The White Chameleon	END	N	Christopher Hampton	Richard Eyre	Bob Crowley	Bob Crowley	Jean Kalman	14-Jan-91	04-Feb-91	29-Aug-91	NT	Alison Rankin	74	271	Richard Hartley
The Fever	END	R	Wallace Shawn						08-Feb-91	09-Feb-91	NT and Royal Court co-presentation	Kate Mailk	3	292	
Invisible Friends	END	R	Alan Ayckbourn	Alan Ayckbourn	Roger Glossop	Roger Glossop	Mick Hughes	11/03/1991 * Delayed due to injury	13-Mar-91	26-Jun-91	NT	Lesley Walmsley	59	292	
Black Snow	LT	NV	Keith Dewhurst from the novel by Mikhail Bulgakov	William Gaskill	Annie Smart	Annie Smart	Rick Fisher	18-Apr-91	25-Apr-91	07-Nov-91	NT	Alison Rankin	71	274	Matthew Scott
The Coup	THR	N	Mustapha Matura	Roger Michell	William Dudley	William Dudley	Rick Fisher	12-Jul-91	18-Jul-91	28-Dec-91	NT	Ernest Hall	70	309	Sound Score Paul
At Our Table	THR	N	Daniel Mornin	Jenny Killick	Bunny Christie	Bunny Christie	Ben Ormerod	12-Sep-91	19-Sep-91	19-Nov-91	NT	Courtney Bryant	29	235	Stephen Warbeck

Cottesloe Theatre Chronology

Play	Staging	Type of Play	Author	Director	Designer Setting	Designer Costume	Designer Lighting	1st preview	Opening or Press Night	Last Performance	Producer	Stage Manager	No of Perfs	No of Seats	Music
The Little Clay Cart	THR	NV	Attributed to Shudraka. Version by	Jatinder Verma	Magdalen Rubalcava	Magdalen Rubalcava	Brian Knox	28-Nov-91	05-Dec-91	07-Mar-92	NT	Ernest Hall	36	251	V Chandran
Blood Wedding	END	R	Federico Garcia Lorca, version by Gwenda Pandolfi	Yvonne Brewster	Kendra Ullyart	Kendra Ullyart	Ian Williams	13-Dec-91	17-Dec-91	05-Feb-92	NT Mobile Production	Diane Willmott	26	261	Matthew Rooke
Angels in America Pt 1 Millennium	THR	R	Tony Kushner	Declan Donnellan	Nick Ormerod	Nick Ormerod	Mick Hughes	17-Jan-92	23-Jan-92	07-Nov-92	NT	Ernest Hall	113	260	Paddy Cuneen
Uncle Vanya	3S	NV	Anton Chekhov, version by Pam Gems	Sean Mathias	Stephen Brimson-Lewis	Stephen Brimson-Lewis	BenOrmerod	20-Feb-92	25-Feb-92	09-May-92	NT Studio Production	Alison Rankin	44	320	Karl Johnson
Needles and Opium	END	V	Robert Lepage	Robert Lepage	Robert Lepage	Robert Lepage	Robert Lepage		30-Apr-92	06-Jun-92	NT co-presentation with Cultural	Robert Beauregard	16	280	Robert Caux
Fuente Ovejuna	LT	RN	Lope De Vega, version by Adrian Mitchell	Declan Donnellan	Nick Ormerod	Nick Ormerod	Mick Hughes		14-May-92	30-Jul-92	NT	David Milling	23	294	
The Rise and Fall of Little Voice	END	N	Jim Cartwright	Sam Mendes	William Dudley	William Dudley	Mick Hughes	10-Jun-92	16-Jun-92	07-Oct-92	NT	David Milling	47	280	Terry Davies
Lloyds Bank Theatre Challenge	THR								16-Jul-92	16-Jul-92	Festival of 4 plays by Young People	Diane Willmott	1	280	
The Street of Crocodiles	THR	N	Bruno Schultz	Simon Mc Burney	Rae Smith	Rae Smith	Paule Constable	06-Aug-92	13-Aug-92	03-Dec-92	NT and Theatre de Complicite co-production	Martin Newcombe	49	274	Gerard McBurney
Kings	END	R	Christopher Logue	Liane Aukin	Sheelagh Killeen	Sheelagh Killeen	Ian Williams		17-Sep-92	29-Oct-92	NT	David Milling	6	290	
Stages	END	N	David Storey	Lindsay Anderson	Jocelyn Herbert	Jocelyn Herbert	Mick Hughes	12-Nov-92	18-Nov-92	17-Feb-93	NT	Trish Montemuro	51	292	Alan Price
Billy Liar	THR	R	Keith Waterhouse & Willis Hall	Tim Supple	Bunny Christie	Bunny Christie	Ben Ormerod with Paule Constable	11-Dec-92	15-Dec-92	17-Mar-93	NT Education Mobile Production	Diane Willmott	33	260	
The Game of Love and Chance	END	NV	Pierre Marivaux, version by Neil Bartlett	Tim Supple	Paul Dart	Paul Dart	Paul Dart	06-Jan-93	11-Jan-93	17-Apr-93	NT/ Cambridge Theatre co./ Gloria co-production	David Milling	39	302	Nicolas Bloomfield
The Day After Tomorrow	THR	R	Roel Adam, version by Noel Clark	Anthony Clark	Kate Burnett	Kate Burnett	Ian Dewar		28-Jan-93	17-Apr-93	NT	Diane Willmott	33	258	Marc Vibrans
Mr A's Amazing Maze Plays	END	R	Alan Ayckbourn	Alan Ayckbourne	Roger Glossop	Roger Glossop	Mick Hughes	25-Feb-93	04-Mar-93	19-Aug-93	NT	Sue Millin	66	290	
Springboards (five plays as below)	THR														
Neighbour, The	THR	N	Meredith Oakes	John Burgess	Jackie Brooks	Jackie Brooks	Chris Toulmin		21-Apr-93	08-May-93	NT Studio Presentation	Diane Willmott	8	250	
Somewhere	THR	N	Judith Johnson	Polly Teale	Stephen Brimson Lewis	Stephen Brimson Lewis			24-Apr-93	11-May-93	NT Studio in association with Liverpool Playhouse	Diane Willmott	8	250	
Hove	THR	N	Devised by NT Studio and Talking Tongues	David Farr	Angela Davies	Angela Davies			28-Apr-93	01-May-93	RNT Studio and Talking Tongues Presentation	Diane Willmott	4	250	Murray Gold

Cottesloe Theatre Chronology

Play	Staging	Type of Play	Author	Director	Designer Setting	Designer Costume	Designer Lighting	1st preview	Opening or Press Night	Last Performance	Producer	Stage Manager	No of Perfs	No of Seats	Music
Baby Doll	THR	NV	Andrew Poppy based on Tenessee Williams	Julia Bardsley	Simon Vincenzi	Simon Vincenzi			05-May-93	10-May-93	NT Studio Presenation in association with Leicester Haymarket Theatre	Diane Willmott	6	250	Andrew Poppy
He Who Saw Everything	THR	NV	The Epic of Gilgamesh, version by Robert Temple	Tim Supple	Ashley Martin Davis	Ashley Martin Davis			12-May-93	15-May-93	NT Studio Presentation	Diane Willmott	4	250	Joanna Bacon, Colin R Campbell, Miranda Foster, Valerie Gogan, Joanne
Sweeney Todd	END	R	Sondheim & Wheeler from	Declan Donnellan	Nick Ormerod	Nick Ormerod	Mick Hughes	22-May-93	02-Jun-93	19-Oct-93	NT	Ernest Hall	83	292	
The Mountain Giants	END	NV	Luigi Pirandello, version by Charles Wood	William Gaskill	Annie Smart	Annie Smart	Andy Phillips	08-Jul-93	14-Jul-93	28-Oct-93	NT	John Caulfield	50	274	Adrian Johnston
Jamais Vu	END	V	Ken Campbell	Colin Watkeys			Iain Dewar		07-Oct-93	23-Oct-93	Ken Campbell	Juan Escandel, Guy Rhodes	8	250	
Recollections of a Furtive Nudist	END	V	Ken Campbell	Gillian Brown			Iain Dewar		09-Oct-93	23-Oct-93	Ken Campbell	Juan Escandel, Guy Rhodes	2	250	
Pigspurt, or Six Pigs from Happiness	END	V	Ken Campbell	Colin Watkeys			Iain Dewar		09-Oct-93	23-Oct-93	Ken Campbell	Juan Escandel, Guy Rhodes	2	250	
Angels in America Part 1: Millennium Approaches	THR	RN					Mick Hughes	03-Nov-93	20-Nov-93	02-Jul-94	NT Revival	David Milling	49	260	Paddy Cunneen
Angels in America Pt 2 Perestroika	THR	R	Tony Kushner	Declan Donnellan	Nick Ormerod	Nick Ormerod	Mick Hughes	12-Nov-93	20-Nov-93	02-Jul-94	NT	David Milling	69	260	Paddy Cunneen
Mother Courage and her Children	END	R	Bertolt Brecht, version by Hanif Kureishi & Sue Davies (lyrics)	Anthony Clark	Kate Burnett	Kate Burnett	Paul McLeish	03-Dec-93	06-Dec-93	15-Jan-94	NT Education Mobile Production	Alison Rankin	26	298	Mark Vibrans
The Skriker	END	N	Caryl Churchill	Les Waters	Annie Smart	Annie Smart	Christopher Toulmin	20-Jan-94	27-Jan-94	26-Apr-94	NT	Alison Rankin	48	204	Judith Weir
Wicked, Yaar!	END	N	Garry Lyons	John Turner	Nigel Prabhavalkar	Nigel Prabhavalkar	Huw Llewellyn		08-Mar-94	19-Mar-94	NT Education Mobile Production	Christopher Sollett	34	292	The West India
The Man Who	3S	V	Oliver Sacks, inspired by his book	Peter Brook	Jean-Guy Lecat	Jean-Guy Lecat	Phillippe Vialatte	04-May-94	05-May-94	21-May-94	NT and Millbrook Productions	Philippe Vialatte	10		
Rutherford and Son	END	R	Githa Sowerby	Katie Mitchell	Vicki Mortimer	Vicki Mortimer	Tina McHugh	26-May-94	02-Jun-94	24-Nov-94	NT	Alison Rankin	81	302	
BT National Connections	END							12-Jul-94	13-Jul-94	14-Jul-94	NT Education Festival of Plays by Young People	Alison Rankin	3	302	
Le Cid	THR	NV	Pierre Corneille, version by Ranjit Bolt	Jonathan Kent	Peter J Davison	Clare Mitchell	Mark Henderson	21 7 94	28-Jul-94	22-Oct-94	NT	Lesley Walmsley	54	292	Richard Rodney Bennett
Two Weeks with the Queen	RND	R	Mary Morris from Morris Gleitzman's novel	Alan Ayckbourn	Roger Glossop	Roger Glossop	Jackie Staines	15-Sep-94	20-Sep-94	16-Feb-95	NT and Stephen Joseph Theatre, Scarborough, co-production	Lesley Walmsley	67	400	Simon Cryer
Alice's Adventures Under Ground		N	Lewis Carroll. Adaptation by Christopher Hampton with Martha Clarke	Martha Clarke	Robert Israel	Robert Israel	Jim Ingolls	01-Nov-94	08-Nov-94	14-Mar-95	NT	Alison Rankin	47	273	

Cottesloe Theatre Chronology

Play	Staging	Type of Play	Author	Director	Designer Setting	Designer Costume	Designer Lighting	1st preview	Opening or Press Night	Last Performance	Producer	Stage Manager	No of Perfs	No of Seats	Music
Landscape	END	R	Harold Pinter	Harold Pinter	Eileen Diss	Joan Bergin	Mick Hughes	22-Nov-94	23-Nov-94	06-Dec-94	NT/ Gate Theatre Dublin co-production	Lesley Walmsley	18	274	
Leave Taking	END	R	Winsome Pinnock	Paulette Randall	Poppy Mitchell	Poppy Mitchell	Mark Ridler	13-Dec-94	04-Jan-95	14-Jan-95	NT Education Mobile Production	Gemma Swallow	16	302	
Dealer's Choice	RND	N	Patrick Marber	Patrick Marber	Bunny Christie	Bunny Christie	Mick Hughes	02-Feb-95	09-Feb-95	22-Apr-95	NT	Trish Montemuro	41	334	
The Blue Ball	RND	N	Paul Godfrey	Paul Godfrey	Stewart Laing	Stewart Laing	Mimi Jordan	23-Mar-95	30-Mar-95	22-Jun-95	NT	Alison Rankin	20	350	
Skylight	END	N	David Hare	Richard Eyre	John Gunter	John Gunter	Mark Jonathan	27-Apr-95	04-May-95	25-Nov-95	NT	Trish Montemuro	81	296	
Richard II	LT	R	William Shakespeare	Deborah Warner	Hildegard Bechtler	Hildegard Bechtler	Peter Mumford	26-May-95	02-Jun-95	17-Feb-96	NT	Alison Rankin	111	274	Arturo Annechino
BT National Connections	END							30-Jun-95	01-Jul-95		NT Education	Trish Montemuro	2	288	
Titus Andronicus	END	R	William Shakespeare	Gegory Doran	Nadya Cohen	Sue Steele	Mark Jonathan		18-Jul-95	22-Jul-95	Market Theatre, Johannesburg/ NT Studio Presentation	Adam Steyn	7	330	MD Dumi Dhlamini
The Machine Wreckers	END	R	Ernst Toller, version by Ashley Dukes	Katie Mitchell	Vicki Mortimer	Vicki Mortimer	Tina McHugh	04-Aug-95	11-Aug-95	02-Dec-95	NT	Alison Rankin	42	302	Helen Chadwick
Cyrano	END	NV	Edmund Rostand, version by Jatinder Verma & Ranjit Bolt	Anurada Kapur	Magdalen Rubalcava	Magdalen Rubalcava	Paul O'Leary	19-Oct-95	25-Oct-95	13-Jan-96	NT and Tara Arts co-production	Charlotte Warner	45	296	Vanraj Bhatia
Violin Time	END	V	Ken Campbell	Colin Watkeys					15-Jan-96	18-Jan-96	Ken Campbell	Andrew Speed	5	322	
Stanley	3S	N	Pam Gems	John Caird	Tim Hatley	Tim Hatley	Peter Mumford	24-Jan-95	01-Feb-96	17-Aug-96	NT	Angela Fairclough	98	299	
The Ends of the Earth	LT	N	David Lan	André Serban	Richard Hudson	Richard Hudson	Simon Corder	23-Feb-96	29-Feb-96	27-May-96	NT	Richard Reddrop	37	271	Adrian Johnston
The Frogs	END	NV	Aristophanes, version by Fiona Laird	Fiona Laird	Mark Leese	Mark Leese	Ian Scott	07-Feb-96	20-Mar-96	01-Apr-96	NT Education Mobile Production	Chris Sollett		256	Fiona Laird
Designated Mourner, The	END	N	Wallace Shawn	David Hare	Bob Crowley	Bob Crowley	Rick Fisher	18-Apr-96	24-Apr-96	01-Jun-96	NT	Angela Fairclough	25	304	
War and Peace	THR	NV	Leo Tolstoy, version by Helen Edmunson, Adapted	Nancy Meckler and Polly Teale	Bunny Christie	Bunny Christie	Chris Davey	07-Jun-96	25-Jun-96	05-Dec-96	NT and Shared Experience Theatre co-production	Alison Rankin	74	253	Peter Salem
Blinded By The Sun	END	N	Stephen Poliakoff	Ron Daniels	Tom Piper	Tom Piper	Rick Fisher	28-Aug-96	03-Sep-96	28-Dec-96	NT	Angela Fairclough	54	283	
Violin TIme	END	V	Ken Campbell	Clin Watkeys			Tim Bray & Huw Llewellyn	30-Sep-96	02-Oct-96	02-Nov-96	Ken Campbell		14	271	
Fair Ladies at a Game of Poem Cards	LT	NV	Chikamatsu Monzaemon. A new verse play by Peter Oswald	John Crowley	Vicki Mortimer	Vicki Mortimer	Rick Fisher	14-Nov-96	20-Nov-96	29-Jan-97	NT	Alison Rankin	30	259	Paddy Cunneen
The Cripple of Inishmaan	END	N	Martin McDonagh	Nicholas Hytner	Bob Crowley	Bob Crowley	Mark Henderson	12-Dec-96	07-Jan-97	23-Apr-97	NT	Angela Fairclough	46	330	Paddy Cunneen
Light Shining in Buckinghamshire	END	R	Caryl Churchill	Mark Wing-Davey	Madeline Herbert	Madeline Herbert	Zerlina Hughes	09-Jan-97	10-Jan-97	04-Mar-97	NT Education Mobile Production	Nigel Mousley	19	303	Stephen Warbeck
Cardiff East	THR	N	Peter Gill	Peter Gill	Alison Chitty	Alison Chitty	Andy Phillips	06-Feb-97	12-Jan-97	19-Apr-97	NT	Courtney Bryant		261	Terry Davies
King Lear	LT	R	Shakespeare	Richard Eyre	Bob Crowley	Bob Crowley	Jean Kalman	21-Mar-97	27-Mar-97	20-Sep-97	NT	John Caulfield	71	266	Dominic Muldowney
Twelfth Night	LT	R	Shakespeare	Brigid Larmour	Nettie Edwards				16-May-97	17-May-97	NT Education Workshop Production	Pippa Dean	3	266	Jack Piner, Gerry Hunt
Closer	END	N	Patrick Marber	Patrick Marber	Vicki Mortimer	Vicki Mortimer	Hugh Vanstone	22-May-97	29-May-97	20-Sep-97	NT	Ernest Hall	58	262	

Cottesloe Theatre Chronology

Play	Staging	Type of Play	Author	Director	Designer Setting	Designer Costume	Designer Lighting	1st preview	Opening or Press Night	Last Performance	Producer	Stage Manager	No of Perfs	No of Seats	Music
BT National Connections								09-Jul-97	12-Jul-97		NT Education Festival of Plays by Young People		3	299	
Othello	THR	R	Shakespeare	Sam Mendes	Anthony Ward	Anthony Ward	Paul Pyant	01-Aug-97	16-Sep-97	06-Jan-98	NT	John Caulfield	60	307	Paddy Cunneen
The Invention of Love	END	N	Tom Stoppard	Richard Eyre	Anthony Ward	Anthony Ward	Peter Mumford	25-Sep-97	01-Oct-97	29-Nov-97	NT	Trish Montemuro	28	299	Dominic Muldowney
Theatre Stories	THR	V	Ken Campbell	Colin Watkeys			Huw Llewellyn	16-Oct-97	17-Oct-97	01-Nov-97	NT	Alison Rankin	8	279	
Mutabilitie	LT	N	Frank	Trevor Nunn	Monica Frawley	Monica Frawley	Andrew Bridge	14-Nov-97	20-Nov-97	17-Feb-98	NT	Lesley Walmsley	48	298	Shaun Davey
Day I Stood Still. The	END	N	Kevin Elyot	Ian Rickson	Mark Thompson	Mark Thompson	Hugh Vanstone	15-Jan-98	21-Jan-98	27-Jun-98	NT	Courtney Bryant	62	287	Stephen Warbeck
Not About Nightingales	LT	N	Tenessee Williams	Trevor Nunn	Richard Hoover	Richard Hoover	Chris Parry	27-Feb-98	05-Mar-98	30-Apr-98	NT	Courtney Bryant	37	234	Steve Edis

TOUR TRANSFER

TRANSFER / TOUR	Cottesloe Theatre	Tours and Transfers				
	Play	Director	Press or Opening Cottesloe	Date	Theatre	City
TR	Illuminatus	Ken Campbell and Chris Langham	04-Mar-77	Apr-77	Roundhouse	London
TR	Half Life	Waris Hussein	17-Nov-77	Mar-78	Duke of Yorks	London
T	Lark Rise	Bill Bryden	21-Apr-77	May-78	Factory Unit	Milton Keynes
T	Early Days	Lindsay Anderson	22-Apr-80	Mar-80	Theatre Royal	Brighton
T	The Passion Part I	Bill Bryden	21-Apr-77	Aug-80	Assembly Hall	Edinburgh Festival
T	The Nativity	Bill Bryden	16-Dec-80	Aug-80	Assembly Hall	Edinburgh Festival
T	The Passion Part II	Bill Bryden		Aug-80	Assembly Hall	Edinburgh Festival
TR	Early Days	Lindsay Anderson	22-Apr-80	Dec-80	Comedy	London
TR	The Crucible	Bill Bryden	30-Oct-80	Mar-81	Comedy	London
T	The Passion	Bill Bryden	21-Apr-77	Jun-81	Kirche San Martin	Cologne
T	The Nativity	Bill Bryden	16-Dec-80	Jun-81	Kirche San Martin	Cologne
T	The Passion	Bill Bryden	21-Apr-77	Jun-81	Centro Palatino Finmedia Studios	Rome
T	The Nativity	Bill Bryden	16-Dec-80	Jun-81	Centro Palatino Finmedia Studios	Rome
T	Mayor of Zalamea, The	Michael Bogdanov	12-Aug-81	Nov-81	Theatre Centre	Denver
TR	Mayor of Zalamea, The	Michael Bogdanov	12-Aug-81	Dec-81	Olivier	NT
TR	Don Juan	Peter Gill	07-Apr-81	Feb-82	Lyttelton	NT
TR	Don Juan	Peter Gill	07-Apr-81	Feb-82	Olivier	NT
T	Don Juan	Peter Gill	07-Apr-81	Mar-82	Theatre Royal	Glasgow
T	One Woman Plays	Michael Bogdanov	26-Jun-81	May-82		Hong Kong
T	One Woman Plays	Michael Bogdanov	26-Jun-81	Jul-82	Theatre Centre	Denver
TV	The Beggars' Opera	Richard Eyre	01-Jul-82	Nov-82	Televison Recording	Cottesloe NT
T	A Midsummer Night's Dream	Bill Bryden	25-Nov-82	Nov-82	Theatre Royal	Bath
T	A Midsummer Night's Dream	Bill Bryden	26-Nov-82	Dec-82	New Theatre	Cardiff
T	A Midsummer Night's Dream	Bill Bryden	26-Nov-82	Jan-83	Theatre Royal	Glasgow
T	The Spanish Tragedy	Michael Bogdanov	23-Sep-82	Mar-83	Theatre Royal	Bath
TR	A Midsummer Night's Dream	Bill Bryden	27-Nov-82	Apr-83	Lyttelton	NT
T	The Beggars' Opera	Richard Eyre	01-Jul-82	Jun-83	Theatre Royal	Bath
T	The Beggars' Opera	Richard Eyre	01-Jul-82	Oct-83	Grand Theatre	Wolverhampton
TR	Master Harold and the Boys	Athol Fugard	24-Nov-83	Feb-84	Lyttelton	NT
TR	The Spanish Tragedy	Michael Bogdanov	22-Sep-82	Jun-84	Lyttelton	NT
TR	Animal Farm	Peter Hall	25-Apr-84	Sep-84	Olivier	NT
T	Animal Farm	Peter Hall	25-Apr-84	Sep-84	Olivier	NT

TOUR TRANSFER

TR	Fool for Love	Peter Gill	04-Oct-84	Feb-85	Lyric, Shafesbury Avenue	London
T	Animal Farm	Peter Hall	25-Apr-84	Feb-85	Theatre Royal	Glasgow
T	The Road to Mecca	Athol Fugard	14-Dec-85	Apr-85	Theatre Royal	Bath
TR	Mysteries Part II Passion	Bill Bryden	20-Sep-80	May-85	Lyceum	London
TR	Mysteries Part III Doomsday	Bill Bryden	09-Jan-85	May-85	Lyceum	London
TR	Mysteries Part I Creation	Bill Bryden	21-Apr-77	May-85	Lyceum	London
TR	Animal Farm	Peter Hall	25-Apr-84	Jul-85	Lyttelton	NT
T	Animal Farm	Peter Hall	25-Apr-84	Aug-85		Helsinki
T	Animal Farm	Peter Hall	25-Apr-84	Sep-85	Lyttelton	NT
T	Animal Farm	Peter Hall	27-Apr-84	Sep-85	Corral	Almagro
T	Animal Farm	Peter Hall	25-Apr-84	Sep-85	Teatro De La Commedia	Madrid
T	Animal Farm	Peter Hall	25-Apr-84	Sep-85	New Theatre	Cardiff
T	Animal Farm	Peter Hall	28-Apr-84	Oct-85	Theatre Centre	Denver USA?
T	Animal Farm	Peter Hall	26-Apr-84	Oct-85	Theatre Royal	Nottingham
T	Animal Farm	Peter Hall	25-Apr-84	Oct-85	Theatre Royal	Norwich
T	Animal Farm	Peter Hall	25-Apr-84	Oct-85	Theatre Royal	Bath
T	Animal Farm	Peter Hall	25-Apr-84	Oct-85	Theatre Royal	Plymouth
T	Animal Farm	Peter Hall	25-Apr-84	Nov-85	Palace Theatre	Manchester
T	Animal Farm	Peter Hall	25-Apr-84	Nov-85	Grand Theatre	Wolverhampon
T	Animal Farm	Peter Hall	25-Apr-84	Nov-85	Opera House	Belfast
T	Animal Farm	Peter Hall	25-Apr-84	Nov-85	New Theatre	Hull
TR	Glen Garry Glen Ross	Bill Bryden	21-Sep-83	Feb-86	Mermaid	London
T	Cherry Orchard, The	Mike Alfreds	10-Dec-85	Mar-86	His Majesties	Aberdeen
T	Animal Farm	Peter Hall	25-Apr-84	Apr-86	Akademie Theatre	Vienna
T	Animal Farm	Peter Hall	25-Apr-84	Apr-86	Shauspielhaus	Zurich
T	Animal Farm	Peter Hall	25-Apr-84	May-86	Royal Alexander	Toronto
T	Cherry Orchard, The	Mike Alfreds	10-Dec-85	May-86	Blackstone	Chicago
T	Animal Farm	Peter Hall	25-Apr-84	Jun-86	Morris A Mechanic	Baltimore
T	Animal Farm	Peter Hall	25-Apr-84	Jun-86	Queen Elizabeth	Vancouver
TR	American Clock, The	Peter Wood	06-Aug-86	Dec-86	Olivier	NT
TR	Three Men on a Horse	Jonathan Lynn	22-Jan-87	Jul-87	Vaudeville	London
TR	View from the Bridge, The	Alan Ayckbourn	12-Feb-87	Oct-87	Aldwych	London
T	Winter's Tale, The	Peter Hall	18-May-88	May-88	Rustaveli	Tbilisi
T	Winter's Tale, The	Peter Hall	18-May-88	May-88	Mhat	Moscow
T	Tempest, The	Peter Hall	19-May-88	May-88	Mhat	Moscow
T	Cymbeline	Peter Hall	20-May-88	May-88	Mhat	Moscow
T	Winter's Tale, The	Peter Hall	18-May-88	Jun-88	Globe	Tokyo
T	Tempest, The	Peter Hall	19-May-88	Jun-88	Globe	Tokyo
T	Tempest, The	Peter Hall	19-May-88	Jun-88	Rustaveli	Tbilisi
T	Cymbeline	Peter Hall	20-May-88	Jun-88	Globe	Tokyo
T	Cymbeline	Peter Hall	20-May-88	Jun-88	Rustaveli	Tbilisi
T	Winter's Tale, The	Peter Hall	18-May-88	Sep-88	Amphitheatre	Epidaurus
T	Tempest, The	Peter Hall	19-May-88	Sep-88	Amphitheatre	Epidaurus

TOUR TRANSFER

T	Cymbeline	Peter Hall	20-May-88	Sep-88	Amphitheatre	Epidaurus
TR	Cymbeline	Peter Hall	20-May-88	Sep-88	Olivier	NT
TR	Winter's Tale, The	Peter Hall	18-May-88	Sep-88	Olivier	NT
TR	Tempest, The	Peter Hall	19-May-88	Sep-88	Olivier	NT
TR	Mrs Klein	Peter Gill	10-Aug-88	Dec-88	Apollo	London
T	Schism in England	John Burgess	26-Jul-89	Aug-89	St Brides	Edinburgh
TR	The Magic Carpet	Chris Barton	25-Sep-89	Oct-89	Olivier	RNT
T	Ma Rainey	Howard Davies	25-Oct-89	Jan-90	Empire	Hackney
TR	Racing Demon	Richard Eyre	08-Feb-90	Aug-90	Olivier	NT
TR	After the Fall	Michael Blakemore	20-Jun-90	Sep-90	Lyttelton	NT
TR	Tartuffe	Jatinder Verma	18-Apr-90	Oct-91	Lyttelton	NT
TR	Racing Demon	Richard Eyre	08-Feb-90	Nov-91	Lyttelton	NT
T	Racing Demon	Richard Eyre	08-Feb-90	Nov-91	Theatre Royal	Newcastle
T	Racing Demon	Richard Eyre	08-Feb-90	Nov-91	Marlowe	Canterbury
T	Racing Demon	Richard Eyre	08-Feb-90	Nov-91	Theatre Royal	Bath
T	Racing Demon	Richard Eyre	08-Feb-90	Dec-91	Alhambra	Bradford
T	Racing Demon	Richard Eyre	08-Feb-90	Dec-91	Theatre Royal	Nottingham
T	The Day After Tomorrow	Anthony Clark	28-Jan-93	Feb-92	Old Bull Arts Centre	Barnet
T	The Day After Tomorrow	Anthony Clark	28-Jan-93	Feb-92	Hemel Hempstead Arts Centre	Hemel Hempstead
T	Mr A's Amazing Maze Plays	Alan Ayckbourn	04-Mar-93	Apr-92	Young Peoples Tour	
T	Fuente Ovejuna	Declan Donnellan	15-Dec-88	Jun-92	Teatro Lope de Vega	Seville
T	Fuente Ovejuna	Declan Donnellan	14-May-92	Jun-92	Templemore Sports Centre	Derry City
T	Fuente Ovejuna	Declan Donnellan	14-May-92	Aug-92	Assembly Hall	Edinburgh
TR	Rise and Fall of Little Voice	Sam Mendes	16-Jun-92	Oct-92	Aldwych	London
T	Sweeney Todd	Declan Donellan	02-Jun-93	Nov-92	Teatro Albeniz	Madrid
TR	Needles and Opium	Robert Lepage	30-Apr-92	Nov-92	Lyttelton	NT
T	Angels in America	Declan Donellan	23-Jan-92	Nov-92	Kleines Schauspielhaus	Dusseldorf
TR	Racing Demon	Richard Eyre	08-Feb-90	Sep-93	Olivier as part of Trilogy	NT
T	Sweeney Todd	Declan Donellan	02-Jun-93	Oct-93	New Theatre	Cardiff
T	Sweeney Todd	Declan Donellan	02-Jun-93	Oct-93	Theatre Royal	Newcastle
T	Sweeney Todd	Declan Donellan	02-Jun-93	Nov-93	Arany Janos Szinhaz	Budapest
T	Sweeney Todd	Declan Donellan	02-Jun-93	Nov-93	New Theatre	Bath
TR	Sweeney Todd	Declan Donnelan	02-Jun-93	Dec-93	Lyttelton	NT
T	Angels in America Part One	Declan Donellan	23-Jan-92	Jan-94	Contact Theatre	Manchester
T	Angels in America Part Two	Declan Donellan	24-Jan-92	Jan-94	Contact Theatre	Manchester
T	Angels in America Part One	Declan Donellan	23-Jan-92	May-94	Teatro Donna Maria II	Lisbon
T	The Day After Tomorrow	Anthony Clark	28-Jan-93	May-94	Young Peoples Tour	UK and Scotland
TR	Racing Demon	Richard Eyre	08-Feb-90	Sep-94	Olivier	NT
T	Racing Demon	Richard Eyre	08-Feb-90	Oct-94	James A Doolittle	Los Angeles
TR	Racing Demon	Richard Eyre	08-Feb-90	Nov-94	Olivier	NT

TOUR TRANSFER

T	Alice's Adventures Under Ground	Martha Clarke	01-Nov-94	Dec-94	Piccolo Studio	Milan
TR	Dealer's Choice	Patrick Marber	09-Feb-95	May-95	Vaudeville	London
T	Skylight	Richard Eyre	04-May-95	May-95	Den Nationale Scene	Bergen
T	Titus Andronicus	Gregory Doran	18-Jul-95	Jul-95	Courtyard West Yorkshire	Leeds
T	Titus Andronicus	Gregory Doran	18-Jul-95	Jul-95	Teatro Municipal	Almagro
T	Richard II	Deborah Warner	02-Jun-95	Jan-96	National Theatre	Bobigny Paris
TR	Skylight	Richard Eyre	04-May-95	Feb-96	Wyndham's	London
T	Dealer's Choice	Patrick Marber	09-Feb-95	Jun-96	Playhouse	Oxford
	Dealer's Choice	Patrick Marber	09-Feb-95	Jul-96	Alliance Theatre	Atlanta USA
	Dealer's Choice	Patrick Marber	09-Feb-95	Jul-96	Theatre Royal	Norwich
T	Richard II	Deborah Warner	02-Jun-95	Jul-96	Perner Insel, Hallein	Salzburg
	Dealer's Choice	Patrick Marber	09-Feb-95	Jul-96	Royal Court	Liverpool
T	Dealer's Choice	Patrick Marber	09-Feb-95	Aug-96	Festival Fringe Society	Edinburgh
	Dealer's Choice	Patrick Marber	09-Feb-95	Sep-96	Queensland Conservatorium	Brisbane
	Dealer's Choice	Patrick Marber	09-Feb-95	Sep-96	Theatre Royal	Bath
	Dealer's Choice	Patrick Marber	09-Feb-95	Sep-96	Yvonne Arnaud	Guildford
	Dealer's Choice	Patrick Marber	09-Feb-95	Oct-96	Marlowe	Canterbury
	Dealer's Choice	Patrick Marber	09-Feb-95	Oct-96	Gaiety	Dublin
T	Violin Time	Colin Watkeys	15-Jan-96	Oct-96	Stary Teatr	Krakow
	Dealer's Choice	Patrick Marber	09-Feb-95	Oct-96	Lyceum	Sheffield
	Dealer's Choice	Patrick Marber	09-Feb-95	Oct-96	Grand Opera House	York
	Dealer's Choice	Patrick Marber	09-Feb-95	Nov-96	Theatre Royal	Newcastle
TR	Stanley	John Caird	01-Feb-96	Feb-97	Circle in the Square	New York
T	Cardiff East	Peter Gill	12-Jan-97	Apr-97	New Theatre	Cardiff
	Skylight	Richard Eyre	04-May-95	Apr-97	Playhouse	Oxford
TR	Cripple of Inishmaan	Nicholas Hytner	07-Jan-97	Apr-97	Lyttelton	NT
	Skylight	Richard Eyre	04-May-95	May-97	Arts Theatre	Cambridge
	Skylight	Richard Eyre	04-May-95	May-97	Yvonne Arnaud	Guildford
	Skylight	Richard Eyre	04-May-95	May-97	Arts Centre	Warwick
T	King Lear	Richard Eyre	27-Mar-97	May-97	Aya Irene Basilica	Istanbul
T	King Lear	Richard Eyre	27-Mar-97	May-97	Dock Store No One	Thessaloniki
	Skylight	Richard Eyre	04-May-95	May-97	Playhouse	Salisbury
	Skylight	Richard Eyre	04-May-95	Jun-97	Royal Court	Liverpool
	Skylight	Richard Eyre	04-May-95	Jun-97	Civic Theatre	Darlington
	Skylight	Richard Eyre	04-May-95	Jun-97	Lyceum	Sheffield
TR	Skylight	Richard Eyre	04-May-95	Jun-97	Vaudeville	London
	Cripple of Inishmaan	Nicholas Hytner	07-Jan-97	Jul-97	Town Hall	Galway
T	Othello	Sam Mendes	16-Sep-97	Aug-97	Perner Insel, Hallein	Salzburg
T	Cripple of Inishmaan	Nicholas Hytner	07-Jan-97	Sep-97	Theatre Royal	Norwich
T	Cripple of Inishmaan	Nicholas Hytner	07-Jan-97	Sep-97	Opera House	Cork
T	Cripple of Inishmaan	Nicholas Hytner	07-Jan-97	Sep-97	Gaiety	Dublin
T	Othello	Sam Mendes	17-Sep-97	Oct-97	Herberger Theatre	Phoenix

TOUR TRANSFER

TR	Closer	Patrick Marber	29-May-97	Oct-97	Lyttelton	NT
T	Othello	Sam Mendes	16-Sep-97	Nov-97	Dramatyczny	Warsaw
TR	Invention of Love, The	Richard Eyre	01-Oct-97	Dec-97	Lyttelton	NT
T	Othello	Sam Mendes	16-Sep-97	Jan-98	Ginza Saison	Tokyo
T	Othello	Sam Mendes	16-Sep-97	Feb-98	Seoul Arts Centre	Korea
T	Othello	Sam Mendes	16-Sep-97	Feb-98	Performing Arts Academy	Hong Kong
T	Othello	Sam Mendes	16-Sep-97	Mar-98	Er Tong Zhu Yoan	Beijing
T	Othello	Sam Mendes	16-Sep-97	Mar-98	Shanghai Centre Theatre	Shanghai
T	Othello	Sam Mendes	16-Sep-97	Mar-98	Stage Opera House	Wellngton
T	Othello	Sam Mendes	16-Sep-97	Mar-98	Her Majesty's	Adelaide
T	Othello	Sam Mendes	16-Sep-97	Apr-98	Brooklyn Acedemy of Music	New York
TR	Othello	Sam Mendes	16-Sep-97	May-98	Lyttelton	NT